TIME ON TWO CROSSES

THE COLLECTED WRITINGS OF BAYARD RUSTIN

Edited by

DEVON W. CARBADO *and* DONALD WEISE

Foreword by

BARACK OBAMA

Afterword by

BARNEY FRANK

Second Edition

CLEiS
PRESS

Cover photo: Rustin with Dr. Martin Luther King, Jr. during the Montgomery Bus Boycott, 1956 (Associated Press/Wide World)

Published in the United States by Cleis Press, an imprint of
Start Midnight, LLC, 375 Hudson Street, Twelfth Floor, New York, New York 10014.
Printed in the United States.
Cover design: Scott Idleman/Blink
Text design: Karen Quigg
Second edition.
10 9 8 7 6 5 4 3 2 1

Trade paper ISBN: 978-1-62779-126-8
E-book ISBN: 978-1-62778-143-5

Library of Congress Cataloging-in-Publication Data for the First Edition

Rustin, Bayard, 1912–1987.
Time on two crosses: the collected writings of Bayard Rustin/edited by Devon W. Carbado and Donald Weise. — 1st ed.
            p. cm.
        ISBN 1-57344-174-0 (alk. paper)
            1. African Americans—Civil rights—History—20th century. 2. Civil rights movements—United States—History—20th century. 3. Nonviolence—United States—History—20th century. 4. Social justice—United States—History—20th century. 5. United States—Race relations. 6. United States—Social conditions—20th century. I. Carbado, Devon W. II. Weise, Donald. III. Title.
        E185.615.R84 2003
        323.1'196073—-dc21   2003007984

ACKNOWLEDGMENTS

THE EDITORS EXTEND A heartfelt thank-you to Walter Naegle and the estate of Bayard Rustin, without whose cooperation, time, and generosity this book would not exist. We also wish to thank David J. Garrow for his expert input.

We would like to acknowledge Rustin biographer John D'Emilio (*Lost Prophet: The Life and Times of Bayard Rustin*), filmmaker Nancy Kates and Bennett Singer (*Brother Outsider: The Life of Bayard Rustin*), and playwright Brian Freeman (*Civil Sex*) for their support and camaraderie in the burgeoning field of Rustin scholarship.

A special measure of gratitude is due to Cleis Press publishers Frédérique Delacoste and Felice Newman for their enthusiasm, input, and support, as well as to the sales and marketing team of Publishers Group West.

Further, we are grateful for the research assistance and support of the Hugh and Darling Library at UCLA and the staff of the San Francisco Public Library. We wish also to acknowledge the kind involvement of Richard Deats and the Fellowship of Reconciliation.

Additional thanks to: Kimberlé Crenshaw, Dale Frett, Laura Gomez, Mitu Gulati, Cheryl Harris, Akasha Hull, Catherine E. McKinley, Jeff Park, Blanche Richardson, Ina Ross, Jerl Rossi and John Serna, Stewart Shaw, Giovanna Tringali, Jim Van Buskirk, Evelyn C. White, and Mariah Wilkins. And especially to Renée Swindle for her inspiration always.

Contents

FOREWORD

THE PRESIDENTIAL MEDAL OF Freedom goes to men and women who have dedicated their own lives to enriching ours. This year's honorees have been blessed with extraordinary talent, but what sets them apart is their gift for sharing that talent with the world. It will be my honor to present them with a token of our nation's gratitude....

Bayard Rustin was an unyielding activist for civil rights, dignity, and equality for all. An advisor to the Reverend Dr. Martin Luther King, Jr., he promoted nonviolent resistance, participated in one of the first Freedom Rides, organized the 1963 March on Washington for Jobs and Freedom, and fought tirelessly for marginalized communities at home and abroad. As an openly gay African American, Mr. Rustin stood at the intersection of several of the fights for equal rights.

Barack Obama

A Word from Walter Naegle

AT BAYARD'S MEMORIAL SERVICE in October of 1987, Democratic Congressman John Lewis began his remarks with *"Bayard Rustin, oh what a life!"* Indeed it was, as John Lewis knew firsthand. As a young activist, he was inspired by Bayard's ideas and example, and worked with him as a member of the group that led the 1963 March on Washington for Jobs and Freedom. That demonstration was a pivotal point both for the African American civil rights movement and for Bayard himself. It brought him from the shadows, where he had often been marginalized because of his radical politics and homosexual identity, and it started the movement on a course from protest to politics, a phrase that was to become the title of Bayard's most influential article. John Lewis and his colleague in the U.S. Congress, Representative Eleanor Holmes Norton, who had also been mentored by Bayard, are the most prominent examples of that journey.

This collection of Bayard's writing covers the full range of his interests and activism, offering a comprehensive portrait of his intellect and talent as a strategist. Reflecting almost a half century of work, these words offer a road map for young activists regardless of their cause. Whether the issue was human rights, labor, disarmament, immigration reform, or civil rights for all, Bayard spoke with a voice that was rooted in his belief in the oneness of the human family.

Walter Naegle is the executor and archivist of the Bayard Rustin Estate. He was Bayard Rustin's partner from 1977 until Rustin's death in 1987.

INTRODUCTION

BAYARD RUSTIN IS REMEMBERED as a consummate civil rights strategist and humanitarian whose staunch advocacy of nonviolent resistance shaped the course of social protest from the 1960s through the close of the twentieth century—and even up to protest movements of today. First as political adviser to Martin Luther King, Jr., in the 1950s and later as organizer of the 1963 March on Washington, Rustin defined the black protest agenda to an extent that few activists had done before him—or would do even after his death in 1987. It was Rustin who helped introduce nonviolent direct action to the civil rights movement, and if he was remembered for nothing more than this, his reputation would be enshrined in African American history. But he was also well-placed among the power brokers of organized labor and the Democratic Party, to say nothing of world leaders like Kwame Nkrumah, Lyndon Johnson, and Golda Meir. Few African Americans engaged in as broad a protest agenda as did Rustin; fewer still enjoyed his breadth of influence in virtually every political sector of American life.

Nevertheless, Rustin remained an outsider in black civil rights circles for much of his life. He was openly gay—and that he was black in addition created a seemingly unprecedented conundrum for African American leaders, who weighed the worth of his tactical expertise and political sophistication against his "deviant" sexual identity. Sometimes his expertise and sophistication won out. At other times, the perceived political cost of his homosexuality outweighed his value to the movement. In these instances, he was dismissed, asked to resign from service, or denied a platform to voice his concerns. Up until quite recently, before the first Rustin biographies appeared in the 1990s, civil rights historians dealt with him—when they have chosen to include him at all—as a "sideline activist" whose principal purpose was to support King and the movement. Perhaps no other figure contributed so much to the civil rights movement yet has been so heavily penalized by it.

Rustin's own point of view in his writings is often outward looking, as if to deflect attention from himself as a man. Given that he came of age under Jim Crow laws and spent much of his life working on behalf of religious-based social protest groups, his reticence around disclosing his true personal feelings, or "coming out," is understandable. *Time on Two Crosses* serves the doubly vital function not only of restoring Rustin's voice to the historical record, but also of refocusing attention on the man himself.

Time on Two Crosses is the first comprehensive collection of Bayard Rustin's writings ever published, comprising forty-eight essays, speeches, and interviews, many of which were never widely available. From the birth of nonviolent direct action to the rise of Black Power, Rustin's writings function as a road map for the meandering course of black protest movements over the past century.

It is impossible to understand the man—his ideological commitments, his political activism, his institutional affiliations—without considering his "time on two crosses": that is, how his race and sexuality shaped his political life, nurtured and sustained his indomitable spirit, and helped him to conceive of civil rights as a struggle for "the human family." As he reminds us, "[O]ne has to fight for justice for all. If I do not fight bigotry wherever it is, bigotry is thereby strengthened. And to the degree that it is strengthened, it will thereby have the power to turn on me."[1]

Bayard Rustin was born in West Chester, Pennsylvania, in March 1912. His mother, Florence Rustin, was sixteen years old and unmarried at the time of his birth. His father, Archie Hopkins, broke off relations with Florence during her pregnancy, never to see his son. Abandoned and unprepared to care for her child, Florence turned to her parents, Julia and Janifer Rustin. The Rustins were a politically progressive, middle-class couple active in the African Methodist Episcopal (AME) Church. Although they were already the parents of eight children, they chose to adopt the infant, naming him Bayard Taylor Rustin. As one of Bayard's sisters recalled, "At first my mother said, 'Oh, I'm just going to let Florence raise that baby by herself.' But one day when she looked down at him in his crib, he smiled up sweetly at her. She decided then and there that Florence could not be a suitable parent, that she would take the baby and raise him properly."[2] To spare him embarrassment, the Rustins concealed from Bayard until adolescence the truth that they were not his parents but in fact his grandparents.

Julia Rustin's activism profoundly shaped Bayard's early thinking. She was a barrier-breaker. Julia served as a charter member of the newly formed National Association for the Advancement of Colored People (NAACP) in 1910, organized a racially integrated garden club, and founded a community center for blacks, who were barred from the West Chester YMCA. When African American luminaries such as W. E. B. Du Bois, James Weldon Johnson, and Mary McLeod Bethune arrived in town to find no guesthouses available to blacks, Julia opened her home to them. Bayard grew up in the presence of these pioneering figures and their stories of lynchings and other acts of racial brutality, though he had no direct childhood experience of the Ku Klux Klan.

It was Julia's Quaker teachings above any other influence that determined her son's notions of nonviolent social protest. As Bayard put it, "My activism did not spring from being black. Rather, it is rooted fundamentally in my Quaker upbringing and the values instilled in me by [my] grandparents.... It is very likely that I would have been involved [in civil rights agitation] had I been a white person."[3] The Quakers, or Society of Friends, taught the concept of a human family within which everyone is equal, contrary to the politics of Jim Crow, which were predicated upon a belief in black inferiority and inhumanity. It was the contradiction between Quaker beliefs and Jim Crow politics that got Rustin involved in the struggle for racial equality. More importantly, his grandmother impressed upon him that it was his social responsibility to combat racial subordination nonviolently.

West Chester, though racially segregated, offered blacks relative serenity. The Rustins lived on the outskirts of a white neighborhood, and many of young Bayard's playmates were white. Although Bayard attended an integrated high school, where he received encouragement from black and white teachers alike, it was clear to him that after high school his opportunities in West Chester would be limited.

In 1932, Rustin left home to attend Wilberforce University, a historically black college in Ohio. There, he earned distinction as first tenor and principal soloist in the Wilberforce Quartet, a musical troupe that performed Negro spirituals. Through the Quartet Rustin became a talented public spokesperson. "[W]hile explaining and describing the songs...I developed a considerable aplomb, a great sense of how to present myself as a speaker. The Wilberforce Quartet gave me status and greater self-assurance."[4]

Yet Rustin left Wilberforce University after only two years—according to him, because he lost his scholarship for refusing to join the ROTC. However, a former classmate offered a very different explanation: that Bayard left Wilberforce because he had fallen in love with the son of the college president.

Rustin became aware of his homosexuality at age fourteen. During an overnight visit to see his mother in 1926, he was forced by the tight living quarters to share a bed with a man who was staying in the same house. They had sex together that night, marking the first of many gay sexual encounters that Rustin would experience throughout his lifetime. Shortly after the incident, he reportedly discussed the matter openly with his grandmother. "[I] never said, 'You know, I'm gay.' I told her I enjoyed being with guys when I joined the parties for dating. And she said, 'Is that what you really enjoy?' I said, 'Yes, I think I do.' Her reply was, 'Then I suppose that's what you need to do.' " While Rustin did not interpret his grandmother's response as "encouragement," he did perceive it to be an acceptance of the fact that he was not heterosexual. Thus, he "never felt it necessary to do a great deal of pretending. And I never had feelings of guilt."[5]

Yet he appears to have felt at least some degree of self-doubt, according to an activist colleague, who recounts a conversation in which Rustin described how his sudden sexual awareness drove him toward high school athletics in a desperate attempt to affirm his masculinity. His self-doubt certainly did not suppress his same-sex desire. Beginning at Wilberforce and continuing at Cheney State Teacher's College, Rustin developed strong attractions for other men. He had sexual relationships with a number of men, particularly at Cheney State. When administrators at that school learned of his sexual orientation and activities, they demanded that he "get the hell out."[6]

And he did, moving to New York in 1937, ostensibly to enroll at City College of New York (CCNY). Instead, Rustin plunged into his exciting new surroundings: New York City and, more particularly, Harlem. Very quickly, he became a part of the city's cultural life. He sang backup for folk singer Josh White, and performed in *John Henry,* the stage musical starring Paul Robeson. Aside from providing Rustin with a source of income, the music scene opened access to Harlem's gay circles. The twenty-five-year-old visited gay musicians, including choir master Hall Johnson, for seemingly professional purposes. But the professional sometimes developed into the personal, because Harlem's black gay cultural elites "could tell what my sexual orientation was, for gay people have a certain telegraph system among themselves."[7]

Like many black gays, Rustin became adept at navigating the social mores of the African American elite, wherein lesbians and gay men were accepted so long as they did not undermine black respectability by flaunting their sexuality. Rustin was determined to be a "New Negro," taking his cues from none other than Alain Locke, the black gay Howard University professor and arbiter of the Harlem Renaissance. "[I] got to know Locke very well. He was gay and he held open house for the literati and for younger writers like Langston Hughes and Richard Wright. I suspect that he was more a model for me than anyone else. He never felt it necessary to discuss his gayness...the most people could say about... [Locke] was that they suspected him of being gay."[8] From Rustin's perspective, Locke was a universalist, a person whose sexual identity defined neither who he was nor whom he associated with. Rustin aspired to manage both his race and his sexual orientation in a similar way.

If gay Harlem (and gay New York) provided Rustin a strategy for navigating race and sexuality, the Communist Party provided him an ideology to realize his commitment to the human family—or so he thought. He joined the Young Communist League (YCL) in 1938, while he was still a student at CCNY. Unlike most liberal proponents of racial equality, the Communists backed up their words with actions. Their unflagging support of the "Scottsboro Boys," nine African American youths sentenced to death on allegations of rape charges in 1936, was unsurpassed among the white radical left—and even among black establishment civil rights groups. The NAACP had been slow to mobilize around the Scottsboro case, because they feared their image would be tarnished and they would lose white patronage. The politics of the Communist Party, Rustin felt, were not chilled by concerns of racial respectability.

Also drawing him to Communism was the party's peace platform against U.S. intervention in World War II. As a young pacifist, Rustin identified strongly with this antiwar position, and his work as Coordinator of the Committee Against Discrimination in the Armed Forces of the YCL converged with broader efforts on the part of black civil rights leaders to integrate the military. The black press had reported countless stories of racial discrimination in the armed forces and raised the question whether segregation was undermining the effectiveness of the U.S. military. However, unlike members of the Communist Party, many in the black civil rights establishment determined to support the war, engaging in the so-called "Double V Campaign": victory against fascism and Nazism abroad and against Jim Crow politics at home.

Hitler's invasion of the Soviet Union in June 1941 reversed the Communist Party's pacifist position. The party did not join the Double V Campaign, but simply insisted that its cadre come to the Soviet Union's defense. This meant "closing ranks"—that is, subordinating concerns about civil rights for the greater good of the nation (not America, but the Soviet Union), which also meant terminating the Committee Against Discrimination. When party officials instructed Rustin to do so, he resigned in protest. "The communists' primary concern was not with the black masses but with the global objectives of the Soviet Union," he said.[9]

A few months earlier, Rustin had refused to acknowledge this very argument when it was pointed out to him by A. Philip Randolph, the revered African American labor leader who, in 1925, created the most powerful African American labor union, the Brotherhood of Sleeping Car Porters. During the spring of 1941, Rustin had walked into the Brotherhood's offices looking for work, but was turned away. "I am sorry to know that you are associated with the Communists," Randolph told him. "I think you'll find that they are not really interested in civil rights."[10] Rustin was not convinced.

After Rustin's break with the Communist Party in June 1941, Randolph asked him to join the planning committee for the March on Washington of Negro Americans. Rustin accepted the invitation. He knew that, in addition to being a committed antiracist, Randolph was deeply concerned with economic equality—and he was a man of action. Randolph had specific plans and timelines. This was all very appealing to Rustin, whose Quaker upbringing suggested to him the importance of *acting* on one's beliefs. What he could not have known, of course, is that his work with Randolph would help to chart a political course that would change the terms upon which the struggle for black civil rights would be fought for years to come.

Almost two decades before the historically decisive 1963 March on Washington, Randolph conceived of a protest march to coerce President Franklin D. Roosevelt to desegregate the armed forces and to promulgate antidiscrimination laws so that blacks could benefit from the thriving defense industry. "Negro America must bring its power and pressure to bear upon the agencies and representatives of the Federal Government to exact their rights in National Defense employment and the armed forces of the United States," Randolph argued. "...One thing is certain and that is if Negroes are going to get anything out of this national defense...WE MUST FIGHT FOR IT AND FIGHT FOR IT WITH OUR GLOVES OFF."[11] Randolph warned that, if Roosevelt was unresponsive, more than 10,000 African Americans would arrive in the capital on July 4. Fearing pandemonium, government officials pleaded with Randolph to call off the event, but to no avail. Unless the President complied with African American demands, Randolph reiterated, the march would go forward.

With less than a week remaining, Roosevelt relented and issued Executive Order 8802, which outlawed employment discrimination based on "race, creed, color or national origin" in defense plants, and established the Fair Employment Practices Committee to enforce the new order. The President's mandate, however, avoided any mention of military desegregation. Randolph insisted that military desegregation had never been the primary objective anyway, and terminated the march. Bayard and other members of the militant youth contingent were dumbstruck. They denounced Randolph, arguing that he had sold out to Roosevelt. This criticism, however, had little traction within the black community; for the most part, African Americans believed that Randolph's decision to cancel the march made sense in light of what they saw as the President's significant concessions.

Dissatisfied with Randolph's decision, Rustin turned to the burgeoning pacifist movement. The impending U.S. entry into World War II had created a new urgency among war resisters. Leading the peace charge was the Fellowship of Reconciliation (FOR), the most influential pacifist organization in America. FOR was headed by A. J. Muste, a firebrand cleric whom *Time* magazine had named the "No. 1 U.S. pacifist." The teachings of Mahatma Gandhi on nonviolent direct action had an especially profound impact on Muste. Whereas pacifism and other forms of nonparticipation involved passive resistance to societal ills, nonviolent direct action required confrontation precisely at those pressure points found to be most oppressive. Central to nonviolent direct action was the idea that only in meeting oppression head on could it be challenged and overcome. Taking his cue from the liberation movement in India, Muste and fellow FOR members introduced nonviolent direct action to America in the 1930s. Sit-down strikes were particularly successful in redressing labor grievances during the Great Depression.

Rustin was an heir to this protest tradition when he became FOR's youth secretary and Muste's chief acolyte in late 1941. In the words of a former member, Rustin was Muste's "hands and feet and eyes." The adoration was mutual. Muste predicted that his protégé would have "a national influence in helping to solve the racial discrimination problem in the United States."[12] Further, the FOR leader served as a father-figure to the younger man, whom one activist labeled Muste's "fair-haired boy."[13] So close were their relations that a portion of the FOR membership even believed Rustin might succeed his elder as national leader.

Rustin's rise to leadership in FOR made him both politically visible and vulnerable. His refusal in 1943 to comply with the Selective Service Act landed him a three-year prison sentence, which he served at the Federal Correctional Institution in Ashland, Kentucky. Almost immediately upon his arrival in prison, he launched a series of civil disobedience campaigns to integrate the prison dining room and chapel. For him, politics was where you found yourself. And because he found himself in prison, he determined to use that location as a site from which to engage in political mobilization and agitation. It was not long before he earned a reputation among prison officials as a troublemaker.

But it was not Rustin's race organizing alone that marked him as a troublemaker. He made frequent passes at fellow prisoners, and participated in numerous sexual encounters. After two inmates complained to administrators, he was diagnosed as "a psychopathic personality" and placed in an isolated cell. Rustin was mortified. He was convinced that he had betrayed the movement, not to mention Muste's faith. Moreover, he was angry with himself for failing to exercise discretion with respect to his sexual orientation, even after he had successfully concealed the true nature of his relationship with an outside lover, Davis Platt—to whom he wrote letters addressed to "Marie." In a letter to Muste, he attributed his lapse in judgment to "my own weakness and stupidity," and he worried that his conduct had "jeopardized immeasurably the causes for which I believe I would be willing to die."[14] Muste's response to Bayard was swift, and did little to ease Bayard's sense of weakness and stupidity. "You have been guilty of gross misconduct, specially reprehensible in a person making the claims to leadership and—in a sense—moral superiority.... You have engaged in practices for which there was no justification."[15] But in the same letter Muste, ever the radical Christian, was also consoling. "My admiration for your courage and estimate of your possibilities has never been greater," he wrote. "God is our refuge and strength."[16]

Muste's confidence and faith in Rustin were prescient. Upon his release from prison in March 1947, he began one of the most productive phases of his life. Chief among his accomplishments during this period was the Journey of Reconciliation, FOR's first attempt to bring nonviolent direct action to the attention of the masses. "There has probably never been a genuine nonviolent campaign against the evil of race prejudice," wrote white FOR member George Houser in 1944. "This is due partly to the fact that the method is not well known. It is impossible to know if the campaign would be successful.... However there are enough persons who have heard of the nonviolent direct action procedure...that there is a good probability of the success of such an organized campaign."[17]

Up until this point, segregation laws had been put to the test in the North in local cases with limited visibility. In 1942, FOR race relations secretary James Farmer founded the Congress of Racial Equality (CORE) with the goal of challenging local restrictions in public accommodations, with sit-ins at restaurants and swimming pools. Farmer hoped his local campaigns would spur on other activists interested in challenging Jim Crow laws in their communities. Houser and Rustin took Farmer's vision a step further. Under the auspices of CORE, they broadened the campaign, spreading the strategy of nonviolent direct action to communities throughout the South.

CORE's mobilization of civil disobedience beyond the North was facilitated by a 1946 Supreme Court decision, *Morgan v. Virginia,* which held that a Virginia statute requiring segregation of interstate buses was unconstitutional. *Morgan* was part of a growing body of Supreme Court cases striking down segregation practices that it perceived either to violate antidiscrimination provisions of the Interstate Commerce Act or to burden commerce. In part, the Journey of Reconciliation was conceived of to exploit the political opportunity these legal developments created. Jointly orchestrated by FOR and CORE, the Journey was to take the form of a series of interracial "freedom rides" through the upper South to determine the extent to which bus companies were complying with the requirements of *Morgan*. In April 1947, a planning committee selected fifteen men—eight of whom were white, the other seven being African American—to travel through fifteen cities in Kentucky, North Carolina, Tennessee, and Virginia. Pairing off in interracial couplings, demonstrators intentionally crossed racial boundaries. Whites sat in black-designated sections of the bus, while blacks chose seats reserved for whites.

Rustin was ideally suited to perform this race-switching strategy. Once, in 1942, more than ten years before Rosa Parks was arrested in Montgomery, Alabama, he had been forcibly removed from a bus after refusing to move to the rear of the vehicle. The arresting officers, in spite of their threats, could not shake his composure. Finally, an exasperated station captain shouted at him, "Nigger, you're supposed to be scared when you come in here!" Rustin's rejoinder was quick and sharp: "I am fortified by truth, justice, and Christ.... There is no need to fear." He exhibited the same defiant spirit in the Journey of Reconciliation. Neither he nor the other protestors were shaken by threats from police, bus drivers, even fellow passengers. Over the course of the two-week trip, twelve of the protestors were arrested, including Rustin, who was sentenced to thirty days on a chain gang for violating various "Jim Crow" ordinances. For Rustin, this kind of direct action, and consequent incarceration, was a necessary predicate to dismantling the legal, social, and political edifice of Jim Crow.

By the late 1940s, Bayard Rustin had become an internationally recognized pacifist, whose opinion on nonviolence in U.S. race relations was sought by antiwar groups around the world. It is a little-known fact that Gandhi himself invited him to attend an international pacifist conference scheduled to take place in India in February 1949. The Mahatma's assassination in 1948, however, nearly led his followers to cancel the pending conference. But Gandhi's son carried on his father's plans, and Rustin was warmly received among pacifist circles. "He sang spirituals that won everybody's heart," remembered one young Indian intellectual. "The Martin Luther King phenomenon had not yet started, but we got the very profound impression that Bayard was doing Gandhi's work in North America."[18]

According to the British FOR ambassador and Gandhi devotee Muriel Lester, Rustin's impact in India was "three times as much as [that of] a white pacifist." In a letter to Muste, she requested that FOR extend Rustin's stay. "He's getting into the very centre of power here, and perhaps no one else could work so effectively with [Indian Prime Minister] Nehru against militarism."[19] Muste declined. He felt Rustin needed "to dig into the American situation, at least for several years, before coming to be regarded as a person who can be called out of that situation for extended periods of time."[20] Further, Muste believed, as did most FOR members, that the organization should prioritize domestic issues above foreign affairs.

But Muste did permit Rustin to be "called out" of the American struggle for short pacifist interventions abroad. The Indian victory over British colonialism suggested to pacifists that nonviolent techniques might also assist West African independence movements. The African National Congress in South Africa organized a civil disobedience campaign to end apartheid in 1952, and the anticolonial struggles in Ghana and Nigeria offered promise for nonviolent movements as well. As a diplomatic gesture, FOR sent Rustin to Africa in 1952 on a mission to foster pacifist coalitions with both Kwame Nkrumah of Ghana and Nigerian independence leader Nnamdi Azikiwe. There, Rustin was once more welcomed as a leading proponent of nonviolent direct action in America. Nkrumah's advocacy of nonviolent resistance impressed the American, even if he remained unconvinced of the Prime Minister's commitment to pacifist ideals. Azikiwe's political debt to Gandhi suggested strong possibilities for a nonviolent independence struggle in Nigeria, too.

And it was not only the pacifist orientation of Nkrumah and Azikiwe, among other African leaders, that connected Rustin to Africa. On a personal level, he discovered what he called "staggering" ancestral links with the continent. For example, in Accra, the "dirty, poor, ambitious" capital of Ghana, he found "much that I find in Harlem. We [African Americans] left here in 1619, yet the people here sing, walk, laugh, cry, dance, and strive in a way that is like 125th Street and Lenox Avenue. I seem to know and to understand them as I do nowhere else but in Harlem."[21] This sense of ancestral ties was one of the reasons he

remained interested in, and committed to, African politics and decolonization efforts. Thus, it was with little difficulty that Rustin accepted
Azikiwe's invitation to return to Nigeria in June 1953. Little did he know
that, in a dramatic turn of events, his plans would be dashed.

To help finance his return to Africa, Rustin embarked on a six-
month fundraising tour of the United States, the centerpiece of which
was a series of public speaking engagements. On January 21, 1953, he
had given a talk to the American Association of University Women in
Pasadena, California. Following the lecture, two white men asked him to
join them for a party. The threesome ended up outside Bayard's hotel in
a parked car, where Bayard engaged in sex with the two strangers. Police
appeared on the scene, and the men were arrested on lewd conduct
charges. The *Los Angeles Times* later announced to readers that Bayard—
"a 40-year-old nationally known Negro lecturer"—was sentenced to sixty
days in county jail.

"To be in prison, but not for something he believed in...broke him,
just broke him," recalled a fellow gay FOR member.[22] Muste was outraged. Although he did not interfere with the private lives of his staff, he
objected to actions that jeopardized the reputation of FOR. No longer
tolerant of what he saw as Rustin's transgressions, Muste accepted his
resignation from FOR. The incident brought Rustin a new understanding of his vulnerability as a gay man. "I know now that for me sex must
be sublimated if I am to live with myself and in this world longer."[23]

At the time of Rustin's arrest in 1953, Martin Luther King, Jr., was a
divinity student at Boston University. King arrived in Montgomery,
Alabama, the following year to assume his first ministerial post as the
pastor of Dexter Avenue Baptist Church. Although a bus boycott in
Montgomery had been discussed for months, NAACP secretary Rosa
Parks set the long-awaited protest in motion with her arrest in December
1955. The boycott was coordinated by the Montgomery Improvement
Association (MIA), a grassroots organization formed by local black
activists to lead some 42,000 African Americans in protest. According to
MIA member Jo Ann Gibson Robinson, King was named president
because of his respected intellect—or, as Robinson put it, "He was the
only minister in Montgomery with a Ph.D. degree."[24] However, when the
twenty-six-year-old was placed in charge he had had no experience with
either nonviolent direct action or social protest. "If M. L. King had never

been born this movement would have taken place. I just happened to be here," King observed. "You know there comes a time when time itself is ready for change. That time has come in Montgomery, and I had nothing to do with it."[25]

A. Philip Randolph thought that black Northerners should be a part of what he viewed as a historic struggle in Montgomery. He communicated as much to Rustin, with whom he had long since reconciled. His thinking was that King could benefit from their (Randolph's and Bayard's) combined "experience in nonviolence."[26] To facilitate this Southern/Northern black political cooperation, Randolph recommended to the black Northern civil rights establishment that Rustin should travel to the South as an emissary. The NAACP leadership objected, arguing that his arrest and former Communist affiliation made him too controversial a figure to represent black northern political interests. Randolph did not indulge this sentiment, and dispatched Rustin to meet with Southern leaders, including King.

Randolph was able to dismiss the concerns of the NAACP because he was arguably the preeminent African American civil rights leader of the time. His victory over racial discrimination in defense industry employment in 1941 was followed by another major triumph in 1948 when he threatened President Harry Truman with mass demonstrations of civil disobedience unless the armed forces were desegregated. Truman succumbed to pressure and issued an order stipulating "equality of treatment" in the armed forces. The President's declaration thrilled Randolph but failed to satisfy the demands of young activists like Rustin, who argued that the order fell short of specifically mandating desegregation. As in 1941, Rustin found himself once again being publicly critical of Randolph. At a press conference, Rustin insisted that the civil disobedience campaign would continue—even against Randolph's wishes—until the President issued a formal declaration of military desegregation.

"We were crazy," Rustin later said of this stance.[27] But at the time, it seemed to him to be the politically principled thing to do. "It was nearly three years before I dared to see Mr. Randolph again, after the terrible thing I had done to him." Randolph was completely forgiving, greeting Rustin by saying, "Bayard, where have you been? You know I've needed you." According to Rustin, from that day "until the day he [Randolph] died he never once said a word about what I had done to him."[28] When

Rustin reached Montgomery in February 1956, he was the first of King's entourage of political advisers from the North to arrive. His sudden appearance marked him as an outsider. White city officials had attempted to diffuse the force of the boycott by charging that civic unrest was the result not of efforts of local African Americans but of the work of northern agitators. In spite of his mission to set up workshops to teach nonviolent direct action—or perhaps because of it—Rustin stayed in the background. He wrote to colleagues in New York that "there must be no talk of my being here, and reports should be made confidential in terms of no one here knowing that I am so closely tied in."[29]

His arrival in Montgomery was well timed. In a new scheme to break the boycott, city commissioners indicted leaders of the Montgomery Improvement Association on criminal charges of illegal organizing. King and fellow members gathered their courage, choosing to continue the protest. Taking civil disobedience one step further, Rustin proposed that in the spirit of Gandhi the accused should turn themselves in to authorities voluntarily before arrest warrants were issued. The tactic proved liberating, as protestors defiantly entered the police station amid cheering crowds of African Americans.

Rustin also discreetly advised the MIA on organizational matters. The group voted to call the demonstration a nonviolent protest rather than a boycott, and perhaps under Rustin's influence adopted the motto "Victory Without Violence." Nevertheless, both King and the MIA had an imperfect understanding of Gandhian principles, employing non-violence strictly as a political means to an end rather than as a way of life. Rustin was dismayed to find King's home secured by a barrage of armed guards, and he once even had to remove a gun from a living room chair before taking a seat. Although King had encountered Gandhi's teachings in college textbooks, the finer points of the Indian philosophy of Satyagraha, or "love force," had eluded him. "I had merely an intellectual understanding and appreciation for the position," King remarked, "with no firm determination to organize it."[30] Rustin explained Satyagraha to him in detail, arguing that the presence of guns in the home of a self-proclaimed leader of a nonviolent struggle was a contradiction of beliefs. "[King] was still working out of the framework of Christian love," Rustin recalled. "His attachment to nonviolence reflected his belief that only the blood of Jesus could clarify the world.... I believe he came soon to see what I had recognized while working with

Gandhi's movement in India—that you ought not separate the secular from the religious."[31] Following Rustin's advice, King banished firearms from his household, marking a radical turn in the moral temper of the movement.

Rustin's position at the center of King's inner circle drew the attention of authorities, who confronted him outside the home of a bus boycott defendant. Officers demanded to know his identity. "I am Bayard Rustin," he stated grandly. "I am here as a journalist working for *Le Figaro* and the *Manchester Guardian.*" In naming two foreign newspapers, he became an even greater source of curiosity for local officials. "This afternoon I received word that the white community has learned that I am in Montgomery, that I am being watched, and that efforts will be made to get me out of town," he wrote. "I was warned under no circumstances to go into the white areas of the city."[32] Sensing that he might be forced to leave at a moment's notice, he telephoned A. J. Muste for support. Although Rustin no longer had ties to his former employer, he knew that FOR would send a representative to Montgomery who could eventually replace him if necessary.

FOR indeed provided a representative as requested, but the group was unwilling to risk further liability by working directly with Rustin. "There are some here who feel the local leaders ought to know about Bayard's personal problem but [we] dare not mention it over the phone," the FOR representative wrote upon his arrival in Montgomery. "They ought to know the risks that are being taken and if they are prepared to accept those risks then it is not our responsibility."[33] Rustin had already disclosed his "personal problem" to King, who felt that the value of Rustin's political acumen, not to mention his access to financial resources in the North, outweighed any threat his gayness or radical past posed to the boycott. The MIA did not agree. When a black reporter threatened to expose him as a homosexual and ex-Communist, Rustin was unceremoniously smuggled out of town in the trunk of a car.

Since Rustin could not participate in the bus boycott in person, he did so by proxy from New York. There, he rallied the support of sympathetic northerners under the banner "In Friendship," an organization he cofounded in March 1956. In Friendship orchestrated a high-profile fund-raiser at Madison Square Garden, where 20,000 people came to hear Eleanor Roosevelt, Harry Belafonte, and Sammy Davis, Jr., speak on civil rights.

If Rustin felt bitterness toward the MIA over his expulsion from Montgomery, he concealed those sentiments. In fact, he kept in steady contact with King by letter and telephone. As with other pacifist leaders who came to King's assistance, Rustin understood that an MIA triumph entailed more than the mere desegregation of city buses, writing: "I felt that without a victory at Montgomery, the southern protest movement, then showing its first signs of life, would die stillborn." Just as critically, however, he saw the boycott as a stepping-stone to mass nonviolent social protest throughout America. He believed that "a victory at Montgomery would have no permanent meaning in the racial struggle unless it led to the achievement of dozens of similar victories throughout the South.... [T]his meant that the movement needed a sustaining mechanism that could translate what we had learned during the bus boycott into a broad strategy for protest in the South."[34]

That sustaining mechanism was born in January 1957 with the inaugural meeting of the Southern Christian Leadership Conference (SCLC). The widely reported events in Montgomery had inspired acts of civil disobedience in other southern states, and the nascent SCLC united the leaders of these neighboring movements. The organization was launched as an assembly of black southern ministers who sought to "redeem the soul of America" through nonviolent direct action. According to Rustin, the SCLC was first discussed with King in fall 1956. "I think Gandhi would very definitely conclude that Montgomery cannot win unless satellite protests take place all over the South, not in one or two places, but a couple of dozen places," he told King. "...[Y]ou've got to set up a South-wide organization, which will support Montgomery AND simultaneously all these other places."[35] At first King did not understand Rustin's intentions in practical terms, but he soon came to share his colleague's vision that the bus boycott was merely an inaugural political event in a long drive to completely desegregate southern politics and everyday life.

In spite of its clerical orientation and regional emphasis, SCLC was conceived by secular-minded activists in New York City. Rustin and In Friendship cofounders Stanley Levison and Ella Baker presented to King a series of working papers that served as the basis for the organization. Their outline called for mass direct action against racial oppression, combined with voter education and outreach. Although Rustin, Levison, and Baker were neither the first nor the only activists to foresee the possibilities for a southern movement beyond Montgomery—among others, FOR proposed replicating the bus boycott elsewhere—the three offered unsurpassed practical expertise, which King readily embraced. Levison was a liberal attorney who belonged to the American Jewish Congress and the NAACP and was supportive of Communist Party politics during the "red-baiting" campaigns of Senator Joseph McCarthy in the early 1950s. Working behind the scenes with Rustin, Levison drafted King's speeches, press releases, and articles and even coordinated his public appearances.

Baker was an outspoken feminist whose grassroots activism dated back to the 1930s. She was the first woman president of the New York chapter of the NAACP, before resigning in 1946 over her assertion that the group was preoccupied with building its coffers rather than leading a mass movement. While Baker had affiliations with the Communist Party, she was not marginalized for that involvement by the civil rights establishment to the extent that Rustin was. In fact, she was appointed Executive Director of SCLC in February 1958.

Baker did, however, encounter sexism in SCLC that mirrored Rustin's political tribulations as a gay man. SCLC ministers, few of whom had ever before taken directions from a woman, resisted her authority, while King disregarded Baker's input on substantive matters. Sharing Rustin's vision for a South-wide movement, she pointed out to King that time was of the essence. It was her sense that SCLC was in a political position to create and sustain the kind of "mass action" required to ensure that legal victories like *Brown v. Board of Education* were respected. She warned that if SCLC failed to perform this function, "some other group will."[36] According to Baker, SCLC was fast becoming a "cult of personality" devoted solely to the upkeep of King's celebrity status. When she raised this concern directly with King, he replied, "Well, I can't help what people do."[37] As Baker explained, "The combination of my being a woman and an older woman presented problems...[and] there would never be any role for me in a leadership capacity."[38] Another woman on the SCLC executive committee, Septima Clark, affirmed Baker's point of view: "[T]hose men didn't have any faith in women, none whatsoever. They just thought that women were sex symbols and had no contribution to make.... Like other black ministers, Dr. King didn't think too much of the way women could contribute. But working in the movement he changed the lives of so many people that it was getting to the place where he would have to see that women were more than sex symbols."[39] Baker resigned from SCLC in April 1960, taking her talents to the burgeoning student protest movement.

At about the same time, Rustin left SCLC as well, but under even more contentious circumstances than did Baker. Once again Rustin's homosexuality was a subject of controversy, only now the accusation directly implicated King: namely, that King and Bayard were sexually involved. Adam Clayton Powell, Jr., the influential African American Congressman from Harlem, threatened to announce to the press a fabricated homosexual coupling of Rustin and King unless their plan to organize a march at the Democratic national convention was called off. The march had been proposed by A. Philip Randolph to keep civil rights issues at the forefront of the 1960 presidential election. He expected 5,000 demonstrators would descend on the convention, and the Democratic Party is believed to have ordered Powell, who hoped to win a cabinet position, to stop the protest. Rather than attack Randolph, the lofty elder statesman of the movement, Powell went after King, who was more vulnerable to blackmail. King had an overwhelming fear of the press, and he was already facing rumors of heterosexual extramarital relations. Rustin recalled that FBI Director J. Edgar Hoover had been "spreading stories, and there were very real efforts to entrap him. I think at a given point he had to reach a decision."[40] Desperate, King solicited advice on Powell's ultimatum from Randolph, who answered, "We simply deny [the allegations] and go about doing our business."[41] But other advisers urged King to sever ties with Rustin.

King procrastinated, unable to reach a decision—or perhaps wishing that Rustin would make the decision for him. When Rustin realized that a decision from King was not forthcoming, he read between the lines. Putting the "greater good" of the movement before his own interests, he voluntarily stepped down from SCLC and quit his position on the march committee. Much to Rustin's bitter surprise, King quickly accepted his resignation. Few observers expected such swift acquiescence from the famed civil rights leader who had exhorted blacks in Montgomery "to let your conscience be your guide."[42] James Baldwin wrote that King had "lost much moral credit...in the eyes of the young, when he allowed Adam Clayton Powell to force the resignation of his extremely able organizer and lieutenant."[43] And Muste, in a political about-turn, said that he was "personally ashamed of Martin."[44]

Although Rustin felt utterly betrayed by King, his bitterness toward him eventually softened. As Rustin later explained in an interview, "Dr. King came from a very protected background. I don't think he'd ever known a gay person in his life. I think he had no real sympathy or understanding. I think he wanted very much to. But I think he was largely guided by two facts. One was that already people were whispering about him. And I think his attitude was, look, I've got enough of my own problems.... Secondly, [by the late 1960s] he was surrounded by people who, for their own reasons, wanted to get rid of me—Andy Young, in particular, and Jesse Jackson."[45] Rustin also described a sexual double standard at work that condoned promiscuity for heterosexual activists but denied the same freedom to gays. "Oh, the crap that was going on in those motels as the movement moved from place to place was acceptable. The homosexual act was not."[46]

Rustin's rift with King was symbolic of an overall political shift occurring in the movement itself in 1960. African American students began to wrest political control away from church leaders with the creation of the Student Nonviolent Coordinating Committee (SNCC). The organization was started in April in alliance with SCLC, and soon challenged King and the rest of the civil rights establishment with an interracial brigade of nonviolent freedom fighters. Ella Baker was instrumental in launching SNCC, and Rustin provided "inestimable help" to the fledgling group.

On the opposite side of the ideological spectrum, Malcolm X added armed militancy to the fray. King was opposed to Malcolm's advocacy of violence, and an SCLC aide was once so overwrought with anger that he was nearly involved in a fistfight with the then-emerging Black Muslim leader. Although Rustin objected to armed self-defense on principle, and rejected Malcolm's by-any-means-necessary mantra, he nevertheless managed friendly relations with the firebrand minister. He was even responsible for bringing Malcolm to speak at Howard University in 1962, after administrators refused him access to students. "I told Malcolm," he recalled, "that I could arrange his appearance on the campus but strictly on my terms. 'What are your terms?' he asked. I said, 'We'll have a debate. You'll present your views, and then I'll attack you as someone having no political, social, or economic program for dealing with the problems of blacks.' He said, 'I'll take you up on that.'"[47] Ultimately, Bayard remained critical of Malcolm's separatist rhetoric. African Americans faced more pressing concerns, he argued, namely jobs and civil rights protection under the law.

Indeed, employment issues and civil rights legislation were the impetus for the March on Washington, which Rustin organized, on August 28, 1963. A. Philip Randolph, acting in the capacity of president of the Negro American Labor Council, had chosen to mark the centennial of the Emancipation Proclamation with a mass demonstration against African American unemployment. Randolph tapped Rustin to lead the march, asking him to draw up an agenda. "We should emphasize the theme that the Emancipation Proclamation of 1863 has failed to bring real freedom for the Negro; no worker in America is genuinely free," Rustin suggested in his blueprint. "We now demand a program of action in 1963 that will ensure the emancipation of all labor, regardless of color, race, or creed." He called for congressional lobbying over two consecutive days of nonviolent direct action, including a ceremonial march down Pennsylvania Avenue followed by a rally at the Lincoln Memorial. Although the gathering began as a labor demonstration, the Emancipation March for Jobs, as the event was originally named, assumed greater breadth of purpose once participation was solicited from the civil rights establishment. The "Big Six" selected by Randolph to cochair the march were: James Farmer, director of CORE; John Lewis, chairman of SNCC; Roy Wilkins, executive director of the NAACP; Whitney Young, president of the National Urban League (NUL); and, of course, King under SCLC. The sixth opening was filled by Randolph himself.

In spite of well-ordered preparations, Rustin's agenda was soon dismantled by political rivalries and personal differences. King, too, had plans for a march on Washington, he told Randolph, adding that the primary concern of SCLC was not unemployment but civil rights. Wilkins and Young expressed similar reservations. Wilkins argued that civil disobedience would jeopardize President John F. Kennedy's comprehensive civil rights bill pending in Congress. Moreover, the President personally warned the Big Six at a White House conference that the march might "create an atmosphere of intimidation," wherein even supporters of his bill would be "forced to vote for it at the point of a gun."[48] Wilkins instead favored "the quiet, patient lobbying tactics that worked best on Congress."[49] As for the NUL, Young reminded Randolph that the tax-exempt status of his organization prohibited his involvement in political lobbying.

Long-standing resentments among the civil rights leaders also divided the committee. "Martin, some bright reporter is going to take a good look at Montgomery," Wilkins said caustically, "and discover that despite all the hoopla your boycott didn't desegregate a single bus. It was the quiet NAACP-type legal action that did it."[50] Still, even Wilkins recognized that King's participation was essential—certainly Randolph did, if only for reasons of prestige. In a gesture to allay some of King's concerns and ensure King's cooperation, Randolph renamed the event the "March on Washington for Jobs and Freedom." He also struck civil disobedience and mass lobbying from the agenda in deference to Wilkins and Young. As it turned out, these changes also mollified President Kennedy, who publicly endorsed the march in July. What later became the 1964 Civil Rights Act moved closer to passage that summer.

Still, the Big Six remained in disharmony. They needed to name a march director, and Randolph's assumption that Rustin would lead the event was hotly contested. Wilkins was worried that Rustin's sexual orientation would "provide ammunition for our enemies, who were doing all they could to attack the march."[51] Rustin discussed the matter privately with him. "I think the time has come when we have to stand up and stop running from these things," he reportedly told the NAACP leader. "And I don't believe that if this is raised by any of the southern Democrats, that it will do anything but spur the people on."[52] Although Wilkins's concern was not unreasonable—after all, Rustin had left SCLC under precisely these circumstances—the rest of the committee, including King, supported Bayard's appointment. "This was going to be a massively complex undertaking, and there was no one more able to pull it together than Bayard Rustin," John Lewis recalled.[53] "The consensus was that he be involved, and Wilkins relented." A compromise was brought about in July, when Young suggested that Randolph be placed in charge. Randolph agreed to the motion, but cautioned, "I want to warn you before I vote that if I'm made leader, I'm going to be given the privilege of determining my staff. I also want you to know that I'll make Bayard my deputy."[54] In reply, Wilkins issued his own warning to Randolph: "We're going to hold you responsible for any embarrassment that might befall the March on Washington."[55]

Wilkins's warning proved to be prescient. With the march only two weeks away, FBI Director Hoover disseminated a transcribed telephone recording in which King made disparaging comments about Rustin.

According to the confidential wire-tapped conversation, King expressed concern to an unidentified colleague that opponents of the march would seize on Rustin's personal life just as Wilkins had feared. "They're going to make a hell of a mess of it," King lamented. Worse, he added that he hoped Rustin would not drink before the march, "and grab one little brother. 'Cause he will grab one when he drinks."[56] Senator Strom Thurmond of South Carolina, a rabid segregationist, denounced Rustin as a sexual degenerate on the floor of Congress. In response, Randolph rushed to his deputy's defense. "I am sure I speak for the combined Negro leadership in voicing complete confidence in Bayard Rustin's character, integrity and extraordinary ability," Randolph asserted. "Twenty-two arrests in the fight for civil rights attests, in my mind, to Mr. Rustin's dedication to high human ideals. That Mr. Rustin was on one occasion arrested in another connection has long been a matter of public record." He continued, "There are those who contend that this incident...voids or overwhelms Mr. Rustin's ongoing contribution to the struggle for human rights. I hold otherwise."[57] Randolph's unconditional support of Bayard was exemplary, and his faith in his protégé remained steadfast for life. As Rustin remembered, an activist was once shocked to find a known homosexual working as Randolph's aide. When the disgruntled activist demanded an explanation, Randolph answered, "Well, well, if Bayard, a homosexual, is that talented—and I know the work he does for me—maybe I should be looking for somebody else homosexual who could be so useful."[58]

The March on Washington was a turning point in American protest history. Under Rustin's direction, the movement peacefully coalesced for the first time ever, articulating its demands for economic empowerment and civil rights with one voice. Even Malcolm X, who had publicly ridiculed "the farce on Washington," attended, telling reporters, "Well, whatever black folks do, maybe I don't agree with it; but I'm going to be there, brother, because that's where I belong."[59] More than 250,000 people attended the march, while millions of television viewers watched from home. However, the proceedings did not lack controversy. In spite of the formative role that Rosa Parks and Ella Baker played in the movement, no woman activist was invited to give a major address. Writer Pauli Murray complained to Randolph, "It is indefensible to call a national March on Washington and send out a Call which contains the name of not a single woman leader."[60]

And there were two unanticipated political fires that Rustin had to put out. One was Attorney General Robert F. Kennedy's objection to what he perceived to be the inflammatory tone of Lewis's speech. At Rustin's request, Lewis modified his comments, ending that conflagration. But there was another: complaints from SCLC that Rustin had purposely marginalized King by placing him last in the program. Rustin denied the accusation, explaining that "almost all the other speakers had asked me to make sure they didn't follow King...they realized that the minute King finished speaking the program would be over, that everybody would be heading home."[61] As it turned out, Rustin was entirely right. King's "I Have a Dream" speech was the pinnacle of the march, if not a symbolic culmination of the movement. While Congress has yet to heed King's call to "let freedom ring," the march helped to secure the passage of the Civil Rights Act in July 1964. Moreover, the gathering created a visible moment of nation building. In Rustin's words, the march "made Americans feel for the first time that we were capable of being truly a nation, that we were capable of moving beyond division and bigotry."[62]

The March on Washington was equally a personal triumph for Bayard. He called the march "the most exciting project I've ever worked on."[63] In only seven weeks, he orchestrated the largest public protest in American history, and discovered that the fanfare surrounding his accomplishment would help open doors previously closed to him. Rustin was pictured along with Randolph on the cover of *Life* magazine, which proclaimed in September 1963, "For all the dissension that has split Negro organizations, the march was an astonishingly well-executed product of leadership." King considered Rustin for an executive role in SCLC, querying an aide in an FBI wire-tapped phone call "whether it would be possible for Rustin to come back in the civil rights movement, inasmuch as he has now received good press publicity as a result of the March on Washington."[64] Although King communicated to Rustin that SCLC was interested in his joining the organization, it is not clear whether SCLC ever presented him with a formal offer.

And it was not only King who made political overtures to Rustin. The NAACP did as well, offering him a permanent position on its staff. However, the prospect of working for Wilkins discomforted Rustin almost as much as that of working with the SCLC; aside from Rustin's troubled past with these groups (not to mention the likelihood that his homosexuality would continue to undermine his authority), he understood that he was ill suited to what he perceived to be their narrow civil rights agendas. As King had explained to Randolph, SCLC was largely disinterested in labor issues, and the NAACP was focused on the courts. Concerned also that the offer from the NAACP was an attempt to control him—and having no formal offer from SCLC—Rustin remained, as the *Saturday Evening Post* put it, "The Lone Wolf of Civil Rights."

In 1965, he took a formal position as executive director of the newly created A. Philip Randolph Institute. Started with a founding grant from the AFL-CIO, the institute marked an important transition in the protest movement. As Rustin explained, "The civil rights movement is evolving from a protest movement into a full-fledged *social movement*— an evolution calling its very name into question. It is now concerned not merely with removing the barriers to full *opportunity* but with achieving the fact of *equality*."[65] The A. Philip Randolph Institute devoted itself to public works and national economic planning, including, among other activities, the development of an apprentice training program that placed people of color in the predominantly white building trade unions. The political strides of nonviolent direct action had dismantled the legal foundation of segregation in America, but landmark legislative victories alone could not create jobs for unemployed blacks. For Rustin, eliminating discrimination under the law was not enough. His new social movement was invested in ending de facto discrimination as well, including discrimination in the opportunities people had to educate themselves and earn a decent living. He asked: "What is the value of winning access to public accommodations for those who lack the money to use them?"[66]

Rustin's quest to broaden the reach of civil rights activism was not uncontroversial. James Farmer of CORE wondered "how Bayard could go to the length he did in saying that the fight against race problems was now secondary to the fight against economic problems?"[67] Other observers felt that Rustin had abandoned the civil rights movement for the AFL-CIO. Still other activists interpreted his transition more generously as an opportunity for forging bonds between the protest and labor movements.

Black militants were especially dismayed by Rustin's new politics, even those activists who at one point deeply respected him. Stokely

Carmichael, for example, recalled that "Bayard was one of the first persons I had direct contact with [of whom] I could really say, 'That's what I want to be.'"[68] But Carmichael wanted nothing to do with the Bayard Rustin of the Randolph Institute. The problem wasn't simply Rustin's commitment to integration, which the emerging Black Power movement was beginning to vigorously contest; more fundamentally, the problem was that he seemed to be against organizing solely around race—and more specifically, blackness. Rustin was a staunch critic of black nationalism and black power. "I contend not only that black power lacks any real value for the civil rights movement, but that its propagation is positively harmful. It diverts the movement from a meaningful debate over strategy and tactics, it isolates the Negro community, and it encourages the growth of anti-Negro forces," he argued.[69] Thus, he even challenged the need and legitimacy of black studies programs, which he thought suffered from a similar separatist orientation. For his part, Carmichael believed that Rustin was distancing himself from African Americans at precisely the moment when black people were beginning to embrace their blackness and claim their rights to political and economic autonomy. As Carmichael saw it, Rustin's economics-first approach undermined black power and threatened the establishment of a community within which blacks could identify as a group.

Carmichael's critique of Rustin was part of broader challenge to what he and other black nationalists perceived to be a reformist approach to civil rights. As SNCC chairman, Carmichael maintained that no national civil rights group represented the concerns of the black underclass. None spoke to the African Americans rioting in the ghettos of Harlem and Watts. Nor could they, Carmichael suggested, as long as these groups were part of an interracial coalition. Carmichael was convinced that "the white man is irrelevant to blacks, except as an oppressive force."[70] Rustin disagreed. "The relevant question," he wrote, "is not whether [a] politician is black or white, but what forces he represents."[71]

Increasingly, this was the question being asked of Rustin, particularly about his reevaluation of pacifism in 1965. He accounted for his evolution as follows: "Whereas I used to believe that pacifism had a political value, I no longer believe that.... I do not believe you can organize a society in which men will refuse to fight, until they have a proven alternative to war. Therefore I'm a pacifist to this extent: I believe that the first and most important thing we can do is to discover the means of defending freedom that men can use. It is ridiculous, in my view, to talk only about peace." Central to Rustin's thinking was the idea that freedom was "more valuable to people than peace." His political project, therefore, was "to find a peaceful way to defend democratic freedom."[72]

Part of the problem with peace activism, as Rustin saw it, was that the movement was structured around a series of vague slogans, such as "end the war." The larger question, he observed, was: how, precisely, does one end war? "[M]any groups in the peace movement fail to provide a step-by-step method by which the US can get out [of Vietnam] and still have national pride," Bayard wrote in the *New York Times* in 1967. "Now it may be that they are right and I am wrong, that there is no way to gradually educate people for a way out. I happen to believe, however, that there is, and therefore I call for sitting down with everybody involved."[73] But when he advised King against merging civil rights concerns with the antiwar movement, pacifists charged Rustin with pandering to the Johnson administration. Certainly some of his offhanded remarks to peace groups ("You guys can't deliver a single pint of milk to the kids in Harlem, and Lyndon Johnson can") did little to dissuade others from this interpretation.[74] Pacifist colleagues, most notably those leading the peace movement to end the war in Vietnam, were aghast. "How can you live with yourself?" one former associate clamored.[75]

While Rustin's political pragmatism alienated him from political radicals, his preoccupation with economic matters was a concern shared by both SCLC leaders and other members of the civil rights establishment. Most notably, King conceived the Poor People's Campaign, an ambitious plan to bring thousands of poor Americans to descend upon Washington, D.C., lawmakers in summer 1968. As was his practice, he first sought input from Rustin, who responded in January that the campaign lacked focus. He cautioned King, "We are not now in the period we were in 1963 at the time of Selma, Birmingham and the March on Washington, when there was absolute clarity in everyone's mind as to objectives. The confusion today around economic questions and the splintering of the movement, I am convinced, requires a clear statement as to objectives, strategy, and tactics." Nonetheless, King remained vague in his course of action, and Rustin politely bowed out.

He then turned his attention to Memphis, Tennessee, where a group of black sanitation workers were on strike against racial discrimination. To support their demands, Rustin joined the Community on the

Move for Equality (COME), and the strike was bolstered further by King's arrival on April 3 to lead a march on their behalf. When the next day King was assassinated outside his motel room, the nation was dealt a tragic blow. Rustin along with millions of Americans was overcome by grief. Unlike the other mourners, however, his anguish was personal, and he was unable to prevent himself from crying during television interviews. Paradoxically, King's murder created a civil rights opportunity, an occasion, Rustin insisted, to remind mourners that "it is up to us, the living, the black and white, to realize Dr. King's dream."[76]

According to Bayard, full employment and a living wage were one important manifestation of that dream. King had told an AFL-CIO audience in 1961 that the African American protest movement and the labor movement were the "two most dynamic and cohesive liberal forces in the country," adding, "I look forward confidently to the day when all who work for a living will be one.... This will...bring into full realization the American dream—a dream yet unfulfilled."[77] Rustin quoted these remarks at length in an article published one month after the assassination. He echoed King's sentiments for the purpose of underscoring that a black/labor coalition was essential to defeat Richard Nixon in the 1968 Presidential election; otherwise, he warned, "we may find ourselves in a decade of vindictive and mean conservative domination."[78]

Although Rustin claimed that unions were "the most integrated institution in American society," organized labor was by no means free from racial discrimination.[79] African Americans were underrepresented in leadership positions, while blacks filled a disproportionate number of low-paying jobs. In spite of these shortcomings, Rustin maintained that of all American institutions the labor movement was the one best equipped to meet the needs of African Americans. "What is needed...is not only a program that would effect some fundamental change in the distribution of America's resources for those in the greatest need of them but a political majority that will support such a program as well," he wrote in 1971. "[T]here is one social force which, by virtue of both its size and its very nature, is essential to the creation of such a majority—and so in relation to which the success or failure of the black struggle must finally turn. And that is the American trade union movement."[80]

Rustin's ties to organized labor, combined with his outspoken dismissal of black nationalism at the height of the Black Power era, earned him a reputation as a political conservative. His reputation would be further undermined by what many perceived to be his uncritical support of Israel. Detractors pointed out that while he opposed black nationalism, he had no problem with nationalism when it came to the state of Israel. Some members of the radical left accused Rustin of having been bought out by "Jewish money."

He countered by saying that many Jews had "stood side-by-side" with the black civil rights movement. "One of the more unprofitable strategies we could ever adopt is now to join in history's oldest and most shameful witch-hunt, anti-Semitism," he told the black press in 1967.[81] Three years later, the A. Philip Randolph Institute ran a full-page advertisement in the *New York Times* calling for U.S. military aid to Israel. Rustin even launched a formal organization, Black Americans to Support Israel Committee (BASIC), in 1975. To those who chanted that Zionism equals racism, he replied, "Zionism is not racism, but the legitimate expression of the Jewish people's self-determination." This in a second advertisement in the *Times* asserting that "blacks and Jews have a common interest in democracy and justice."[82]

By this time, former allies were openly hostile to Rustin's position on Israel; former comrades suggested that his support was "probably good business for the APRI Institute."[83] For his part, he maintained that the issue was indeed economics but of another sort: the creation of jobs. As he explained to the Anti-Defamation League, "We must get on with the fight for a coalition of labor forces, of religious forces, of businessmen, of liberal and civil rights groups standing together. White fear, Negro frustration, and anti-Semitism will disappear not because we rail against them but because we bring about a social and economic program to neutralize them."[84]

By the late 1970s Rustin's humanitarian concerns encompassed not only Israel but also human rights matters throughout the world. Whereas he had traveled widely during his years as a representative to FOR and later as an adviser to King, his trips abroad were now no longer undertaken to carry the message of the American civil rights struggle to foreign countries. He became an internationally recognized proponent of free elections everywhere, as well as of aid to Southeast Asian refugees. Under the auspices of Freedom House, an international human rights group, he served as an election observer in Barbados, El Salvador, Grenada, and Zimbabwe. As vice chairman of the International Rescue Committee (IRC), a nonpartisan refugee aid organization, he visited Pakistan, Puerto Rico, and Somalia. However, his most pro-longed engagement overseas was under the Citizens Commission on Indochinese Refugees, which provided refugee camps with IRC moni-tors, doctors, and provisions. Over the next ten years Bayard traveled to Thailand five times; notably in February 1980, when he participated in a March for Survival with Joan Baez, Liv Ullmann, and Elie Wiesel, among others. Rustin was also credited with uniting human rights groups with American labor unions. Aside from offering IRC financial support, the AFL-CIO was instrumental in persuading President Jimmy Carter to liberalize immigration restrictions for Southeast Asians. Rustin ran a full-page ad in the *New York Times,* imploring "President Carter and the United States Congress to facilitate the entrance of these refugees into the United States in the same spirit that we have urged our country to accept the victims of South Africa's apartheid."[85]

Rustin witnessed apartheid first-hand when he made his first visit to South Africa at the invitation of Zulu Chief Gatasha Buthelezi in 1983. Disregarding leftist orthodoxy of the day, Rustin espoused the politically unpopular position of limited sanctions for South Africa, arguing that total sanctions might devastate its economy and harm the movement for democracy. According to him, the primary objective was ensuring a nonracial democracy in postapartheid South Africa. He was particularly concerned about who might lead the South African government after apartheid had ended. A second visit under the auspices of IRC in 1986 did not allay his concerns about leadership. It was his sense that the African National Congress (ANC) was only "fairly democratic." He qual-ified his views in this way because of the organization's practice of guerilla warfare, which, he pointed out, was not "the democratic process."[86] As for Nelson Mandela, Rustin did not think that he was a viable leader. For one thing, Mandela was still imprisoned. For another, even if Mandela was released from prison, his advanced age and failing health would prevent him from effectively leading the nation. Finally, with respect to the candidacy of Buthelezi, Rustin described him as a man who "had great leadership qualities" but "cannot stand any form of crit-icism."[87] This suggested to Rustin that Buthelezi was unlikely to be a proponent of democratic rule. Unable to play a direct role in facilitating the establishment of democratic leadership in South Africa, Rustin played an indirect role by coordinating a foreign aid program in 1986 called Project South Africa, which matched U.S. humanitarian groups with some seventy South African grassroots organizations dedicated to the furtherance of democracy through peaceful means.

In the late 1980s, at the same time he was working internationally, Rustin became publicly vocal about his homosexuality. Of course, his gayness had been well-known throughout civil rights and humanitarian circles for years, and he never denied the truth of his sexual orientation when asked. But his "coming out" in the national press of the 1980s marked an important transition. "[T]here is a double responsibility for people like myself to come out. Because we are highly respected in a number of areas," Rustin told the *Village Voice* in 1987. "I think the gay community has a moral obligation...to do whatever is possible to encourage more and more gays to come out of the closet."[88]

Rustin turned to the gay press to elaborate on his motivations for coming out, telling black gay editor Joseph Beam, "[E]very gay who is in the closet is ultimately a threat to the freedom of gays. I don't want to seem intolerant to them, and I think we have to say that to them with a great deal of affection, but remaining in the closet is the other side of prejudice against gays. Because until you challenge it, you are not play-ing an active role in fighting it."[89] Speaking specifically to African American lesbians and gay men, Rustin recommended that they "try to build coalitions of people for the elimination of *all* injustice."[90]

As a gay elder statesman of the African American civil rights strug-gle, Rustin was often called upon by gay people to compare the black movement with the gay rights struggle. "The gay movement is much simpler; it only seems harder," he explained. "The homosexual struggle is only to fight prejudice under the law. It does not require billions of dollars for an economic program."[91] It was his view that since gays and lesbians as a group were not economically disadvantaged, the gay rights struggle was for symbolic, not substantive, equality. The black civil rights movement, on the other hand, was forced to direct its energy at elimi-nating not only the formal laws of Jim Crow but also the poor economic conditions that Jim Crow laws had helped to create and sustain.

Notwithstanding Rustin's sense that meaningful differences existed between the gay rights and the black civil rights movements, it was his view that the two were deeply connected. Although he had not partici-pated in the Mattachine Society, the first national gay organization in the United States, nor in other gay protest groups of the pre-Stonewall era, he believed that his contributions to the black civil rights movement indirectly helped to launch the gay liberation movement. According to him, the black civil rights movement had created the social conditions and political strategies that made the gay rights movement possible. Put another way, Montgomery helped to produce Stonewall. Rustin thought it was important that contemporary gay civil rights leaders draw lessons from the black civil rights movement, particularly the lesson that "unless you are out here fighting for yourself, then nobody else will." He became convinced that gay rights rather than black civil rights had become *the* "barometer for social change." At a 1986 gathering of Black and White Men Together, an interracial gay organization, he explained that "[t]wenty-five years ago, if you were to know whether a person was truly for democracy, you asked a simple question, 'What about blacks?'... To ask that question now about blacks...is no longer the central question. If you want to know whether today people believe in democracy...the question to ask is, 'What about people who are gay?' Because that is now the litmus paper by which this democracy is to be judged."[92] He reasoned that, given the vanguard social status of gay identity, the gay movement had a unique social responsibility to the world. Thus he was "very hard with the gay community, not because I want to be hard with my fellow gays, but because we stand in the center of the progress towards democracy." While he did not practice narrow identity politics, he did believe that there was a relationship between identity and politics. He had difficulty understanding how a gay person could be an anti-Semite, or why "many of the gays in New York...[didn't] want blacks coming into their bars."[93] He genuinely held the view that there was a fundamental contradiction between being gay and being prejudiced.

As prescient as Rustin often was about politics, even he could not have predicated the new battlefront for gay activism in the 1980s: the AIDS/HIV epidemic. Black civil rights leaders were slow to respond to the growing pandemic. Bayard helped to change that by publicly commenting on the epidemic and sensitizing groups like the NAACP, the National Urban League, and the Black Medical Association to social and racial implications of AIDS. As a result of his efforts, the civil rights establishment by 1987 was, in his words, "reluctantly coming to see the reality" of AIDS/HIV.[94] Still, it wasn't until 1989 that the NAACP mentioned AIDS/HIV in its literature, by which point more than 17,000 black people had died from the disease. And it would take almost another decade before the organization seriously engaged AIDS as a social and civil rights problem that affected the well-being of the black community. In the meantime, Rustin urged black gays and lesbians to confront black civil rights leaders and churches for failing to respond to AIDS. "You cannot expect the white gay community to challenge blacks about AIDS," he insisted. "It has to be the black gay community.... [B]lack gays have a dual responsibility—to fight in the black community against AIDS, and fight in the white gay community as well."[95]

While Rustin's limited involvement in AIDS activism helped to solidify his public identity as a black gay man, this "coming out" was less politically charged than it might appear to be from his comments to the press. As his partner, Walter Naegle (whom he met in 1977 and with whom he remained lovers until his death a decade later), attested, Rustin's gay activism consisted primarily of delivering speeches, attending conferences, and giving interviews. Most of his political attention focused on operating the A. Philip Randolph Institute, whose primary function throughout the 1980s was to place African Americans in the trade unions. And when he was not pursuing this agenda, he devoted his time to international human rights work.

The fall of Haiti's dictators in 1987 served as the impetus for Rustin's humanitarian visit in July, when he and other Freedom House representatives arrived to monitor the possibilities for democratic elections. Shortly after his return home, he experienced intense nausea. Doctors prescribed medication but were unable to diagnose his condition. Finally, exploratory surgery in August revealed that his appendix was perforated. He was recovering from the operation when his condition worsened suddenly. Rustin died from cardiac arrest on August 24 at age seventy-five.

The next day, his death was headlined in the *New York Times* with a full-page obituary lauding his contributions to Martin Luther King, Jr., and the March on Washington. The newspaper chose to overlook his most recent accomplishments (including his gay rights advocacy and refugee work), mentioning only his support for Israel. A more fitting tribute was offered at the Community Church in New York City, where a thousand colleagues, admirers, and loved ones recalled his extraordinary life. In the words of National Urban League director Vernon Jordan, "His lifetime of devotion to the cause of civil rights and human rights invokes the words of Oliver Wendell Holmes, who wrote that, as life is action and passion, it is required of a man to share the action and passion of his time or risk being judged not to have lived. Bayard Rustin truly lived."[96]

With the 1990s came a wave of new and more in-depth tributes that began the long-neglected task of considering Rustin's contributions and controversies in detail. Two groundbreaking biographies, Jervis Anderson's *Bayard Rustin: Troubles I've Seen* and Daniel Levine's *Bayard Rustin and the Civil Rights Movement,* in addition to James Haskins's young-adult book *Bayard Rustin: Behind the Scenes of the Civil Rights Movement,* presented readers with the fullest chronicles to date of Rustin's life and legacy. John D'Emilio's recent biography, *Lost Prophet: The Life and Times of Bayard Rustin,* enhanced this notoriety. And in 2002, a feature-length documentary film, *Brother Outsider: The Life of Bayard Rustin,* brought unprecedented awareness to the man.

Bayard Rustin's past remains a point of contention even today. Only last year, the public school district in his hometown of West Chester, Pennsylvania, weathered a firestorm of debate over whether to name a high school after the city's most famous native son. Once again, critics dug out his Communist Party affiliation and homosexuality, which were put before the public as justification for denying him much-deserved credit due. The school board stood its ground, however, and voted in favor of the newly named Bayard Rustin High School, marking another battle won on his behalf. *Time on Two Crosses* takes its place in line with these honors.

Devon W. Carbado and Donald Weise
March 2003
San Francisco

NOTES

1. Redvers Jeanmarie, "An Interview with Bayard Rustin," in *Other Countries: Black Gay Voices,* vol. 1 (Other Countries Collective, 1988).
2. Jervis Anderson, *Bayard Rustin: Troubles I've Seen* (HarperCollins, 1997), 7.
3. Anderson, 19.
4. Anderson, 34–35.
5. George Chauncey, Jr., and Lisa Kennedy, "Time on Two Crosses: An Interview with Bayard Rustin," *Village Voice,* June 30, 1987.
6. Anderson, 38.
7. *Open Hands.*
8. *Open Hands.*
9. Anderson, 56.
10. Anderson, 59.
11. Jervis Anderson, *A. Philip Randolph: A Biographical Portrait* (University of California, 1986), 248–49.
12. Anderson, 67.
13. Daniel Levine, *Bayard Rustin and the Civil Rights Movement* (Rutgers, 2000), 31.
14. Levine, 45.
15. Levine, 45.
16. Levine, 45.
17. Levine, 50.
18. Anderson, 131.
19. Anderson, 133.
20. Anderson, 134.
21. Anderson, 146.
22. Levine, 70.
23. Levine, 71.
24. Jo Ann Gibson Robinson, *The Montgomery Bus Boycott and the Women Who Started It: The Memoir of Jo Ann Gibson Robinson* (University of Tennessee, 1987), 67.
25. David J. Garrow, *Bearing the Cross: Martin Luther King, Jr., and the Southern Christian Leadership Conference* (Morrow, 1986), 56.
26. Levine, 78.
27. Anderson, 128.
28. Anderson, 128.
29. Levine, 81.
30. Anderson, 186.
31. Anderson, 188.
32. Bayard Rustin, *Down the Line: The Collected Writings of Bayard Rustin* (Quadrangle, 1971), 60.
33. Garrow, 69.
34. Bayard Rustin, *Strategies for Freedom: The Changing Patterns of Black Protest* (Columbia, 1976), 38.
35. Levine, 94.
36. Joanne Grant, *Ella Baker: Freedom Bound* (Wiley, 1998), 109.
37. Grant, 108.
38. Anderson, 199.
39. Septima Clark, *Ready from Within: Septima Clark and the Civil Rights Movement* (Wild Trees Press, 1986), 77–79.
40. Jeanmarie, 5.
41. Garrow, 140.
42. Garrow, 74.

43. Anderson, 231.
44. Garrow, 140.
45. Chauncey and Kennedy.
46. Chauncey and Kennedy.
47. Anderson, 237.
48. Garrow, 270.
49. Roy Wilkins and Tom Matthews, *Standing Fast: The Autobiography of Roy Wilkins* (Penguin, 1982), 291.
50. James Farmer, *Lay Bare the Heart: An Autobiography of the Civil Rights Movement* (New American Library, 1985), 216.
51. Wilkins and Matthews, 292.
52. Chauncey and Kennedy.
53. John Lewis and Michael D'Orso, *Walking with the Wind: A Memoir of the Movement* (Simon & Schuster, 1998), 208.
54. Jeanmarie, 6.
55. Anderson, 248.
56. Taylor Branch, *Parting the Waters: America in the King Years 1954—1963* (Touchstone, 1988), 861.
57. Levine, 142.
58. *Open Hands.*
59. Anderson, 253–54.
60. Anderson, 259.
61. Anderson, 261.
62. Anderson, 264.
63. Anderson, 265.
64. Anderson, 273.
65. Rustin, *Down the Line,* 115.
66. Rustin, 112.
67. Anderson, 288.
68. Milton Viorst, *Fire in the Streets* (Touchstone, 1979), 350.
69. Rustin, 154.
70. Jonathan Birnbaum and Clarence Taylor, eds., *Civil Rights Since 1787: A Reader on the Black Struggle* (New York University, 2000), 613.
71. Rustin, 154–55.
72. Anderson, 292.
73. Anderson, 293–94.
74. Levine, 203.
75. Levine, 198.
76. Rustin, 229.
77. Rustin, 228.
78. Rustin, 229.
79. Anderson, 235.
80. Rustin, 338.
81. Bayard Rustin, "The Premise of the American Stereotype," *Amsterdam News,* April 8, 1967.
82. *New York Times,* Nov. 23, 1975.
83. Levine, 225.
84. Rustin, *Down the Line,* 237.
85. Levine, 236.
86. Anderson, 343.

87. Anderson, 343.

88. Chauncey and Kennedy.

89. Joseph Beam, "The Elder of the Village: An Interview with Bayard Rustin," *Blackout,* 1987.

90. Beam.

91. Chauncey and Kennedy.

92. Bayard Rustin, "Talk to Black and White Men Together: Philadelphia Chapter," March 1, 1986, 2–3.

93. Rustin, "Talk to Black and White Men Together."

94. Jeanmarie.

95. Chauncey and Kennedy.

96. Anderson, 358.

PART ONE

◆ ◆ ◆

THE MAKING OF
A MOVEMENT

Nonviolence vs. Jim Crow

◆ ◆ ◆

[1942]

RECENTLY I WAS PLANNING to go from Louisville to Nashville by bus. I bought my ticket, boarded the bus, and, instead of going to the back, sat down in the second seat. The driver saw me, got up, and came toward me.

"Hey, you. You're supposed to sit in the back seat."

"Why?"

"Because that's the law. Niggers ride in back."

I said, "My friend, I believe that is an unjust law. If I were to sit in back I would be condoning injustice."

Angry, but not knowing what to do, he got out and went into the station. He soon came out again, got into his seat, and started off.

This routine was gone through at each stop, but each time nothing came of it. Finally the driver, in desperation, must have phoned ahead, for about thirteen miles north of Nashville I heard sirens approaching. The bus came to an abrupt stop, and a police car and two motorcycles drew up beside us with a flourish. Four policemen got into the bus, consulted shortly with the driver, and came to my seat.

"Get up, you ——— nigger!"

"Why?" I asked.

"Get up, you black ———!"

"I believe that I have a right to sit here," I said quietly. "If I sit in the back of the bus I am depriving that child—" I pointed to a little white child of five or six— "of the knowledge that there is injustice here, which I believe it is his right to know. It is my sincere conviction that the power of love in the world is the greatest power existing. If you have a greater power, my friend, you may move me."

How much they understood of what I was trying to tell them I do not know. By this time they were impatient and angry. As I would not move, they began to beat me about the head and shoulders, and I shortly found myself knocked to the floor. Then they dragged me out of the bus and continued to kick and beat me.

Knowing that if I tried to get up or protect myself in the first heat of their anger they would construe it as an attempt to resist and beat me down again, I forced myself to be still and wait for their kicks, one after another. Then I stood up, spreading out my arms parallel to the ground, and said, "There is no need to beat me. I am not resisting you."

At this three white men, obviously Southerners by their speech, got out of the bus and remonstrated with the police. Indeed, as one of the policemen raised his club to strike me, one of them, a little fellow, caught hold of it and said, "Don't you do that!" A second policeman raised his club to strike the little man, and I stepped between them, facing the man, and said, "Thank you, but there is no need to do that. I do not wish to fight. I am protected well."

An elderly gentleman, well dressed and also a Southerner, asked the police where they were taking me.

They said, "Nashville."

"Don't worry, son," he said to me. "I'll be there to see that you get justice."

I was put into the back seat of the police car, between two policemen. Two others sat in front. During the thirteen-mile ride to town they called me every conceivable name and said anything they could think of to incite me to violence. I found that I was shaking with nervous strain, and to give myself something to do, I took out a piece of paper and a pencil, and began to write from memory a chapter from one of Paul's letters.

When I had written a few sentences, the man on my right said, "What're you writing?" and snatched the paper from my hand. He read it, then crumpled it into a ball and pushed it in my face. The man on the other side gave me a kick.

A moment later I happened to catch the eye of the young policeman in the front seat. He looked away quickly, and I took renewed courage from the realization that he could not meet my eyes because he was aware of the injustice being done. I began to write again, and after a moment I leaned forward and touched him on the shoulder. "My friend," I said, "how do you spell 'difference'?"

He spelled it for me—incorrectly—and I wrote it correctly and went on.

When we reached Nashville, a number of policemen were lined up on both sides of the hallway down which I had to pass on my way to the captain's office. They tossed me from one to another like a volleyball. By the time I reached the office, the lining of my best coat was torn, and I was considerably rumpled. I straightened myself as best I could and went in. They had my bag, and went through it and my papers, finding much of interest, especially in the *Christian Century* and *Fellowship*.

Finally the captain said, "Come here, nigger."

I walked directly to him. "What can I do for you?" I asked.

"Nigger," he said menacingly, "you're supposed to be scared when you come in here!"

"I am fortified by truth, justice, and Christ," I said. "There's no need for me to fear."

He was flabbergasted and, for a time, completely at a loss for words. Finally he said to another officer, "I believe the nigger's crazy!"

They sent me into another room and went into consultation. The wait was long, but after an hour and a half they came for me and I was taken for another ride, across town. At the courthouse, I was taken down the hall to the office of the assistant district attorney, Mr. Ben West. As I got to the door I heard a voice, "Say, you colored fellow, hey!" I looked around and saw the elderly gentleman who had been on the bus.

"I'm here to see that you get justice," he said.

The assistant district attorney questioned me about my life, the *Christian Century*, pacifism, and the war for half an hour. Then he asked the police to tell their side of what had happened. They did, stretching the truth a good deal in spots and including several lies for seasoning. Mr. West then asked me to tell my side.

"Gladly," I said, "and I want *you*," turning to the young policeman who had sat in the front seat, "to follow what I say and stop me if I deviate from the truth in the least."

Holding his eyes with mine, I told the story exactly as it had happened, stopping often to say, "Is that right?" or "Isn't that what happened?" to the young policeman. During the whole time he never once interrupted me, and when I was through I said, "Did I tell the truth just as it happened?" and he said, "Well...."

Then Mr. West dismissed me, and I was sent to wait alone in a dark room. After an hour, Mr. West came in and said, very kindly, "You may go, *Mister* Rustin."

I left the courthouse, believing all the more strongly in the non-violent approach. I am certain that I was addressed as "Mister" (as no Negro is ever addressed in the South), that I was assisted by those three men, and that the elderly gentleman interested himself in my predicament because I had, without fear, faced the four policemen and said, "There is no need to beat me. I offer you no resistance."

The Negro and Nonviolence

◆ ◆ ◆

[1942]

SINCE THE UNITED STATES entered the war, white–Negro tension has increased steadily. Even in normal times, changes in social and economic patterns cause fear and frustration, which in turn lead to aggression. In time of war, the general social condition is fertile soil for the development of hate and fear, and transference of these to minority groups is quite simple.

Organized violence is growing in the North and South. The Ku Klux Klan is riding again, employing more subtle methods.

Negroes and whites in Southern iron ore mines, as well as in Mobile, Alabama, shipyards, are going armed to work.

Negro soldiers often are forced to wait at Jim Crow ticket windows while whites are being served, frequently missing their buses and trains. Often bus drivers refuse to pick up any Negroes until all whites are seated, sometimes causing them hours' delay. Scores of Negroes have been beaten and arrested in Memphis, Tennessee; Beaumont, Texas; Columbus, Georgia; and Jackson, Mississippi, for insisting on transportation on buses overcrowded because of war conditions. Beaumont has threatened severe punishment for violation of Jim Crow bus laws.

There have been numerous wildcat strikes, in both North and South, where white employees refuse to work with Negroes. Several white and Negro CIO officials have been attacked. One was twice assaulted by white workers for trying to get jobs for Negroes.

Negro soldiers and civilians have been killed by whites. On June 27, Walter Gunn of Macon County, Alabama, wanted on a charge of drunkenness, was shot in the leg, stripped of his clothes, and beaten to death by a deputy sheriff in the presence of Gunn's wife and children. A similar police brutality occurred on the streets of New York City when a liquor-dazed young Negro was killed for refusing to remove his hand from his pocket.

A soldier was shot in the streets of Little Rock, Arkansas, because he refused to tip his hat to a local policeman and address him as "sir."

The world-famous singer Roland Hayes was beaten and jailed because his wife, who had taken a seat a "few yards forward" in a Georgia shoe store, insisted upon being served "where she was" or trading elsewhere.

On July 28, two Texas policemen, Clyde and Billy Brown, forced Charles Reco, a Negro soldier, into the back seat of a police car and drove him to the police station because in a Beaumont bus he took a vacant seat reserved for a white. During the ride they shot him once in the shoulder and once in the arm.

Racial feeling has increased since June 1942, when the Fair Employment Practices Committee began hearings on anti-Negro discrimination in Birmingham, Alabama. It has been fed by the anti-Negro propaganda stirred up by Governor Dixon of Alabama, Governor Talmadge of Georgia, and Representative John Rankin of Mississippi. This propaganda has encouraged such minor politicians as Horace C. Wilkinson, who has suggested developing a "League of White Supremacy," to make sure "that this menace to our national security and our local way of life will disappear rapidly."

Governor Dixon, in refusing to sign a government war contract because it contained a nondiscrimination clause, said, "I will not permit the citizens of Alabama to be subject to the whims of any federal committee, and I will not permit the employees of the state to be placed in the position where they must abandon the principles of segregation or lose their jobs." Following this statement, Alabama's Senator John Bankhead wrote General Marshall, army chief of staff, demanding that no Negro soldiers be brought South for military training.

These and other humiliations have had a very marked effect on great masses of Negroes, who are being told by the press that "equality of opportunity and social and political recognition will come *now or never,* violently or nonviolently." The *Pittsburgh Courier* and the *People's Voice,* typical of the general Negro press, constantly remind the masses that greater economic and political democracy was supposed to have followed

World War I. Instead, they pointed out, the Negro found himself the scapegoat, "last hired and first fired," in a period of economic and social maladjustment that has lasted until the present time. Thus the average Negro is told, "There can be no delay. What achievement there will be must come now."

An increasingly militant group has it in mind to demand *now*, with violence if necessary, the rights it has long been denied. "If we must die abroad for democracy we can't have," I heard a friend of mine say, "then we might as well die right here, fighting for our rights."

This is a tragic statement. It is tragic also how isolated the average Negro feels in his struggle. The average Negro has largely lost faith in middle-class whites. In his hour of need he seeks not "talk" but dynamic action. He looks upon the middle-class idea of long-term educational and cultural changes with fear and mistrust. He is interested only in what can be achieved immediately by political pressure to get jobs, decent housing, and education for his children. He describes with disgust the efforts in his behalf by most middle-class Negro and white intellectuals as "pink tea methods—sometimes well-meanin' but gettin' us nowhere." It is for this reason, in part, that the March on Washington movement, aiming to become a mass movement, has tended toward "black nationalism." Its leadership, originally well motivated, now rejects the idea of including whites in its constituency or leadership. One local official said, "These are Negroes' problems and Negroes will have to work them out."

The March on Washington movement is growing but at best is only a partial answer to the present need. While the movement already exerts some real political pressure (President Roosevelt set up the FEPC at its request), it has no program, educational or otherwise, for meeting immediate conflict. To demand rights but not to see the potential danger in such a course, or the responsibility to develop a means of meeting that danger, seems tragic.

Many Negroes see mass violence coming. Having lived in a society in which church, school, and home problems have been handled in a violent way, the majority at this point are unable to conceive of a solution by reconciliation and nonviolence. I have seen schoolboys in Arkansas laying away rusty guns for the "time when." I have heard many young men in the armed forces hope for a machine-gun assignment "so I can turn it on the white folks." I have seen a white sailor beaten in

Harlem because three Negroes had been "wantin' to get just one white" before they died. I have heard hundreds of Negroes hope for a Japanese military victory, since "it don't matter who you're a slave for."

These statements come not only from bitterness but from frustration and fear as well. In many parts of America the Negro, in his despair, is willing to follow any leadership seemingly sincerely identified with his struggle if he is convinced that such leadership offers a workable method. In this crisis those of us who believe in the nonviolent solution of conflict have a duty and an opportunity. In all those places where we have a voice, it is our high responsibility to indicate that the Negro can attain progress only if he uses, in his struggle, nonviolent direct action— a technique consistent with the ends he desires. Especially in this time of tension we must point out the practical necessity of such a course.

Nonviolence as a method has within it the demand for terrible sacrifice and long suffering, but, as Gandhi has said, "freedom does not drop from the sky." One has to struggle and be willing to die for it. J. Holmes Smith has indicated that he looks to the American Negro to assist in developing, along with the people of India, a new dynamic force for the solution of conflict that not merely will free these oppressed people but will set an example that may be the first step in freeing the world.

Certainly the Negro possesses qualities essential for nonviolent direct action. He has long since learned to endure suffering. He can admit his own share of guilt and has to be pushed hard to become bitter. He has produced, and still sings, such songs as "It's Me, Oh Lord, Standin' in the Need of Prayer" and "Nobody Knows the Trouble I've Seen." He follows this last tragic phrase by a salute to God—"Oh! Glory, Hallelujah." He is creative and has learned to adjust himself to conditions easily. But above all he possesses a rich religious heritage and today finds the church the center of his life.

Yet there are those who question the use of nonviolent direct action by Negroes in protesting discrimination, on the grounds that this method will kindle hitherto dormant racial feeling. But we must remember that too often conflict is already at hand and that there is hence a greater danger: the inevitable use of force by persons embittered by injustice and unprepared for nonviolence. It is a cause for shame that millions of people continue to live under conditions of injustice while we make no effective effort to remedy the situation.

Those who argue for an extended educational plan are not wrong, but there must also be a plan for facing *immediate* conflicts. Those of us who believe in nonviolent resistance can do the greatest possible good for the Negro, for those who exploit him, for America, and for the world by becoming a real part of the Negro community, thus being in a position to suggest methods and to offer leadership when troubles come.

Identification with the Negro community demands considerable sacrifice. The Negro is not to be won by words alone, but by an obvious consistency in words and deeds. The *identified* person is the one who fights side by side with him for justice. This demands being so integral a part of the Negro community in its day-to-day struggle, so close to it in similarity of work, so near its standard of living that when problems arise he who stands forth to judge, to plan, to suggest, or to lead is really at one with the Negro masses.

Our war resistance is justified only if we see that an adequate alternative to violence is developed. Today, as the Gandhian forces in India face their critical test, we can add to world justice by placing in the hands of thirteen million black Americans a workable and Christian technique for the righting of injustice and the solution of conflict.

LETTER TO THE DRAFT BOARD

◆ ◆ ◆

[1943]

Local Board No. 63
2050 Amsterdam Avenue
New York, N.Y.

Gentlemen:

For eight years I have believed war to be impractical and a denial of our Hebrew–Christian tradition. The social teachings of Jesus are: (1) Respect for personality; (2) Service the "summum bonum"; (3) Overcoming evil with good; and (4) The brotherhood of man. These principles as I see it are violated by participation in war.

Believing this, and having before me Jesus' continued resistance to that which he considered evil, I was compelled to resist war by registering as a Conscientious Objector in October 1940.

However, a year later, September 1941, I became convinced that conscription as well as war equally is inconsistent with the teachings of Jesus. I must resist conscription also.

On Saturday, November 13, 1943, I received from you an order to report for a physical examination to be taken Tuesday, November 16, at eight o'clock in the evening. I wish to inform you that I cannot voluntarily submit to an order springing from the Selective Service and Training Act for War.

There are several reasons for this decision, all stemming from the basic spiritual truth that men are brothers in the sight of God:

1. War is wrong. Conscription is a concomitant of modern war. Thus conscription for so vast an evil as war is wrong.

2. Conscription for war is inconsistent with freedom of conscience, which is not merely the right to believe, but to act on the degree of truth that one receives, to follow a vocation which is God-inspired and God-directed.

   Today I feel that God motivates me to use my whole being to combat by nonviolent means the ever-growing racial tension in the United States; at the same time the State directs that I shall do its will; which of these dictates can I follow—that of God or that of the State? Surely, I must at all times attempt to obey the law of the State. But when the will of God and the will of the State conflict, I am compelled to follow the will of God. If I cannot continue in my present vocation, I must resist.

3. The Conscription Act denies brotherhood—the most basic New Testament teaching. Its design and purpose is to set men apart— German against American, American against Japanese. Its aim springs from a moral impossibility—that ends justify means, that from unfriendly acts a new and friendly world can emerge.

   In practice further, it separates black from white—those supposedly struggling for a common freedom. Such a separation also is based on the moral error that racism can overcome racism, that evil can produce good, that men virtually in slavery can struggle for a freedom they are denied. This means that I must protest racial discrimination in the armed forces, which is not only morally indefensible but also in clear violation of the Act. This does not, however, imply that I could have a part in conforming to the Act if discrimination were eliminated.

   Segregation, separation, according to Jesus, is the basis of continuous violence. It was such an observation which encouraged him to teach, "It has been said to you in olden times that thou shalt not kill, but I say unto you, do not call a man a fool"—and he might have added: "for if you call him such, you automatically separate yourself from him and violence begins." That which separates man from his brother is evil and must be resisted.

I admit my share of guilt for having participated in the institutions and ways of life which helped bring fascism and war. Nonetheless, guilty as I am, I now see as did the Prodigal Son that it is never too late to refuse longer to remain in a non-creative situation. It is always timely and virtuous to change—to take in all humility a new path.

Though joyfully following the will of God, I regret that I must break the law of the State. I am prepared for whatever may follow.

I herewith return the material you have sent me, for conscientiously I cannot hold a card in connection with an Act I no longer feel able to accept and abide by.

Today I am notifying the Federal District Attorney of my decision and am forwarding him a copy of this letter.

I appreciate now as in the past your advice and consideration, and trust that I shall cause you no anxiety in the future. I want you to know I deeply respect you for executing your duty to God and country in these difficult times in the way you feel you must. I remain

Sincerely yours,
Bayard Rustin

P.S. I am enclosing samples of the material which from time to time I have sent out to hundreds of persons, Negro and white, throughout our nation. This indicates one type of the creative work to which God has called me.

We Challenged Jim Crow

◆ ◆ ◆

[1947]

ON JUNE 3, 1946, THE SUPREME COURT of the United States announced its decision in the case of Irene Morgan versus the Commonwealth of Virginia. State laws demanding segregation of interstate passengers on motor carriers are now unconstitutional, for segregation of passengers crossing state lines was declared an "undue burden on interstate commerce." Thus it was decided that state Jim Crow laws do not affect interstate travelers. In a later decision in the Court of Appeals for the District of Columbia, the Morgan decision was interpreted to apply to interstate train travel as well as bus travel.

The executive committee of the Congress of Racial Equality and the racial–industrial committee of the Fellowship of Reconciliation decided that they should jointly sponsor a "Journey of Reconciliation" through the upper South, in order to determine to how great an extent bus and train companies were recognizing the Morgan decision. They also wished to learn the reaction of bus drivers, passengers, and police to those who nonviolently and persistently challenge Jim Crow in interstate travel.

During the two-week period from April 9 to April 23, 1947, an interracial group of men, traveling as a deputation team, visited fifteen cities in Virginia, North Carolina, Tennessee, and Kentucky. More than thirty speaking engagements were met before church, NAACP, and college groups. The Morgan decision was explained and reports made on what was happening on buses and trains in the light of this decision. The response was most enthusiastic.

To clarify the incidents described below, it will be necessary to list the sixteen participants by race.

Negro. Bayard Rustin, of the Fellowship of Reconciliation and part-time worker with the American Friends Service Committee; Wallace Nelson, freelance lecturer; Conrad Lynn, New York attorney; Andrew Johnson, Cincinnati student; Dennis Banks, Chicago musician; William Worthy, of the New York Council for a Permanent FEPC; Eugene Stanley, of A. and T. College, Greensboro, North Carolina; Nathan Wright, church social worker from Cincinnati.

White. George Houser, of the FOR and executive secretary of the Congress of Racial Equality; Ernest Bromley, Methodist minister from North Carolina; James Peck, editor of the Workers Defense League *News Bulletin;* Igal Roodenko, New York horticulturist; Worth Randle, Cincinnati biologist; Joseph Felmet, of the Southern Workers Defense League; Homer Jack, executive secretary of the Chicago Council Against Racial and Religious Discrimination; Louis Adams, Methodist minister from North Carolina.

During the two weeks of the trip, twenty-six tests of company policies were made. Arrests occurred on six occasions, with a total of twelve men arrested.

The Test Trips

The report of what happened on the test trips should be much more complete than is here possible. For purposes of brevity, many important comments and psychological reactions have had to be omitted.

Between eight and ten men participated in simultaneous tests. This made it possible to split the group into two parts—either for two separate tests on the same bus line or for testing both Greyhound and Trailways buses when both companies ran buses to the next point on the itinerary.

Washington, D.C., to Richmond, Virginia, April 9

No difficulties were encountered. On both the Trailways and Greyhound buses the Negroes in the group sat up front and the whites in the rear. Other passengers tended to cross the color line too. A white couple sat on the back seat of the Greyhound with two Negroes. A Negro woman sat beside a young white man in the center of the bus when she could have taken a vacant seat by a Negro man. Rustin gave his seat, third from

the front, to an elderly Negro woman, then sat by a white lad directly
behind the driver. Nothing was said.

Richmond to Petersburg, Virginia, April 10

Because there have been so many cases in the Richmond courts testing
segregation in interstate travel, no more arrests were being made there.
Both the Greyhound and Trailways groups reached Petersburg without
incident. The Trailways bus was local, running only between the two
cities. The tickets used were interstate, of course. The Greyhound bus was
a crowded through-bus, but no attempt was made to force Rustin and
Johnson to move from the front. Nelson and Lynn rode in front on the
Trailways bus. A Negro man in the rear spoke to Houser and Roodenko,
saying a Negro might be able to get away with riding up front here, but
some bus drivers are crazy, "and the farther South you go, the crazier
they get." Two Negro women talking about Peck, sitting in the rear of
the Greyhound reading his *New York Times,* said, "He wouldn't know
what it was all about if he was asked to move." Then they laughed.

Petersburg to Raleigh, North Carolina, April 11

Before the Trailways bus left the station Lynn was arrested for sitting in
the second seat from the front. The bus driver was courteous but insis-
tent. Lynn explained the Morgan decision quietly. The driver countered
that he was in the employ of the bus company, not the Supreme Court,
and that he followed company rules about segregation. He said aloud,
so all passengers could hear: "Personally, I don't care where you sit,
but I have my orders. Are you going to move?" Lynn said that he could
not. The driver got the police. There were no threats nor abusive language. It took about an hour and a half to get a warrant for Lynn's
arrest. The magistrate in Petersburg would not sign the warrant until the
bus company attorney in Richmond had been called, and dictated the
statement of the warrant over the telephone. The warrant read that
Lynn was guilty of disorderly conduct for not obeying the reasonable
request of the bus driver to move to the rear, in compliance with the
company rules. The bus operator apologized for having to arrest Lynn.
A policeman, referring to equality for Negroes, said, "I'm just not
Christian enough." Passengers on the bus were patient, and relatively
neutral, while they waited almost two hours. A Negro porter made the
only fuss when he boarded the bus. Looking at Lynn, he said, "What's

the matter with him? He's crazy. Where does he think he is? We know how to deal with him. We ought to drag him off." Lynn was released on $25 bond.

Petersburg to Durham, North Carolina, April 11

On the Greyhound to Durham there were no arrests. Peck and Rustin sat up front. About ten miles out of Petersburg the driver told Rustin to move. When Rustin refused, the driver said he would "attend to that at Blackstone." However, after consultation with other drivers at the bus station in Blackstone, he went on to Clarksville. There the group changed buses. At Oxford, North Carolina, the driver sent for the police, who refused to make an arrest. Persons waiting to get on at Oxford were delayed for forty-five minutes. A middle-aged Negro schoolteacher was permitted to board and to plead with Rustin to move: "Please move. Don't do this. You'll reach your destination either in front or in back. What difference does it make?" Rustin explained his reason for not moving. Other Negro passengers were strong in their support of Rustin, one of them threatening to sue the bus company for the delay. When Durham was reached without arrest, the Negro schoolteacher begged Peck not to use the teacher's name in connection with the incident at Oxford: "It will hurt me in the community. I'll never do that again."

Raleigh to Chapel Hill, North Carolina, April 12

Lynn and Nelson rode together on the double seat next to the very rear of the Trailways bus, and Houser and Roodenko in front of them. The bus was very crowded. The one other Negro passenger, a woman seated across from Nelson, moved to the very rear voluntarily when a white woman got on the bus and there were no seats in front. When two white college men got on, the driver told Nelson and Lynn to move to the rear seat. When they refused on the basis of their interstate passage, he said the matter would be handled in Durham. A white passenger asked the driver if he wanted any help. The driver replied, "No, we don't want to handle it that way." By the time the group reached Durham, the seating arrangement had changed and the driver did not press the matter.

Durham to Chapel Hill, April 12

Johnson and Rustin were in the second seat from the front on a Trailways bus. The driver, as soon as he saw them, asked them to move to the rear. A station superintendent was called to repeat the order. Five minutes later the police arrived and Johnson and Rustin were arrested for refusing to move when ordered to do so. Peck, who was seated in about the middle of the bus, got up after the arrest, saying to the police, "If you arrest them, you'll have to arrest me, too, for I'm going to sit in the rear." The three men were held at the police station for half an hour. They were released without charge when an attorney arrived on their behalf. A suit will be pressed against the company and the police for false arrest. The conversation with the Trailways official indicated that the company knew there was an interracial group making a test. The official said to the police: "We know all about this. Greyhound is letting them ride. But we're not."

Chapel Hill to Greensboro, North Carolina, April 13
Johnson and Felmet were seated in front. The driver asked them to move as soon as he boarded. They were arrested quickly, for the police station was just across the street from the bus station. Felmet did not get up to accompany the police until the officer specifically told him he was under arrest. Because he delayed rising from his seat, he was pulled up bodily and shoved out of the bus. The bus driver distributed witness cards to occupants of the bus. One white girl said: "You don't want me to sign one of those. I'm a damn Yankee, and I think this is an outrage." Rustin and Roodenko, sensing the favorable reaction on the bus, decided they would move to the seat in the front vacated by Johnson and Felmet. Their moving forward caused much discussion by passengers. The driver returned soon, and when Rustin and Roodenko refused to move, they were arrested also. A white woman at the front of the bus, a Southerner, gave her name and address to Rustin as he walked by her. The men were arrested on charges of disorderly conduct, for refusing to obey the bus driver, and, in the case of the whites, for interfering with arrest. The men were released on $50 bond.

The bus was delayed nearly two hours. Taxi drivers standing around the bus station were becoming aroused by the events. One hit Peck a hard blow on the head, saying, "Coming down here to stir up the niggers." Peck stood quietly looking at them for several moments, but said nothing. Two persons standing by, one Negro and one white, reprimanded the cab driver for his violence. The Negro was told, "You keep out of this." In the police station, some of the men standing around could be heard saying, "They'll never get a bus out of here tonight." After the bond was placed, Reverend Charles Jones, a local white Presbyterian minister, speedily drove the men to his home. They were pursued by two cabs filled with taxi men. As the interracial group reached the front porch of the Jones home, the two cabs pulled up at the curb. Men jumped out, two of them with sticks for weapons; others picked up sizable rocks. They started toward the house, but were called back by one of their number. In a few moments the phone rang, and an anonymous voice said to Jones, "Get those damn niggers out of town or we'll burn your house down. We'll be around to see that they go." The police were notified and arrived in about twenty minutes. The interracial group felt it wise to leave town before nightfall. Two cars were obtained and the group was driven to Greensboro, by way of Durham, for an evening engagement.

Greensboro to Winston-Salem, North Carolina, April 14

Two tests were made on Greyhound buses. In the first test Lynn sat in front; in the second, Nelson. A South Carolinian seated by Bromley on the first bus said, "In my state he would either move or be killed." He was calm as Bromley talked with him about the Morgan decision.

Winston-Salem to Asheville, North Carolina, April 15

From Winston-Salem to Statesville the group traveled by Greyhound. Nelson was seated with Bromley in the second seat from the front. Nothing was said. At Statesville, the group transferred to the Trailways, with Nelson still in front. In a small town about ten miles from Statesville, the driver approached Nelson and told him he would have to move to the rear. When Nelson said that he was an interstate passenger, the driver said that the bus was not interstate. When Nelson explained that his ticket was interstate, the driver returned to his seat and drove on. The rest of the trip to Asheville was through mountainous country, and the bus stopped at many small towns. A soldier asked the driver why Nelson was not forced to move. The driver explained that there was a Supreme Court decision and that he could do nothing about it. He said, "If you want to do something about this, don't blame this man [Nelson]; kill those bastards up in Washington." The soldier explained to a rather large, vociferous man why Nelson was allowed to sit up front. The large man commented, "I wish I was the bus driver." Near Asheville the bus became very crowded, and there were women standing up. Two women spoke to the bus driver, asking him why Nelson was not moved. In each case the driver explained that the Supreme Court decision was responsible. Several white women took seats in the Jim Crow section in the rear.

Asheville to Knoxville, Tennessee, April 17
Banks and Peck were in the second seat on the Trailways. While the bus was still in the station, a white passenger asked the bus driver to tell Banks to move. Banks replied, "I'm sorry, I can't," and explained that he was an interstate passenger. The police were called and the order repeated. A twenty-minute consultation took place before the arrest was made. When Peck was not arrested, he said, "We're traveling together, and you will have to arrest me too." He was arrested for sitting in the rear. The two men were released from the city jail on $400 bond each.

Knoxville to Nashville, Tennessee, April 17
Wright and Jack sat at the front of a Greyhound bus. Before the driver boarded, a redheaded soldier asked him if he was going to move Wright. The driver approached Wright and asked him politely, "Would you like to move?" Wright said he would not. The driver disappeared for fifteen minutes. Two Negroes in the rear of the bus discussed the situation audibly, saying, "They are going to get the police, and they'll probably hit him." The other said, "When in Rome, I believe in doing as the Romans do." When the bus driver returned, he drove off without raising any more questions. This bus trip was at night.

Knoxville to Louisville, Kentucky, April 18
Worthy and Roodenko sat in the front of a Greyhound bus. The bus reached Corbin, Tennessee, some hundred miles from Knoxville, before Worthy was asked to move. The driver hinted that there would be violence from the crowd if Worthy did not move. A white woman from Tennessee talked with the officials in the bus station and to the bus driver, protesting threatened arrests. The bus driver received orders to drive on.

Nashville to Louisville, Kentucky, April 19
Wright and Jack had reserved seats on an all-coach reserved train of the Louisville and Nashville railroad. There was no difficulty in getting on

the train. Two conductors approached to collect the tickets. One asked Jack if Wright were his prisoner. Learning they were friends, he told Wright that company rules meant he would have to move to the Jim Crow car. "This is the way it is done down here," he concluded. When Wright refused to move, he said he would be back later. When he came back he said, "If we were in Alabama, we would throw you out of the window." He threatened to have Wright arrested in Bowling Green, Kentucky, but no arrest took place. A woman sitting in the second seat behind the men approached them after the conductor left, giving them her name and address and saying that they could call on her for help.

Weaversville, North Carolina, to Bristol, Virginia, April 19

No test was made. Banks was the only Negro on the bus, and he was on the rear seat. The bus was extremely crowded. The driver asked Banks to move from the rear seat to the double seat in front of the rear seat so that only one white person, and not four, would have to sit beside him, Banks complied. He had a friendly conversation with a young white farmer who sat beside him.

Bristol to Roanoke, Virginia, April 19

Banks and Peck rode together on a Greyhound. The driver approached them twice, but on neither occasion insisted that they move.

Cincinnati, Ohio, to Roanoke, April 19

Worthy and Houser had coach reservations on the Norfolk and Western. The railroad man at the gate expressed consternation that Worthy had a seat in a white coach, but no attempt was made to keep him from taking it.

Roanoke to Washington, D.C., April 20

Worthy and Bromley sat together in a white coach on the Norfolk and Western. No questions of any kind were raised. Bromley got off at Charlottesville, Virginia. For the last part of the trip to Washington, a white girl sat beside Worthy rather than sit on her suitcase in the aisle.

Roanoke to Lynchburg, Virginia, April 21

Banks and Houser sat together in the front of a Greyhound bus. No incident occurred.

Lynchburg to Washington, D.C., April 22

Nelson and Houser were seated at the front of the Trailways bus. The driver did not see Nelson until the bus was about five miles out of the station. When he stopped at a service station, he asked Nelson to move to the rear. Nelson refused on the ground that he was an interstate passenger. Houser explained that they were traveling together. The driver said they could ride in the rear. Houser asked whether that too would not be breaking the Jim Crow rules of the company, by which the driver said he was guided. The driver then said that Houser would have to sit one seat in front of Nelson in the rear. It took more than an hour to get a warrant for Nelson's arrest. State police took Nelson to the small town of Amherst, where he was held for $50 bail. The bus driver apologized profusely for his action when Houser got off at Amherst to put up the bond for Nelson. The passengers were very patient, rather neutral in attitude.

Amherst, Virginia, to Washington, D.C., April 22

Nelson and Houser took a train on the Southern Railway at Amherst. They asked the conductor where they could ride together. He asked if Nelson were Houser's prisoner. Upon learning that they were friends, he said it was against the rules for them to ride together on that train. He said, "I'll turn you over to the officials at Charlottesville if you sit together." They sat together in the Jim Crow car, where the conductor asked Houser if he refused to move. Again he threatened arrest in Charlottesville, but no arrest was made.

Charlottesville, Virginia, to Washington, D.C., April 23

Banks rode alone in the front of the Trailways bus. Peck and Randle were riding on the rear seat. For two hours out of Charlottesville there was no incident. In the small town of Culpeper, Virginia, the driver told Banks to move to the rear. It took about an hour and a half to get a warrant issued for Banks's arrest. A Negro woman who had a concession selling bus tickets in town came on board the bus and offered to help Banks in any way she could. The warrant read that Banks was guilty of not obeying the order of the driver. Nothing was said to Peck or Randle, in spite of the fact that the rules of the company state that white persons shall not sit in the rear. Banks was released on $25 bond.

The Trials

By July 6, 1947, four trials had been held. In Petersburg, Virginia, Conrad Lynn received a $10 fine. In Chapel Hill, North Carolina, Bayard Rustin and Igal Roodenko were found guilty of violating the state Jim Crow law. Rustin was sentenced to thirty days on the road gang, while Roodenko was given sixty days. The judge said he purposely discriminated against the white person involved. Likewise, when Andrew Johnson and Joe Felmet were tried on June 24, Felmet was given the maximum sentence of thirty days on the road gang, while Johnson received a $25 fine. The judge tried to give Felmet six months, only to discover this was beyond the maximum permitted. The indictment for the four arrested in Chapel Hill was changed from disorderly conduct and interfering with arrest to a violation of the state Jim Crow law, on the ground that since the men were planning stopovers in three cities within the state, they were not interstate passengers.

The Asheville case against Peck and Banks came up for trial in the police court before Judge Sam Cathay. Curbs Todd of Winston-Salem was their attorney. (There were no Negro attorneys in Asheville, and this was the first time a Negro attorney had appeared in the court.) The indictment was that the men had violated the Jim Crow law. The two witnesses for the state—the bus driver and the policeman—testified so accurately that it was not necessary to call defense witnesses. They both said there was no disorder on the part of the arrested men. Neither the judge nor the state's attorney knew about the Morgan decision, and they had to borrow Attorney Todd's copy of it. When the judge learned the maximum sentence was thirty days, he gave thirty-day sentences, to be served under the supervision of the highway commissioner. Pending appeal, the men were released on $250 bonds.

The cases in Amherst and Culpeper were scheduled for trial pending the outcome of another case involving the same legal principles.

All convictions were appealed.

General Observations

The one word which most universally describes the attitude of police, of passengers, and of the Negro and white bus riders is "confusion."

Persons taking part in the psychological struggle in the buses and trains either did not know of the Morgan decision or, if they did, possessed no clear understanding of it. Thus when police officers and bus drivers in authority took a stand, they tended to act on the basis of what they knew—the state Jim Crow law. In the South, where the caste system is rigidly defined, this confusion is extremely dangerous; it leads to frustration, usually followed by aggression in some form.

The great majority of the passengers were apathetic and did not register their feelings, even when their faces clearly revealed how they felt about the action the group was taking.

It was generally apparent that the bus companies were attempting to circumvent the intentions of the Supreme Court in the Irene Morgan decision by reliance on state Jim Crow laws, by company regulations, and by subtle pressures. Negro passengers tended to follow the dominant reaction of the other riders. There were exceptions to this, of course, but generally they showed fear first, then caution. When cautious Negroes saw resistant Negroes sitting in the front of the bus unmolested, many moved forward too.

There were no acts of violence on the buses. The most extreme negative reactions were verbal, but without profanity. Typical was the young Marine who said, "The KKK is coming up again, and I guess I'll join up." The one act of violence against a member of the group was on the part of a taxi driver outside the bus station at Chapel Hill. This act—a single but hard blow to the head—was directed against a white man.

On three occasions when Negro members of the group protested discrimination by sitting in the front, other Negroes—a porter, a school-teacher, and a day laborer—urged the resisters in very emotional terms to comply with the law. Their request was either the result of fear or, as in the case of the Negro porter, an attempt to ingratiate themselves with white authorities. Such reactions are to be expected in a caste system and represent the kind of personal degradation which ought to spur us on to eliminate caste.

Policemen and bus drivers have a great responsibility in social change of this kind. Success or failure, violence or peaceful change is in large part determined by the position they take. White persons generally ignored Negroes riding in the front of buses or in the non–Jim Crow cars on trains until the bus drivers or train conductors raised the issue. We are of the opinion that in most cases if the bus drivers had not taken action, the passengers would have continued to ignore the Negroes sitting in the front of a bus or in coaches for whites. Between Statesville and Asheville, North Carolina, a clear statement from the driver explaining the Morgan decision quieted protesting white passengers. It is our belief that when those in authority take a clear stand, passengers who might otherwise resent a Negro's presence in a nontraditional position will accept the situation with a typical shrug of the shoulder: "Well, this is the law. What can you do?"

In no case of arrest was there a single example of police inconsideration. The police were polite and calm, and if any of them were anti-Negro there was no indication of it. In fact, one officer, when pressed for a reason for his unwillingness to sit beside a Negro, said, "I'm just not Christian enough, I guess." This would not necessarily be true in the lower South.

Without exception those arrested behaved in a nonviolent fashion. They acted without fear, spoke quietly and firmly, showing great consideration for the police and bus drivers, and repeatedly pointed to the fact that they expected the police to do their duty as they saw it. We cannot overemphasize the necessity for this courteous and intelligent conduct while breaking with the caste system. We believe that the reason the police behaved politely was that there was not the slightest provocation in the attitude of the resisters. On the contrary, we tried at all times to understand *their* attitude and position first.

Another reason for the lack of tension was the interracial character of the group. We did not allow a single situation to develop in which the struggle seemed to be between white and Negro persons; rather it appeared that progressives and democrats, white and black, were working by peaceful means to overcome a system which they felt to be wrong.

Much was gained when someone in our group took the lead in discussion with bus drivers or train conductors and when police appeared. Those who seemed certain of their facts, and who spoke clearly and assuredly, set the tone. Attitudes were greatly accelerated in the proper direction whenever a person of liberal sentiments spoke up first.

As the trip progressed it became evident that the police and bus drivers were learning about the Irene Morgan decision as word of the "test cases" was passed from city to city and from driver to driver. We see here again the need for incidents as "teaching techniques." The following paragraph from a letter written by a student at Chapel Hill supports this contention: "I don't know whether all the stir has been in vain or not. Everyone on this campus now knows about the Fellowship of Reconciliation, the Congress of Racial Equality, and the Supreme Court decision. What is more important, many people, including my two very conservative roommates, are thinking seriously about the whole nonviolent approach to social problems."

The incident at Chapel Hill indicates that one of the chief dangers of violence arises when crowds gather outside buses. Such persons are unable to hear the discussion or to know and debate the facts given inside the bus. They merely pick up bits of hearsay and false rumors. It is also true that taxi drivers, pool-room fellows, and idlers are likely to be in the groups which hang around bus terminals. Many of them depend on Jim Crow for personal status. No matter how poor they are, they can "feel better than the niggers."

It is our belief that without direct action on the part of groups and individuals, the Jim Crow pattern in the South cannot be broken. We are equally certain that such direct action must be nonviolent.

It appeared that women are more intelligently inquisitive, open for discussion, and liberal in their sentiments than men. On several occasions women not only defended those who broke with Jim Crow, but gave their names and addresses, offering to act as witnesses. In appealing for aid in the psychological struggle within the bus one might do well to concentrate on winning over women.

All the arrests occurred on Trailways buses. It is difficult to account for the difference between the two bus lines. One possible reason might be the fact that Trailways largely serves Southern states, and is not used so universally in interstate travel as the Greyhound lines.

If the attitude of those Southerners who did speak up could be put in a nutshell, it was expressed by one Southerner, who said, "The South is the South and will always be this way. We don't care about the Supreme Court decision." This is not so much an attitude of resistance to change as one of despair and cynicism.

We believe that the great majority of the people in the upper South are prepared to accept the Irene Morgan decision and to ride on buses and trains with Negroes. One white woman, reluctantly taking a seat beside a Negro man, said to her sister, who was about to protest, "I'm tired. Anything for a seat."

Persons who did not wish to see change, particularly the bus drivers, became more angry with the white participants than with the Negroes. This is an important observation, since, except in extreme cases, white resisters may have to bear the brunt of hostility.

The situation in the upper South is in a great state of flux. Where numerous cases have been before the courts recently, as in northern Virginia, the barriers are already down, and Negroes can, in general, ride without fear of arrest. Repeated arrests have occurred in other parts of Virginia as well as North Carolina, eastern Tennessee, and Kentucky.

Civil Disobedience, Jim Crow,
and the Armed Forces

◆ ◆ ◆

[1948]

IT IS A REAL OPPORTUNITY TO SPEAK with American citizens who seriously seek to remove racial and religious intolerance from our national life, for recent history amply reveals that America cannot gain moral leadership in the world until intolerance of minority groups has been eliminated at home. The Journey of Reconciliation was organized not only to devise techniques for eliminating Jim Crow in travel, but also as a training ground for similar peaceful projects against discrimination in such major areas as employment and in the armed services.

The use of these methods against Jim Crow military service is a regrettable necessity. Today no single injustice more bitterly stands out in the hearts and minds of colored people the world over, or continues more successfully to frustrate the United States' efforts abroad, than the continuation of discrimination and segregation in our military forces.

As a follower of the principles of Mahatma Gandhi, I am an opponent of war and of war preparations and an opponent of universal military training and conscription; but entirely apart from that issue, I hold that segregation in any part of the body politic is an act of slavery and an act of war. Democrats will agree that such acts are to be resisted, and more and more leaders of the oppressed are responsibly proposing nonviolent civil disobedience and noncooperation as the means.

On March 22, 1948, A. Philip Randolph and Grant Reynolds, trusted Negro leaders, told President Truman that Negroes "do not propose to shoulder another gun for democracy abroad while they are denied democracy here at home." A few days later, when Mr. Randolph testified before the Senate Armed Services Committee, he declared that he openly would advise and urge Negro and white youth not to submit to Jim Crow military institutions. At this statement, Senator Wayne Morse interrupted and warned Mr. Randolph that "the Government would apply the legal doctrine of treason to such conduct."

This is a highly regrettable statement for a United States Senator to make. Certainly throughout Asia and Africa millions must have agreed with the lovers of freedom here who reasoned that if treason is involved, it is the treason practiced by reactionaries in the North and South who struggle to maintain segregation and discrimination and who thus murder the American creed. The organizers and perpetuators of segregation are as much the enemy of America as any foreign invader. The time has come when they are not merely to be protested. They must be resisted.

The world and the United States should know that there are many younger leaders, both black and white, in positions of responsibility who, not wishing to see democracy destroyed from within, will support Mr. Randolph and Mr. Reynolds.

We know that men should not and will not fight to perpetuate for themselves caste and second-class citizenship. We know that men cannot struggle for someone else's freedom in the same battle in which they fasten semi-slavery more securely upon themselves. While there is a very real question whether any army can bring freedom, certainly a Jim Crow army cannot. On the contrary, to those it attempts to liberate, it will bring discrimination and segregation such as we are now exporting to Europe and to South America. To subject young men at their most impressionable age to a forced caste system, as now outlined in the Universal Military Training and Selective Service bills, not only is undemocratic but will prove to be suicidal.

Segregation in the military must be resisted if democracy and peace are to survive. Thus civil disobedience against caste is not merely a right but a profound duty. If carried out in the spirit of good will and nonviolence, it will prick the conscience of America as Gandhi's campaigns stirred the hearts of men the world over.

Therefore, in the future I shall join with others to advise and urge Negroes and white people not to betray the American ideal by accepting Jim Crow in any of our institutions, including the armed services.

Further, I serve notice on the government that, to the extent of my resources, I shall assist in the organization of disciplined cells across the nation to advise resistance and to provide spiritual, financial, and legal aid to resisters.

If Senator Morse and the government believe that intimidation, repression, prison, or even death can stop such a movement, let them examine past struggles for freedom. If the government continues to consider such action treason, let it recall the advice that Justice Jackson gave the German people at the opening of the Nuremberg trials: "Men," he said, "are individually responsible for their acts, and are not to be excused for following unjust demands made upon them by governments." Failure of the German citizens to resist antisocial laws from the beginning of the Hitler regime logically ended in their placing Jews in gas furnaces and lye pits. Justice Jackson indicated in conclusion that individual resistance to undemocratic laws would have been a large factor in destroying the unjust Nazi state.

I believe that American citizens would do well to ponder Mr. Jackson's remarks. Civil disobedience is urged not to destroy the United States but because the government is now poorly organized to achieve democracy. The aim of such a movement always will be to improve the nature of the government, to urge and counsel resistance to military Jim Crow in the interest of a higher law—the principle of equality and justice upon which real community and security depend.

I sincerely hope that millions of Negroes and white people who cherish freedom will pledge themselves now to resist Jim Crow everywhere, including the military establishments. Thereby the United States may, in part, achieve the moral leadership in world affairs for which we so vigorously strive. I urge you to register this intention now with your Senators and Congressmen.

It is my supreme desire that those who resist will do so in that spirit which is without hatred, bitterness, or contention. I trust that all resisters will hold firm to the true faith that only good-will resistance, in the end, is capable of overcoming injustice.

Twenty-Two Days
on a Chain Gang

◆ ◆ ◆

[1949]

LATE IN THE AFTERNOON of Monday, March 21, 1949, I surrendered to the Orange County court at Hillsboro, North Carolina, to begin serving a thirty-day sentence imposed two years before for sitting in a bus seat out of the Jim Crow section. As afternoon waned into evening, I waited alone in a small cell of the county jail across the street. I had not eaten since morning, but no supper was forthcoming, and eventually I lay down on the mattressless iron bed and tried to sleep. Next morning I learned that only two meals were served daily—breakfast at seven A.M. and lunch at noon.

That morning I spent reading one of the books I had brought with me and wondering where I would be sent to do my time. At about two P.M. I was ordered to prepare to leave for a prison camp. Along with two other men I got into the "dog car"—a small, brown enclosed truck with a locked screen in the rear—and began to travel through the rain. An hour later we stopped at the state prison camp at Roxboro, and through the screen I could see the long, low building, circled by barbed wire, where I was to spend the next twenty-two days.

The camp was very unattractive, to put it mildly. There were no trees, grass only near the entrance and to one side. There was not one picture on the walls and no drawer, box, or container supplied for storing the few items one owned. While an effort was made to keep the place clean, there was always mud caked on the floor as soon as the men got in from work, since there was no change of shoes. Roaches were everywhere, though I never saw a bedbug. Once a week the mattresses were aired.

In the receiving room, under close supervision, I went through the routine of the new inmate: receiving a book of rules and a change of clothing, fingerprinting, and—"You'll have to have all your hair cut off."

An inmate barber gleefully shaved my head and, with an expression of mock sadness, surveyed me from various angles. Finally he brought a small mirror and ceremoniously held it up for me. The final touch was his solemn pretense of brushing some hairs from my shirt. Then he told me to go out to the corridor, where an officer would show me to my bed. As I left, the three inmates who were in the room doubled up with laughter. Apparently they had discovered the reason for my schoolboy nickname, "Pinhead"!

Wordlessly the officer outside unlocked the dormitory door and motioned for me to go through.

Inside I found myself in one of two rooms into which a hundred men were crowded. Double-decker beds stood so close together that one had to turn sidewise to pass between them. Lights bright enough to read by remained on all night. The rule book states: "No inmate may get out of bed after lights are dimmed without asking permission of the guard," and so all night long men were crying out to a guard many yards away: "Gettin' up, Cap'n," "Closing the window, Cap'n," "Goin' to the toilet, Cap'n." I did not sleep soundly one night during my whole stay at Roxboro, though I went to bed tireder than I had ever been before.

The camp schedule at Roxboro began with the rising bell at five-thirty. By seven beds had been made, faces washed, breakfast served, and lines formed for leaving the camp for the ten-hour-day's work. We worked from seven until noon, had a half-hour for lunch, resumed work at twelve-thirty, and worked until five-thirty. Then we were counted in and left immediately for supper, without so much as a chance to wash hands and face. From six o'clock we were locked in the dormitory until lights were dimmed at eight-thirty. From then until five-thirty A.M. we were expected to sleep.

On the morning of March 23, my second day at camp, I shaved hurriedly. When I had finished, Easy Life, an inmate who had a nearby bed, apologetically asked if he might borrow my razor. He had a week's growth of hair on his face.

"Most of us ain't got no razors and can't buy none," he said. "But don't they give you a razor if you can't afford one?" I asked.

He looked at me and smiled. "We don't get nothing but the clothes we got on and a towel and soap—no comb, no brush, no toothbrush, no razor, no blades, no stamps, no writing paper, no pencils, nothing." Then he looked up and said thoughtfully, "They say, 'Another day, another dollar,' but all we gets for our week's work is one bag of stud."

I suppose my deep concern must have been reflected in my face, for he added, "Don't look so sad. T'ain't nothin! The boys say 'So round, so firm, so fully packed,' when you roll your own."

The guard swung open the doors for breakfast, and as Easy Life rushed to the front of the line he yelled back, "But the damn stuff sure does burn your tongue—that's why I like my tailor-mades," meaning factory-made cigarettes. He winked, laughed heartily, and was gone. I picked up my toothbrush and razor, and slowly walked to my bed to put them away.

A week later I was to remember the conversation. The one towel I had been given was already turning a reddish gray (like the earth of Persons County) despite the fact that I washed it every day. That towel was never changed as long as I stayed at Roxboro. Some of the men washed their towels but once a week, just after they bathed on Saturday.

Each week we were given one suit of underclothing, one pair of pants, a shirt, and a pair of socks. Even though we worked in the mud and rain, this was the only clothing we would get until the next week. By Tuesday, the stench in the dormitory from sweating feet and encrusted underclothing was thick enough to cut. As one fellow said, "Don't do no good to wash and put this sweat-soaked stuff on again."

Two weeks later I saw Easy Life borrowing my toothbrush. "My old lady's coming to visit today and I gotta shine my pearls somehow," he apologized.

I offered him thirty-five cents for a toothbrush. He accepted the money, thanked me, and said, "But if you don't mind I'll buy stamps with it. I can write my old lady ten letters with this. I can borrow Snake's toothbrush if I wanna, but he ain't never got no stamps, and I ain't never got no money."

I started from the camp for my first day's work on the road with anything but an easy mind. Our crew of fifteen men was met at the back gate by the walking boss, who directed the day's work, and by a guard who carried both a revolver and a shotgun. We were herded into the rear of a truck where we were under constant scrutiny by the armed guard, who rode behind in a small, glass-enclosed trailer. In that way we rode each day to whatever part of Persons County we were to work in. We would leave the truck when we were ordered to. At all times we had to be within sight of the guard, but at no time closer than thirty feet to him.

On this first day I got down from the truck with the rest of the crew. After several moments of complete silence, which seemed to leave everyone uneasy, the walking boss, whom I shall call Captain Jones, looked directly at me.

"Hey, you, tall boy! How much time you got?"

"Thirty days," I said politely.

"Thirty days, Sir."

"Thirty days, Sir," I said.

He took a newsclipping from his pocket and waved it up and down.

"You're the one who thinks he's smart. Ain't got no respect. Tries to be uppity. Well, we'll learn you. You'll learn you got to respect us down here. You ain't in Yankeeland now. We don't like no Yankee ways." He was getting angrier by the moment, his face flushed and his breath short.

"I would as lief step on the head of a damyankee as I would on the head of a rattlesnake," he barked. "Now you git this here thing straight," and he walked closer to me, his face quivering. "You do what you're told. You respect us, or…." He raised his hand threateningly but, instead of striking me, brought the back of his hand down across the mouth of the man on my left. Then he thrust a pick at me and ordered me to get to work.

I had never handled a pick in my life, but I tried. Captain Jones watched me sardonically for a few minutes. Then he grabbed the pick from me, raised it over his head, and sank it deep into the earth several times.

"There, now," he shouted. "Let's see you do it."

I took the pick and for about ten minutes succeeded in breaking the ground. Then my arms and back began to give out. Just as I was beginning to feel faint, a chain-ganger called Purple walked over and said quietly, "O.K. Let me use dat pick for a while. You take the shovel and, no matter what they say or do, keep workin', keep tryin', and keep yo' mouth shut."

I took the shovel and began to throw the loose dirt into the truck. My arms pained so badly that I thought each shovelful would be the last. Then gradually my strength seemed to return.

As Purple began to pick again, he whispered to me, "Now you're learnin'. Sometimes you'll give out, but you can't never give up—dat's chain-gangin'!" An hour later we moved to another job. As I sat in the truck I racked my mind for some way to convince Captain Jones that I was not "uppity," and at the same time to maintain self-respect. I hit upon two ideas. I would try to work more willingly and harder than anyone in the crew, and I would be as polite and considerate as possible.

When the truck stopped and we were ordered out, I made an effort to carry through my resolution by beginning work immediately. In my haste I came within twenty feet of the guard.

"Stop, you bastard!" he screamed, and pointed his revolver at my head. "Git back, git back. Don't rush me or I'll shoot the goddamned life out of you."

With heart pounding I moved across the road. Purple walked up to me, put a shovel in my hand, and said, "Follow me and do what I do."

We worked together spading heavy clay mud and throwing it into the truck. An hour later, when the walking boss went down the road for a Coca Cola, I complained to Purple about my aching arms. Purple smiled, patted me on the back, and said as he continued to work, "Man born of black woman is born to see black days."

But my first black day was not yet over. Just after lunch we had begun to do what the chain-gangers call "jumpin' shoulders," which means cutting the top from the shoulders of the road when they have grown too high. Usually the crew works with two trucks. There is scarcely a moment of delay and the work is extremely hard. Captain Jones was displeased with the rate of our work, and violently urged us to greater effort. In an attempt to obey, one of the chain-gangers struck another with his shovel. The victim complained, instantly and profanely. The words were hardly out of his mouth before the Captain strode across the road and struck the cursing chain-ganger in the face with his fist again and again. Then Captain Jones informed the crew, using the most violent profanity, that cursing would not be tolerated. "Not for one goddamned moment," he repeated over and over.

No one spoke; every man tried to work harder yet remain inconspicuous. The silence seemed to infuriate the Captain. He glared angrily at the toiling men, then yelled to the armed guard.

"Shoot hell out of the next one you find cursin'. Shoot straight for his feet. Cripple 'em up. That will learn 'em."

The guard lifted his rifle and aimed it at the chest of the man nearest him.

"Hell, no!" he drawled. "I ain't aimin' fer no feet. I like hearts and livers. That's what really learns 'em."

Everyone spaded faster.

On the ride back to camp that evening, I wondered aloud if this were average behavior for Captain Jones.

"Well," said Easy Life, "that depends on how many headache powders and Coca Colas he takes. Must of had a heap today."

Back in camp Easy Life continued the conversation.

"Dat was nothin', really," he said. "Cap'n might have done them up like the Durham police did that old man over there."

He pointed to a small, thin man in his middle fifties, dragging himself slowly toward the washroom. His head was covered with bandages and one eye was discolored and bruised.

"Dad," as the men already were calling him, had come up from the country to Durham a few days before for a holiday. He had got drunk, and when the police tried to arrest him he had resisted, and they had beaten him with blackjacks. After three days in jail he was sentenced to Roxboro. When he got to the prison camp he complained that he was ill, but nonetheless was ordered to go out on the job. After working an hour, Dad told the walking boss that he was too sick to continue and asked if he could be brought in. He was brought in and the doctor summoned, but he had no temperature and the doctor pronounced him able to work. When he refused to go back to his pick and shovel he was ordered "hung on the bars" for seventy-two hours.

When a man is hung on the bars he is stood up facing his cell, with his arms chained to the vertical bars, until he is released (except for being unchained periodically to go to the toilet). After a few hours, his feet and often the glands in his groin begin to swell. If he attempts to sleep, his head falls back with a snap, or falls forward into the bars, cutting and bruising his face. (Easy Life told me how Purple had been chained up once and gone mad, so that he began to bang his head vigorously against the bars. Finally the night guard, fearing he would kill himself, unchained him.)

The old man didn't bang his head. He simply got weaker and weaker, and his feet swelled larger and larger, until the guard became alarmed, cut the old man down, and carried him back to bed.

The next day the old man was ordered out to work again, but after he had worked a few minutes he collapsed and was brought back. This time the doctor permitted him to be excused from work for a week. At the end of the week, when Dad came back to work, he was still very weak and tired but was expected to keep up the same rate of work as the other members of the crew.

A few days later, I told several of the boys that I had decided to talk to the Captain to try to improve relations on the job, since I was sure the guards were taking it out on the men because of me. They urged me to keep still. "Quiet does it," they said. "No need to make things worse," they admonished. "He'll kick you square in the ass," Purple warned.

Nevertheless I stopped the Captain that morning and asked to speak with him. He seemed startled. I told him that I knew there were great differences in our attitudes on many questions but that I felt we could be friends. I said that on the first morning, when I had failed to address him as "Sir," I had meant no disrespect to him and if he felt I had been disrespectful I was willing to apologize. I suggested that perhaps I was really the one who deserved to be beaten in the face, if anyone did. I was willing to work as hard as I could, and if I failed again at my work I hoped he would speak to me about it and I would try to improve. Finally I said I could not help trying to act on the basis of my own Christian ideals about people but that I did try to respect and understand those who differed with me.

He stared at me without a word. Then after several moments he turned to the gun guard and said in an embarrassed tone, "Well, I'll be goddamned." Then he shouted, "O.K., if you can work, get to it! Talk ain't gonna git that there dirt on the truck. Fill her up." (Later I learned that the Captain had said to one of the chain-gangers that he would rather I call him a "dirty-son-of-a-bitch" than to look him in the face "and say nothin'.")

That evening he called us together.

"This Yankee boy ain't so bad," he said. "They just ruined him up there 'cause they don't know how to train you-all. But I think he'll be all right and if you-all will help him I think we can learn him. He's got a strong back and seems to be willing."

The chain-gangers glanced at one another. As we piled into the truck one of them turned to me and said, "When he says he'll learn you, this is what he means:

> "When you're white you're right,
> When you're yellow you're mellow,
> When you're brown you're down,
> When you're black, my God, stay back!"

The chain-gangers laughed. We pulled the canvas over our heads to protect us from the rain that had begun to pour down, and headed back to camp to eat supper.

The book of regulations said: "No talking will be permitted in the dining hall during meals." Not until I experienced it did I realize what a meal is like when a hundred men are eating in one room without a word spoken. The guards stood with clubs under their arms and watched us. I had the feeling they too were unhappy in the uneasy silence.

At one evening meal, I was trying by signs to make the man next to me understand that I wanted the salt. I pointed toward the salt and he passed the water, which was close by. I pointed again, and he passed the syrup. When I pointed again, he picked up the salt and banged it down angrily against my plate. Forgetting the rule, I said quietly, "I'm sorry." One of the guards rushed across the room to our table and, with his stick raised, glared at me and said, "If I catch you talking, I'll bust your head in." The spoons and forks were no longer heard against the aluminum plates. The dining room was perfectly quiet. The guard swung his club through space a couple of times, then retired to a corner to resume his frustrating vigil. The tin spoons and forks rattled again on the aluminum plates.

The morning after my conversation with Captain Jones we were instructed to go to the cement mixer, where we were to make cement pipe used in draining the roads and building bridges. We had been working twenty minutes when the Captain came to me carrying a new cap. He played with the cap on the end of his finger for a while and stared at my shaved head.

"You're gonna catch your death of cold," he said, "so I brought you a cap. You tip it like all the other boys whenever you speak to the Captain and the guards, or whenever they speak to you."

I had noticed the way the men bowed obsequiously and lifted their hats off their heads and held them in the air whenever they spoke to the guard. I had decided I would rather be cold than behave in this servile way. I thanked the Captain, put the cap on my head, and wore it until lunchtime. After lunch I put it in my pocket, never to wear it again in the presence of the Captain or the guards.

Some of the men left their caps in the camp rather than wear them on the job, and for good reason. There was a rule that when leaving for work in the morning a man was not permitted to wear his hat until he was beyond the barbed-wire fence that surrounded the camp. On several occasions, men going to or coming from work would rush thoughtlessly through the gates with their caps on, and be struck severely on the head with a club. As Softshoe, a chain-ganger distinguished for his corns and bunions, said, "No use courting trouble. If you don't wear no hat, you ain't got to doff it."

One day the chain-gangers were on fire with the news that an old prisoner had returned. Bill was slender, tall, good-looking and sang very well. Some three years before he had raped his own three-year-old daughter and been put in jail for a year. This time he was "up" for having raped his eight-year-old niece.

It was difficult to believe all the tales the men told about Bill. One evening he came to me and asked me if I had time to talk with him. We talked for almost two hours. He was quite different from the description I had heard. He had provided well for his family, he had gone to church, but, as he pathetically admitted, he had "made some terrible mistakes." It was apparent that he wanted to wipe the slate clean, but in Roxboro jail he could never discover the reason for his unhappiness and troubles.

As I lay awake that night I wondered how ten hours a day of arduous physical labor could help this young man to become a constructive citizen. The tragedy of his being in the prison camp was highlighted by the extraordinary success that good psychiatrists and doctors are having today with men far more mixed up than Bill. I thought of the honesty with which he had discussed himself, of the light in his eyes when he had heard for the first time of the miracles modern doctors perform—and I knew that Bill deserved the best that society could offer him: a real chance to be cured, to return to his wife and children with the "devils cast out."

Then there was a young boy who had been arrested for stealing. It was obvious from his behavior that he was a kleptomaniac. I would see him spend half an hour going from one section of the dormitory to another, waiting, plotting, planning, and conniving to steal many small and useless items. Although he did not smoke, I saw him spend twenty minutes getting into a position to steal a box of matches, which he later threw away.

One day, after I had written a long letter for him, he began to tell me that he had stolen even as a child but that now he wanted to stop. As tears came to his eyes, he explained that he had been able to stop stealing valuable things but that he could not stop stealing entirely. I asked him if he really wanted to change. He said he thought so. But he added: "It's such a thrill. Just before I get my hands on what I'm gonna take, I feel so excited."

After that, as I watched him evening after evening, I wondered how many men throughout the world were languishing in jails—burdens to society—who might be cured if only they were in hospitals where they belonged. One thing was clear. Neither this boy, who reluctantly stole by compulsion, nor Bill could be helped by life on the chain gang. Nor could society be protected, for in a short time these men and thousands like them return to society not only uncured but with heightened resentment and a desire for revenge.

Early one morning Easy Life was talking with one of his friends, who had done time for stealing and was to be released that day. To the despair of those trying to get a few last winks, Easy Life was singing:

> "Boys, git up, grab your pone,
> Some to the right-a-ways, some to the road—
> This fool's made it and he's headin' home."

Easy Life's companion smiled and said for all to hear:

> "Boys, you stole while I took,
> Now you roll [work hard] while I look."

"I can work," Easy Life said, "and I can work plenty, for work don't bother me none. No sir! Boys, it's the food that gits me down." And he went to rhyming one of his spontaneous verses:

"Kick me, shout me, pull ma teet',
But lemme go home where I can eat.'

As I lay in bed for a few last minutes' rest, I began to think about the food. We had beans—boiled beans, red beans, or lima beans—every day for lunch. Every day, after five long hours of hard physical labor, we had beans, fatback (a kind of bacon without lean meat), molasses, and corn pone. Many of the men who had spent years on the road were no longer able to eat the beans at all, and I saw several men, working for ten hours day after day, with nothing to eat after breakfast for the entire day but molasses and corn pone. One of the most frequently quoted bits of folk poetry described the lunch:

Beans and cornbread
Every single day.
If they don't change
I'll make my getaway.
How long, Oh Lord,
How long?

For breakfast we usually had oatmeal without sugar or milk, a slice of fried baloney, stewed apples, and coffee. In the evening the two typical meals were cabbage and boiled white potatoes, and macaroni and stewed tomatoes. On Sundays the meal consisted of two vegetables, Argentinean corned beef, and apple cobbler. Except for being struck with clubs, the thing that the men complained most about was the food. They often recited another bit of folk poetry:

The work is hard,
The boss is mean,
The food ain't done,
And the cook ain't clean.

Actually both the cooks and the dining room were relatively clean; the protest was against the monotony of the food.

The hour was getting near for Easy Life's companion to depart. They brought in the pillowcase in which his clothes had been stored three months earlier. As he dumped his clothes onto the bed, they made one shapeless lump. He opened out his pants and began to get into them. They had a thousand creases. Then he put on the dirty shirt he had worn when he came in, and dressed in this way he left to begin a new life. He had no comb or toothbrush or razor, nor a penny in his pocket. The "dog cart" would come to pick him up and drop him somewhere near the railroad station in Durham.

I looked at him, his face aglow, happy that he would once again be "free," and wondered how he could be so happy without a cent, with no job, and with no prospects. I wondered what he would go through to get his first meal, since he had no home. I wondered where he would sleep. He said he knew a prostitute who might put him up. Prostitutes and fairies, he had said, "will always give a guy a break." I wondered where he would find a decent shirt or a pair of pants. Would he beg or borrow or steal?

I wondered if he would return. One day on the job the Captain had offered to bet ten to one that the man would be back before the week was up. As I saw him start forth, so ill prepared to face life in the city, I too felt that he would return. I asked Easy Life what he thought his friend would do when he got to town. Easy Life said, "He'll steal for sure if they don't get him first." I asked him what he meant. He said, "If the bulls don't get him for vagrancy 'fore sundown, he'll probably snatch something for to eat and some clothes to cover his ass with for the night."

"For vagrancy?" I asked.

"For vagrancy! Sure enough for vagrancy," Easy underlined. He then told me the story of a friend from South Carolina who had been on the chain gang. He, like all the others, was released without a penny in his pocket. While thumbing his way home, he was arrested for vagrancy soon after he crossed into South Carolina, and was back in jail for ninety days, less than two days after being released.

Between supper and "lights out" was our time for recreation. But for most of the men it was not a creative period. The rules permitted "harmless games," but there was not one set of checkers or chess or dominoes available, no material for the development of hobbies, and no books, only an occasional comic book. One newspaper came into the place, and few men had access to it. There were no organized sports, no library, no entertainment other than one motion picture a month.

Under these circumstances, recreation was limited to six forms, five of them definitely destructive. The first of these was *"dirty dozens,"* a game played by one or two persons before an audience. Its object was to outdo one's opponent in grossly offensive descriptions of the opponent's female relatives—mother, sister, wife, or aunt. If a "player" succeeded in making a clever combination of obscene and profane words, the audience burst into laughter, and then quieted down to await the retaliation of the opponent. He in turn tried to paint a still more degrading picture of the relatives of his partner. No recreation attracted larger crowds or created more antagonism, for often men would be sucked into the game who actually did not want to play and became angered in the course of it.

Another form of recreation was the *telling of exaggerated stories about one's sex life*. These included tales of sexual relations with members of the same sex, with animals, with children and close relatives, and with each other. It was generally recognized that 70 percent of these tales were untrue, but the practice led to lying, to experimentation in abnormal sex relations, and to a general lowering of the moral standards of younger inmates, who continually were forced into the position of advocating strange practices as a means of maintaining status with the group.

Stealing "for the thrill of it" was yet another way in which numbers of men entertained themselves. One of the best friends I had in the camp had stolen stamps from me, returned them, and then described to me how he had done it. He had sent a friend to talk with me and had given the man who slept in the bed next to mine an old comic book to reduce the possibility of being detected. I asked him why he went to all that trouble, only to return my stamps. He explained that he had stamps, but, having nothing else to do, he wanted to "keep my hands warm."

Gambling was perhaps the chief form of recreation for those who had anything to gamble with. Men gambled for an extra sock stolen on the day of clothing exchange, or a sandwich smuggled from the kitchen, or a box of matches. The three games most widely used for gambling were Tonk and Skin, games played with an ordinary deck of cards, and throwing dice. Cheating was simple and common and led to constant arguments.

There was little or no effort to control the gambling, though it was against the rules. When a new night guard came on duty and complained to an old hand that the boys were playing dice in the rear of the dormitory, the older guard was overheard to say, "What da hell do I care! They gotta do sumpin, and dice keep 'em quiet."

Gossip and talking about one's sentence also consumed a great deal of time. Over and over again men related the story of their trial and told one another how they were "framed on bum raps." The gossip session was the stool pigeon's chief means of getting information to carry "up front." Even though men feared talking about one another, they did so because they felt that the gossip-mongers had to have something to tell the superintendent. As one of the chain-gangers expressed it, "That stool pigeon has got to sing sumpin, so it's better for me to give him sumpin good [i.e., helpful information for the authorities] to carry about somebody else, before somebody gives him sumpin bad to carry about me." This created an atmosphere of universal mistrust.

The most creative form of recreation was *rhyming and singing*. There were several quartets and trios and much informal singing, both on the job and in the dormitory. The poetry was almost always a description of life in the camp or of the desire for women or of the "fear of time." Occasionally it was the bragging of a tough guy:

> I was born in a barrel of butcher knives,
> Sprayed all over with a forty-five.
> Bull constrictor bit me.
> He crawled off and died.
> I hoboed with lightnin'
> And rode the black thunder,
> Rode through the graveyards
> And caused the dead folks to wonder.
> Sixty-two inches across my chest,
> Don't fear nothin' but the devil and death.
> I'll kick a bear in the rear
> And dare a lion to roar.

Much of the best poetry was directed against those who complained. The following is an excellent example:

> Quit cryin'!
> Quit dyin'!

Give dat white man
Sumpin on your time.

I would-a told you,
But I thought you knowed,
Ain't no heaven
On the county road.

Six months ain't no sentence,
Twelve months ain't no time,
Done been to penitentiary
Doing ninety-nine.

Quit cryin'!
Quit dyin'!
Give dat white man
Sumpin on your time.

The following verses are some of the more imaginative statements about the relationship between the chain-gangers and the walking bosses and guards.

Cap'n got a pistol and he thinks he's bad;
I'll take it tomorrow if he makes me mad.

What I want for dinner they don't serve here.
Thirty-two thirty and some cold, cold beer.

Cap'n says hurry. Walker say run.
Got bad feet—can't do more 'n one.

One of the most stifling elements of life on the road gang is the authoritarianism. The prisoner's life is completely regulated. He is informed that obedience will be rewarded and disobedience punished. Section 1 of the rules and regulations makes this clear.

Every prisoner upon arrival at any prison after being sentenced by the court shall be informed of the

rules and regulations of the camp and advised what
the consequences will be if he violates these rules. He
shall also be informed as to what privileges he will
receive if he obeys the rules and conducts himself
properly.

Such unquestioning obedience may appear to be good and logical
in theory, but in experience authoritarianism destroys the inner resource-
fulness, creativity, and responsibility of the prisoner and creates, in wardens
and prisoners alike, an attitude that life is cheap. The following illustra-
tions indicate the degree to which respect for personality is violated.

—One day when we were digging ditches for draining Highway
501, we were working in water about a foot deep. A chain-ganger who had
very large feet could not be fitted to boots. After attempting to do as
much as he could from the dry banks of the ditch, he finally tried to
explain to the Captain that he could not work in water over his shoe
tops. "Get the hell in that water—I don't give a good goddamn if it is up
to your ass," the Captain yelled at him. "You should have thought about
that before you came here. The judge said ninety days, and he didn't say
nuthin' about your havin' good ones."

—The walking boss was heard commenting on one of his ace workers who had come back for the third time. "Now ain't that a shame—and
he only got a year. I sure wish he had ten or more."

—Every day after lunch the walking bosses and armed guards
would send the food remaining in their lunch kits to the chain-gangers.
After the kits had been emptied, I noticed that the water boy always
filled one of them with the corn pone from the prisoners' meal. One day
I asked the water boy why he did this. He explained that the Captain fed
that "stinkin' pone to his pigs." For a moment no one spoke. Then
Softshoe said, "Pigs and convicts."

—Visiting days were the first and third Sundays of the month; visiting hours, from one to four. The visiting took place in the prison yard.
There were two wire fences about five feet apart. The convicts stood in
front of one, the visitors behind another. There in the yard, in summer,
winter, rain, snow, sleet, they talked—if they could be heard. Visiting
day was an event both longed for and dreaded because, as one of the
chain-gangers so aptly put it, "We gotta meet the home folks like animals
in the zoo."

—The supreme authority in a state prison camp is the superintendent. The superintendent at Roxboro was a silent man who appeared chiefly at mealtimes. His major contacts with the men came when he observed them as they ate and when he directed them to their work in the morning. One of the few times I heard him speak to the men was when a newly arrived inmate violated one of the many petty rules of the dining hall and came down the wrong aisle. The superintendent raised his club and said, "Get around there before I knock the shit out of you."

We must bear in mind that one result of the authoritarian system is to develop in the prisoners many of the same attitudes they themselves decry in the officials. The majority of the prisoners accept the idea that punishment can be just. In fact they share this basic premise with most of the judges whom they eternally criticize. Many prisoners would be more severe than judges in making the punishment fit the crime. In discussing a young man who had raped two children I heard Easy Life say, "The no-good bastard should have got ninety-nine years and one dark day." When a young man came into the camp who reportedly had stolen eight hundred dollars, his mother's life savings, a prisoner suggested, "They should have built a jail on top of him." To which another replied, "That's too damn good for the bastard. They should have gassed him, but quick."

The prisoners, like the judges, hold the superstition that two wrongs can make a right. A chain-ganger claims that his incarceration clears him; hence the deprivations of prison life are equal to his crime. He feels he is doubly absolved when he gets the worst of the bargain. But any punishment that affects his body or causes him to fear while in prison, he looks upon as unjustified. Consequently he feels, often while in prison and certainly upon release, that he is entitled to avenge this injustice by becoming an enemy of society. Thus the theory that two wrongs make a right becomes a vicious circle, destructive to wardens, prisoners, and society.

Let us see what the punishments are on the chain-gang. Section 5 of the rules book states:

> *For Minor Offenses*—[The superintendent will be permitted to] handcuff [the prisoner] and require [him] to remain in standing or sitting position for a reasonable period of time.

This form of punishment produces swollen feet and wrists, muscular cramps, and physical fatigue. During the period, if the prisoner is standing up, he does not eat but is taken down for fifteen or twenty minutes every few hours to urinate, defecate, and relax.

> *For Major Offenses*—Corporal punishment, with the approval of the Chairman of the State Highway and Public Works Commission, administered with a leather strap of *the approved type* and by some prison officer other than the person in immediate charge of said prisoner and only after physical examination by a competent physician, and such punishment must be administered either in the presence of a prison physician or a prison chaplain.

Another section of the rules book dealing with punishment and discipline states that the superintendent may place a prisoner on "restricted diet and solitary confinement, the period of punishment to be approved by the disciplinarian."

One chain-ganger whom I got to know very well had recently finished a period of such confinement in "the hole." For fourteen days James had been without any food except three soda crackers a day. "The bastards gave me all the water I could drink, and I'll be damned if I wasn't fool enough to drink a lot of it. Soon I began to get thinner, but my gut got bigger and bigger till I got scared and drank less and less till I ended by drinking only three glasses a day."

Although he was very weak, he was forced to go to work immediately. He was expected to work as hard as the others and be respectful to the same captain he felt was responsible for his hardship.

James had been sentenced to sixty days for larceny, which good behavior would have reduced to forty-four days. Because of one surly remark he not only had to spend fourteen days in that unlighted hole, on crackers and water, but also lost the sixteen days of good time. Actually James had begun to hate himself as much as he hated the Captain. "A man," he said, "who tips his hat to a son-of-a-bitch he hates the way I hate him ain't no man at all. If I'd-a been a man, I'd-a split his head wide open the minute I got half a chance."

Some punishments were administered that were not listed in the rules book, as when officers kicked, punched, or clubbed the inmates.

One day when we were working at the cement mixer I heard the Captain yelling to an elderly man that he had better increase his rate and do more work. The old man attempted to work faster. "Cap'n says I'm lazy, but I'm plumb wore out," he complained. Then I noticed the Captain rushing toward him. "You goddamn lazy bastard," the Captain shouted. "I told you to get to work. When I work a man, I expect a man's work." As the old fellow turned to the Captain and began to explain that he was tired, the Captain kicked him heavily and said, "Don't talk, work." When the Captain had gone away, the old man said over and over, in mixed fear and resignation, "The Captain says I'm lazy, but I'm plumb wore out."

One chain-ganger, a man named Joe, aged about fifty-two, was at the camp for thirty days—his fifth or sixth time to receive that same sentence for drunkenness. He said he was tired all the time, that he had pains in his back. Some of the chain-gangers said he was "damn lazy." For two days the Captain urged him to work harder. "Get some earth on that spade. I'm getting tired of you, Joe. You'd better give me some work." All the second day the Captain kept his eye on Joe. In midafternoon he walked over to Joe and said, "You're not going to do no work till I knock hell out you." He calmly struck Joe several times vigorously in the face. "Now maybe that will learn you," the Captain said as he walked away. Joe took off his cap, bowed obsequiously, and said, "Yessa, yessa, that sure will learn me." When the Captain had walked away Joe spat on the ground and said, "He's a dirty son-of-a-bitch and I hope he rots in hell."

The first thing a man did when he awoke in the morning was to look out the window. "How's the weather?" was always the first question. A heavy rain meant a day without work, and the fellows prayed for "sweet rain." It was not just because the work was hard but also for four other reasons, all having to do with working conditions:

1. The work was never done.
2. Thought and creativity in any form were not permitted.
3. Staying "under the gun" made for crowded, tense conditions.
4. The men felt like "things" rather than people on the job.

I believe they most disliked the feeling that no matter how hard they toiled, "the work on the highway ain't never done." When one job was finished there was always another. "Let's ride," the Captain would say, and off we would go. One fellow complained, "If we only knew that we had so much to do in a day, then I wouldn't mind the aches so much 'cause I could look to some rest at the end."

I had never before realized the importance, even to men doing the most monotonous manual labor, of knowing clearly the reasons for doing a job, and the dejection of spirit that subconsciously creeps in when men cannot see a job completed. One day when we dug out patches in the road which another crew would fill in, Purple expressed this feeling: "I reckon these holes will be filled by some fool 'rrested in Durham tonight, and he'll wonder where the hell they come from."

On the job the men were not permitted to use the kind of imagination that they put into their rhymes. Over and over again the walking boss would say, "Don't try to think. Do what I tell ya to do." Once when a resourceful chain-ganger offered a suggestion that might have improved or simplified the task, the walking boss said, "I'm paid to think; you're here to work." Softshoe used to say,

> "When you're wrong, you're wrong,
> But when you're right, you're wrong anyhow."

On two or three occasions when the Captain was away, the assistant walking boss was in charge of the crew. He was quite inexperienced as compared with one of the chain-gangers, James, who knew almost as much about the job as the Captain. One day in the Captain's absence James suggested to the assistant that a ditch should be cut a certain way. The assistant captain ordered otherwise. So fifteen men spent three and a half hours in water and mud digging a ditch forty feet long, four feet wide, and in places five feet deep. The next day the Captain told us that the work would have to be redone. The men looked knowingly at one another and started digging.

There was a regulation that each prisoner, except the trusties, must at all times be within eyeshot and gun range of the armed guard. The prisoners called this "under the gun." Another regulation was that at no time could a chain-ganger be seen to rest during his ten-hour day except during the two fifteen-minute smoking periods. These regulations made for continuous tension.

When digging or clearing ditches, our crew of fourteen to sixteen men was usually divided, half of them assigned to each side of the road. Since the amount of work on each side was seldom equal, the logical thing would have been for the crew that finished first to move on down the road. They could not do so because then they would not have been "under the gun." Or the crew that finished first could have rested for a few minutes and then moved on with the group. But the regulation that "all must be busy at all times" precluded such a step. The solution accepted was to put all fourteen men on one side, where we were jammed in so tightly on one another that work was dangerous, slow, and inefficient. We got on one another's nerves and often struck each other with tools.

Certain men in the crew, to avoid hardship and to give the impression they were working harder than the others, indulged in hiding other men's tools, pushing, or criticizing one another's work in loud voices in order to place themselves in more favored working positions or to get in a good light with the Captain for informing. Whenever we worked on ditches, tension in the evenings in the dormitory often ran high.

To me the most degrading condition of the job was the feeling that "I am not a person; I am a thing to be used." The men who worked us had the same attitude toward us as toward the tools we used. At times the walking bosses would stand around for hours while we worked, seeming to do nothing—just watching, often moving from foot to foot or walking from one side of the road to the other. It was under these conditions that they would select a "plaything." One boy, Oscar, was often "it." Once the bored gun guard ordered Oscar to take off his cap and dance. With a broad smile on his face, he warned Oscar, "I'll shoot your heart out if you don't." As the guard trained his rifle on Oscar's chest, Oscar took off his cap, grinned, and danced vigorously. The guard and the walking boss screamed with laughter. Later most of the crew told Oscar that they hated him for pretending he had enjoyed the experience. But almost any of them would have reacted the same way.

To return to the story of my relations with Captain Jones. He had learned of my case and knew I was from the North. Several chain-gangers agreed that the newsclipping he waved about on the day he first lectured me was

the Durham *Sun*'s article on my surrender. At any rate I am sure he felt
that I was going to shirk and be difficult—that I would try to show off
and challenge his authority.

My aims were really far different. I wanted to work hard so I would not
be a burden to other chain-gangers. I wanted to accept the imprisonment
in a quiet, unobtrusive manner. Only in this way, I believed, could the
officials and guards be led to consider sympathetically the principle on
which I was convicted. I did not expect them to agree with me, but I did
want them to believe I cared enough about the ideals I was supposed to
stand for so I could accept my punishment with a sense of humor, fairness, and constructive good will.

It would have been easy to be either servile or recalcitrant. The difficulty was to be constructive, to remove tension, and yet to maintain my
balance and self-respect, at the same time giving ample evidence of respect
for the Captain's personality.

I found him to be a very fine craftsman, who knew well the skills of
his trade. I noted, too, that when it began to rain hard he was much more
careful to leave immediately for the dormitory than were most of the
other captains. Soon after our first unfortunate encounter, I mentioned
these facts to him.

One morning when he came toward me with what I considered a
hostile expression on his face (I was unskillfully making cement pipe),
I decided to take the initiative. Before he could teach me I called over
to him, "Captain Jones, I seem to need help. Would you have the time
to show....?" I could not finish my sentence.

"Damn well you need help," he said, but already I could notice a
difference in his expression. He showed me how to scrape the steel
forms and how to oil them. Thanking him politely, I told him that if he
saw me doing poorly I hoped he would speak to me because I wanted to
use the rest of my sentence to pick up as much knowledge as possible.
He said, "Well, I can learn you," and walked away.

An hour later he returned, looked over my work, found it satisfactory, and said, "Well, Rusty, you're learnin'." That was the first time he
had not called me "tall boy" or "hey-you-there."

For three days our relations improved, but on the fourth day when
I reported for work he seemed very agitated. It turned out that an
informer among the prisoners had told him I was urging the men not to
wear caps so as not to have to tip them. Actually I did look upon the tipping

of caps as degrading, for most of the men did it as a gesture of respect while inwardly they not only cursed the captains but also lost self-respect. When asked, I had told the men about my attitude but also had made it clear that my first concern was what the tipping did to them inside.

That same day I had another talk with the Captain. He seemed very impatient, but he did listen as I explained my position on wearing caps. Although he said nothing more to me, I later heard that he informed several men who had recently begun to go bareheaded that they should wear caps the year round or not at all. One of the prisoners said, "There is goin' to be some coldheaded spooks 'round here next January!" After that there was no further discussion of the caps and no effort to get men to wear them.

The next morning the Captain offered us cigarettes during smoking period. Since I did not smoke, I felt I should not take any and attempted to return them. "Rusty," he said, "they're for you whether you smoke or not." I accepted the cigarettes and gave them to another chain-ganger. This seemed to me a logical way to behave, but the Captain attached real significance to my having offered to return the cigarettes. That afternoon he told one of the men that I was filled with a lot of bad ideas but at least I was polite. Later he said to the armed guard, in the presence of Easy Life, that it was probably not my fault that I was "mixed up about so many things." He concluded, "Everything those damyankees touch the bastards spoil."

The Captain and I continued to disagree on many points, but as time went on, I felt, we came to recognize that despite our different attitudes we could work together and learn from each other.

One day toward the end of my sentence, the Captain stopped me.

"Well, how are you getting along, Rusty?" he said.

"Quite all right, Captain," I answered, "but I feel that some of the fellows need things. I hope to send in some toothbrushes, combs, and razors when I get home."

"Well, you got a surprise, didn't ya?" he asked.

"A surprise?" I said.

"Yes, indeed. You thought we was going to mistreat ya—but bad, didn't ya?"

"I didn't know what to expect," I said, "but I have learned a good deal here."

"Well, we can all learn something," he said, and walked away. That afternoon he treated the crew to a bottle of Royal Crown Cola.

Before I left, I decided to write the Captain a letter. The prisoners were astounded. "You can't write the Captain." "What do you think you're doin'?" "They ain't goin' to do nothin' but throw it in the shit pot."

I explained to the men that I was sure they could write anyone connected with the camp or the Prison Bureau. But even the more enlightened were skeptical. "I bet the Captain don't never get it," Purple said.

At any rate, I sat down and wrote the following letter to Captain Jones.

Camp #508
Roxboro, North Carolina
Sunday, April 10, 1949

Dear Captain Jones:

If all goes well, I understand that I may be released this coming Wednesday morning. But before I go I want to say that I am pleased to have been placed in your work crew.

Never having done similar work before, I am afraid I was not very apt, so all the more I want to thank you for all the help you gave me on the job. I feel that I learned a great deal.

I want to thank you and Captain Duncan for the treats to cigarettes and soft drinks. As you probably know better than I do, life has not always been easy for most of the men who come to this camp. And such kindnesses mean more to us than words can express.

I trust that your cold will have cleared up soon.

Sincerely,
Bayard Rustin

The Captain's reaction to the letter was very interesting. He was seen passing it around to the other captains and to several guards. He never mentioned it to me, but he did seem to have an honest, friendly feeling toward me during my last days at the camp.

Now most of the inmates were pleased that I had written the letter. On my last night in camp one of the chain-gangers asked me if I would help him compose a letter to an official.

"Your letter sure done some good," he said. "Guess it won't hurt me none to try."

This one successful attempt to modify the authoritarian setup should not, however, carry undue weight. There was much working in my favor. Many persons wrote and visited me; people outside sent packages to the community kit; I had a short sentence; and I got on well with the other chain-gangers. All this made it easier for me to approach the Captain and to do so with some degree of confidence. On the other hand, this experience does indicate that even in trying circumstances (for both the Captain and me) it was possible to reach a working solution without losing one's self-respect or submitting completely to outside authority.

There are three methods of dealing with offenders against society once they are apprehended: retribution, deterrence, and rehabilitation. Prison officials and men generally lay claim more or less to advocating all three. At present the public thinks that offenders should be punished. There are many different reasons why this is so, among them the belief that the average criminal responds to nothing but fear and penalties. Yet there is some real evidence that only through the very opposite of fear and punishment—intelligent good will—can men be reached and challenged and changes brought about.

Three experiences during my stay at Roxboro exemplify Auden's statement, "What can be loved can be cured," and suggest that we can expect true rehabilitation only when we have rejected punishment, which is revenge, and have begun to utilize the terrific healing and therapeutic power of forgiveness and nonviolence.

On the final Saturday of my stay, the Captain was away and his assistant directed the work. While the assistant was not so skillful as the Captain, he was more gentle, more considerate, and willing on occasion to consult the crew on procedure. Before we began work he explained clearly what was to be done. For five hours that morning, in the presence of a director who was not tense, who did not curse, and who permitted the men to help plan the work, many constructive things occurred. The men were cooperative, they worked cheerfully, tension was reduced, and the time passed more quickly than usual. When we returned to the dormitory, Purple, who had a way with turning phrases, referred to the morning's work as a "halfday of heaven."

Stealing was the chief problem in the dormitory. The night I arrived, my fountain pen, stamps, razor, and twenty blades were stolen. The next morning my writing paper disappeared. All these things had been locked away in a box, so I decided to follow the policy of not locking up my belongings. I announced that in the future all my stamps, money, food, writing paper, etc., were for the use of the community, but that in order to divide things according to need, I hoped that before anyone took anything he would consult me. As small boxes of food and other things were sent to me, they were added to the community kit. Gradually the following things occurred:

1. After a week, except for four candy bars, there was no stealing from the community kit.
2. Other men made contributions to the community kit.
3. Inmates began to unlock their unsafe strongboxes and bring things to the open community kit for safekeeping. As one of the fellows said, "If anyone is caught snatching from that box, the boys won't think much of him."
4. Two packages of cigarettes were stolen from a chain-ganger. Then it was announced that unless they turned up, money would be taken from the community kit to pay for them. The cigarettes were found on the floor the next morning.

Finally there is the example of our party. Near the end of my second week in camp several boxes of candy, cookies, cakes, dates, peanuts, and fruit juice were sent in to be added to the community kit. It was suggested that we have a party, but practically all the inmates were against it. They said, "The fellows will behave like pigs." It would be impossible to keep order, they added, and a few husky people would get all the food.

The decision was that I should select the committee to put on the party. I purposely chose the three men known to be the biggest thieves in the camp, and they accepted. The others were disheartened. "Now we know the party is wrecked. Those guys will eat half the stuff themselves before it even starts!" they groaned.

Nevertheless the boxes were turned over to them to be kept for two days until the party. Except for the disappearance of the four candy bars already mentioned, all the food was kept intact, and six candy bars were

donated to replace the four stolen ones. The party itself was well organized and orderly, and the left-over food was returned to the community
kit. Perhaps more significant was the fact that one man, noted for stealing, became known as one of the most capable men in the camp. He was
so thorough that he appointed a sergeant-at-arms for the party, whose
business was to patrol the floor to watch for stealing or disorder.
Fortunately the sergeant-at-arms had no business at all and gave up his
job before the party was half over.

I certainly do not want to imply that we had in any real sense
dealt with the problem of stealing in the camp. However, the stimuli of
expectancy, trust, and responsibility had, for the moment at least,
brought about positive responses—faithfulness to duty, imagination,
and sharing. Would more such gentle stimuli over longer periods of
time, accompanied by proper diet, medical care, music education,
good quarters, and respectful treatment, be more effective finally than
retribution and punishment? If the law of cause and effect still operates
in human relations, the answer seems clear.

MONTGOMERY DIARY

◆ ◆ ◆

[1956]

February 21, 1956

I arrived in Montgomery this morning and had an interview with Reverend Abernathy, one of the leaders of the nonviolent protest. The situation is so tense that men watch his home in shifts while he and his family sleep. I was warned that I will be watched while in town and that it is important that I have the bolts tightly drawn on the windows in my hotel. As one person put it, "This is like war. You can't trust anyone, black or white, unless you know him."

This afternoon I talked with E. D. Nixon, whose home was bombed on February 1. For years he has been a fearless fighter for Negro rights. He suspects that his home will be bombed again but says, "They can bomb us out and they can kill us, but we are not going to give in."

Later I sat in on a conference with a committee of the Montgomery Improvement Association, which coordinates the protest activities. Three recommendations were accepted:

1. The movement will always be called a nonviolent protest rather than a boycott in order to keep its fundamental character uppermost.
2. A pin should be designed for all those who do not ride the buses, to wear as a symbol of unity, encouragement, and mutual support.
3. The slogan for the movement will be "Victory Without Violence."

Tonight I walked past Reverend King's house. Lights are strung all around the house, and it is being carefully guarded by Negro volunteers.

White police patrol the Negro section of town, two by two. A hotel employee advised me not to go into the streets alone after dark. "If you find it necessary to do so, by all means leave in the hotel everything that identifies you as an outsider. They are trying to make out that Communist agitators and New Yorkers are running our protest."

February 22
One hundred leaders of the protest received word that they had been indicted. Many of them did not wait for the police to come but walked to the police station and surrendered. E. D. Nixon was the first. He walked into the station and said, "You are looking for me? Here I am." This procedure had a startling effect on both the Negro and the white communities. White community leaders, politicians, and police were flabbergasted. Negroes were thrilled to see their leaders surrender without being hunted down. Soon hundreds of Negroes gathered outside the police station and applauded the leaders as they entered, one by one. Later those who had been arrested were released on $300 bail. They gathered at the Dexter Avenue Baptist Church for a prayer meeting and sang for the first time a song which had been adopted that morning as the theme song for the movement. The four stanzas proclaim the essential elements of a passive struggle—protest, unity, nonviolence, and equality. Sung to the tune of the spiritual, "Give Me That Old-Time Religion," the text is:

> We are moving on to vict'ry
> With hope and dignity.

> We shall all stand together
> Till every one is free.

> We know love is the watchword
> For peace and liberty.

> Black and white, all are brothers
> To live in harmony.

> We are moving on to vict'ry
> With hope and dignity.

After the prayer meeting I went to the home of Mrs. Jeanette Reeve, a Negro woman who had informed the police that she had not known what she was doing when she signed legal papers to challenge bus discrimination in the courts. A few days earlier her attorney, one of the two Negro lawyers in Montgomery, had been arrested for fraud because of Mrs. Reeve's retraction. Although the police had provided no protection for King and Nixon after their houses had been bombed, I found two squad cars parked before Mrs. Reeve's home. In addition, a policeman was patrolling the area with a machine gun. After ten minutes of negotiation, the police finally permitted me to see Mrs. Reeve. Her only comment was, "I had to do what I did or I wouldn't be alive today." I felt sorry for her.

February 23

This morning Reverend King invited me to attend a meeting of the protest committee. The committee decided not to hold any more mass meetings but only prayer meetings. This was to emphasize the moral nature of the struggle. The meetings will center around five prayers:

A prayer for the success of the meeting.
A prayer for strength of spirit to carry on nonviolently.
A prayer for strength of body to walk for freedom.
A prayer for those who oppose us.
A prayer that all men may become brothers to live in justice and equality.

This afternoon at three-thirty the Negroes began to fill the church for the seven o'clock prayer meeting. From four o'clock on, without leadership, they sang and prayed. Exactly at seven the one hundred who had been arrested worked their way to the pulpit through five thousand cheering men, women, and children. Overnight these leaders had become symbols of courage. Women held their babies to touch them. The people stood in ovation. Television cameras ground away, as King was finally able to open the meeting. He began: "We are not struggling merely for the rights of Negroes but for all the people of Montgomery, black and white. We are determined to make America a better place for all people. Ours is a nonviolent protest. We pray God that no man shall use arms."

February 24

Forty-two thousand Negroes have not ridden the buses since December 5. On December 6, the police began to harass, intimidate, and arrest Negro taxi drivers who were helping to get these people to work. It thus became necessary for the Negro leaders to find an alternative—the car pool. They set up twenty-three dispatch centers where people gather to wait for free transportation.

This morning Rufus Lewis, director of the pool, invited me to attend the meeting of the drivers. On the way, he explained that there are three methods, in addition to the car pool, for moving the Negro population: hitchhiking, the transportation of servants by white housewives, and walking.

Later he introduced me to two men, one of whom has walked seven miles and the other fourteen miles every day since December 5.

"The success of the car pool is at the heart of the movement," Lewis said at the meeting. "It must not be stopped."

I wondered what the response of the drivers would be, since twenty-eight of them had just been arrested on charges of conspiring to destroy the bus company. One by one they pledged that, if necessary, they would be arrested again and again.

This afternoon the coordinating committee rejected a proposal that people be asked to stop work for one hour on March 28. I was impressed with the leaders' response, which adhered to the Gandhian principle of consideration for one's opponents. As King put it, "We do not want to place too much of a burden upon white housewives nor to give them the impression that we are pushing them against the wall."

This evening a few of the leaders got together to consider a constructive program for inculcating the philosophy of nonviolence in the community. After hours of serious discussion, several proposals were accepted. The following impressed me as being particularly significant:

An essay contest for high school students on the subject "Why We Should Use Nonviolence in Our Struggle."

The distribution of a pamphlet on nonviolence.

The importance of preaching nonviolence in the churches.

The possibility of a workshop on the theory and practice of nonviolence. This meeting concluded with agreement that the committee should do everything possible to negotiate the issues. The Montgomery Improvement Association is asking for these assurances:

Greater courtesy on the part of drivers.

Accepting first-come, first-served seating within the pattern of segregation while the question of intrastate segregation is being decided in the courts.

The employment of some Negro drivers on predominantly Negro routes.

February 25

This morning I had a long talk with Reverend Hughes, a white Southerner who is executive secretary of the Alabama Interracial Council, with offices in Montgomery. Hughes indicated that his association with an interracial group has always tied his hands in dealing with the conservative whites, who distrust anything interracial. Now the liberals, to whom his group normally appeals, are also alienated because of the psychological confusion in the changed situation.

For generations the status quo has been based on violence, with the Negro as victim. A few whites have managed to be liberal without feeling a direct threat to their social position. Now, as the Negroes reach the stage where they make specific, if minimum, demands, a new and revolutionary situation has developed. There is little middle ground on which to maneuver and few compromises that are possible. For the first time, the white liberals are forced to stand for racial justice or to repudiate the liberal principles which they have always wanted to believe in.

The one definite principle they can cling to is to condemn overt violence. Even the nonviolence of the Negroes has not counterbalanced their horror of the violence which they fear will break out sooner or later. The result is that they are immobilized by confusion and fear.

This afternoon I was finally able to get an original copy of a handbill I had been hearing about since I reached Montgomery. It was distributed by unidentified individuals at a meeting sponsored by the White Citizens Council at Montgomery's State Coliseum on February 10. Twelve thousand people attended and Senator Eastland spoke. There's no proof that the leaflet was in any way a part of the official proceedings, but it is reliably reported that thousands of copies were distributed in the meeting hall and that none of the speakers denounced its distribution.

I cannot believe that this leaflet reflects the thinking of all white people in Montgomery. Thousands of them no doubt would be nauseated by it. Yet I report its distribution because such hate literature, against both Negroes and Jews, is being circulated in Alabama and unfortunately is an aspect of the emotional climate in which grave problems must be solved.

The leaflet called for the annihilation of Negroes in these terms:

> When in the course of human events it becomes necessary to abolish the Negro race, proper methods should be used. Among these are guns, bow and arrows, slingshots and knives.
>
> We hold these truths to be self-evident: that all whites are created equal with certain rights; among these are life, liberty and the pursuit of dead niggers.
>
> In every stage of the bus boycott we have been oppressed and degraded because of black, slimy, juicy, unbearably stinking niggers. The conduct should not be dwelt upon because behind them they have an ancestral background of Pygmies, Head hunters and snot suckers.
>
> My friends it is time we wised up to these black devils. I tell you they are a group of two legged agitators who persists in walking up and down our streets protruding their black lips. If we don't stop helping these African flesh eaters, we will soon wake up and find Reverend King in the white house.
> LET'S GET ON THE BALL WHITE CITIZENS

This evening I met with several women of the community who were setting up an artistic wing of the movement to carry the philosophy of nonviolence to the community. They designed a pin with a cross (to show that the movement is Christian) and a heart (for nonviolence). Two feet are superimposed as a symbol of walking for freedom. On the branches of the cross will appear the words RESISTANCE, NONVIOLENCE, BROTHERHOOD, AND LOVE.

February 26 (Sunday)
Together with a number of Negro and white reporters, I attended King's packed church. He spoke simply, emphasizing the nonviolent nature of the struggle, and told his congregation: "We are concerned not merely to win justice in the buses but rather to behave in a new and different way—to be nonviolent so that we may remove injustice itself, both from

society and from ourselves. This is a struggle which we cannot lose, no matter what the apparent outcome, if we ourselves succeed in becoming better and more loving people."

This afternoon I received word that the white community has learned that I am in Montgomery, that I am being watched, and that efforts will be made to get me out of town. I was warned under no circumstances to go into the white areas of the city.

Tonight I spent discussing the protest campaign with Reverend and Mrs. King over coffee in their kitchen. I asked King if he felt that the activities of the White Citizens Council would lead to further bombings and other violence and whether he felt some elements in the Negro community would return violence with violence. He said that he felt the behavior of the White Citizens Council could very easily lead to serious violence and that the results might be catastrophic. "But," he added, "give us six weeks. The spirit of nonviolence may so have permeated our community by that time that the whole Negro community will react nonviolently."

February 27

I learned this morning from reliable sources that there is some indication that the bombing of the King and Nixon homes was not the work of irresponsible youth or cranks, but had the support of powerful vested interests in the community. There is some evidence that even the dynamite used passed through the hands of some people in the community who should be responsible for the maintenance of order.

This afternoon I attended another meeting of the working committee, which has been up against great problems because the protest, originally planned for one day, is now running into the twelfth week. I am impressed with the seriousness and determination of these people. They are handling their money very carefully and anyone who contributes can be certain that the funds will be spent carefully.

Reverend Abernathy concluded the meeting with a statement which was unanimously adopted:

1. We have all worked hard to make our protest known around the world.
2. We have kept our struggle Christian and nonviolent and intend to keep it so.

3. Although many have been arrested, we continue our protest, for none of our actions has been illegal.
4. The car pool continues.
5. All who were arrested are out on bail, thanks to our community's fine spirit.
6. We have received moral support and encouragement from all over the United States.
7. The NAACP will help us carry on the legal aspects of the struggle.
8. We shall have occasional days of prayer and pilgrimage.
9. We pray God for strength to carry on nonviolently.

As I watched the people walk away, I had a feeling that no force on earth can stop this movement. It has all the elements to touch the hearts of men.

Fear in the Delta

◆ ◆ ◆

[1956]

THE 1950 UNITED STATES CENSUS records that there are about two million people in Mississippi. Almost half of these are Negroes, living predominantly in the northwestern corner of the state. This section, the cotton producing Delta, is the backbone of the state. There the real economic and political power is concentrated. Much of the remainder of Mississippi is poor and the people depressed.

It was with these facts in mind that Senator Eastland recently said at a meeting of the White Citizens Council: "Whoever controls the Delta controls Mississippi." The Senator made this remark in discussing the potential registration and voting power of Negroes in the state. Before him stood a large map of the twenty counties in and around the Delta where the Negro population is two and three times larger than the white.

After carefully impressing these "frightful figures" upon his audience he concluded, "We must not be overrun; our way of life must not be taken away by usurping courts or by the subversive NAACP." What he really meant was this: Under no circumstances must the Negro in the Delta vote. While numerically white men can control him forever in the remainder of the state, they could not in the Delta. If the Negro votes there, he will outvote the whites, integration will come, white economic privileges resting on segregation will be destroyed and, according to Eastland, the whites therefore enslaved.

The Senator has spent this summer building fences and making similar talks in crowded halls throughout the Delta. One must see through the political demagoguery and understand the Senator's aims, tactics, and appeal if one is to understand the elements of reaction in the South today, to feel the pressure upon confused white workers, to sense the businessmen's fear of the NAACP, and to appreciate the position of white liberals. In a profound sense the Senator speaks for the Delta. It is the voice of fear: first, the white men's fear of losing their favored position; then, their fear that if ever the Negro wins equality, he will use his overwhelming political power to give the white man the same kind of treatment he has given the Negro—and which the white man feels he himself deserves.

Fear in the Delta is Kenya's fear; reaction to fear in the Delta is South Africa's reaction. If one is fully to understand the forces at work in the Southern mind and heart today, one must know what fear has wrought upon the Delta:

—Emmett Till was kidnapped and brutalized there, and his confessed kidnapers and proved murderers released as "innocent."

—The NAACP is feared by many black men and hated by almost all white people.

—The legislature has provided for a private school system at state expense.

—Economic pressure is brought against the eight thousand Negroes who have dared to register and attempted to vote.

—Negro leaders are systematically driven from the state or murdered in cold blood.

—Negro farmers are driven from their land by intimidation and by economic double-dealing.

—Police brutality is widespread.

—The state has recently passed an amendment raising voter qualifications in an effort to disfranchise the Negro further.

—Federal agencies such as the Farm Home Administration are locally misused as a means of controlling and harassing Negro workers and farmers.

All this has begun in the Delta. It was, moreover, at Indianola, in the heart of the Delta, that the White Citizens Council was founded in 1954. Today this organization dedicated to white supremacy holds the state in its grip and dares pulpit, labor, press, or citizens openly to defy it. No one does. Fear has settled over the Delta.

Ku Klux Klan in Business Suits

On May 17, 1954, the United States Supreme Court outlawed segregation in public education. By October 12, 1954, the White Citizens Council
of Indianola, Mississippi, had become a state-wide organization. Today
its first major report of accomplishments boasts:

> In less than two years of activity, 65 of our 82 coun-
> ties in Mississippi have been organized with a
> membership of 80,000.... The state office has pub-
> lished over two million pieces of literature in the 48
> states...which give concrete, convincing reasons for
> the absolute necessity of maintaining segregation
> in the South. —REPORT TO EXECUTIVE COMMITTEE,
> AUGUST 1956

The report then calls the committee's attention to the declaration
of March 12, 1956, by 101 Southern Congressmen attacking the Supreme
Court decision, and concludes:

> The Citizens Council is proud of the part it played
> in the expression of this sentiment against the
> tyrannical actions of the Supreme Court.

Section two of the report deals with the NAACP:

> We have proven to our Negro citizens that the
> NAACP is a left-wing, power-mad organ of destruc-
> tion that cares nothing about the Negro. We have
> the support of the thinking, conservative Negro
> people who believe in segregation. We want to help
> them develop social pride in a segregated society.

There is no shame expressed in the report as to how this "support of
the thinking, conservative Negro people" was in part obtained. It was
done by the use of paid Negro agents who have carried tales, some true
and many false, creating confusion and discord until no one knows whom
he can trust. Many are thus afraid to act at all. The report puts it this way:

> Information is received by the Council concerning all activities of the NAACP. Sources of this information cannot be divulged. It is important that the NAACP leaders in all vicinities be known. A list of the NAACP membership is being compiled.
>
> This compilation of the NAACP list has numerous ramifications. Professional Negroes in the Delta are afraid of economic reprisals and do not now join the NAACP. Teachers, doctors, pharmacists, and businessmen are kept under terrific pressure.

A teacher in Cleveland, Mississippi, would receive me only after dark if I walked to her home. "That NAACP man's car you ride in will cause a commotion. Anyhow, you're a stranger, and somebody may think you are from the NAACP. Come late and walk." At the close of our conversation, she said: "Well, I really don't know what to think, but I know Mr. Smith [a white businessman and member of the WCC] is correct. He said that integration can't happen in Mississippi and if I lose my job the NAACP can't give me one. You can't give me one either, so please don't come here any more and don't speak to me if you see me on the street."

A businessman in Charleston, Mississippi, who is not an NAACP member, told a story too long to repeat in detail. It classically illustrates the forces faced by someone who is even *reported* to be an NAACP member.

Family pressure. His wife finally divorced him and left the South for Chicago.

Harassment. At night his telephone rings constantly. Often no one speaks when he answers it. Occasionally all he hears is "Nigger, nigger" and then silence.

Ostracism. Most of the middle-class Negroes in the town and many of the more prosperous farmers in the county do not speak to him on the street. No one calls at his home any more.

Economic pressure. He cannot buy at wholesale prices in the area.

Fear. A "liberal" white man who had lent him money over the years recently refused to do so again. He said, "Amos, you're a good boy, but I don't know why you won't get out of that NAACP. Don't you have no pride in your race? Anyhow, I can't lend you money. I don't want to be called a nigger-lover."

This pressure is applied to white people also. Some months ago Dr. Alan Knight Chalmers, a white minister long associated with the NAACP, visited Cleveland, Mississippi. He was not on NAACP business. He came out of Christian concern to see if an interracial ministers' committee could be set up to discuss integration. His mission failed, but while in Cleveland he called upon Reverend Duncan Gray, a white Episcopal rector. After Dr. Chalmers left town, the rector was threatened, members of his church are reported to have resigned, and he was told, "Leave the state or behave yourself."

The Council not only threatens the progressive Negroes and white people in the community, but, as its report makes clear, it

> has given backing to the conservative class of Negro
> in the area and has given them courage to speak
> out in opposition to the radical NAACP element.

In the Delta the Negro church is bought and paid for by the Council, with very few exceptions. Many ministers are in debt to members of the Citizens Council. These clergymen denounce the NAACP as radical and misguided. They call for "a new Booker T. Washington—someone to lead who is not interested in racial equality."

On September 30, I was invited to speak at a county-wide song contest at Mt. Moria Baptist Church near Bobo, Mississippi. At the end of the meeting I told the story of the Montgomery protest and related the walking of Negroes there to Moses walking with the Hebrew children out of slavery in Egypt. The talk was received by the rural population with enthusiasm. But no sooner had I sat down than Reverend J. A. Butler was on his feet urging the people to remember that God alone, in his own good time, could lead the Negro to freedom. The congregation sat in absolute silence as he spoke. When the service was over, some of the country people got in their old cars and drove away while the rest walked. Reverend Butler kissed a few children, climbed into his Cadillac, warned me not to stir things up lest I get his flock into trouble, and drove away.

As he picked up speed well down the road, a young sharecropper turned to me and said: "I liked your sermon, Brother Rustin. Now don't you pay Reverend Butler no mind. The white folks pays for his car and he's satisfied. But you better be careful. He's headin' toward Mr. Smith's now to tell him what you been preachin'."

Where the bought clergy and frightened middle class don't pay off, stronger methods are used. A good example is the careful plan carried out by the WCC in Charleston, Mississippi.

Three years ago Charleston had a small but thriving NAACP group; today it has only four members. They operate as the underground did in Nazi Germany. On the surface all is well, and recently nobody has tried to vote or to discuss integration. What caused this group, so active a short time ago, to become so quiet now?

The militant leader in Charleston, Robert Smith, had urged the Negroes to vote, had said integration was inevitable, so why not now? He was a good farmer and collected burial insurance. He was prosperous.

Then one day he was seen talking to a white man downtown. The woman who saw him said he looked mighty scared. That night he left town. Nobody yet knows why. All anyone will say is, "Don't know how they got him out. It must have been something terrible, 'cause he was a good man and he always stood up and fought for his people." But Robert Smith is gone. Behind him he left a business, a house, a truck, and his farm. No one, not even his sister, knows for sure where he is. "Some folks," she says, "tell me he's in Chicago. God knows. He might be dead."

A few weeks after Robert Smith disappeared, John Wesley Logan was sitting in a dingy Negro cafe talking with his wife. The waitress called him to the phone. When he returned to the table he told his wife that he had to "see some white man about a job." The next day they pulled him out of Tilletopa Creek. All his wife could say was, "He sure beat up a poor white man who insulted him a while back. I guess the white folks done got him." Everyone in town knew John Wesley Logan was the only day laborer who would not say "Sir," and who bragged that "I hits white folks if they hits me."

"John Wesley Logan weren't cold in the ground yet," an old man said, "before Professor J. R. Gray lost his job at Sherman Creek, down the road a piece." For "his great learnin'," Professor Gray was greatly beloved by Negroes all over the county, but, they say, "He sure made two bad mistakes." He gave the impression that he was against segregation and he bought a car outside the county because he could get it cheaper. But nobody knows for sure, because Professor Gray has never said. He left school after many years and started to farm. "Folks say he doin' fairly well. Got two bales of cotton this year. But," said the old man, "he done lost his purpose and his self-respect. You can see dat in his face. Poor man, he don't look like the same person."

Five miles down the road from Professor Gray's farm, the Reverend L. Terry used to have his rural church and a neat cabin alongside it. Every morning during the Emmett Till trial, Reverend Terry put on his best clothes and drove over to Sumner. He sat erect in the court. One day he paused and shook hands with Representative Diggs of Michigan, who was at the trial, and the following Sunday he told his congregation that Diggs was one of the "smartest and most politest men" God had given him the pleasure to gaze upon. The following Wednesday Reverend Terry called a meeting of his board and told them that for the good of the community he was leaving town. Six carloads of white men with shotguns had told him to get out or innocent people would suffer with him. He sold his cabin and his car. He left the next day for Arkansas. "Some weeks later," the old man said, "one of those same crackers who run him off bought his plantation for half what it was worth. It's a sin, son. It's a sin."

Now Charleston is quiet. Robert Smith, symbol of integration, is gone. John Wesley Logan, symbol of dignity, is dead, Reverend Terry is gone, and whatever militancy the Negro church has went with him. Yes, Charleston on the surface is quiet. And some fearful Negro businessmen have been given courage to speak out in opposition to the radical NAACP element. The WCC further reports that "inroads of NAACP upon local Negro sentiment have been severely crushed." This is true. But outside this sentiment and beneath the quiet are four Negroes who love their race, who respect the NAACP, and who are quietly carrying on in Charleston—underground.

Another and similar method of keeping Negroes from pressing for equality in the Delta was made clear by Edward Pemberton, Bolivar County chairman of the White Citizens Council. After he had ruthlessly driven a family of "uppity niggers" from his land, he told them: "Now you'll go to the NAACP and see if they can take care of you. You niggers can't live unless we let you. Your food, your work, and your very lives depend on good-hearted white people. When the likes of you learn your place, race relations can be cordial. Trouble is, you don't respect your race." In other words, if you want to eat, to work, and to live, denounce integration for all to hear.

The most servile Negroes are suspect, and every means is used to impress upon them the power of the White Citizens Councils. Even police brutality can be put to good use. An incident in Ruleville, Sunflower County, birthplace of the Council, will illustrate the point. Preston Johns, Negro renter on Senator Eastland's plantation near Blane, is a "good nigger who knows his place." One day in May 1955, Preston's wife got into a fight with another Negro woman in the Jim Crow section of the Ruleville theater. The manager threw the women out and notified the police. While the police were questioning the women, Preston's daughter came up to see what was happening to her mother. Without warning, a policeman struck her over the head with the butt of his gun. She fell to the pavement bleeding badly. The police left her there. Someone went for her father. When he came up, the police threatened to kill him. Preston left and called Mr. Scruggs, one of Eastland's cronies. After half an hour, Scruggs came and permitted the girl to be lifted from the street and taken to the hospital.

When Scruggs left, he yelled to the Negroes across the street: "You'll see who your friend is. If it wasn't for us Citizens Council members, she'd have near about died." One old Negro answered back, "I been tellin' these niggers Mr. Scruggs and Mr. Eastland is de best friends dey got." A few days later, Senator Eastland came to Ruleville to look the situation over. Many Negroes lined the streets and beamed at their "protector."

Mr. Patterson's Master Plan

Among the group of fourteen men who formed the first White Citizens Council in the living room of Dave Hawkins of Indianola, Mississippi, was one Robert Patterson. Patterson later became secretary of the Citizens Councils of Mississippi, and, in January 1956, he became executive secretary of the Citizens Councils of America upon its formation in New Orleans. The national headquarters is at Patterson's office in Greenwood, Mississippi.

According to its stated purpose, the national movement is "dedicated to the maintenance of peace, good order and domestic tranquility in our communities and our state and to the preservation of states' rights."

According to documents smuggled from Patterson's headquarters, read by this reporter, and hurriedly returned, it appears that his idea of the "maintenance of peace, good order and domestic tranquility" begins with what he calls the master plan. The plan has what a wise old Negro woman described as a "smart but ignorant" introduction in which Patterson finally concludes that tens of thousands of Negroes will vote in Mississippi within ten years "as the result of congressional, judicial and executive action which the South cannot stop short of widespread violence." He has no illusions that cloture can be maintained in the United States Senate.

These are not surprising admissions, since on Thursday, August 30, Senator Eastland, speaking before the Cleveland, Mississippi, Rotary Club, had said:

> The South has absolutely no influence with the Judiciary of the United States and is losing ground on cloture in the Senate. We have nineteen sure votes and we need thirty-four to block civil rights legislation. The control of the legislative machinery enjoyed by the South, due to seniority, is our only source of power.

What is surprising, however, is Patterson's bold solution to this problem. His plan calls for at least 500,000 Negroes to leave Mississippi by 1966. About 200,000 will leave voluntarily, having been forced out by the tractor, the mechanical cotton picker, the desire of the younger generation to head for the cities, and the decline of the small independent farmer. Another 100,000 will leave "if industries coming into the state are made to understand that Negroes are not to be hired." The remaining 200,000 may need to be "assisted to leave through economic pressure."

For those who are concerned lest the absence of Negro labor create problems, the Patterson plan is reassuring. Plantations will grow in size. Skeletal groups of "Negroes who have pride in their race"—that is, who believe in segregation—will be kept on "under the supervision of strict and carefully trained white supervisors." They will live in "modern but strictly segregated compounds." They will have good housing, hot water, bathrooms, and be permitted to establish their own churches. Just as Southern industry now has chaplains paid by management, so large farmers will be encouraged to hire "good spiritual leadership" for the segregated compounds. In other words, of the 70 percent of the Negro population who are tenants and sharecroppers, over half, according to the Patterson plan, are to leave the state.

Already thousands of Negroes are leaving the Delta. Last year 240 Negro families were tenants on the R. M. Dakin plantation, one of the largest in the Delta. This fall all but forty families have been told to leave. Machinery and the Patterson plan are replacing them.

The plan also calls for driving the radical NAACP element out of the state immediately. It is argued that the masses of Negroes "will do what is for the common good" if only the dangerous leaders are curbed or driven out first. To understand how completely in earnest Mr. Patterson undoubtedly is requires only the most cursory recital of the fate of Negroes who have stood up for their rights in the Delta:

—On May 6, 1954, the Reverend George Lee of the Belzoni, Mississippi, NAACP was shot and killed on the street after refusing to stop distributing literature urging Negroes to vote.

—In November 1955, Gus Courts, chairman of the Belzoni NAACP, was shot for carrying on the fight in which Reverend Lee was killed. After a month in the hospital and a short stay in Jackson, Mississippi, he left the state for Texas.

—In Columbus, Mississippi, a cafe thought to belong to Dr. Emmett Stringer was forced to close. His wife was threatened night after night.

—Shots were fired into the home of Dr. McCoy, the president of the state NAACP conference, in Jackson.

—Professor Hennington, principal of the Negro school at Merigold, Mississippi, was found dead in Long Lake, near Whitney, Mississippi. Although spies accused him of NAACP membership, he did not actually belong to the organization.

In other words, to accept leadership in the NAACP means signing one's own death warrant. There was nothing specific in the master plan about killing and shooting men, and Patterson claims that he is opposed to both force and violence. However, the plan does call for driving out the radical elements. With respect to methods of accomplishing this aim, the plan states: "The organization in each city and town is independent and autonomous." Patterson has provided only the outline: 500,000 Negroes out of Mississippi by 1966.

One point in Patterson's careful plan has already been achieved— the establishment of the Mississippi Sovereignty Committee. Set up by the legislature in the summer of 1956, it aims to sell segregation to the public. The committee has $250,000 appropriated for its use. Some small part of this has gone to pay Negroes and white people who spy on the NAACP. The committee, composed completely of WCC legislators, has power to seize records, sends speakers over the state and into the North, publishes anti-Negro literature, holds hearings, attacks the NAACP and the Urban League, and works with the press. On October 2, 1956, at the committee's expense, ten journalists were invited from the New England states to tour Mississippi and to see for themselves how peaceful race relations are in the state.

How the committee operates in the Negro community is revealed by the case of Aaron Henry. Henry has been one of the few militant Negro leaders. Vice-president of the local NAACP, owner of a thriving pharmacy, a leader in the struggle of Negroes for the vote, he had the respect of the Negro day laborers and farmers in his area. However, when the Myrtle Hall Parent Teacher Association at Clarksville, Mississippi, began to discuss school facilities, Henry appeared to be a totally different man than the one the community had known. He had drawn up a document calling for "separate but equal" schools in the entire Cohoma County school district and urged the parents to support it.

A few days later, R. L. Drew of Clarksdale reported to Amzie Moore of the Cleveland NAACP that Henry was a very troubled man. He had been visited by a representative of the Sovereignty Committee. Henry told Drew that of course he felt as he always had, but the economic position of the Negro made it impossible to put up a fight in the Delta. Furthermore, he argued, "We can't really depend on any help from the outside. We can't fight against impossible odds. We had better forget integration for the present and try to get equalization of teachers' salaries, decent libraries, gyms, tennis courts, and the like. I know Eastland will agree to do all these things."

Drew felt that Henry had been told by the committee to cooperate or give up his drugstore and leave the state. Henry, however, was only one of the six men who had worked on the "separate but equal" statement. Drew, president of the United Order of Friendship, admitted that the following persons, in addition to himself and Henry, had agreed to the statement:

—H. H. Humes, president of the General Baptist Convention.

—J. H. White, president of Mississippi Vocational College, one of the state's three institutions of higher learning for Negroes.

—James Gillian, grand master of the Free and Accepted Masons.

—John Melcher, executive vice-president of the Regional Council of Negro Leadership.

Drew was ashamed of himself and kept repeating, "What can a man do, up against such pressure?"

Amzie Moore's reply was, "A man can try to be a man."

Economic Pressure

The Keenan Case

Theodore Keenan is a tall, well-built brown man forty-eight years old. He was reared in the Delta and is a good farmer. He is proud that he has never been arrested, has four children, and goes every Sunday "to hear the word of God." He has believed in integration, has taught his children "to look white folks in the face," and has tried to help his neighbor when the need arises.

Everyone will tell you that Ted Keenan is a brave man—for in 1955 he did a brave thing. He walked to town, signed an affidavit that a number of Negroes' voting ballots had been destroyed, and sent it to the FBI. This was the first time a Negro in the Delta had done such a thing. He even gave the names of the poll-keepers who destroyed the ballots: C. K. Fisackerly and Claud Fisackerly. And for the first time the FBI came into the county to investigate. "Nothing was done, but Theodore Keenan did a brave thing by calling them," the people in the county will tell you.

Whenever Keenan prayed aloud at church, he asked God to "remove all segregation and discrimination from the land." The minister warned him long ago to hold his tongue. But instead of listening to his pastor, he "kept moving," joined the NAACP, and worked to get others to join it whenever his work was done on the farm. Keenan's farm is a great responsibility. He owns 240 acres and has three tenants and their families helping to run it. There are four houses, a car, two trucks, three tractors, one combine, a hay baler, twenty-five head of cattle, and all the little things to take care of. But Keenan is used to hard work and he has prospered. Only two other Negroes in the county own anything comparable—

J. W. Lee and George Hall, both of Indianola. Neither will have any dealings with the NAACP, and they used to warn Theodore Keenan that he was "headin' for trouble, sure."

In 1954, Keenan had a "short crop" and borrowed $10,000 from a bank. In 1955 he had a "fair crop" and paid $6,000 on the previous year's debt. He then went to another bank in the county to borrow $4,000 on a second mortgage, but they turned him down. "Niggers that work with the NAACP ain't welcome here," they said. Keenan tried several other banks and was refused everywhere. Finally, early in August, Keenan went to the Farm Home Administration and requested a disaster loan of $4,000 in order to repay the balance on the 1954 bank loan. The agency promised to grant the loan, but when he returned a few days later, the FHA local representative said the county had used up all its disaster funds. Keenan was desperate.

When he got home he received a call from Eugene Fisackerly, local leader of the White Citizens Council. Fisackerly said he had called him on advice of Keenan's friend and offered to lend him the $4,000 at 6 percent interest *if* Keenan would not vote in the August 23, 1956, second primary. Keenan was noncommittal.

The next day W. P. Scruggs, Eastland crony and spokesman for the Citizens Council, sent for Keenan. He was rude and blunt and made three things clear:

1. Since June 1956 the WCC had been working to see that Keenan would get no credit or loans anywhere in Mississippi.
2. Keenan must resign from the NAACP.
3. He must sign a statement that he would immediately resign from the NAACP; if not, he had better "leave Mississippi before the sun comes up."

Keenan admits that he was terrified and confused. He wanted to stand and fight, but he thought about his wife, his children, and his tenants. Reluctantly he signed to renounce the NAACP. When he left, Mr. Scruggs smiled and said, "You'll see, you'll get on without trouble if you keep your promise. And if you don't...well, I know you will."

The next day Keenan asked that his request for the FHA disaster loan be reopened. He waited and waited but got no reply. Then he went to see Mr. Scruggs and reminded him that he needed the money badly.

Scruggs picked up the telephone and told the superintendent of the FHA, Malcolm French, that he was sure Keenan was now O.K., so "Let him have the money."

Scruggs hung up the phone and told Keenan, "Mr. French says he will be glad to let you have the money." Keenan said, "I went there yesterday and he wouldn't even see me." Scruggs replied, "You get on over there. You'll get it. You're truthful. We like that. We had to take time to check on you. We checked on whether you were at the big meeting [the state NAACP meeting in Jackson]. I'm going to see you over the hump. You'll have no worries as long as you're a good boy."

Following this talk, Keenan was also able to borrow $475 on open notes from the Bank of Ruleville, whereas earlier he could not get a $100 loan for seed even though he had security.

Shortly after Scruggs had sent for Keenan, the White Citizens Council sent J. H. White, Negro president of the Mississippi Vocational College at Itta Bena, to see Keenan. President White came quickly to the point: "Mr. Keenan, I want you to line up with the aims and purposes of the Council. Vocational College has a great role to play and I need your help." Keenan refused.

Later Scruggs told Keenan that White was working with the Council, and "he is doing all right for himself and for your people." Scruggs wanted Keenan to function for the Council as a spy on the NAACP and the activities and plans of other Negro leaders in the radical element. Keenan said he had left the NAACP and that was all he could do. Scruggs suggested that he "think the matter over...carefully...very carefully."

A short while afterward, President White visited Keenan again and literally begged him to give him a list of all the local Negro leaders associated with the NAACP. Keenan told him, "The only man I know in Mississippi associated with the NAACP's Amzie Moore of Cleveland" (Moore was so well known that Keenan knew he was not divulging any secret). White asked Keenan to try to get Moore to sign a pledge that he would cease his NAACP activities. Keenan replied, "I can't do nothing with Moore. Why don't you see him?" White replied, "I guess it's no use. Mr. Scruggs says that Moore got a big loan from the NAACP. I can't reach him yet."

About a week later, Malcolm French, the FHA superintendent who earlier had refused Keenan the disaster loan, called Keenan and offered to buy him forty acres of land. He further offered Keenan a loan to build a house on a separate eighty acres Keenan already owned. Keenan thanked him but refused the offer on the pretext that he was already overburdened with property.

I asked Ted Keenan what he had learned from the experience. Here are his answers:

1. Negroes in the South cannot stand up to economic pressure without help from outside.
2. The WCC wants to create a situation in which only those who give up NAACP membership and go along with the Council can live, be protected, and prosper.
3. The federal government's agencies, including farm relief, are being used at the county level to break the Negroes' will and to build the WCC.
4. He had jumped from the frying pan into the fire, and any day he could end up in the river.

What Keenan meant by the last point was this: After signing the statement that he would leave the NAACP in order to save his land and his family, he had continued to contribute to the NAACP, to collect memberships from "safe people," and to work quietly with Amzie Moore and the NAACP regional secretary. He knew his every move was watched, but he says, "Amzie Moore is right. A man may be forced part of the way but he has to do the best he can—a man is still a man. But if they find out what I'm doin', I'm a dead duck. Pray for me!"

The Moore Enterprises

In the winter of 1953, Ruth and Amzie Moore were deeply troubled. They had been watching the steady flow of young Negroes out of the Delta. "There is nothing to keep them here," Ruth told Amzie. "We need more Negro businesses, more people for them to see owning something." Amzie got to thinking. He talked some more with Ruth and they came up with an idea: the Moore Enterprises. The plan called for a service station, restaurant, and a beauty shop on a good piece of land on the main highway running through town.

In January 1954 Ruth and Amzie, with little more than their hands and a good idea, started working. They bought a lot 130 by 65 feet on Highway 61 South, Cleveland, Mississippi, for $1,500. Then they leveled it off with 200 loads of dirt costing $800. The $2,300 to do this was borrowed from J. O. Alexander, a Negro minister. On February 1, they borrowed $6,600 at 6 percent interest and a 10 percent brokerage fee from J. T. Smith, a white attorney in Cleveland. A few days later, construction was started, but within two weeks their funds had been exhausted on steel, brick, labor, etc. For six weeks they waited for another loan and finally in April J. T. Smith lent them another $1,500.

Meanwhile Amzie Moore, on the basis of his credit rating and home, negotiated a loan of $17,000 from the Standard Life Insurance Company of Jackson, on completion of the Moore Enterprises building on July 17, 1954. This money was immediately paid out for back bills and toward air-conditioning, which cost $10,000.

Now there were no funds for operational equipment for the gas station, the restaurant, or the beauty parlor. So Amzie tried to arrange for a loan of $7,500 from the Tri-State Bank in Memphis, Tennessee. The bank offered to lend him $1,600, but the Moores could find no one in Mississippi with such a balance in the Tri-State Bank to endorse the loan. So Moore wangled the most basic materials on credit.

At this point, Dr. Howard, president of the Regional Council of Negro Leadership, publicly announced in October 1955 that Moore was so deep in debt that foreclosure was inevitable. He then appealed for Negroes all over the country to deposit funds in the Tri-State Bank to help save Negro business in Mississippi. Although more than $200,000 was deposited with the bank, Moore could not use any of it for failure to obtain endorsers. He was in even deeper trouble because Howard's appeals in Northern papers angered Southerners who had lent Moore money.

In December 1955, following Dr. Howard's dramatic appeal in Moore's name, Cleveland City Alderman Hutchinson, County Tax Assessor Chriss, and Local Policeman Noel came to Moore and demanded that he put a "For Colored Only" sign on the building housing the three enterprises. Moore refused. Thereupon the local banks which had given him small loans on a short-term credit basis—for operational needs such as gas, oil, light, and water bills—were instructed by the White Citizens Council not only to refuse further loans but also to cut off his credit.

With the receipts from the restaurant, gas station, and beauty shop, and funds raised by the Moores themselves, doing side jobs, they were able on November 1 to pay J. T. Smith all the $8,100, plus interest and fees, except $900. But on December 1, 1955, the WCC sent word that Moore could get no more day labor in the county. A few days later, J. T. Smith posted a notice at the courthouse that Moore's house, on which he had a second mortgage for $900 and on which the Veterans Administration had a mortgage of $6,000, was to be sold at auction. An appeal was made to the NAACP, which lent Moore $1,200 to pay J. T. Smith in full.

As the result of the pressure of the WCC, the agencies which had given Moore time to get money for equipment delivered on credit threatened to remove it. Moore applied to the National Sharecroppers Fund for help. Although the NSF cannot make such loans itself, it did get certain individuals to place $4,000 in escrow with the Tri-State Bank in Memphis, to help liquidate Moore's indebtedness on real estate and personal property.

In the summer of 1956 a special fund of the American Friends Service Committee sent Moore $900. He planned to spend this to stock his business, but instead had to use it to bring his building loans up to date, or else lose everything.

Of the $30,400 borrowed to build the Moore Enterprises, Moore has repaid all but $15,000. In addition to this sum still owed on the building, he owes the Tri-State Bank $4,000 and equipment firms (for the three enterprises) $2,000, making a total of $21,000 owed on the enterprises.

Since 1954 no funds have been available from local banks or private citizens for stocking the business. At the end of the 1955 business year Moore took the Enterprises' books to a white certified public accountant, who turned them over to the state tax examiner rather than post the books and file the proper income and sales tax returns for the last quarter of 1955. The tax examiner multiplied the gross income by 3 percent and told Moore that this sum, $586, represented the balance due the state sales tax commission. This was too high, and, after checking with the American Friends Service Committee and the NAACP, Moore decided nothing could be done. He wanted to instigate a legal suit, but the Negro business community urged him not to, lest the action be used as a pretext for economic reprisals against all Negro business and Moore, on whom they depended, be driven out. Moore agreed to try to raise the funds elsewhere.

J. A. Faduccia, a white attorney, appealed in Moore's behalf to the National Sharecroppers Fund, which referred the matter to an organization and saw that Moore received a check for $586, the total delinquent sales tax for 1955.

Moore could not pay the sales tax for the first quarter of 1956. He had used the money to buy gas and oil after the WCC had made it impossible for him to obtain these commodities on a credit basis.

In order to try to hold on to the Enterprises, Moore is at present working at the U.S. Post Office as a mail handler. The remainder of his time he gives to the Enterprises and to NAACP work all over the Delta. At present his financial situation is this:

1. There are no funds to employ qualified labor for the Enterprises.
2. There are no funds for stock such as batteries, seal-beam headlights, fan belts, tires, tubes, and parts—all items on which substantial profit is made.
3. The cost of gas and oil is too high. Moore must pay $19.90 and sell at $34.50. Dealers fix wholesale prices and do not wish to sell to Moore so he can make a profit.
4. Both Negro and white businessmen have advised him to sell out.

The WCC is stepping up pressure. Moore feels it is imperative not to sell for the following reasons:

1. Some Negro leaders must stand firm in the face of WCC economic pressure and harassment.
2. As one of the four militant Negroes in the Delta, he owes it to the people to try to stay on against all odds.
3. If Moore sells, other businessmen who look to his leadership will also sell and run.
4. A Negro businessman who defies the WCC is a necessity in the situation.
5. Moore cannot remain militant, or chairman of the NAACP, unless he can finally build up a business and remain independent of WCC pressure.
6. The experience he gains in attempting to do this will be invaluable for others who, if a new course is not found, must either run away or submit.

Druggist Without Drugs
Claude Bariol was a poor boy who worked his way through Xavier College in New Orleans as a paint sprayer. After college he came back to

Cleveland, Mississippi, married, and worked as a poorly paid pharmacist for M. D. Ragsdale. Ragsdale is anti-Negro, but certainly not hypocritical. He frankly told Claude that he hired him because he could get him cheap and "anyhow there ain't nobody else around." Yet Ragsdale was always polite and never called Claude "boy."

But Claude had been talking with Amzie Moore and had decided he should do something, on his own, with his education. Furthermore, he did not like the idea of working for a man who belonged to the White Citizens Council. So when a Negro businessman suggested putting up the capital for a drugstore, Claude jumped at the chance even though he would have to support his wife and family on $25 a week for a year or so. Claude felt good, for the contract stated that if after a year business flourished, his salary would gradually rise to $100 a week and, if he desired it, he could buy up to 50 percent of the business.

In May 1955 the store opened. There was very limited operating capital, so Claude did all the advertising posters by hand and carried them around the neighborhood. Arrangements had been made with Ellis-Bagwell Drug Company of Memphis, Tennessee, to stock the store with drugs. Members of the firm had come to see Claude, looked over the plans, and told him, "Of course we will handle your supply. Get in touch with us a couple of weeks before you open." They left a good supply of order blanks and showed Claude how to fill them out. Two weeks before the announced opening, Claude sent in his order. By return mail he got a short note saying, "We cannot fill your order, and there is no further need for you to contact us." Claude later learned that the very day they came to look at the store, they had gone uptown and been told by the WCC: "We don't want that nigger drugstore in this town."

Next Claude tried McKesson and Robbins in Memphis. They refused to open a regular account but said they would ship what he needed from time to time COD. This would not be easy, for he had used every penny in fixing up the store.

Finally, he wrote Standard Drug at Meridian, Mississippi. They replied, "You are too far outside our regular territory." So Claude started ordering COD from McKesson and Robbins.

At first pharmaceutical firms would not send their salesmen to the store; then finally Upjohn, Sharp and Dohme, Massengill, and Tilden did agree to sell Claude prepared medicines. But getting drugs for prescriptions was a real problem. Druggists in a town are usually cooperative. If one is out of a drug, the others are happy to fill a pre-scription at cost. There were three white druggists in Cleveland. At first, Simmons Drug Company was helpful, but after a week they said here was an agreement not to sell him anything and they did not feel they could break it. Claude then telephoned Owens Drug Store and asked the owner's assistant for two ounces of sulfose suspension. But he hung up when he heard the owner yell to his helper, "Tell the nigger we ain't got none."

So he gathered his courage and called Mr. Ragsdale, his former boss. Ragsdale refused, saying he did not like the NAACP crowd Claude was hanging out with. But a few days later he called back and asked Claude to come to his home that night. He told Claude how the Citizens Council had laid down the law, how they planned to freeze him out, and how the Negro schoolteachers had been warned to stay out of his store. But he added, "We can work together on the quiet. I don't have anybody to fill my prescriptions and you sure need drugs."

At this point Claude and his partner began trying to negotiate a loan through the local banks. But although the building and land are worth $10,000, they have not been successful.

So Claude is limping along with the makeshift arrangement which depends on Ragsdale's whims.

As I left the store, Claude looked at a bottle Ragsdale had sent to his house the night before, and said: "Worst thing is, in a way I am still working for Mr. Ragsdale of the White Citizens Council."

The Wrinkled Uniform
In 1949 the lily-white Cleveland City Hospital turned over an $1,800 contract for laundering nurses' uniforms to Watson's Laundry. To this day there has been no complaint about the work done for the hospital. Later Charles Watson got all the laundry for the Friendship Clinic at Mound Bayou, an all-Negro town. When the Cleveland Motel, for whites only, was set up in 1953, it too gave Watson its laundry. Encouraged, Watson expanded when he won a $21,721 contract for the laundry at Greenville Army Air Base for the fiscal year 1955–1956. He took on four new workers and bought $3,000 worth of new machinery to handle the job.

There were regular inspections of the work, and all seemed to be in order until July. Just after Independence Day, July 4, someone reported that Watson was an active member of the NAACP. Everywhere he went, white people mentioned the NAACP and pressed him for his views of it and its activities. Then his telephone began to ring late at night. Finally, Watson said he was not a member and did not know who was. The white folks frankly did not believe him.

In August he began to hear reports from the air base that his work was not neat. He was upbraided because a sheet from the Negro hospital got mixed in with the air base laundry. Then he received a registered letter from Major William P. Johnson, air force contracting officer, saying in part:

> An official complaint has been registered by Chief Nurse 3505th USAF Hospital to the effect that the type of service being rendered on nurses' uniforms is thoroughly unsatisfactory.... We must insist that finished work be of first-class quality.... Complaints... certainly indicate that such is not the case. This letter is your notification that failure to correct discrepancies that now exist in the quality of your work, and failure to maintain acceptable standards of work, will be cause for termination of part or all of your contract consistent with provisions of Clause 7 of your contract entitled "Default." Request that receipt of this letter be acknowledged in the space provided therefor, and a copy be returned.

The next day the owner of the Cleveland Motel called Watson in. After some embarrassment, he said he had no choice but to turn his work over to the Cleveland Laundry, a firm owned by a member of the WCC. He promised Watson that he would return to him, if he could, "after all this fuss about you and the NAACP dies down, if it ever does."

Watson was sure the letter from the air base would lead to his losing the contract. It was a well-known fact that officers from the base attended Citizens Council meetings. It was also known that the base was doing everything possible to keep on the friendliest terms with the leading citizens of Cleveland.

Were Watson to lose the contract, he would be over $8,000 in debt. Already he had been told that no bank in the state would lend him money. In addition, he would have to lay off six workers. All his labor, operations, equipment, and maintenance budget had been geared to the air base contract.

When I suggested he try the Tri-State Bank in Memphis, he said, "But $8,000! Who will sign for that much money?" I told him I did not know but to keep up his spirit, for the contract was not broken yet.

The next day I stopped in to pick up two shirts. I asked Watson if I could see some of the nurses' uniforms. He smiled and took me into a clean room where they hung in long, neat lines. I looked at them carefully—there was not a wrinkle to be seen. "I'm watching them carefully," he said. "God knows we can't have a single wrinkle." Then he paused, took my hand, and said, "Son, please pray for me. I need that contract."

A Journey into the Till Country

On the last Saturday of September 1956, Amzie Moore, president of the Cleveland, Mississippi, NAACP, drove me through the three counties that Negroes call the "Till Country": Le Flore County, where Emmett Till was abducted; Sunflower County, where he was killed; and Tallahatchie County, where Milam and Bryant dumped his scarred body into the river.

Amzie knows that country well. As an adventurous boy he had roamed through the area, swum in the Tallahatchie River, and visited churches, singing with a quartet. He had sadly investigated the Till murder, got the first facts on the case, and telephoned them to the NAACP in New York.

"First," he said, "I want you to see the barn where they murdered that boy. It's just the other side of Ruleville—on a farm where Milam's brother used to live. He ain't there no more; white folks drove him out. A man named Wyman lives there now. He's a mean cuss—don't let nobody go near that barn. But I think we can see it from the road." "You mean," I asked, "that we have to go close to a white man's farm to see it?" "Well," he said, "I'm not sure. I think, if I remember right, there's a public road that goes by it."

At that moment the barn came in sight. "Yes," Amzie said, "this is the road." We turned into it, only to discover we were going up the driveway to Mr. Wyman's house. There was no public road past the barn. "Perhaps we had better get out of here quick," I said. We were almost at the house and could see the barn some fifty feet away. In front of it stood Mr. Wyman, shotgun in hand.

"This is no time to turn back," Amzie said quietly, and slowly stopped the car at the rear of the house. He opened the car door, got out, walked deliberately over to a white woman near the garage, tipped his hat, and politely asked for directions to Ruleville. At this point Mr. Wyman, who had been moving toward us, stopped about twenty feet away and stood, legs apart, shotgun in hand. The woman looked at us uneasily, then at him, and paused in bewilderment. A tall, well-built young Negro man ran from behind the house and stood next to her. Then she relaxed and pointed out the road to Ruleville. Amzie thanked her politely and came back to the car. We turned and drove ever so slowly down the dirt road. "Man!" Amzie said, "If we had turned back or looked nervous, we'd sure have got shot. He's a mean one." I looked back and saw Mr. Wyman still standing in front of the barn with his gun.

"Did you get a good look at that Negro?" Amzie asked. Before I could answer he continued, "Well, he was actually milkin' in the barn and heard Till being murdered. He ran down the road to a Negro woman to get help, but they was all scared. He told us about it. We tried to get him to testify, but he wouldn't or, I guess, couldn't. Scared to death. They was all scared."

"But how could he go on working there after that?" I asked. Amzie thought for a moment and replied: "Some of these folks don't know nothing but this farm. They'd be afraid to leave. Been working here all their lives. They don't know no better. They're conditioned." He paused. "But do you see all these empty cabins along this road?" I looked; practically every cabin was empty. "Well," Amzie continued, "those folks left after the murder. They were conditioned too, for a long time, but that boy's death sure unconditioned them. They're gone. I don't say they did the best thing—running—but at least they did something."

We drove on for a while in silence. Then Amzie said, "Just down the road we will be able to see the Tallahatchie River, where they threw him." In a few minutes we were on the banks of the river. The water was dirty, and the spot a lonely one. I told Amzie that the trees leaning toward the river would make a beautiful picture and suggested that he take one. "Yeah," he said bitterly as he reached for the camera, "these trees are beautiful, but they bear some strange fruit." In a moment he was smiling. "You know," he said, "I've heard of this river all my life. There's an old man down the way claims to be over a hundred. Says more than 1,100 Negroes been thrown in here since 1900. Could you believe it?" "I don't know," I said. "I don't either," he replied as he shook his head, "but sometimes you can believe almost anything."

We climbed back in the car and headed for Money, where the Till drama had begun. I asked Amzie if he had read the *Look* article and if there was any truth to the report that Till had made advances to Mrs. Milam (Bryant?). "I wouldn't say advances," he said. "I'd say what the kids who was with him reported was true. Some of them dared him to go in and ask her for a date. You know kids, especially him being from the North and needing to show off. He walked right in and acted like he was in Chicago—speaking fresh and friendly-like. He was kinda big for his age and he scared that woman plenty. She ran out and got a gun from her car. When the other kids saw the gun, they knew they was in for trouble. They called Till and all of them beat it fast."

"Pity they did not get him out of town," I said. "They should have known that, scared as you say she was, she would certainly start trouble."

"Wait," said Amzie. "You have to give credit where it's due. That woman never told her husband. Seems like she didn't want him to know. It was the colored boy who worked there that told him. I don't suppose the boy wanted to get anybody hurt. He was just trying to prove he was a 'good nigger'—or maybe just trying to protect himself."

By now we were in Money—a small town with one main street. On one side of the street runs the railway. The other side looks like a Hollywood set for a western—a small town with its flat-topped, square buildings poorly painted. We parked the car by the railway tracks and passed through small knots of Negro shoppers, who turned to look at us strangers as we passed. We walked into the small store where Till had agreed to take that dare and thereby signed his death warrant.

A white man and woman with sour, tight faces sat in rocking chairs before a dirty spittoon. When we entered, they looked at us and kept their eyes on us until we left. I bought a candy bar from the tall, red-faced man behind the counter, and we walked out. He came to the window and watched us until we got in the car. As we walked back to the car, I noticed a large sign before a drygoods store. It read, "Do unto others what you would have them do unto you." I called it to Amzie's attention. He smiled and said, "That ain't up there for them. It's for us."

As we drove out of Money, I asked Amzie if the man who waited on us was Milam. "No," he said, "the white folks ran him out of town shortly after the trial." "Ran him out?" I asked. "Yes, sir," Amzie replied. "Seems like the city fathers told him he was a disgrace and to get out right away. 'We don't want you here.' That's what they said. And he left, too. He left real quick." "How do you explain that?" I asked. "Well," Amzie said, "white folks is hard to explain. For one thing, they are all tied up inside. Seems as if they considered what he'd done a bad thing—but at the same time, mind you, they were defending him for all they was worth. I guess their running him out just shows how mixed up they are about this whole question." It was dark now and we decided to go back to Cleveland.

Two days later we went to Summer, where the trial had taken place. We parked in the square in front of the courthouse. Amzie had been there throughout the trial. Before we got out of the car he pointed out the main rear door. "That's where they searched us," he said. "Yes, sir, every Negro who came to town was searched just by that door. They searched the cars, too. Far as I know they never found a Negro with a gun on him. But some had them hid, 'cause all the white males from thirteen on had guns and carried them where you could see them. They meant business, too."

"What is that statue?" I asked. "A Civil War general—probably Lee's," Amzie said. "What else on the courthouse lawn?" The statue stood on one side of the entrance and a beautiful tree on the other. "What kind of tree is that?" I asked. "I don't know for sure," Amzie replied, "but I think it's an oak. Big, ain't it? Strong, too. Been there a long time."

For a moment he sat still and full of thoughts. "Let's look around town," I said. "Wait," he replied. "You just gave me a thought. *There's* a picture of the South if I ever saw one. That Southern general and that tree. One is the dead past and the other the living present. This South is sure caught in between—between life and death."

We got out of the car and Amzie took me to see the restaurant where Negro leaders and Representative Diggs of Michigan ate during the days of the trial. On an unpaved street behind the courthouse, Jessie Griffin's Cafe was still trying to stand up. Plaster was falling off the walls, roaches walked about with freedom, flies were plentiful, and a loud juke-box blared wild music. The floor was strewn with beer cans and bottles. At three tables men were gambling. A woman came running in, hysterical with anger, and dared a man sitting alone to slap her. He looked at her with compassion and said, "Git home, Mary, you's done and got drunk again. You ought to be 'shamed yo'self." As Mary continued to rant at him, he got up and walked out, muttering, "My people, my people."

Amzie pointed to a corner of the room and said, "There, at that table, with the jukebox going, with people running in and out, the lawyers planned their strategy during the trial. Diggs and I ate lunch here with them every day." I asked him if this was the only place where Negroes could eat in town. "No," he said, "this ain't the only place, but it's the best."

We left the restaurant and walked around the square. In every store there were ten to fifteen Negro shoppers. Amzie pointed out that the shopkeepers there depend upon Negroes for about 85 percent of their business. "But," he said, "you know one thing. These sales people treat Negroes like dogs. Trouble is, these Negroes don't own nothing. Think what changes would be made if a few Negroes owned some business here, and had sense enough to buy where they are treated like human beings. But they're mostly sharecroppers and they're afraid."

We ambled back to the car and Amzie drove around the town. He pointed out a house in which a white man was living with a Negro woman. "They got three little bastards, but nobody says anything about that. The Negroes keep quiet about her, and the white people dismiss him as crazy."

Just then I saw a strange-looking factory on the left and asked Amzie what it was. He explained that it was a cotton oil mill. "They employ mostly Negroes. It's hard work and poor pay," Amzie said. "After the Till murder so many Negroes left this county that they were short sixty hands. I hear they ain't running full yet."

We turned up a small dirt road and onto the highway. Amzie was suddenly very quiet. "What's on your mind?" I asked. "I was thinking about Twotype and Logan," he said. "They used to hang out around here." It developed that they were the two Negro witnesses who disappeared and could not be found until after the Till trial was over. Amzie explained that the sheriff had picked them up and held them in the county jail at Charleston, Mississippi, so they could not testify for the state. This seemed hard to believe. But a few days later in Charleston, an old Negro man said: "Yes, they were here, all right. At night they slept in the jail and by day they worked nearby. I was as close to them once or twice as I am to you. But we knew it was best not to get mixed up in that mess. So we kept quiet. God will take care of them and those white folks too. He sure will and in his own good time. We all pays for what we do in this world."

As we drove down the highway and out of the Till country, we passed a large, well-kept graveyard. At one end of it there was a section in very bad condition, separated from the rest by a high iron fence. "That's the Negro section," Amzie remarked, "but I don't get excited about that. The graveyard is the only place where things can be separate... *and* equal."

Nellie Puts Her Trust in God

Just east of Ruleville, Mississippi, south of Herman Lucas' small farm, lie sixty-four acres of rich soil worth $300 an acre. They belong to Nellie Lenor, a Negro woman just past sixty. Nellie's father was a hard-working man and managed to pull through the depression by doing day labor as well as farming. When Nellie's mother died last year, her last words were, "Don't let them take this land away from you."

After her mother's death, J. T. Smith, white banker and attorney, called Nellie into his office. He explained to her that he had always taken care of the family and would do the same for her. He showed Nellie a pile of papers, old bills, and the like—but Nellie "didn't pay no 'tention to them," for she didn't read much and couldn't understand what he said. Furthermore, she said, "Mr. Smith had always done business and kept things straight for my mother. I trusted him. I didn't have to remember."

But there were some things Nellie did remember. She knew that her family and two neighboring families together borrowed $780 annually from Mr. Smith. She knew that Mr. Smith asked 60 percent interest and 2 percent "broking" fee, for many was the time her mother mentioned that it seemed "a bit steep." But before her father died, he told her mother that Mr. Smith was as good a white man as any in the county and to let him take care of her. So each time Nellie asked her mother why she didn't try someone else, her mother would say, "Your father knowed these men. We better do as he say." Nellie knew that they always turned over the cotton to Mr. Smith to sell, and she remembered how many bales they got each year. For example, Nellie remembered that the first year Mr. Smith was paid in full, but "'course there wasn't no receipt 'cause we trusted Mr. Smith."

Year after year, Nellie had paid Mr. Smith what she could. Mostly it had been according to the price of cotton—but she was not sure. Things went along all right, and Mr. Smith's loan money, $130 a month for the three families, came between November and April when life was difficult on the farm.

This year Nellie had a fairly good crop and assumed everything was all right. But on September 24, Mr. Smith called her into his office and told her that she owed him $4,290.22. He went over the record. Nellie did not understand it, but she knew something was wrong. "He just didn't look right," she said over and over. "There was somethin' funny about his lips. He just didn't look right."

With no records available we tried to help Nellie reconstruct what had and had not been paid. It was a hopeless and impossible task. But figuring cotton at the low price of $150 a bale, and counting in the exorbitant tax and broker's fee, it was clear that Nellie had twice repaid the loan—except for two factors.

First, two years ago Mr. Smith had sent out an old John Deere "B" tractor, equipped with secondhand plow, middle buster, cultivator, planter, and a broken harrow. Although the most modern model cost only $1,800 new and no more than $1,000 secondhand, Mr. Smith told Nellie on September 24, 1956, that he had charged her $2,500 when he had brought it to her two years before. "But," he added, "that of course included price of delivery."

Second, he had arranged all matters when Nellie's mother died. He told Nellie, "As your lawyer I get a fee for all that work." But Nellie did not know she was supposed to pay for such help from Mr. Smith. To her he was a trusted friend and adviser.

Finally, Mr. Smith told Nellie he was sorry she had let the debt get so large. He said he would hate to turn her out, but he had to pay *his* debts, too. So if she couldn't pay in full by November 25, he would have to foreclose. Nellie was stunned. But she didn't think Mr. Smith really would turn her out. She went home and prayed.

Two days later she went back and talked with Mr. Smith again. This time she knew he was in earnest. Then she got to thinking. Nellie said, "I says to myself, that land's worth $300 an acre. If I sell some of it, I can pay him off. But I been lookin' and nobody wants to buy it." What Nellie did not know was that Mr. Smith had already made a deal with other white men in the county. If and when Nellie's land were sold, Mr. Smith himself would buy it at a fraction of its worth.

I asked Nellie what she planned to do if she could not keep the farm. She pulled herself up straight and said, "I'll kill that white man." Then she settled back and said, "I've lived here all my life." Tears came to her eyes and she continued, "I guess I'd beg him for an acre to die on. My preacher told me you can't trust man. He's a weak vessel. Now I know I can't put my trust in nobody but God. He'll take care of me!"

New South...Old Politics

◆ ◆ ◆

[1956]

FEW AREAS IN THE WORLD are witnessing such a drastic and far-reaching transformation as is under way in the South today. American industry, in its flight from outmoded methods, uneconomical plants, and stultifying industrial traditions in the North and East, is migrating to the South on a large scale. The transition of the South from a culture and economy basically agrarian to urban industrialization has acquired the dimension of a revolution.

Between 1940 and 1950, two million white workers were added to Southern industry. During the same period, over three million Negro workers quit the South, thus turning the problem of race relations from a sectional to a national one. In ten years, the number of Negroes outside the South rose 60 percent.

The really significant development, however, is that over one-third of poor white and Negro labor has moved from farms to cities. Cotton, oil, chemicals, and textiles have created a new economy and a new urban middle class. Yet despite this economic transformation, the South has clung to its old agrarian and feudal attitudes and sought to incorporate them in the new emerging industrial society.

The confusing and frustrating major party setup in this country, marked by the "solid" Democratic South, stems largely from this Southern "backwardness." Not only Negro leaders but Southern politicians of every complexion are well aware that the South cannot play a part that makes sense in national political life so long as a one-party pattern exists. Genuine national unity of either major party will come only as the Southern vote is divided between them, or, what would be more significant, between one of the old parties and a new political entity. This would, however, entail a thorough political regrouping in the entire country.

The questions which now arise in every presidential election as to whether certain Southern states may go Republican, whether Southerners are well advised to support the Democratic party nationally or might more advantageously put up Dixiecrat candidates, and so on, reflect the South's transitional situation.

The growing influence of the Republican party in the South stems from the fact that in the struggle between Northern industry and Northern labor to extend their power in the South, industry has so far triumphed and hence has determined the nature of the rising white urban middle class. Composed of new plant managers, technicians, doctors, tradesmen, lawyers, newspaper publishers, and Realtors, this middle class has assumed the role of rebel in Southern politics. Its Republican sympathies have engendered real pressure for two-party politics. Locally cornered and nationally homeless, this group's revolt against the old agrarianism may draw still other Southerners into the Republican fold.

At the moment it appears that Eisenhower may get fewer Southern votes this year than in 1952. It is unlikely, however, that the Republican party in the country as a whole will move to the left. It seems, therefore, that Southern industrial and financial elements will eventually find a home in the GOP—despite memories of "the War Between the States."

The Democratic party, on the other hand, cannot in the long run accommodate sufficiently to the increasing conservatism of considerable sectors of its Southern wing without alienating its Northern following. The leaders of organized labor cannot repeatedly make the shabby compromises which they made in Chicago this year and keep their following. The Democratic party has to remake itself radically or fall apart.

The behavior of the Negro will be the determining factor in the political revamping of the South because the economic and social position of the Negro has been the foundation of the reactionary one-party system in the South. In his rise to a new status the Negro can exert sufficient pressure to determine the nature of the new alignments. The Negro masses can break—and have an immense stake in breaking— the existing political pattern, which obviously is detrimental to the nation as a whole through the hold of Southern Democrats over key Congressional committees and in other ways.

The significance of the nonviolent protests in Montgomery and Tallahassee is thus national. The refusal of Negroes to tolerate further segregation will, if it continues to grow, decisively influence all our lives. The Negro may force the South to choose between true democratic support for social revolution and the suppression of it by a movement to the extreme right. In either case, the South will be transformed. Nationally, unless one of the major parties genuinely supports the Negro, a strong impetus will be given for a new party composed of farmers, white industrial workers, and Negroes to emerge in the South. These will be the decisive element in any new national party.

In his political thinking about strategy today the Negro must take cognizance of two dangers. The first is that the industrial revolution of the South may make him less important economically. It is significant that before the Second World War, Southern white businessmen sought to discourage the northward migration of Negroes, but after the war they encouraged it. In 1940 one-fourth of the labor force was Negro. Ten years later it had fallen off to one-fifth. Industrialization, the effect of mechanized cotton pickers and harvesters, the ease with which part-time white farmers have moved into the factories, the difficulties surrounding Negro membership in unions, and the failure to pass the Fair Employment Practices Act have tended to weaken the position of the Negroes in relation to whites.

The second danger is that when the present economic boom slackens, the Negro will be the hardest hit by unemployment and will be further displaced from the land. The full effects of agricultural mechanization are yet to be seen, and it is doubtful that Southern industry will be able to absorb the rapid growth of the population even with the northward Negro migration.

Under the shadow of these two dangers the Negro people must move carefully but swiftly while the initiative is theirs, or they may discover that they and the democratic impulses for which they stand are on the defensive or even forced to retreat. Whether consciously or unconsciously, the response of Negro leaders in Montgomery and Tallahassee indicates their realization that to go slow is to go backward.

Considering his political course and deciding, for example, how to vote, the Negro should not lose sight of the basic weapon of nonviolent noncooperation and protest. It is difficult to assess the importance of a one-shot performance at the polls in November. But the tremendous effects of day-to-day nonviolent protest go on through the year. There can be no doubts about the profoundly positive response of the entire nation to the nonviolent direct action in Montgomery and elsewhere. Such action exerts immediate social and economic pressure to which the South has no choice but to accommodate itself. The more widespread it becomes, the greater will be its effectiveness as real political action.

It is true that direct action has profoundly disturbing effects within a locality. To a large extent, however, the fears roused are modified and ultimately dispelled if the action is nonviolent. In any case, the fact that resistance to injustice is bound to have a disturbing effect cannot be the basis for inaction and submission. We therefore urge the Negro people to extend their nonviolent protest against segregation now. Action patterned after Montgomery and Tallahassee is a truly total vote of infinitely greater importance than any ballot cast in November.

Insofar as the Negro retains the nonviolent approach he will be able to win white sympathy and frustrate the aims of the White Citizens Council. Nothing is so terrifying to white supremacists as the fear that if Negroes gain power they will visit upon their former masters violence and oppression similar to that employed by whites against Negroes in the past. Nothing can so thoroughly disarm their terror as the determined adherence of Negroes to nonviolence. The initial reaction of the whites will be one of distrust, since deceit and violence form the larger part of their experience of intergroup relations. But in time the fact that Negroes have eschewed retaliation of this nature will be borne in upon them.

This will not be easy. The Councils dimly recognize this coercive psychological power of nonviolence and will be bent on inciting violence from Negroes. Should they succeed, the Negroes will lose their moral initiative, liberals will become even more frightened and inactive, and a deeper wedge will be driven between white and black workers. If, on the other hand, despite this provocation, the Negro holds fast to the spirit of Montgomery he will be able to work with white workers and farmers to create a new political force for social progress.

All this does not mean that the Negro can or should struggle alone to achieve freedom for himself. The mass of Negroes are farmers or workers, and their interests are fundamentally allied to those of other farmers and workers. The role of the Negro is unique only in that his especially demeaned position and, consequently, unprecedented new drive for dignity and self-respect lend him a momentum and initiative lacked by Southern white workers. The Negro is, therefore, now pivotal to the resolution of the major problems confronting all classes in the South.

The historical facts of segregation shed a flood of light upon the basic nature of the relationship of black and white labor in the South. During the period of Reconstruction following the Civil War, Negro and white workers, many of them illiterate, worked together effectively in Southern legislatures for progressive legislation of all sorts, such as the present laws providing for free universal education in North Carolina. Not until 1876 did Northern and Southern capital realize the threat such a progressive union of black and white workers offered to its own interests. At that time it conspired to destroy this unity by the resurrection of the doctrine of white supremacy. From 1880 to 1890 such efforts met with small success, although from this period dates the transformation of the remnants of the Confederate underground into the Ku Klux Klan. In 1890 prejudice was legislated in the form of segregation laws. Jim Crow laws date primarily from the period between 1890 and the First World War. This stratagem on the part of Northern and Southern capital has continued till today.

When the industrial revolution began to accelerate in 1940, the American labor movement, primarily concerned with wages and hours, faced a dilemma. On the one hand, it could attempt to oppose the powerful capitalist-inspired program of segregation by organizing white and Negro labor into integrated unions. On the other, it could more expediently organize separate white and Negro locals, and sacrifice the strength of true solidarity. Where Negroes were brought into the factories, labor chose the latter course and for a number of years this system seemed to work.

Today, however, organized labor faces a quite different situation. The White Citizens Councils—the KKK in gray flannel suits—are well aware that organized labor is part and parcel of the racial and economic progressive forces they loathe. The Councils' prejudice against Negroes, Catholics, and Jews is superficial in comparison with their main objective—to castrate the labor movement by preventing a coalition of Negro and white workers. The forces behind the Councils have thrived by keeping white workers poor and Negro workers poorer, and, as in the past, their prime device against any strong union of laborers is to fan the flames of religious and racial intolerance.

This situation is as critical for all American labor as it is for the Negro. For labor now to sidestep the Southern racial issue means suicide. Already in Mississippi, Alabama, and Georgia, local labor leaders, influenced by the White Citizens Councils, are urging unions to withdraw from the AFL-CIO. They want to create a Southern Labor Organization of lily-white, strictly segregated company unions. As the South becomes more and more an industrial center, it takes little imagination to see how an unorganized, company-unionized South would undermine the unions throughout the whole nation.

American labor is as yet oblivious to this danger or is unwilling to face it. But enlightened American workers must bring their unions to understand that the time for equivocation is past. Sooner or later labor will have to accept the Negro as a first-class citizen. To attempt now to organize white workers in a position of superiority or privilege is to play into the hands of the White Citizens Councils by pushing Negroes, one-fifth of the labor force, into the position of potential scabs.

But when the unions finally embrace the Negro they can no longer expect to limit their attention to wages and hours. The effort to organize Negro and white workers on a basis of equality in the face of political splintering and racial upheaval will make it imperative for labor, as it deals with these issues, to evolve a political philosophy. The combination of Southern white farmers, workers, and Negroes in a political alliance which will also draw in labor and progressive elements from the rest of the country will create a new labor movement. Labor then will no longer be obliged to seek favors from existing political groups and, in exchange for them or in fear of losing them, support an adventurist and warlike foreign policy.

Negro and white workers face essentially the same dilemmas and inevitably, if they are intelligent, experience the same frustration in trying to find a party worth voting for. The Negro is nevertheless in one respect in a unique position. For him, disfranchised as he now is for the most part, the mere act of casting his ballot constitutes in a sense a revolutionary achievement. It is imperative for him to register as widely as possible, pay his poll tax where necessary, and vote. The fight for the ballot is integral to the revolt against oppression.

Yet the bitter resentment of the Negroes at the handling of the civil rights issue, both at Chicago and at San Francisco, and their marking time in deciding for whom to vote, clearly indicate that no real and satisfactory choice is open to them. There is something fantastically unreal and at the same time tragic about fighting desperately at the risk of one's livelihood, or even life itself, to gain admission to a polling booth in a typical Southern state, and then having to use this hard-won achievement to indicate a choice between the present Democratic and the present Republican party.

It would be presumptuous for us to attempt to make specific suggestions, much less to lay down directions, for Negro voters. The situation will inevitably remain profoundly unsatisfactory until basic attitudes on the race question are altered and labor is effectively organized. What is clear in the meantime is that the paramount object when making up one's mind how to vote must be to make the vote instrumental in the disruption of the "solid South." In some areas Negroes will probably decide that the reconstitution of Southern politics will be best served by voting Republican, in others by voting Democratic. In areas where there is a sizable Negro population, it has been suggested that a write-in vote might be cast for a Negro candidate, such as Martin Luther King, Jr. In all cases, the Negro vote should be designed as effectively as possible to confuse the old guard and to diminish and rapidly destroy its power.

When the Negro comes back from the polls he must face problems that cannot be solved by voting. Northern Negroes have had the right to vote for years without gaining economic or social equality. The same is true of most workingmen, regardless of their color. More often than not, reliance on voting in periodic elections has sidetracked them from using the more powerful weapons of direct action.

Labor, both white and Negro, must address itself to the real economic issues by organizing fully integrated locals; aiding the struggle for racial equality in Montgomery, Tallahassee, and elsewhere; supporting the victims of economic boycott in Mississippi and South Carolina; fighting the Smith Act and similar repressive measures; and opposing restrictive immigration laws. By engaging in the continuous struggle for justice and human welfare, workers will gain a realistic political education and will cast the only ballot worth casting—the daily ballot for freedom for all.

EVEN IN THE FACE OF DEATH

◆ ◆ ◆

[1957]

"NOT ONE HAIR OF ONE HEAD of one white person shall be harmed in the campaign for integration."

At first this sounds like the defensive slogan of a Southern White Citizens Council. Instead it is the motto adopted unanimously by sixty Negro leaders to serve as a rallying point for a South-wide campaign for nonviolent integration.

At the close of the meeting in Atlanta, on January 11, 1957, at which this slogan was adopted, a press conference was held. The *New York Times* correspondent asked, "Do you mean that all of you accept this motto?"

"We do," came the answer.

Turning to Martin Luther King, Jr., chairman of the conference, the correspondent continued, "Do you mean it, even if others start the violence?"

"Individuals had better speak for themselves on that," said King. "But *I* mean it."

The correspondent queried the others. One by one, all sixty said "Yes," or nodded their heads in assent.

Last November, when the Supreme Court confirmed its earlier ruling that segregation in bus transportation is illegal, the Negro people of Montgomery, Alabama, were jubilant. After several prayer meetings, much planning, and a week of rededication to nonviolence, they returned to the buses on December 24 for the first time in over a year. For the first time in Montgomery history they "rode like men."

Within a few days, protests similar to the one in Montgomery swept the South. In Atlanta, Birmingham, Baton Rouge, New Orleans, Norfolk, Tallahassee, and many other cities, Negroes "moved up front." Most Southern white persons accepted integration; there were only a few acts of violence on the part of a tiny minority. But by the beginning of January, the occasional beating or shooting had grown into organized terror. The terror was supported by legal subterfuge. It became clear that the opposition was planning to frustrate the court decision by organized violence and "a century of hopeless litigation."

At this point, Reverend Martin Luther King, Jr., of Montgomery, Reverend F. L. Shuttlesworth of Birmingham, and Reverend C. K. Steele of Tallahassee, leaders of the three major protests, began consultations. They came to several conclusions:

> None of the other protests were apt to succeed if the one at Montgomery was defeated. For whites and Negroes alike, Montgomery had become a symbol.
>
> Integration might not win at Montgomery unless the protests continued to spread throughout other areas of the South.
>
> The increasing violence was being carefully planned and organized on the theory that the Negroes would back down when faced with such incidents. *Therefore* Negroes had no alternative but to extend and intensify this struggle.
>
> The majority of white persons were "teetering" between a desire to cling to the pattern they had always known and a feeling that integration must take place. Any hesitation or temporary retreat on the part of Negroes would confuse white persons and drive them back to the old pattern.
>
> The time had come for Negro leaders to gather from all over the South to "share thinking, discuss common problems, plan common strategy, and explore mutual economic assistance."

King, Steele, and Shuttlesworth issued a call on January 5 for a two-day conference to be held in Atlanta, beginning five days later.

Despite the daily emergencies that each of the leaders had to face, the conference was well planned. It was not to be a matter of coming together simply to exchange details about the bombings and shootings most of them had undergone. Papers were prepared in advance, not only on the practical problems of coordination and planning but on such underlying questions as the relationship of the major economic groups to the struggle for integration; how to encourage and maintain a nonviolent attitude among all Negroes; and the relationship between state power and a nonviolent movement. As violence has mounted, the leaders have been under pressure to call for FBI investigations, for the use of the National Guard or other army units to maintain order. Is this compatible with the spirit of a nonviolent movement?

King and Abernathy arrived at Atlanta the night before the conference was scheduled to open. But neither was present when the first session began. At 5:30 in the morning they had been roused from their beds with notice that four churches and two ministers' homes had been bombed in Montgomery during the night. Taking the next plane for Montgomery, they left word that they would return as soon as possible.

Meanwhile, as the hour approached for opening the conference, the streets adjacent to Ebeneezer Baptist Church, site of the meeting, bristled with city police and plainclothesmen. Five minutes before the scheduled beginning, Detective Clarence M. Nelms gave me an urgent message at the door of the church, then rushed away to supervise the deployment of two carloads of newly arrived detectives. As the men disappeared within a few seconds into side streets and alleys, I stood for a moment in the doorway and pondered the words he had just spoken:

"Be careful. We got word that a carload of white men has started up from Florida to break up your meeting and raise hell in general. If you see anything suspicious, call this number and be damn quick about it."

By 2:30 that afternoon, no hell had been raised, but something of greater significance had happened. Sixty Negro leaders had come from twenty-nine localities of ten Southern states for the first session of the Negro Leaders Conference on Nonviolent Integration.

Every major protest leader was present. Leaders struggling with economic boycotts and reprisals in South Carolina were standing in a corner exchanging views with the "strong men" from the Mississippi Delta, who are forced to carry on their work at night, underground.

The first person to take the floor was a man who had been shot because he had dared to vote. Some had come for technical advice, others to find out more about the spirit and practice of nonviolence. But all of them were determined to respond to the call "to delve deeper into the struggle."

The next day King returned. He reported that there had been great damage in the six bombings at Montgomery but that no one had been hurt. He told how, at a sympathetic white minister's home, twelve sticks of dynamite had failed to go off and had been found on the lawn near a window, in the morning. Then he said: "Let this be a sign unto you. God is truly our protector. He permits men the freedom to do evil. He also has His way to protect His children."

For a time there was a great silence. Then a minister began to pray. At the end of the prayer, King spoke movingly on the power of nonviolence. After this the session broke up in silence.

The final meeting of the conference may go down in history as one of the most important meetings that have taken place in the United States. Sixty beleaguered Negro leaders from across the South voted to establish a permanent Southern Negro Leaders Conference on Nonviolent Integration.

This was the beginning of a South-wide nonviolent resistance campaign against all segregation.

The leaders indicated the price they themselves might have to pay:

> We must continue to stand firm for our right to
> be first-class citizens. Even in the face of death, we
> have no other choice. If in carrying out this obliga-
> tion we are killed, others more resolute will rise to
> continue.

They then made the following appeal to Negroes in both North and South:

> We call upon all Negroes...to assert their human
> dignity.... We know that such an assertion may cause
> them persecution; yet no matter how great the
> obstacles and suffering, we urge all Negroes to reject
> all segregation.

They expressed their realization that "equality" is not enough if it merely means Negroes' fighting for equality of opportunity within a corrupt and competitive social order. Time and again, speakers said that they must struggle against the things in their own hearts that might breed future violence and inequality:

> We ask them to seek justice and to reject all injustice, *especially that in themselves.* We pray that they will refuse further cooperation with the evil elements which invite them to collude against themselves in return for bits of patronage.

Perhaps the most moving part of the statement is that which urged the Negro people to adhere to nonviolence "in word, thought and deed":

> We call upon them to accept Christian Love in full knowledge of its power to defy evil....Nonviolence is not a symbol of weakness or cowardice, but, as Jesus and Gandhi demonstrated, nonviolent resistance transforms weakness into strength and breeds courage in face of danger.

It was at this point that the conference voted to accept as the slogan of the broader movement the motto:

> Not one hair of one head of one white person shall be harmed.

At the press conference that followed, representatives of all the press services and many of the major papers raised questions for more than an hour. The Negro leaders explained how they had called upon white Southerners to realize that the treatment of Negroes is a basic spiritual problem, and how they had urged Southern Christians to speak out with conviction. They reminded the South that the major choice may no longer be between segregation and integration, but between chaos and law.

> People control their destinies only when order prevails. Disorder places all major decisions in the

> hands of state or federal police. We do not prefer
> this, for our ultimate aim is to win understanding
> with our neighbors.

King read a telegram that the conference had sent to President Eisenhower, asking him to "come South immediately to make a major speech in a major Southern city urging all Southerners to accept and to abide by the Supreme Court's decisions as the law of the land." He referred to another telegram sent to Vice-President Nixon urging him "to make a tour of the South similar to the one he made on behalf of Hungarian refugees."

Every major paper in the country carried references to these telegrams, but did not point up the real significance of the conference. The press did not seem to realize that this conference, which solidified the Southern Negroes on the twin platforms of freedom and nonviolence, gave impetus to a movement which will help change the economic and social structure of Southern culture.

As King and I left, we discussed a prophetic statement made by Gandhi. In 1935, Dr. Howard Thurman of Howard University had asked him to come to America—not for white America, he said, but to help the American Negro in his fight for civil rights.

"How I wish I could," Gandhi said, "but I must make good the message here before I bring it to you.

"It may be that through the American Negro the unadulterated message of nonviolence will be delivered to the world."

PART TWO

◆ ◆ ◆

THE POLITICS OF PROTEST

THE MEANING OF BIRMINGHAM

◆ ◆ ◆

[1963]

AS THIS PAMPHLET *[Civil Rights: The True Frontier]* goes to press, the civil rights movement has reached yet a new step in its development. For the first time a thoroughgoing revolution is occurring in the South. From progressive Greensboro, to industrial Birmingham, to semi-rural Jackson the movement includes all levels of the Negro community. It is a movement that consciously intends to transform the white power structure in this country; a movement that has taken the initiative away from the Kennedy administration (and the forces that would contain the movement with moderate concessions); a movement that will not be satisfied with integrated lunch counters and promises but that is demanding jobs and freedom now.

Birmingham has taught white America many lessons—not the least of them that Negroes were serious when they said they would fill the jails until Southern cities were impoverished and that social dislocation is a reality that confronts all segregated institutions. It ought now to be perfectly clear that Negroes will not wait another twenty-five years. No longer can white liberals merely be proud of those well-dressed students who are specialists in nonviolent action; now they are confronted by a Negro working class that is demanding equal opportunity and full employment.

The Negro community is now fighting for total freedom. It took three million dollars and a year of struggle simply to convince the powers that be that one has the right to ride in the front of a bus. If it takes this kind of pressure to achieve a single thing, then one can just as well negotiate fully for more—for every economic, political, and social right that is presently denied. That is what is important about Birmingham: tokenism is finished.

The Negro masses are no longer prepared to wait for anybody: not for elections, not to count votes, not to wait on the Kennedys or for legislation, nor, in fact, for Negro leaders themselves. They are going to move. Nothing can stop them from moving. And if that Negro leadership does not move rapidly enough and effectively enough they will take it into their own hands and move anyhow.

And out of this we can see a new phase for the civil rights movement. It is the phase of the use of mass action—nonviolent disobedience and nonviolent noncooperation.

Birmingham has proved that no matter what you're up against, if wave after wave of black people keep coming prepared to go to jail, sooner or later there is such confusion, such social dislocation, that white people in the South are faced with a choice: either integrated restaurants or no restaurants at all, integrated public facilities or none at all. And the South then must make its choice for integration, for it would rather have that than chaos.

This struggle is only beginning in the North, but it will be a bitter struggle. It will be an attack on business, on trade unions, and on the government. The Negro will no longer tolerate a situation where for every white man unemployed there are two or three Negroes unemployed. In the North, Negroes present a growing threat to the social order that, less brutally and more subtly than in the South, attempts to keep him "in his place." In response, moderates today warn of the danger of violence and "extremism" but do not attempt to change conditions that brutalize the Negro and breed racial conflict. What is needed is an ongoing massive assault on racist political power and institutions.

The mood of the black community is one of anger and confidence of total victory. The victories to date have given added prestige to nonviolent resistance as a method. One can only hope that the white community will realize that the black community means what it says: jobs and freedom now!

PREAMBLE TO THE
MARCH ON WASHINGTON

◆ ◆ ◆

[1963]

1. The one hundred years since the signing of the Emancipation Proclamation have witnessed no fundamental government action to terminate the economic subordination of the American Negro. Today the ratio of unemployment among Negroes and whites remains two-to-one, while the income of Negroes is roughly half that of whites. Not only have these disparities remained constant over decades, but in the present period they have absolutely widened. Their effect on race relations generally can only frustrate the limited gains recently registered in school integration and in equal accommodations in public facilities and transportation.

2. The condition of Negro labor is inseparable from that of white labor; the immediate crisis confronting black labor grows out of the unresolved crisis in the national economy. History shows that the peculiar disadvantages suffered by the Negro as the result of segregation and discrimination are alleviated in times of relatively full employment and aggravated when employment is high. So far the federal government has produced no serious answers to the problem of rising unemployment; each succeeding recession has produced an upward revision of minimal unemployment rates, and Congress and the White House appear complacent in the face of current unemployment figures of 6 percent.

3. The current crisis is overwhelmingly the result of structural unemployment. Thousands of workers have been displaced by

automation, rendered economically functionless in modern industrial society. Negroes have been disproportionately victimized,
for automation has attacked precisely those unskilled and semi-
skilled jobs to which Negroes have traditionally been relegated.
Moreover, the persistence of racial discrimination on a national
scale has closed to Negroes who have lacked the training to compete for skilled jobs, even the limited opportunities for job
retraining available to whites. Statistics speak clearly: 25 percent of
the long-term unemployed are Negroes.

4. Automation coupled with a tremendous population increase is
seriously limiting job opportunities for all youth particularly
Negroes in the 16–21 age group. Fifty percent of Negro youth
16–21 are idle. A disproportionate number of the eight million
school dropouts a year are Negroes.

5. These indisputable facts dictate certain strategies for the overall
progress of the Negro in the present period:

   a.   Integration in the fields of education, housing, transportation,
        and public accommodations will be of limited extent and dura-
        tion so long as fundamental economic inequality along racial
        lines persists. Already the slowdown in the rate of progress in
        many of these fields is evident in the widespread characterization
        of recent gains as "tokenism." An economically disprivileged
        people is not able to utilize institutions and facilities geared to
        middle-class incomes and to an inflated economy. They cannot
        afford to patronize the better restaurants, integrated or not;
        their own financial circumstances segregate them from middle-
        class housing; they cannot afford to travel, whether buses are
        integrated or not, or send their children to college.

   b.   The demand for "merit hiring" practices is obsolete. When a
        racial disparity in unemployment has been firmly established
        in the course of a century, the change-over to "equal opportu-
        nities" merely prevents a further divergence in the relative status
        of the races but does not wipe out the cumulative handicaps
        of the Negro worker. In addition, "equal opportunities" in a
        declining national economy means, at best, only an equal
        opportunity to share in the decline.

   c.   Clearly there is no need for Negroes to demand jobs that do
        not exist. Nor do Negroes seek to displace white workers as

both are being displaced by machines. Negroes seek instead, *as an integral part of their own struggle as a people,* the creation of more jobs for all Americans. Therefore, the project described below must be a massive effort involving coordinated participation by all progressive sectors of the liberal, labor, religious, and Negro communities. Only such an all-embracing effort can call for a broad national governmental action on a scale adequate to meet the problem of unemployment, especially as it relates to minority groups. At the same time, we believe that the Negro community has an especially important role to play. For the dynamic that has motivated Negroes to withstand with courage and dignity the intimidation and violence they have endured in their own struggle against racism, in all its forms, may now be the catalyst which mobilizes all workers behind demands for a broad and fundamental program of economic justice.

Nature of the Project

1. Program:
   a. The project should call for action by the President and Congress, listing concrete *demands* (to be drawn up).
   b. We should emphasize the theme that because the Emancipation Proclamation of 1863 has failed to bring real freedom for the Negro, no worker in America is genuinely free. We now demand a program of action in 1963 that will ensure the emancipation of all labor, regardless of color, race, or creed.
2. Action: We envision a two-day action program divided as follows:
   a. A Friday in June—a mass descent on Congress and a carefully chosen delegation to the White House. The objective in Congress would be to so flood all Congressmen with a staggered series of labor, church, and civil rights delegations from their own states that they would be unable to conduct business on the floor of Congress for an entire day. Just as these delegations would present, in part, our list of legislative demands, so would the White House delegation seek to put before the President,

as leader of his party and as Chief Executive, our proposals for both legislative and executive action.

b.   A Saturday in June—a mass protest rally with the two-fold purpose of projecting our concrete "Emancipation Program" to the nation and of reporting to the assemblage the response of the President and Congress to the action of the previous day.

Organizational Steps

1. The following two documents should be drawn up immediately:
    a.   A clear statement of our purpose.
    b.   A simple factual analysis of the present job situation in the United States, with special attention to minority group workers.
2. Mr. Randolph should clear the above statements, as well as this memorandum, with his colleagues.
3. The entire idea should receive a vote of approval by the Negro American Labor Council.
4. Mr. Randolph should then be in touch with Dr. King, Roy Wilkins, and James Farmer to secure their endorsement of the plan and a commitment of whatever resources they can make available.
5. Having secured the support of these elements, a combined State of the Race and Labor conference should be convened, including representation from relevant labor, civil rights, church, women, and civic organizations.
6. This conference, having formulated the precise demands we shall take to Washington and established the broad base of the effort, should be terminated with a press conference at which the project would be officially announced.
7. Project committees should be set up in major cities.

From Protest to Politics:
The Future of the Civil
Rights Movement

◆ ◆ ◆

[1964]

THE DECADE SPANNED BY THE 1954 SUPREME COURT decision on
school desegregation and the Civil Rights Act of 1964 will undoubtedly
be recorded as the period in which the legal foundations of racism in
America were destroyed. To be sure, pockets of resistance remain; but it
would be hard to quarrel with the assertion that the elaborate legal
structure of segregation and discrimination, particularly in relation to
public accommodations, has virtually collapsed. On the other hand, without making light of the human sacrifices involved in the direct-action
tactics (sit-ins, Freedom Rides, and the rest) that were so instrumental to
this achievement, we must recognize that in desegregating public accommodations we affected institutions which are relatively peripheral both
to the American socioeconomic order and to the fundamental conditions
of life of the Negro people. In a highly industrialized twentieth-century
civilization, we hit Jim Crow precisely where it was most anachronistic,
dispensable, and vulnerable—in hotels, lunch counters, terminals,
libraries, swimming pools, and the like. For in these forms, Jim Crow
does impede the flow of commerce in the broadest sense; it is a nuisance
in a society on the move (and on the make). Not surprisingly, therefore,
the most mobility-conscious and relatively liberated groups in the Negro
community—lower-middle-class college students—launched the attack
that brought down this imposing but hollow structure.

The term "classical" appears especially apt for this phase of the civil rights movement. But in the few years that have passed since the first flush of sit-ins, several developments have taken place that have complicated matters enormously. One is the shifting focus of the movement in the South, symbolized by Birmingham; another is the spread of the revolution to the North; and the third, common to the other two, is the expansion of the movement's base in the Negro community. To attempt to disentangle these three strands is to do violence to reality. David Danzig's perceptive article "The Meaning of Negro Strategy" (*Commentary*, February 1964), correctly saw in the Birmingham events the victory of the concept of collective struggle over individual achievement as the road to Negro freedom. And Birmingham remains the unmatched symbol of grass-roots protest involving all strata of the black community. It was also in this most industrialized of Southern cities that the single-issue demands of the movement's classical stage gave way to the "package deal." No longer were Negroes satisfied with integrating lunch counters. They now sought advances in employment, housing, school integration, police protection, and so forth.

Thus the movement in the South began to attack areas of discrimination which were not so remote from the Northern experience as were Jim Crow lunch counters. At the same time, the interrelationship of these apparently distinct areas became increasingly evident. What is the value of winning access to public accommodations for those who lack money to use them? The minute the movement faced this question, it was compelled to expand its vision beyond race relations to economic relations, including the role of education in modern society. And what also became clear is that all these interrelated problems, by their very nature, are not soluble by private, voluntary efforts but require government action—or politics. Already Southern demonstrators had recognized that the most effective way to strike at the police brutality they suffered from was to get rid of the local sheriff. That meant political action, which in turn meant, and still means, political action within the Democratic party, where the only meaningful primary contests in the South are fought.

And so in Mississippi, thanks largely to the leadership of Bob Moses, a turn toward political action has been taken. More than voter registration is involved here. A conscious bid for *political power* is being made, and in the course of that effort a tactical shift is being effected.

Direct-action techniques are being subordinated to a strategy calling for the building of community institutions or power bases. Clearly, the implications of this shift reach far beyond Mississippi. What began as a protest movement is being challenged to translate itself into a political movement. Is this the right course? And if it is, can the transformation be accomplished?

The very decade which has witnessed the decline of legal Jim Crow has also seen the rise of *de facto* segregation in our most fundamental socioeconomic institutions. More Negroes are unemployed today than in 1954, and the unemployment gap between the races is wider. The median income of Negroes has dropped from 57 percent to 54 percent of that of whites. A higher percentage of Negro workers is now concentrated in jobs vulnerable to automation than was the case ten years ago. More Negroes attend *de facto* segregated schools today than when the Supreme Court handed down its famous decision; while school integration proceeds at a snail's pace in the south, the number of Northern schools with an excessive proportion of minority youth proliferates. And behind this is the continuing growth of racial slums, spreading over our central cities and trapping Negro youth in a milieu which, whatever its legal definition, sows an unimaginable demoralization. Again, legal niceties aside, a resident of a racial ghetto lives in segregated housing, and more Negroes fall into this category than ever before.

These are the facts of life which generate frustration in the Negro community and challenge the civil rights movement. At issue, after all, is not *civil rights*, strictly speaking, but social and economic conditions. Last summer's riots were not race riots; they were outbursts of class aggression in a society where class and color definitions are converging disastrously. How can the (perhaps misnamed) civil rights movement deal with this problem? Before trying to answer, let me first insist that the task of the movement is vastly complicated by the failure of many whites of good will to understand the nature of our problem. There is a widespread assumption that the removal of artificial racial barriers should result in the automatic integration of the Negro into all aspects of American life. This myth is fostered by facile analogies with the experience of various ethnic immigrant groups, particularly the Jews. But the analogies with the Jews do not hold for three simple but profound reasons. First, Jews have a long history as a literate people, a resource which has afforded them opportunities to advance in the academic and professional worlds, to achieve intellectual status even in the midst of economic hardship, and to evolve sustaining value systems in the context of ghetto life. Negroes, for the greater part of their presence in this country, were forbidden by law to read or write. Second, Jews have a long history of family stability, the importance of which in terms of aspiration and self-image is obvious. The Negro family structure was totally destroyed by slavery and with it the possibility of cultural transmission (the right of Negroes to marry and rear children is barely a century old). Third, Jews are white and have the *option* of relinquishing their cultural-religious identity, intermarrying, passing, etc. Negroes, or at least the overwhelming majority of them, do not have this option. There is also a fourth, vulgar reason. If the Jewish and Negro communities are not comparable in terms of education, family structure, and color, it is also true that their respective economic roles bear little resemblance.

This matter of economic role brings us to the greater problem—the fact that we are moving into an era in which the natural functioning of the market does not by itself ensure for every man with will and ambition a place in the productive process. The immigrant who came to this country during the late nineteenth and early twentieth centuries entered a society which was expanding territorially and/or economically. It was then possible to start at the bottom, as an unskilled or semi-skilled worker, and move up the ladder, acquiring new skills along the way. Especially was this true when industrial unionism was burgeoning, giving new dignity and higher wages to organized workers. Today the situation has changed. We are not expanding territorially, the western frontier is settled, labor organizing has leveled off, our rate of economic growth has been stagnant for a decade. And we are in the midst of a techno-logical revolution which is altering the fundamental structure of the labor force, destroying unskilled and semi-skilled jobs—jobs in which Negroes are disproportionately concentrated.

Whatever the pace of this technological revolution may be, the *direction* is clear: the lower rungs of the economic ladder are being lopped off. This means that an individual will no longer be able to start at the bottom and work his way up; he will have to start in the middle or on top, and hold on tight. It will not even be enough to have certain spe-cific skills, for many skilled jobs are also vulnerable to automation. A broad educational background, permitting vocational adaptability and flexibility, seems more imperative than ever. We live in a society where, as Secretary of Labor Willard Wirtz puts it, machines have the equivalent of a high school diploma. Yet the average educational attainment of American Negroes is 8.2 years.

Negroes, of course, are not the only people being affected by these developments. It is reported that there are now 50 percent fewer unskilled and semi-skilled jobs than there are high school dropouts. Almost one-third of the twenty-six million young people entering the labor market in the 1960s will be dropouts. But the proportion of Negro dropouts nationally is 57 percent, and in New York City, among Negroes twenty-five years of age or over, it is 68 percent. They are without a future.

To what extent can the kind of self-help campaign recently prescribed by Eric Hoffer in the *New York Times Magazine* cope with such a situation? I would advise those who think that self-help is the answer to familiarize themselves with the long history of such efforts in the Negro community, and to consider why so many foundered on the shoals of ghetto life. It goes without saying that any effort to combat demoralization and apathy is desirable but we must understand that demoralization in the Negro community is largely a common-sense response to an objective reality. Negro youths have no need of statistics to perceive, fairly accurately, what their odds are in American society. Indeed, from the point of view of motivation, some of the healthiest Negro youngsters I know are juvenile delinquents. Vigorously pursuing the American dream of material acquisition and status, yet finding the conventional means of attaining it blocked off, they do not yield to defeatism but resort to illegal (and often ingenious) methods. They are not alien to American culture. They are, in Gunnar Myrdal's phrase, "exaggerated Americans." To want a Cadillac is not un-American; to push a cart in the garment center is. If Negroes are to be persuaded that the conventional path (school, work, etc.) is superior, we had better provide evidence which is now sorely lacking. It is a double cruelty to harangue Negro youth about education and training when we do not know what jobs will be available for them. When a Negro youth can reasonably foresee a future free of slums, when the prospect of gainful employment is realistic, we will see motivation and self-help in abundant enough quantities.

Meanwhile, there is an ironic similarity between the self-help advocated by many liberals and the doctrines of the Black Muslims.

Professional sociologists, psychiatrists, and social workers have expressed amazement at the Muslims' success in transforming prostitutes and dope addicts into respectable citizens. But every prostitute the Muslims convert to a model of Calvinist virtue the ghetto replaces with two more. The Muslims, dedicated as they are to maintenance of the ghetto, are powerless to effect substantial moral reform. So too with every other group or program which is not aimed at the destruction of slums, their causes and effects. Self-help efforts must be geared, directly or indirectly, to mobilizing people into power units capable of effecting social change. That is, their goal must be genuine self-help, not merely self-improvement. Obviously, where self-improvement activities succeed in imparting to their participants a feeling of some control over their environment, those involved may find their appetites for change whetted; they may move into the political arena.

Let me sum up what I have thus far been trying to say. The civil rights movement is evolving from a protest movement into a full-fledged *social movement*—an evolution calling its very name into question. It is now concerned not merely with removing the barriers to full *opportunity* but with achieving the fact of *equality*. From sit-ins and Freedom Rides we have gone into rent strikes, boycotts, community organization, and political action. As a consequence of this natural evolution, the Negro today finds himself stymied by obstacles of far greater magnitude than the legal barriers he was attacking before: automation, urban decay, *de facto* school segregation. These are problems which, while conditioned by Jim Crow, do not vanish upon its demise. They are more deeply rooted in our socioeconomic order; they are the result of the total society's failure to meet not only the Negro's needs but human needs generally.

These propositions have won increasing recognition and acceptance, but with a curious twist. They have formed the common premise of two apparently contradictory lines of thought which simultaneously nourish and antagonize each other. On the one hand, there is the reasoning of the *New York Times* moderate who says that the problems are so enormous and complicated that Negro militancy is a futile irritation, and that the need is for "intelligent moderation." Thus, during the first New York school boycott, the *Times* editorialized that Negro demands, while abstractly just, would necessitate massive reforms, the funds for which could not realistically be anticipated; therefore the just demands were also foolish demands and would only antagonize white people. Moderates of this stripe are often correct in perceiving the difficulty or impossibility of racial progress in the context of present social and economic policies. But they accept the context as fixed. They ignore (or perhaps see all too well) the potentialities inherent in linking Negro demands to broader pressures for radical revision of existing policies. They apparently see nothing strange in the fact that in the last twenty-five years we have spent nearly a trillion dollars fighting or preparing for wars, yet we throw up our hands before the need to overhaul our schools, clear the slums, and really abolish poverty. My quarrel with these moderates is that they do not even envision radical changes; their admonitions of moderation are, for all practical purposes, admonitions to the Negro to adjust to the status quo, and are therefore immoral.

The more effectively the moderates argue their case, the more they convince Negroes that American society will not or cannot be reorganized for full racial equality. Michael Harrington has said that a successful war on poverty might well require the expenditure of $100 billion. Where, the Negro wonders, are the forces now in motion to compel such a commitment? If the voices of the moderates were raised in an insistence upon a reallocation of national resources at levels that could not be confused with tokenism (that is, if the moderates stopped being moderates), Negroes would have greater grounds for hope. Meanwhile, the Negro movement cannot escape a sense of isolation.

It is precisely this sense of isolation that gives rise to the second line of thought I want to examine—the tendency within the civil rights movement to pursue, despite its militancy, what I call a "no-win" policy. Sharing with many moderates a recognition of the magnitude of the obstacles to freedom, spokesmen for this tendency survey the American scene and find no forces prepared to move toward radical solutions. From this they conclude that the only viable strategy is shock; above all, the hypocrisy of white liberals must be exposed. These spokesmen are often described as the radicals of the movement, but they are really its moralists. They seek to change white hearts—by traumatizing them. Frequently abetted by white self-flagellants, they may gleefully applaud (though not really agreeing with) Malcolm X because, while they admit he has no program, they think he can frighten white people into doing the right thing. To believe this, of course, you must be convinced, even if unconsciously, that at the core of the white man's heart lies a buried affection for Negroes—a proposition one may be permitted to doubt. But in any case, hearts are not relevant to the issue; neither racial affinities nor racial hostilities are rooted there. It is institutions—social, political, and economic institutions—which are the ultimate molders of collective sentiments. Let these institutions be reconstructed *today,* and let the ineluctable gradualism of history govern the formation of a new psychology.

My quarrel with the "no-win" tendency in the civil rights movement (and the reason I have so designated it) parallels my quarrel with the moderates outside the movement. As the latter lack the vision or will for fundamental change, the former lack a realistic strategy for achieving it. For such a strategy they substitute militancy. But militancy is a matter of posture and volume and not of effect.

I believe that the Negro's struggle for equality in America is essentially revolutionary. While most Negroes—in their hearts—unquestionably seek only to enjoy the fruits of American society as it now exists, their quest cannot *objectively* be satisfied within the framework of existing political and economic relations. The young Negro who would demonstrate his way into the labor market may be motivated by a thoroughly bourgeois ambition and thoroughly "capitalist" considerations, but he will end up having to favor a great expansion of the public sector of the economy. At any rate, that is the position the movement will be forced to take as it looks at the number of jobs being generated by the private economy and if it is to remain true to the masses of Negroes.

The revolutionary character of the Negro's struggle is manifest in the fact that this struggle may have done more to democratize life for whites than for Negroes. Clearly, it was the sit-in movement of young Southern Negroes which, as it galvanized white students, banished the ugliest features of McCarthyism from the American campus and resurrected political debate. It was not until Negroes assaulted *de facto* school segregation in the urban centers that the issue of quality education for *all* children stirred into motion. Finally, it seems reasonably clear that the civil rights movement, directly and through the resurgence of social conscience it kindled, did more to initiate the war on poverty than any other single force.

It will be—it has been—argued that these by-products of the Negro struggle are not revolutionary. But the term "revolutionary," as

I am using it, does not connote violence; it refers to the qualitative transformation of fundamental institutions, more or less rapidly, to the point
where the social and economic structure which they comprised can no
longer be said to be the same. The Negro struggle has hardly run its
course; and it will not stop moving until it has been utterly defeated
or won substantial equality. But I fail to see how the movement can be
victorious in the absence of radical programs for full employment, the
abolition of slums, the reconstruction of our educational system, new
definitions of work and leisure. Adding up the cost of such programs,
we can only conclude that we are talking about a refashioning of our
political economy. It has been estimated, for example, that the price of
replacing New York City's slums with public housing would be $17 billion.
Again, a multibillion-dollar federal public works program, dwarfing the
currently proposed $2 billion program, is required to reabsorb unskilled
and semi-skilled workers into the labor market—and this must be done
if Negro workers in these categories are to be employed. "Preferential
treatment" cannot help them.

I am not trying here to delineate a total program, only to suggest
the scope of economic reforms which are most immediately related
to the plight of the Negro community. One could speculate on their
political implications—whether, for example, they do not indicate the
obsolescence of state government and the superiority of regional structures as viable units of planning. Such speculations aside, it is clear that
Negro needs cannot be satisfied unless we go beyond what has so far
been placed on the agenda. How are these radical objectives to be
achieved? The answer is simple, deceptively so: *through political power.*

There is a strong moralistic strain in the civil rights movement
which would remind us that power corrupts, forgetting that the absence
of power also corrupts. But this is not the view I want to debate here, for
it is waning. Our problem is posed by those who accept the need for
political power but do not understand the nature of the object and
therefore lack sound strategies for achieving it; they tend to confuse
political institutions with lunch counters.

A handful of Negroes, acting alone, could integrate a lunch counter
by strategically locating their bodies so as *directly* to interrupt the operation of the proprietor's will; their numbers were relatively unimportant.
In politics, however, such a confrontation is difficult because the interests
involved are merely *represented.* In the execution of a political decision

a direct confrontation may ensue (as when federal marshals escorted James Meredith into the University of Mississippi—to turn from an example of nonviolent coercion to one of force backed up with the threat of violence). But in arriving at a political decision, numbers and organizations are crucial, especially for the economically disenfranchised. (Needless to say, I am assuming that the forms of political democracy exist in America, however imperfectly, that they are valued, and that elitist or putschist conceptions of exercising power are beyond the pale of discussion for the civil rights movement.)

Neither that movement nor the country's twenty million black people can win political power alone. We need allies. The future of the Negro struggle depends on whether the contradictions of this society can be resolved by a coalition of progressive forces which becomes the *effective* political majority in the United States. I speak of the coalition which staged the March on Washington, passed the Civil Rights Act, and laid the basis for the Johnson landslide—Negroes, trade unionists, liberals, and religious groups.

There are those who argue that a coalition strategy would force the Negro to surrender his political independence to white liberals, that he would be neutralized, deprived of his cutting edge, absorbed into the Establishment. Some who take this position urged last year that votes be withheld from the Johnson–Humphrey ticket as a demonstration of the Negro's political power. Curiously enough, these people who sought to demonstrate power through the non-exercise of it also point to the Negro "swing vote" in crucial urban areas as the source of the Negro's independent political power. But here they are closer to being right: the urban Negro vote will grow in importance in the coming years. If there is anything positive in the spread of the ghetto, it is the potential political power base thus created, and to realize this potential is one of the most challenging and urgent tasks before the civil rights movement. If the movement can wrest leadership of the ghetto vote from the machines, it will have acquired an organized constituency such as other major groups in our society now have.

But we must also remember that the effectiveness of a swing vote depends solely on other votes. It derives its power from them. In that sense, it can never be independent, but must opt for one candidate or the other, even if by default. Thus coalitions are inescapable, however tentative they may be. And this is the case in all but those few situations in which Negroes running on an independent ticket might conceivably win. Independence, in other words, is not a value in itself. The issue is which coalition to join and how to make it responsive to your program. Necessarily there will be compromise. But the difference between expediency and morality in politics is the difference between selling out a principle and making smaller concessions to win larger ones. The leader who shrinks from this task reveals not his purity but his lack of political sense.

The task of molding a political movement out of the March on Washington coalition is not simple, but no alternatives have been advanced. We need to choose our allies on the basis of common political objectives. It has become fashionable in some no-win Negro circles to decry the white liberal as the main enemy (his hypocrisy is what sustains racism); by virtue of this reverse recitation of the reactionary's litany (liberalism leads to socialism, which leads to communism), the Negro is left in majestic isolation, except for a tiny band of fervent white initiates. But the objective fact is that Eastland and Goldwater are the main enemies—they and the opponents of civil rights, of the war on poverty, of Medicare, of social security, of federal aid to education, of unions, and so forth. The labor movement, despite its obvious faults, has been the largest single organized force in this country pushing for progressive social legislation. And where the Negro–labor–liberal axis was weak, as in the farm belt, it was the religious groups that were most influential in rallying support for the Civil Rights Bill.

The durability of the coalition was interestingly tested during the election. I do not believe that the Johnson landslide proved the "white backlash" to be a myth. It proved, rather, that economic interests are more fundamental than prejudice: the backlashers decided that loss of social security was, after all, too high a price to pay for a slap at the Negro. This lesson was a valuable first step in reeducating such people, and it must be kept alive, for the civil rights movement will be advanced only to the degree that social and economic welfare gets to be inextricably entangled with civil rights.

The 1964 elections marked a turning point in American politics. The Democratic landslide was not merely the result of a negative reaction to Goldwaterism; it was also the expression of a majority liberal consensus. The near unanimity with which Negro voters joined in that expression was, I am convinced, a vindication of the July 25 statement by Negro leaders calling for a strategic turn toward political action and a temporary curtailment of mass demonstrations. Despite the controversy surrounding the statement, the instinctive response it met with in the community is suggested by the fact that demonstrations were down 75 percent as compared with the same period in 1963. But should so high a percentage of Negro voters have gone to Johnson, or should they have held back to narrow his margin of victory and thus give greater visibility to our swing vote? How has our loyalty changed things? Certainly the Negro vote had higher visibility in 1960, when a switch of only 7 percent from the Republican column of 1956 elected President Kennedy. But the slimness of Kennedy's victory—of his "mandate"—dictated a go-slow approach on civil rights, at least until the Birmingham upheaval.

Although Johnson's popular majority was so large that he could have won without such overwhelming Negro support, that support was important from several angles. Beyond adding to Johnson's total national margin, it was specifically responsible for his victories in Virginia, Florida, Tennessee, and Arkansas. Goldwater took only those states where fewer than 45 percent of eligible Negroes were registered. That Johnson would have won those states had Negro voting rights been enforced is a lesson not likely to be lost on a man who would have been happy with a unanimous electoral college. In any case, the 1.6 million Southern Negroes who voted have had a shattering impact on the Southern political party structure, as illustrated in the changed composition of the Southern congressional delegations. The "backlash" gave the Republicans five house seats in Alabama, one in Georgia, and one in Mississippi. But on the Democratic side, seven segregationists were defeated while all nine Southerners who voted for the Civil Rights Act were reelected. It may be premature to predict a Southern Democratic party of Negroes and white moderates and a Republican party of refugee racists and economic conservatives, but there certainly is a strong tendency toward such a realignment; and an additional 3.6 million Negroes of voting age in the eleven Southern states are still to be heard from. Even the *tendency* toward disintegration of the Democratic party's racist wing defines a new context for presidential and liberal strategy in the congressional battles ahead. Thus the Negro vote (North as well as South), while not *decisive* in the presidential race, was enormously effective. It was a dramatic element of a historic mandate which contains vast possibilities and dangers that will fundamentally affect the future course of the civil rights movement.

The liberal congressional sweep raises hope for an assault on the seniority system, Rule Twenty-two, and other citadels of Dixiecrat-Republican power. The overwhelming of this conservative coalition should also mean progress on much bottlenecked legislation of profound interest to the movement (e.g., bills by Senators Clark and Nelson on planning, manpower, and employment). Moreover, the irrelevance of the South to Johnson's victory gives the President more freedom to act than his predecessor had and more leverage to the movement to pressure for executive action in Mississippi and other racist strongholds.

None of this *guarantees* vigorous executive or legislative action, for the other side of the Johnson landslide is that it has a Gaullist quality. Goldwater's capture of the Republican party forced into the Democratic camp many disparate elements which do not belong there, big business being the major example. Johnson, who wants to be President "of all the people," may try to keep his new coalition together by sticking close to the political center. But if he decides to do this, it is unlikely that even his political genius will be able to hold together a coalition so inherently unstable and rife with contradictions. It must come apart. Should it do so while Johnson is pursuing a centrist course, then the mandate will have been wastefully dissipated. However, if the mandate is seized upon to set fundamental changes in motion, then the basis can be laid for a new mandate, a new coalition including hitherto inert and dispossessed strata of the population.

Here is where the cutting edge of the civil rights movement can be applied. We must see to it that the reorganization of the "consensus party" proceeds along lines which make it an effective vehicle for social reconstruction, a role it cannot play so long as it furnishes Southern racism with its national political power. And nowhere has the civil rights movement's political cutting edge been more magnificently demonstrated than at Atlantic City, where the Mississippi Freedom Democratic party not only secured recognition as a bona fide component of the national party, but in the process routed the representatives of the most rabid racists—the white Mississippi and Alabama delegations. While I still believe that the FDP made a tactical error in spurning the compromise, there is no question that they launched a political revolution whose logic is the displacement of Dixiecrat power. They launched that revolution within a major political institution and as part of a coalitional effort.

The role of the civil rights movement in the reorganization of American political life is programmatic as well as strategic. We are challenged now to broaden our social vision, to develop functional programs with concrete objectives. We need to propose alternatives to technological unemployment, urban decay, and the rest. We need to be calling for public works and training, for national economic planning, for federal aid to education, for attractive public housing—all this on a sufficiently massive scale to make a difference. We need to protest the notion that our integration into American life, so long delayed, must now proceed in an atmosphere of competitive scarcity instead of in the security of abundance which technology makes possible. We cannot claim to have answers to all the complex problems of modern society. That is too much to ask of a movement still battling barbarism in Mississippi. But we can agitate the right questions by probing at the contradictions which still stand in the way of the Great Society. The questions having been asked, motion must begin in the larger society, for there is a limit to what Negroes can do alone.

Some Lessons from Watts

◆ ◆ ◆

[1965]

IN ORDER FOR ME TO TALK ABOUT WATTS, it is necessary for me to talk first about the nature of the revolution through which we are moving. Europeans find it very difficult to accept the term "the civil rights revolution," because a revolution usually is thought of as having aspects that this revolution does not have.

In general usage, a revolution means an attempt, by force, by a group not in power to take power, and to exercise it. That is not what Negroes want. Contrary to some things that Mr. James Baldwin and Leroy Jones have written, I do not know any sizable number of Negroes who think in terms of seizing power. Secondly, a real revolution postulates a political philosophy which is different from that held by the major groups with which they are contending. I know of no sizable group of Negroes in this country who want to revise American institutions. They want to be part of those institutions, for good or ill, as they now exist.

Thirdly, revolutions as we have known them invariably have used any form of power and in any degree—whatever it can get into its hands—for the accomplishment of its aim, the achieving of power. By and large, the Negro revolt has denied that it is interested in, nor has it used, violence. It has limited itself in tactics and stratagems to nonviolence.

Now, if this be true, how can we use the term "civil rights revolution"? In the Greek—and true—meaning of the term, "revolution" means to go to the roots of things and turn them upside down. There is a revolution, that is, a going to the bottom of things and turning them topsy-turvy, in that the Negro subjectively, inwardly, psychologically, declares himself a man, no longer looks upon himself as an inferior.

This is important because the history of top and bottom, the history of slave and master, shows that slavery cannot in fact continue far beyond the point at which slaves no longer looked upon themselves as slaves and accommodated to it—as in America we accommodate to two distinctly different but important concepts, that of Uncle Tom and that of Sambo.

Needed: A Democratic Constitutional Convention

There is another sense in which we are in a revolutionary stage—an inner revolution that has nothing to do with the Negroes' objectives. It grows out of the fact that what the American Negro now wants to achieve with nonrevolutionary objectives cannot in fact be achieved unless there is a democratic constitutional revolution in the economic and social life of this country. That is what is truly revolutionary. Now, this is already quite clear in its pre-revolutionary form. I do not for a moment think that the changes I am about to enumerate are due exclusively to the Negro in motion; but if other forces did exist and the Negro were not in motion, these changes could not have come about. The ecumenical movement in religion—Catholics, Protestants, and Jews cooperating—emerged essentially from Negroes in movement. It is, in fact, only around Negroes that Catholics, Protestants, and Jews have been able to coalesce for social objectives. I believe we would not now be examining our school systems and doing what Dr. Cronin—and many other educators—have asked us to do for years except for Negroes in motion. It took Negro school boycotts to get this nation to realize that the school system itself is not training people for the age of automation and cybernation and a technological revolution through which we are passing. I do not believe there would be a war on poverty today if Negroes had not been in motion. I do not believe that there would be the student movement concerned with peace and civil rights and academic freedom had that movement not been inspired by the movement of Negro students in 1960.

A Warning and an Appeal

It is important to note that I say we are in a pre-revolutionary state precisely because the Negro will no longer consent to look on himself as be has done for 350 years; and because, unless something profound happens, we not only will be unable to solve what we think of as the Negro problem, but we are preparing for a continuous siege, a continuous social dislocation of a violent nature in this country if we are not able to move rapidly. And this is so precisely because if the Negro's being in motion nonviolently causes a number of creative things to happen, if his frustration then causes him to be in motion violently, we will discover that a number of extremely violent things will be visited upon the total nature of our society.

This analysis is important because Watts was a warning and an appeal. If a few Negroes get drunk and go berserk, that is criminal behavior. If an entire community goes berserk, it signals the presence of a social sickness that has sprung from social germs. A young man in Watts said to me and Dr. King, "You know, we won."

I said, "What do you mean, you won?"

He said, "They finally listened to our manifesto." And he kept talking about the manifesto.

And I said, "Young man, what do you mean, the manifesto? Would you mind letting me and Dr. King see a copy of it?"

He pulled out a matchbox; he pulled out a single match; he lit it. He said, "Daddy, that was our manifesto, and the slogan was 'Burn, baby, burn.'"

I said, "But you haven't told me how you won."

He said, "Well, I'll tell you how we won. We were four years telling these white folks peacefully what we needed. We asked them to come and talk with us. They didn't come. We tried to get some war on poverty. It didn't come. But after our manifesto, daddy, the Mayor, the Governor, you, Dr. King, everybody came."

Now, this is amusing, but it is terribly serious, because Watts has caused thousands of young Negroes in this country to speak, not what is untrue but what is precisely true—that the great majority of white people in this country, and particularly those with political power, did in fact, after they had burned, bring in the war on poverty; did in fact, after they had pillaged, pay attention to them; did in fact, after the rampaging and the looting, finally say, "Well, something must be done." The danger is not so much from the looting or the burning; the real danger is that, objectively, from what these youngsters have seen happen, they now believe that looting and burning have become a legitimate means for forcing social change. If anyone is at fault, it is the authorities who have failed to see the first aspect of this revolution, which is dignity.

In Watts, I learned what I had been fearing for some time from the response to Malcolm X and to other black nationalist groups: that the Negro in this country no longer will do what Dollard and others described them as doing in their study at Yale on frustration and aggression. Mr. Dollard and others pointed out that frustration generates aggression, in direct proportion. They cited the great number of fights between Negro women and their husbands during weekends, the number of razor duels in the streets, the fights over gambling, the murders as evidence that Negroes (apart from the Uncle Tom–Sambo concept) turn their aggressive violence in upon themselves. Watts proved to me conclusively that Negroes no longer are going to express frustration in self-aggression; but that they will turn it against the people they feel are responsible for their status.

No Law and Order in a Vacuum

Watts taught us that, any way one turns it, no law and order are possible in a vacuum. It is pointless to cry, "Let us maintain law and order," for order does not proceed from the accumulation of law. Law is neutral. Order springs from just law and the pursuit of justice—and where there is neither justice nor evidence of its pursuit, disorder is inevitable. Let me give some concrete examples of what I mean by this. I do not want to discuss police brutality in this context. If every policeman in Watts or Bedford-Stuyvesant or Harlem behaved as an ideal creature, there still would be disorder and it would be directed at the policeman, because people in Watts refer to Watts as the zoo, and the policeman as the zoo-keeper—the blue-coat zoo-keeper. The youngsters in Watts would not have been able to analyze their meaning—and it took me some time to apprehend fully what they were saying, which was something like this:

"Mr. Rustin, they hem us into this zoo on four sides, then they tell Charlie Bluecoat to come in here and keep us still. We don't like the zoo. We intend to break out of it."

And in Watts, in the ten-mile stretch from the center of that community all that way to three or four blocks from City Hall, is complete devastation attesting to the strength of that intention. Even the direction that the destruction took has meaning to those people. When the police officers come in and say to them, "Behave yourselves in this condition," the people say the same thing they said to me and Dr. King—and if they say it to me and Dr. King, how much more do they mean it to the policemen?—those boys said to me:

"Mr. Rustin, don't you and Dr. King come in here and tell us to behave ourselves. We are sick of Negro leaders telling us to behave ourselves; 'cause, daddy, when you tell me to behave myself, you are asking me to accept this condition, and I don't intend to accept it."

There is another aspect: a young boy came to me and said, "Mr. Rustin, I have been trying for weeks and weeks and weeks to get a job. Whitey is not going to give me a job."

I said, "Well, now, son, what do you mean by that?"

He said, "I'll tell you what I mean, Mr. Rustin—I mean that I am so sick of Whitey and his lording it over me and not giving me any work, that I've been selling pot on the street and making me $60 a week. What that Bluecoat Whitey doesn't know is that when he comes in here and tells me not to sell pot, when he isn't going to let me work when I'm able to work and want to work, when that sonofabitch asks me to be lawful, he's trying to take my goddam job away from me."

One of the boys said, "We know that those policemen are scared of us. We had for once to prove to them that they were scared of us, because they come walking in here six at a time and beat us up whenever they want."

White Stereotype Fear of Negroes

What the boy did not know was the basis of that fear. White people are always afraid of Negroes when there are more than two present. I am quite serious. What else would explain why—when the FBI knew all our plans, when every department of government knew, because we bad been meeting with them for eight weeks straight—they continued, before the March on Washington, as did every newspaper, to predict that Negroes had to misbehave?

It is very simple: psychologically, it is projection. The average white policeman says to himself, "Look at these conditions they live in. Look how many of them are unemployed. Look at the condition of the schools. Look what we do to them, and how we beat them. Aha! If I were one of them, I wouldn't take it, I would fight back." Therefore he assumes that we are going to make the same kind of response that he would, because inwardly he knows that we are and react in the same way as human beings.

Those kids smelled this, and they had to bring it out.

It is a tragedy that there is not a major civil rights problem to be solved in the North. When one comes up against decent housing and the destruction of slums, quality integrated education, and work, one is not dealing with Negro problems; one is dealing with contradictions in a society which happen most grievously to affect the Negro. I am aware that segregation and discrimination are not totally responsible for the conditions that I shall now describe—but the average Negro in Watts is not any more analytical than the average Jew on the lower East Side or the average Italian on Mott Street; he does not want to know the causes; the shoe pinches; there is a monkey on his back; he wants to get it off. Since 1954, the ghettos have gotten larger; there are more rats and more roaches in them. Negro employment is infinitely worse than it was in 1954. Since 1954 there are more Negro children in segregated class-rooms than there were. But in addition, all the legislative action, all the Presidential action, all the Supreme Court decisions—excepting the FEPC provisions of the 1964 [civil rights] bill—were not designed to do anything about the North. They were all designed to do something about the South.

My prediction: there is not a major city in this country—given the revolutionary mood of the Negro youth and their alienation and their separation from the leadership—which may not have a Watts, unless we are prepared to build a coalition of forces, including labor, religious groups, church groups, and others, that will come forward with a truly revolutionary plan—a nonrevolutionary plan is never adequate for a revolutionary situation.

Grandiose Planning Needed

There are times when only that which appears to be grandiose is capable of dealing with a situation which is desperate. And therefore this coalition of forces must now demand that where the private sector of the economy cannot provide work, the public sector do so. We need a massive public works program, *with training*. We need to understand that automation and cybernation cannot affect human services to humans. Therefore in addition to having the kinds of work programs that Franklin Delano Roosevelt had, training must be built into them. The unskilled must be given useful work in the wide area of human services to humans; such people can be employed in that realm with very little training. We must face up to the fact that this nation has got to plan, not go on acting as if somehow or other planning is un-American (by which we seem to mean that planning to give billions to the railways is American; planning to give to the poor is socialism or communism).

Let me give you an illustration. I am all for the war on poverty and all it is doing; but the war on poverty is no answer to the basic revolutionary situation we are in. What is Mr. Shriver going to do with those Negro boys he sends to camp, after he upgrades their reading rates, gives them a feeling of being somebody, in a society where there's so little planning that we could not possibly know what is going to be automated next so that we could really train them to go into a job? I'll tell you what those boys are: they are sticks of dynamite with a time fuse, planted in the ghetto with their frustrated expectations—a major part of the future trouble. It is a dangerous thing to take a seventeen-year-old boy off the streets of Harlem and lead him to believe that when he goes to one of these camps for the year and raises his reading rate to the seventh grade, he is then going to make it, when in fact he cannot make it in a society where there are not jobs for anybody with his skills.

Jobs As a Remedy

A recent Sunday issue of the *New York Times* had two extremely interesting articles: one related that the Negroes in Miami were up in arms because they were fearful that more of their jobs will be lost to Cubans who will work for nothing. (That is quite understandable, especially in a state where there is no minimum wage.) The other story related that Mexican-Americans in California are up in arms because, as they saw it, the Negroes rioted and got something while they remained peaceable and got nothing. The basic problem is not the poor Cubans; it is not the Negroes who may be getting jobs; it is not the Mexican-Americans who rightfully feel resentful. The problem is that in a society where the government does not see to it that every man who wants work can have it, the government, whether it knows it or not, is pitting those men against one another to fight like dogs over a bone for the few jobs that do exist. Nothing less than full and fair employment will get us out of this problem.

Michael Harrington reports that 50 percent of the people of Watts were without work. If 50 percent of the American people were out of work, we would not only have rioting and revolt; we would have revolution. Therefore why are we surprised that these people do this? And how chagrined we should be that, having done it, the government then makes a half-hearted effort and a response leading young Negroes to feel that this is one of the ways now to legitimize it.

Political Agitators

A word about political leadership: a riot—or riots—as I have studied them (I've studied the Detroit riots by going to Detroit; I've studied the Cicero riot by going there for the American Friends Service Committee and making a study), whether black or white rioting, happens in the same way. There is frustration, leading to aggression. For no good reason, riots always start over silly things—something bursts. The next step is that the police, with this fear I've been talking about, come in with power far beyond what is needed to the disorders. The community reacts to that extraordinary amount of power. That is always the second stage. The third stage is when the worms come out of the woodwork— that is, the thieves in the community see that they can take advantage of the situation; they start breaking windows and stealing. Toward the end of that stage, perfectly respectable people get caught up in the looting. The next stage is when certain political groups—I will not name the ones in Los Angeles because they are still under examination, but will refer back to Harlem where they were Chinese-Maoist Communists— come in and try to keep it going. This is the way it develops.

Now, the important thing about this development is that, after it's gone a certain distance, there is really nothing to do but let it burn out. I myself was booed, shot at, stoned, and finally run off the streets of Harlem last summer trying to stop the riot there. What we discovered is that if the right groups in the community can be reached, and they can reach some of the young people, they can stop it. We have heard a great deal of ugliness about Watts; but the primary reason that it finally boiled down to was not because the police came in with more and more power but because finally two youth groups decided that they were going to organize to stop it.

Every paper in this country said that the Watts riot was the worst in American history; everything that the Negro does is the worst. A judge sits on the bench for twenty years and in that time sends ten men to their deaths. Each time, he says, "This was the most heinous crime in the annals of man." In the year 1863, in New York, the Irish were called "shanties," which means "nigger." In the year 1863, amongst the Irish in New York there was 44 percent unemployment. In the year 1863, Irish could not buy property in certain parts of New York. In the year 1863, policemen used to come into the Irish district five and six together. In the year 1863 the Irish were dirty, they didn't wash, they stank, they were ugly, they were all the things that Negroes are called today. And in the year 1863, the Irish rioted in New York. They killed over 300 people, lynched over 31 Negroes, did much more property damage than was done in Watts.

Do I recall this because I have animosity toward the Irish? No. I only say that poor frustrated people will riot. And yet, I have yet to hear anyone other than myself recall these facts in connection with Watts.

The Irish got out of the situation they were in because following the Civil War there was a great development, an industrialization, the use of semi-skilled workers which put men back to work. If Negro rioting is to be avoided in the future, it will be because Negroes are enabled to get out of the vicious cycle of frustration that breeds aggression; because this country proves that it is capable of creating a new economic way of life without unemployment, without slums, without poverty. We have the means. Will we find the way to use them wisely, while there is still time?

The Mind of the Black Militant

◆ ◆ ◆

[1967]

THE PROBLEMS OF THE SCHOOL, we have been told, are intimately related to those of the city. Commissioner [of Education Harold] Howe said that we cannot have good schools if we have bad cities. I would agree with this statement, but I would carry it a step further: we cannot have good cities unless we have a good nation. And to have a good nation, we must face, once and for all, the problems of poverty and race. Only through the formulation of a national program to eliminate poverty and racial discrimination can we lay the basis for a good, let alone a great, society.

There is no longer any denying that this country is in the throes of a historic national crisis. Its implications for education are so frightening that even now the American people have not yet fully grasped what is happening to them.

The grim data are still coming in. In the summer of 1967, thirty of our cities, big and small, were wracked by racial disorder. Scores of citizens, almost all of them black, were killed; thousands were injured and even more arrested. Property damage exceeded a billion dollars; total income loss is incalculable.

The greatest toll, however, is not in property damage or even in lives lost. Nor is the greatest danger that the violence will go on indefinitely, any more than the Civil War did. It is that the aftermath of that war will be repeated—that, as in the Compromise of 1877, the country will turn its back on the Negro, on the root causes of his discontent, on its own democratic future.

Why does the republic find itself at a crossroads? What is actually happening?

Several newspaper columnists and television commentators have already begun to draw comparisons between the ghetto uprisings and the French, Russian, Algerian, Irish, and Black African independence revolutions. Some black power advocates have proclaimed the beginnings of guerrilla warfare and see the urban Negro as a counterpart to the Viet Cong. And in Paris it has become fashionable to speak of the *révolution des noires* in the United States.

The preconditions for an authentic independence revolution are completely lacking, however. American Negroes have no geographical focus for nationalist sentiment, nor do they constitute a popular majority struggling against a relatively small, white colonial group. More aptly, the situation can be described as a form of social revolution. The phrase "social revolution"—widely used by civil rights leaders—designates fundamental changes in social and economic class relations resulting from mass political action. Such action would be democratic. That is, it would aim to create a new majority coalition capable of exercising political power in the interest of new social policies. By definition, the coalition must be interracial.

As a minority, Negroes by themselves cannot bring about such a social revolution. They can participate in it as a powerful and stimulating force, or they can provoke a counterrevolution.

If, however, the comparison between Harlem and Algeria is misleading, the term "race riot" is similarly unilluminating and anachronistic.

Any real effort to understand the educational meaning of these events must begin with an examination of the mentality of the black activist and the psychological factors that will inevitably face those who attempt to do anything constructive about ghetto conditions and specifically ghetto schools. The mentality of the activist influences both those who, by their constructive, concrete behavior, are attempting to influence the schools in a positive direction and those who, by virtue of their militancy, exercise a substantial veto over anyone else who attempts to act in the community.

At the outset, it is essential to understand that Negroes are not only "exaggerated Americans," as Gunnar Myrdal said; they are also inevitably ambivalent. A good illustration of this is the total confusion surrounding my friend Stokely Carmichael, who has been accused of being a racist. I happen to disagree with Mr. Carmichael's strategy and tactics, but he is not a racist. He is *ambivalent,* and so appears to be fostering a new form of black nationalist racism.

The racist says, "No matter who you are, what you have done, what your capabilities are, what you have accomplished, you are like that and I am like this. Stay away from me. I do not choose to recognize you as a man."

This is not what Stokely Carmichael says about white people. You have to know him and to know the dynamics of ambivalence to understand what he is saying. Actually, he is saying, "I recognize you for your accomplishments and for what you really are, but, knowing from experience that you are not going to recognize me, I cannot endure another injury from you. Therefore, before you have an opportunity to injure me, get the hell out of my way. I hate you. I do not want to have anything to do with you." This is protective negativism, but it is not racism.

Unless one understands that this basic negativism is an effort to be loved, one cannot understand ghetto psychology. Those who are teachers will understand this, and so will those who are mothers, because ghetto rioting can be compared, fundamentally, to a child's tantrum. The child in tantrum ought not to be slapped by his mother, for the child is simply saying, "Mother, something hurts. You do not understand me. I need to be loved. There is something wrong and I need your help." And so he kicks and screams in order to get the attention he needs.

The "tantrums" of the underprivileged are caused by a series of problems. Ghetto people, for example, feel that they have been boxed in by other people—not because they deserve it but because other people disrespect them. Consider Harlem. With wealthy Westchester to the north, Central Park to the south, the East River on one side, and the Hudson River on the other, there is no way for the community to expand. Already overcrowded, its population continues to grow. The same is true elsewhere as well. In fact, the population of our urban ghettos is increasing by half a million each year. Within these tightly confined areas, the whites—whether they are wanted, loved, or loathed—must fight the ghetto's sense of compression.

So long as people lack mobility—economically, socially, and politically—intruders from the outside world will be regarded ambivalently. Police, teachers, and small businessmen comprise the fundamental outside groups that the Negro community depends on and, therefore, in a certain sense, likes. Resentment at being boxed in, however, turns this liking into loathing.

- Resentment of the policeman—because telling a man in a box to behave is tantamount to telling him to accept his unemployment, his lack of education, and his slum housing.
- Resentment of the teacher—because, no matter how great his or her contribution, the ghetto child still lags years behind in reading and mathematics.
- Resentment of the white small businessman, Jewish or otherwise, because, no matter how good a man he may be, his installment selling (which makes buying possible for the poor) also means an overall higher price.

All such resentments stem from, and contribute to, this boxed-in feeling from which the Negro in the ghetto can find no escape. The constriction, the sense of no place to go, the lack of outlet, sharpen resentment and amplify every petty dislike into instant hate.

Black activists know, too, that the problems in education are staggering, and they see still less progress in coping with them. The fact is that the educational system is no longer as capable as it once was when it comes to preparing ordinary, uneducated citizens for productive roles in society. People from Eastern Europe who came here in 1900 could, when given a minimal public education, find jobs and become part of the productive system. Today, however, people coming out of Mississippi, even though they know the language and the culture of the United States, need more than a minimal education to take their place in the advanced technological society. The present automation revolution is so pervasive and complex as to leave no room for the uneducated or the semi-skilled. A once-over-lightly education is not enough.

Technology, in short, demands a higher level of competence from both schools and people than it did a mere generation ago. Activists know this, and for that reason they recognize that ordinary measures to improve the schooling of ghetto children are not enough. This accounts for the intensity of their concern with education. This is why the schools have become a primary target of the ghetto activist.

The black militants, looking at housing, looking at employment, looking at health care, looking at education, also understand something else that many whites do not. They recognize that in the great period of civil rights struggle, between 1955 and 1965, all efforts were directed toward the Negroes in the South—that the 1963 March on Washington, the

1964 civil rights bill, and the 1965 civil rights bill were all directed toward the Southern Negro. In fact, there has not been a single victory for ghetto Negroes in the past fifteen years, not a single thing they might point to that makes the ghetto look different, that means more money is coming in or that their children are being better educated. Is it surprising, then, that activists in the ghetto are thoroughly convinced our society does not intend to do away with racism and economic disadvantage?

From this conviction flows a series of corollaries. First, the Negro sees this society as one that responds only to violence. The chief lesson that young Negroes are learning today in the ghetto is to achieve, create violence.

To illustrate their contention, they point to A. Philip Randolph, a most respected Negro, who for five years headed a committee in New York for upgrading the police in the Harlem and Bedford-Stuyvesant areas. For five years, I was secretary to that committee and nothing happened. However, two weeks after the riot in Harlem, a Negro, Lloyd Sealey, was promoted to police captain.

Or they cite the situation in Chicago, where Negroes rioted because they wanted to use the fire hydrants to keep cool. Dr. Martin Luther King had been in Chicago two years. He had won not a single concession, except a housing commitment on paper, which was subsequently not honored. But, less than twenty-four hours after the Negroes rioted, Mayor Daley was traipsing through the ghetto, distributing eight-dollar sprinklers and promising two new swimming pools.

Again, they mention Watts. There, a bus line had been sought for many years because there was no decent transportation system. After the rioting, the Establishment rushed in, talking about building a hospital and a decent transportation system. One of the young men said to me at the end of the riot, "Mr. Rustin, I don't know what you have been here for. You should go back to New York because we won, and, if you don't believe me, go out into that street. There are so many sociologists, educators, and economists here, you will trip over them." I would certainly not have tripped over them before the riot.

What is happening is simple. Society, by waiting for riots to occur before responding to needs, deprives the more responsible Negro leaders of any possibility of leadership. Why should anyone join the NAACP or the Southern Christian Leadership Conference? Society has systematically taught ghetto people that the methods used by Roy Wilkins and Martin Luther King, Jr., are useless.

Reduced to violence and robbed of leadership, the Negro activist is struck by still another reality—the shift of public attention away from these problems. White America, instead of turning its energies toward a solution of these problems, has turned away. After about 1965, most intelligent Americans would have argued that civil rights represented America's most pressing problem. Today, however, attention has shifted to Vietnam. Here again the Negro finds himself the victim of discrimination, for the war has diverted more than attention—it has diverted resources that might have been used to eliminate the ghetto from American life.

Worse yet, the Negro activist looks at Vietnam and finds proportionally more Negro Americans there than whites. He sees society, which is unwilling or incapable of dealing with racism and unwilling or incapable of dealing with poverty, pouring its youth and its money into war. The activist concludes that this society is dirty and rotten and that it ought to be wiped from the face of the earth—a drastic conclusion, which results finally in what might be called "frustration politics."

Those who are frustrated, who feel they cannot free themselves and cannot escape from the box in which they find themselves, turn on those who visibly represent the outside world. Since teachers are, in fact, among the most visible representatives of the outside world, they often bear the brunt of the attack. Pressure tactics will not solve unemployment or eradicate slums, but they can give the local board of education and the teachers a hard time—a substitute satisfaction. It may be impossible to get at those in the Pentagon who are sending the boys to Vietnam, but it is relatively easy to strike back at those who run the schools. Thus frustration politics results in such demands as:

- Get rid of all white teachers in the ghetto.
- Employ only Negro principals in the ghetto.
- Win the right to establish the curriculums in ghetto schools.
- Take over the ghetto schools completely, and destroy all central control over urban school systems.

I do not agree with all these demands, particularly the last; if control of ghetto schools can be captured by a local group of Negroes, the same sort of thing could be done by any other minority group.

What would some other groups that I can think of do if they gained control of the schools? Put in a John Birch curriculum? Insist on only white principals who are Catholic or Protestant, but not Jewish? I cannot agree with this in principle.

Even if one did, however, there is an even more fundamental problem with the politics of frustration—a sense of the hopelessness of it all. Ghetto radicals see the problems of housing, schools, jobs, health, and police as so interrelated and so complex that it appears to them that *no* program is, in fact, workable.

In New York, for example, this negativism is based on the history of the local school situation over the past ten years. Every year there has been a new gimmick. First it was buses; the next year it was the Allen Plan. Now these are forgotten. The following year it was talk about education parks. Last year it was the More Effective Schools program. This year it's decentralization. Next year it will be still another gimmick. The fundamental reason educators have become involved in this gimmickry is that they do not seem to understand that unless there is a *master plan* to cover housing, jobs, and health, every plan for the schools will fall on its face. No piecemeal strategy can work.

There must be a diversion of federal funds simultaneously to schools, housing, jobs, and health. We must eradicate our worst poverty—not the poverty in Harlem or Watts, but the poverty in men's imaginations. The middle classes who think that string, Scotch tape, and spit will get us out of our present dilemma must be convinced otherwise. Even compensatory education, isolated from adequate housing, decent living conditions, and good neighborhoods, is useless.

What is needed is something more far-reaching, more imaginative. We must begin by accepting the idea of a *national plan to eradicate the ghetto*. We must have national priorities and we must adjust the scale of our thinking to the scale of the problem.

Economic and social deprivation, if accepted by its victims as their lot in life, breeds passivity, even docility. The miserable yield to their fate as divinely ordained or as their own fault. And, indeed, many Negroes in earlier generations felt that way.

Today young Negroes aren't having any of this. They don't share the feeling that something must be wrong with them, that they are responsible for their own exclusion from this affluent society. The civil rights movement—in fact, the whole liberal trend beginning with John Kennedy's election—has told them otherwise.

These young Negroes are right. The promises made to them were good and necessary and long, long overdue. The youth were right to believe in them. The only trouble is that the promises were not fulfilled.

What they and the American people absolutely must understand now is that these promises cannot be revoked. They were not made to a handful of leaders in a White House drawing room; they were made to an entire generation, one not likely to forget or to forgive.

Unless the nation is prepared to rearrange its priorities, to set a timetable for achieving them, and to allocate its resources accordingly, it will not be taking its own commitments seriously. Surely it cannot then turn in amazement to responsible Negro leaders, whose pleas for large-scale programs it has failed to heed, for an explanation of the consequences.

Guns, Bread, and Butter

♦ ♦ ♦

[1967]

PUBLIC ORGANIZATIONS IN THE UNITED STATES tend, by and large, to be monistic in their interests—that is, they tend to function on behalf of specific causes. However, for some the task of concentrating attention on their special interests is more difficult than it is for others. For instance, it may not be too difficult for the AMA to concern itself exclusively with problems affecting the medical profession. But particularly for politically oriented organizations, the problem is somewhat different. On the one hand, they recognize their obligation to focus upon their stated objective; on the other, they are forced to deal with the fact that marginal issues impinge upon and affect the attainment of their own objectives. Thus we find liberal and civil rights organizations keeping attuned to and in touch with the diverse political, economic, and ideological sounds of the society. And we find the peace movement engaging at times in dialogue over what ought or ought not to be its singular area of interest.

Since for most of my life I have been engaged in peace and civil rights activities, I know something about these problems and conflicts. In my years with the War Resisters League, there were frequent discussions about the amount of time I was spending with the civil rights movement. It was not so much a debate over my personal right to participate in civil rights activities, but rather over my own view that nonviolence was not simply a philosophical stance for the peace movement, but was indeed a fundamental way of life. The implication of this view, therefore, was that wherever there was a possibility of violence, the War Resisters League had some obligation to work against that violence.

Many of my colleagues were inclined to agree with me, but many others remained convinced that nonviolence was the exclusive strategy of the peace movement.

The question is a very difficult one that becomes even more meaningful in the context of a broad and engaged conscience in our time: how can we continue to pay tender and exclusive attention to shoring up our own special furrow when the rest of the field is eroding all around us?

It is somewhere in this context that we must examine the problem of what is the responsibility of the civil rights movement to the peace movement, or whether the civil rights movement, per se, has any official responsibility in the peace movement at all.

When all is said and done, we are all citizens of a world in crisis. The universe of human suffering is everybody's universe. Moreover, it may well be that the solution of one problem has implications for the solution of another. This being so, there is a role for citizens to play in the solution of different problems that converge and impinge upon their personal situation. All of which means that if there is not a part for the civil rights movement to play in the peace struggle, there is certainly a part for Negroes to play, by joining peace groups all around the country.

What's more, many Negroes do take a deep and genuine interest in the problems of war and peace, and are trying to find some ground on which they can make a contribution. As I travel across the country, speaking before religious, liberal, civil rights, trade union, and campus groups, I am invariably asked by a large number of Negroes what they can do for peace. On such occasions, I always advise them to become members of peace organizations. When young Negro boys come up to me and say they are conscientiously opposed to war, I advise them to contact the War Resisters League, the Central Committee for Conscientious Objectors, or the American Friends Service Committee.

Of course I am aware that there is not going to be a tremendous onrush of Negroes into the peace movement. The immediate problems of Negroes' lives in America are so vast as to allow them very little time or energy to focus upon international crises. What is still crucial in the thinking and experience of Negroes in our society is that even in some of the most liberal cities they have a hard time finding a job, living in a decent neighborhood, sending their children to quality integrated schools, or even getting a taxi. We have also got to realize that politically

Rustin on the high school football team, 1931.

The Wilberforce Quartet, 1933. Rustin pictured at far right.

A moment of relaxation in the early 1940s.

Rustin at a protest in Washington DC during the mid-1940s.

Posing with the lute he taught himself to play while incarcerated as a conscientious objector, 1947.

Rustin along with a handful of his fellow participants in The Journey of Reconciliation, 1947. Left to right: Worth Randle, Wally Nelson, Ernest Bromley, James Peck, Igal Roodenko, Rustin, Joe Felmet, George Houser, Andrew Johnson.

Meeting with Indian Prime Minister Nehru at the All India Congress Party, 1948.

Rustin with Muriel Lester, International FOR traveling secretary and friend of Gandhi, in India, 1948.

Rustin at an antiwar demonstration in Philadelphia, 1950.

Meeting with Kwame Nkrumah in Accra, Ghana, 1952.

Rustin and Nnamdi Azikiwe, the Nigerian independence leader, 1952.

Taking a break with Malcolm X and debate moderator Michael R. Winston at Howard University, October 1961.

With the March on Washington less than a month away, Rustin poses in front of the National Headquarters office on West 130th Street, August 1, 1963.

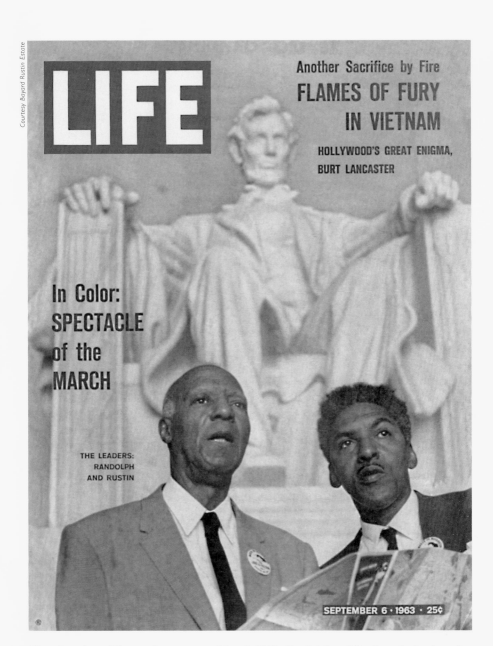

Another Sacrifice by Fire
FLAMES OF FURY IN VIETNAM

HOLLYWOOD'S GREAT ENIGMA, BURT LANCASTER

In Color: SPECTACLE of the MARCH

THE LEADERS: RANDOLPH AND RUSTIN

SEPTEMBER 6 · 1963 · 25¢

The triumphant *Life* magazine cover, crediting A. Philip Randolph and Rustin as the leaders of the March on Washington.

Rustin and author James Baldwin calling on President Kennedy to send troops into Alabama to "break the hold" of segregationist Governor George Wallace. The arm bands pictured were worn to protest the murder of African American children in Birmingham, September 1963.

Rustin at the A. Philip Randolph Institute, 1972.

Meeting with Golda Meir, Prime Minister of Israel, 1976.

Under the auspices of Freedom House, Rustin attends a political rally in Zimbabwe/Rhodesia, April 1979.

Rustin with children displaced by civil unrest in El Salvador, 1983.

An exuberant Rustin at age seventy-one in London's Trafalgar Square, 1983.

Negroes have carried a great national burden for the past ten years. Almost all of the progressive developments during this period have been the result of Negroes' marching in the streets, demonstrating for equal treatment under the law. Negroes helped end McCarthyism on U.S. campuses because the freedom struggle attracted and awakened the best moral instincts of our college youth. An American ecumenical movement came into being primarily because the religious conscience had to respond to the struggle for human rights in our country. Therefore, one must be careful, while examining the extent of Negro involvement in causes beyond civil rights, not to demand that they ought, with equal ardor, to be catalysts in the struggle for social and human rights at home and the quest for peace abroad.

The peace movement finds itself in a peculiar position. On the one hand, it would like to protect the integrity of its activities and objectives; on the other, it is somewhat unhappy over the fact that the civil rights movement does not openly ally itself with peace efforts. The answer to the latter problem is for Negroes to ally themselves individually with the peace struggle without committing the civil rights movement. And if this is true, then members of the peace movement have an obligation to ally themselves with certain objectives of the civil rights struggle without committing their organizations to any official involvement.

There is one other problem, with relation to war, that Negroes find difficult to resolve. Traditionally Negroes have made some of their more significant strides in American society during periods of military crisis. During World War I, hundreds of thousands of Negroes migrated out of the oppressed conditions of the South to find jobs in the North. During World War II, tremendous employment opportunities opened up for them in Detroit and other large industrial centers. And even during this horrible Vietnam war, many Negro young men who would have no alternative but to stand on street corners in Mississippi, Alabama, or New York are convinced that by joining the armed forces they can learn a trade, earn a salary, and be in a position to enter the job market on their return.

All this means that thousands of Negroes, in order to rehabilitate themselves, are forced to take a stand beyond morality and exploit the opportunities presented to them by their country's military involvement. I myself can afford the luxury of drawing those moral lines, but it is more difficult to suggest to people who are hungry, jobless, or living in slums that they turn their backs on opportunities that promise them a measure of economic betterment.

If this attitude on the part of thousands of Negroes horrifies the peace movement, then perhaps the peace movement might well conclude that it must give a large part of its energy to the struggle to secure the social and economic uplift of the Negro community. Needless to say, that is not what peace workers conclude, and this fact reveals the problem. I am not saying that they must, but if they object to what Negroes are forced to do in this situation, then they should follow the clear implication of their objection.

THE ANATOMY OF FRUSTRATION

♦ ♦ ♦

[1968]

THE UNITED STATES IS IN A DEEP MORAL CRISIS—and I speak with a heavy heart. Many younger Negroes today, in deep frustration, sincerely, gropingly, tragically, have adopted some of the negative and degrading concepts which have brutalized and enslaved them, believing somehow that these concepts can bring them freedom.

We must try to analyze the problem.

We would be mistaken to think that the only desires of young Negroes today are to have a job, to have a decent house, to be well educated, to have medical care. All these things are very important, but deeper and more profound is the feeling of young Negroes today—through all classes, from the *lumpenproletariat* to the working poor, the working classes, the middle classes, and the intelligentsia—that the time has come when they must demand recognition of their dignity and when they should have power, a voice in the solution of problems which affect them.

The tragedy is that those who are in deepest revolt are responding not only to the frustrations of their objective situation, but more fundamentally to the morality of a society which is teaching them that violence is the only effective force for social change. This society is systematically teaching them that it will respond only to tactics of desperation and violence.

This is not only true for Negroes. Many of us have been concerned for years about Columbia University taking all the land around its Harlem site and running people out of their homes to build high-rise structures exclusively for white people. We warned Columbia officials that a problem would occur. But the great educators at Columbia did not respond to our pleas. They waited until two hundred students, using the tactics of desperation, closed down the university. Then they were ready to talk. Then they were ready to discuss whether there ought to be a building where Columbia students, predominantly white, would enter from the top into one gym and where Negroes from Harlem would enter at the bottom of the same structure into a separate gym. They should have known that such separated facilities would create problems.

In New York, A. Philip Randolph and I had for five years tried to get the police department to upgrade Negro patrolmen. We urged that a Negro be made head of the police force in Harlem for psychological reasons. It was not done. But two weeks after the riot in 1964, they upgraded a Negro lieutenant, made him a captain, and put him in charge of the Central Harlem precinct. I then received a letter from a youth group saying, "You and Randolph failed. You should roll over and get the hell out of the way for your methods don't work. *We* upgraded a Negro policeman with sticks and stones and Molotov cocktails."

So this is the lesson we are teaching—that when the liberal forces of this nation join in coalition and urge that something be done, they are ignored; but when people riot, something is done. Basic needs may not be met, yet minor and often insignificant concessions are made.

Negro women in Watts making fifty-five and sixty dollars a week as maids were spending up to twenty-six of those dollars on taxis from the Negro ghetto to the white homes where they worked, all because no one had provided a transportation system for Watts. When Martin Luther King and I went to Watts and told the young Negroes they must put an end to rioting, that it was destroying their own community, they said, "Go back where you came from. We are winning." One of them lit a match, held it up, and said, "This is our manifesto and it's winning." And he went on to say that if you went out into the streets you would find sociologists, economists, city planners, hospital experts, transportation experts, "all there because of our manifesto." The fact is that before the riot there were groups in Watts which urged the city to do something about conditions. They were ignored.

The action for dealing with the problem of justice must come quickly, and before more rioting, lest we further teach people that the only viable method of social change is an act of desperation.

What I know, and what you ought to know, is the tragedy of a society which will not make basic changes but will make promises and token concessions—so long as the rioting goes to point X. But when it reaches X plus one, we are all in trouble, for then there will be the most vigorous repression. Then there will be vigilantism. Even more important, you cannot repress one-tenth of the population, no matter how badly elements of it behave, without threatening the civil liberties of everyone in the nation. Where there are not civil liberties, we cannot make social progress.

What must be understood is the anatomy of frustration, and here is where the Jewish problem can be put into focus. I am not one who goes around apologizing for or explaining away Negro anti-Semitism. It is here, it is dangerous, it must be rooted out. We cannot say it is somehow different or not really important. We cannot sweep it under the rug. What we can and had better do is understand it if we are to deal with it.

The first thing about those who are frustrated is that their frustration causes them to adopt a psychology, an economics, and a sociology based on the thinking of the frustrated. It goes like this: the United States is no longer viable. Negroes are never going to get their rights. All institutions must be destroyed and new ones established.

The death of Dr. Martin Luther King spurred that philosophy to its logical conclusion. Stokely Carmichael is reported to have said: "If they wanted to brutalize a black man, why didn't they get me or Rap Brown? We're the really dangerous ones to this social order. The fact that they got King indicates that Negroes will never get anything in this society and they are out to exterminate us all."

So the first point of the frustrated is that the society is not viable. Second, if the society is not viable, then no program needs to be projected because to project a program is to fool the masses of Negroes. So they viciously attack the Freedom Budget put forth by A. Philip Randolph. To them Randolph and I became the major enemies because we were putting forth a program, and to put forth a program, when you know nothing will move, is dishonest.

Third, if the nation is not viable and no program is needed, then all those people who have worked over the years for civil rights, and are still working for integration into this society, become the enemy. Not the Ku Klux Klan, not the John Birch Society, but those closest to you.

This is what Jews need to understand: that in the list of whom you attack, those you love come first. You attack those you have expected something from. You attack those who have in fact carried the banner. Before King's death, he and his nonviolence were the first enemy precisely because he had done the most. The argument went that if, after all the bloodshed, the bombings, the tear-gas, the water-hosings, and the dogs, King could not produce real victories, then he had fooled his people, exposed them to useless sacrifice. After his death, of course, a new situation was created. Now they had the opportunity to shift gears, to say that the greatest Negro was killed by a white. But when King was alive, it was a different story.

Next in the list of enemies of the frustrated come Roy Wilkins, Whitney Young, A. Philip Randolph. They are now the traitors to the cause. Listed too are the liberal community, which has fought side by side with us, and the Jews, who have made greater contributions than anybody else in the liberal community. Because of this reverse hate–affection syndrome, Martin Luther King, Roy Wilkins, Whitney Young, A. Philip Randolph, the liberals, the Jews, the labor leaders who lifted almost two million Negroes out of the *lumpenproletariat* into the working classes are all bastards now.

The point is that if Jews are under attack by the extreme left in the Negro community, they are in the same basket with Negro leaders and even the most progressive political leadership. Jews are not likely to feel better simply because others are also under attack; nevertheless there ought to be an understanding of what the problem really is.

In the anatomy of frustration, the long-time leadership is rejected. But heroes must be found somewhere, and so the frustrated adopt heroes of foreign revolutions—not because they believe in their philosophy but because they want to adopt the extreme tactics that they believe have worked for those heroes. Thus Che Guevara, Mao Tse-tung, Castro, and Fanon become heroes. This doesn't make the militants Communists. It means, rather, that they are so desperate for new methods that they reach into completely different kinds of situations, hoping that those tactics can be applied here. Of course, they cannot be, but the frustrated, by the anatomy of frustration, are convinced that the only thing left to do is to give everybody hell, to denounce everybody, and to call for revolt.

Consider the question of the Jew in the ghetto. Nothing that I say is justification for anti-Semitism, for I know that in a situation where anti-Semitism exists none of us is safe. Anti-Semitism must be rooted out. We have, however, an obligation to try to understand Negro anti-Semitism without excusing it.

If you happen to be an uneducated, poorly trained Negro living in the ghetto, and particularly if you live by your wits selling numbers, selling dope, engaging in prostitution, then you only see four kinds of white people: the policeman, the businessman, the teacher, and the welfare worker. In many cities, three of those four are predominantly Jewish. Except for the policeman, the majority of the businessmen, teachers, and welfare workers are Jewish. Here again is the hate–love syndrome.

Ninety percent of the crimes that Negroes commit are against other Negroes in the ghetto. Negroes, therefore, both hate and depend on policemen. To have to depend on someone whom you dislike and who often brutalizes you is ghastly.

Then comes the businessman. Many ghetto Negroes know nothing about capitalization. The fact is, if you walk up 125th Street you will see what Negroes say you will see: a television set that sells in department stores for $79.50 costs $132 in Harlem. But the ghetto dweller does not know that the department store is able to sell the TV set at $79.50 because the buyer makes a considerable down payment and is required to finish payments within one year, while the ghetto buyer is often given, with no down payment, three or four years in which to pay. He may not understand that as the length of time for payment is increased, the interest is increased. He does not always understand that only such long-term capitalization makes it possible for him to have a TV set at all.

Many people are kept alive for three and four weeks at a time by local businessmen who let them pile up a debt until they hit the numbers or something and can pay for what they bought. But if you hit the numbers once in a year and have to give most of the money to the grocer for things you have already eaten, when there are still more things you need, you hate him for taking your money even though you know it belongs to him.

The chief characteristic of every ghetto and of every major poor area is that people operate on the principle of immediate gratification. If you have little money, you operate on immediate gratification. You don't buy a new sheet until the old sheet is in shreds. You don't buy salt until you're at dinner and the salt runs out. Nobody can save up enough money to take advantage of a sale; you've got to buy things when you need them. The tragedy is that the need to live always on the principle of immediate gratification can sometimes be frightening.

A young fellow I got a job for came to see me a week after receiving his first two weeks' pay—$125. He came to thank me for the job and to show me what he had bought for himself: he had gone into a store on 125th Street and paid $67.50 for a pair of alligator shoes.

Now, this may shock you, unless you never had anything but sneakers, usually with holes in them, and day after day you had been walking past the shoestore seeing something beautiful there. To pay $67.50 for shoes may be uneconomical, but it is psychologically understandable. He held those shoes to his breast waiting for me to rave about them. And I did. I knew that at a later time I would have to talk to him about the wise use of money, but I wasn't going to destroy his moment of immediate gratification—for him a moment of great beauty.

Next comes the teacher. In the ghetto one does not lay the blame on the board of education and the whole corrupt system or realize that no matter how much a teacher wants to teach she cannot in those conditions. One does not realize that it is not the teacher's fault that a child has no breakfast and may not have lunch, that he may have to go to the poolroom to bum money for potato chips and an orange soda, which may be all he eats that day. How can you teach such a child? How can you teach children when you have forty in a class and two disruptive children who need psychiatric care? The ghetto mother knows only that the teacher is there and is Jewish. And she does not think the Jewish teacher cares whether her child learns or not.

Then comes the welfare worker. If you know anything about welfare you know that spying is part of the system. Sneaking around on weekends to find out if there are men's shoes or pants hanging in the closet, or whether a man has been in the house for the weekend, is part of the job. One method by which the relief rolls are decreased is finding a man in the house.

We must get at these problems not on the basis of urging people merely to change their attitudes or of misinterpreting the Kerner Report on civil disorders. That report does not say that Americans are racist. If it did, the only answer would be to line everybody up, all 200 million of us, then line up 200,000 psychiatrists, and have us all lie on couches for ten years trying to understand the problem and for ten years more learning how to deal with it. All over the country people are beating their breasts crying *mea culpa*—"I'm so sorry that I am a racist"—which means, really, that they want to cop out because if racism is to be solved on an individual psychological basis, then there is little hope.

What the Kerner Report is really saying is that the *institutions* of America brutalize not only Negroes but also whites who are not racists but who in many communities have to use racist institutions. When it is put on that basis, we know we cannot solve the fundamental problem by sitting around examining our innards, but by getting out and fighting for institutional change.

I am all in favor of Jewish businessmen's doing what they can to find jobs here and there for Negroes. But if the choice were between putting energy into that effort and putting the weight of affluent Jewish businessmen behind fundamental social change—in which the government becomes the employer of first and last resort for the hard-core poor—then I would propose the latter choice. Neither individuals nor the private sector of the economy has, or can take, responsibility for full employment in American society. This is the responsibility of all segments of the society and thus, finally, of the government.

The Negro and the poor can be lifted out of poverty only when the government takes the responsibility of creating work for those whom the private sector can no longer use, given the impact of automation and cybernation. American business will not buy sheer muscle power. The sale of muscle power began to diminish when sweatshops began to disappear. American capital is not going to put the undereducated back to work; the society must collectively do that. Private enterprise should do what it can, but there are extreme limitations.

For example, we are not going to find homes for the poor until we have a national land-use policy, as well as a national migration policy. We talk about the urban crisis while Negroes in Mississippi, Georgia, and Alabama are being run off the farms and forced by our present farm policy to Chicago, St. Louis, and New York. One-half million Negroes are leaving the South annually, coming to New York, Chicago, and other ghettos—one-half million coming in while only about 30,000 a year are going out of the ghettos into the suburbs. For those who don't take the trouble to find out, that is how the ghettos grow larger, with more frustration and more despair.

Here are some of the things we are going to have to do in order to deal with white fear and Negro frustration. We must have a two-dollar minimum wage in this country: And small businessmen who cannot afford to pay this wage should be subsidized by the government, just as it subsidizes millionaire railway men and millionaire farmers with price supports.

We are going to have to have public works programs to put these people back to work and to do it without a lot of talk about pre-training. These people don't have to be pre-trained. All they need is to know that there are jobs. John Dewey said that a man learns by doing. I want to go Dewey one better: we must put these people to work learning *while* doing, and while being paid. In World War II we did not ask whether people were too black, or too old, or too young, or too stupid to work. We simply said to them this is a hammer, this is a tool, this is a drill. We built factories and sent these people into the factories. We paid them extraordinarily good wages and in two months they created the miracle of making planes that flew. We can find a peacetime method for doing this—public works for schools, hospitals, psychiatric clinics, new modes of transportation, of cleaning the air, of cleaning the rivers. All of these improvements would benefit not only the poor but also the affluent.

Furthermore, those who cannot work because they are too young, too old, or too sick or who are female heads of large families must have guaranteed incomes. In addition, we must supply free medical care, and we must pay a salary to those capable of going through school. Beyond this we must realize that the ghettos, with their high density of people per room, cannot be improved. We must create new towns and destroy the ghettos, providing work through construction projects and human services to human beings. Nothing short of this will be effective.

These programs will cost us $18.5 billion a year beyond the present level of expenditure and that money can come from the gross national product. But I want to assure businessmen that the people who benefit from the programs are not going to sit on the money when they get it. They are going to act like Americans. They are going to buy all the junk that is advertised, thereby raising the GNP, raising the economic production and growth of the country, and fundamentally adding to its economic stability.

The way things are now, we are twice damned. We are paying $15 billion a year for the support and misdeeds of those who cannot find work and end up in prison or on welfare. If they are provided with work and improve the economy, then we have additional growth plus the $15 billion we are now paying for keeping them on welfare and in jail.

For the things which must be done, I request the understanding, the cooperation, and the aid of Jews. I do so knowing that there is Negro anti-Semitism and knowing how Jews must feel when they hear some Negro extremists talk. To hear these young Negroes spouting material directly from *Mein Kampf* must bring terrible memories, shocking inner turmoil. But in times of confusion, I recommend to Jews what I do for myself in times of confusion. I go back and read the Jewish prophets, mainly Isaiah and Jeremiah. Isaiah and Jeremiah have taught me to be against injustice wherever it is, and first of all in myself. There is a moral problem in abandoning the fight against injustice merely because less than 2 percent of the Negroes in this country are engaging in anti-Semitism. It is a problem which Isaiah and Jeremiah would be the first to point out. The issue never was, and never can be, simply a problem of Jew and gentile or black and white. The problem is man's inhumanity to man and must be fought from that basic principle regardless of race or creed. We must get on with the fight for a coalition of labor forces, of religious forces, of businessmen, of liberal and civil rights groups standing together. White fear, Negro frustration, and anti-Semitism will disappear not because we rail against them but because we bring about a social and economic program to neutralize them.

What is truly at stake is whether we can band together in a great political movement to bring about the socialization of this nation where it needs to be socialized, or whether we are going to permit the nation we love to be torn asunder in a race war in which people who don't want to be on either side may be forced to take sides. That is our problem. That is our challenge.

From an address to the Anti-Defamation League of B'nai B'rith, given on May 6, 1968.

No More Guns

◆ ◆ ◆

[1969]

BLACK PEOPLE HAVE KNOWN VIOLENCE IN AMERICA. They have known the Ku Klux Klan and the White Citizens Councils. They have seen the white mobs in Mississippi and in Cicero, Illinois. They have understood that violence is synonymous with oppression and destruction. Therefore, the use of guns on the Cornell University campus by a group of black students should come as a great shock—and a great sorrow—to all black Americans struggling for freedom and social justice.

Those black students who paraded so arrogantly with their guns will not bring progress to the black community or reform to the universities by imitating the tactics of the Klan. Nothing creative can emerge from their mindless use of force. Rifles will not enhance their education, nor will bullets enlighten their minds. And guns will not provide them with the knowledge and skills they need to help uplift their black brothers who are still suffering in the ghetto.

Those black students were not interested in reforming the university. Otherwise they would not have acted in such a way as to destroy the university. The fundamental cause of their actions lies not in the failure of the university to provide them with the means of obtaining an adequate education. I say this in full knowledge of the tremendous changes which must be made in policy and curriculum if universities are to meet the profound needs of black students—and white students—in our urban and technological society. In this regard Cornell is far ahead of most universities in responding to that challenge.

Those students acted as they did because they are under severe psychological stress. They have come to a predominantly white university from predominantly black high schools where they were brutalized by inferior, segregated education. They now not only find themselves in an alien social environment, but they are being asked to perform academically at a level they have not been prepared to reach. On top of this, they are undergoing a difficult quest for black identity which is aggravated by feelings of guilt at having deserted the ghetto.

Caught in a strange and pressured environment and deprived of the psychological security they had in the ghetto, their impulse is to withdraw from the challenges of the university and establish a separate world for themselves. Once a situation of racial separatism has been established, racial hostility becomes inevitable. Mutual misunderstanding and fear predominate. A psychology of warfare develops, guns are procured, and the university is transformed into an armed camp.

The black students at Cornell only displayed their arms. They used them to intimidate the administration. But built into the situation is the logic of escalation. Violence that is threatened with bravado will become violence used with viciousness, and the main victims will not be the administration but the black students—and the university.

I, therefore, find those guilt-ridden and nihilistic white students who encouraged the blacks in this madness to be equally culpable. So too is the indecisive and flaccid administration, which has abdicated its responsibility to ensure that reason prevails in our institutions of higher learning. Cheap accommodationism will only bring greater violence in the future.

Moreover, by their irresponsible actions, these black students have strengthened the reactionary forces in the society which will obstruct any progress for black Americans. The fear in the white community which produced George Wallace has also been the source of resistance to programs to rebuild our cities, educate our youth, and employ all our adults. These students have increased that fear and have thus further obstructed efforts for real social progress. They have not done a service to their black brothers in the ghetto.

Finally, the central and most profound difficulty was well articulated by Kenneth Clark, who perceived in the confrontation tactics of these students "the destruction of the institutions and the total rejection of the rational and democratic process as a basis for redress of grievances." Thus it is not only the university which is being threatened by these students but all our democratic institutions. And if democracy is destroyed and violence prevails, those who will suffer most will be black Americans. This has been true in the past, and it remains true today. We must repudiate such violence if we are to achieve our liberation.

PART THREE

◆ ◆ ◆

AFRICAN AMERICAN LEADERSHIP

Bayard Rustin Meets Malcolm X

◆ ◆ ◆

[1960]

IN NOVEMBER 1960, Malcolm X and Bayard Rustin discussed their perspectives on race relations in the United States on Radio Station WBAI in New York.

MALCOLM X: In the past two years, the Honorable Elijah Muhammad has become the most talked about black man in America because he is having such miraculous success in getting his program over among the so-called Negro masses. *Time* magazine last year [1959] wrote that he has eliminated from among his followers alcohol, dope addiction, profanity—all of which stems from disrespect of self. He has successfully eliminated stealing and crime among his followers. *Time* also pointed out that he has eliminated adultery and fornication, and prostitution, making black men respect their women, something that has been characteristically absent among our men. *Time* also pointed out that Muslims, followers of Elijah Muhammad, have eliminated juvenile delinquency.

When you think about it, *Time* was giving Mr. Muhammad credit for being one of the greatest moral reformers that has appeared among the so-called Negroes yet. A few months later, *US News and World Report* pointed out that Mr. Muhammad was successful in stressing the importance of economics. The point behind his program—farms to feed our people, factories to manufacture goods for ourselves, businesses to create jobs for ourselves—is to be economically independent rather than sit around waiting for the white man to give us jobs.

What the Honorable Elijah Muhammad has been teaching is not what we have been accused of: nationalism. Nationalism is the political approach to the problems that are confronting the so-called Negro in

America. The aim of the black nationalist is the same as the aim of the Muslim. We are pointing toward the same goal. But the difference is in method. We say the only solution is the religious approach; this is why we stress the importance of a moral reformation. I would like to stress that Mr. Muhammad is not a politician. He does not believe politics is the solution to the so-called Negro's problem. It will take God. God will have to have a hand in it, because the problem of the so-called Negro is different from the problems of any other black people anywhere on this earth since the beginning of time. Every condition of the so-called Negro was pre-ordained and prophesied. And we believe that we are living in the fulfillment of that prophecy today. We believe that our history in America, our experiences at the hands of slave masters, is in line with Biblical prophecy. And we believe that Mr. Muhammad's presence among so-called Negroes here in America is in line with Biblical prophecies.

HOST: Does this involve the creation of a separate state in America?

X: It involves the creation of a black state for the black man if not in America then somewhere on this earth. If not abroad, then here in America. Primarily it involves acquiring some land that the black man can call his own. If the powers that be don't want it here, then they should make it possible for us to do it somewhere else.

HOST: It does involve politics, then?

X: Any religion that does not take into consideration the freedom and the rights of the black man is the wrong religion. But politics as such is not the solution. But the divine solution would have to have that ingredient in it. You can call it politics if you want, but the overall problem of the so-called Negro in America is not a political problem as such, it is an economic problem, a social problem, a mental problem, and a spiritual problem. Only God can solve the whole problem.

BAYARD RUSTIN: I am very happy to be here and I think Malcolm X can clarify some of the questions he has brought up in my mind. I believe the great majority of the Negro people, black people, are not seeking anything from anyone. They are seeking to become full-fledged citizens.

Their ancestors have toiled in this country, contributing greatly to it. The United States belongs to no particular people, and in my view the great majority of Negroes and their leaders take integration as their key word—which means that rightly or wrongly they seek to become an integral part of the United States. We have, I believe, much work yet to do, both politically and through the courts, but I believe we have reached the point where most Negroes, from a sense of dignity and pride, have organized themselves to demand to become an integral part of all the institutions of the U.S. We are doing things by direct action which we feel will further this cause. We believe that justice for all people, including Negroes, can be achieved.

This is not a unique position, and while a controversial one it is certainly not as controversial as the one Malcolm X supports. Therefore I would like to ask him this question: the logic of your position is to say to black people in this country: "We have to migrate and set up some state in Africa." It seems to me that this is where you have to come out.

X: Well, Mr. Rustin, let me say this about "full-fledged" or as they say "first-class" citizenship. Most of the so-called Negro leaders have got the Negro masses used to thinking in terms of second-class citizenship, of which there is no such thing. We who follow the Honorable Elijah Muhammad believe that a man is either a citizen or he is not a citizen. He is not a citizen by degree. If the black man in America is not recognized as a first-class citizen, we don't feel that he is a citizen at all. People come here from Hungary and are integrated into the American way of life overnight, they are not put into any fourth class or third class or any kind of class. The only one who is put in this category is the so-called Negro who is forced to beg the white man to accept him. We feel that if 100 years after the so-called Emancipation Proclamation the black man is still not free, then we don't feel that what Lincoln did set them free in the first place.

RUSTIN: This is all well and good but you are not answering my question.

X: I am answering your question. The black man in America, once he gets his so-called freedom, is still 9,000 miles away from that which he can call home. His problem is different from that of others who are striving for freedom. In other countries they are the majority and the oppressor is the minority. But here, the oppressor is the majority. The white man can just let you sit down. He can find someone else to run his factories.

So we don't think the passive approach can work here. And we don't see that anyone other than the so-called Negro was encouraged to seek freedom this way. The liberals tell the so-called Negro to use the passive approach and turn the other cheek, but they have never told whites who were in bondage to use the passive approach. They don't tell the whites in Eastern Europe who are under the Russian yoke to be passive in their resistance. They give them guns and make heroes out of them and call them freedom fighters. But if a black man becomes militant in his striving against oppression then immediately he is classified as a fanatic.

The white man is posing as the leader of the so-called Free World, and the only way he can be accepted as the leader of the so-called Free World is to be accepted by the majority of the people on this earth, the majority of whom are not white people. And they measure him by the way he treats the nonwhite people here in America. This integration talk is hypocrisy, meant to impress our brothers in Africa or Asia.

RUSTIN: Then what you are saying is that you are opposed to integration because it is not meaningful and can't work. If you believe that integration is not possible, then the logic of your position should be that you are seeking to find a piece of territory and go to it. Either you are advocating the continuation of slavery, since you feel we cannot get integration by the methods that I advocate—which is to say the slow, grinding process of integration—or you are proposing separation.

X: We believe integration is hypocrisy. If the government has to pass laws to let us into their education system, if they have to pass laws to get the white man to accept us in better housing in their neighborhoods, that is the equivalent of holding a gun to their head, and that is hypocrisy. If the white man were to accept us, without laws being passed, then we would go for it.

RUSTIN: Do you think that is going to happen?

X: Well, your common sense tells you, sir, that it's not going to happen.

RUSTIN: But if you cannot do it through the constitutional method, and you cannot do it through brotherhood, then what do you see as the future of black people here and why should they stay?

X: As any intelligent person can see, the white man is not going to share his wealth with his ex-slaves. But God has taught us that the only solution for the ex-slave and the slave master is separation.

RUSTIN: Then you do believe in separation.

X: We absolutely do believe in separation.

RUSTIN: Well, are you being logical by saying, "Let's take over a territory, a part of the U.S." or are you saying, "Let's go outside"?

X: I think both are logical. The land could be anywhere. When the Honorable Elijah Muhammad teaches us that we have to have some land of our own, it means just that; that we have to have some land of our own. Now if the master's intention is good, since we have been faithful workers, I should say faithful servants, all these years, then it seems he should give us some of these states.

RUSTIN: All right, now it is clear that you are advocating separation.

X: Separation not integration.

RUSTIN: All right, now that is clear we can put that out of the way and move on to other things. Isn't there an inconsistency in your economic position? Where are they going to move to? When Moses took his people into the desert, he had a pretty clear idea of where he was going.

X: Well, mentioning Moses is just right. The people that Moses was leading were probably the closest parallel to the problems confronting the so-called Negro. Moses' people were slaves in a land that was not theirs. Moses' people had a slave mentality, they were worshipping a god that was not their own. The Negro in America is the same way, he worships the white man's god, and he is following the white man's religion. They are in the same fix—socially, mentally, politically, spiritually—as the people whom Moses grew up amongst 4,000 years ago. Now, if you'll recall, Moses didn't advocate integration. Moses advocated separation. Nowhere in the Bible will you find that Moses told his people to integrate themselves with Pharaoh. His one doctrine was: Let my people go. That meant separate, not seek integration in the house of bondage. It did not mean to seek the acceptance of the slave master. He said: if you follow me, I will lead you to a land flowing with milk and honey. He never told anyone where that land was. He never told the people where he was taking them, or what they would have to go through. And if you go back to that time you will see that some of them believed in him but many were afraid of the slave master. They didn't believe they could get along without Pharaoh. They didn't believe anybody would give them a job if Pharaoh didn't. They didn't believe they could have an economic system free of Pharaoh. Remember, Pharaoh himself never opposed Moses. He always got magicians to oppose Moses. And today the modern slave master gets a lot of so-called Negro politicians to oppose Elijah Muhammad and work a lot of magic to make the so-called Negroes think he is a crazy man, just as Pharaoh had magicians to make the Hebrews think Moses was some kind of crazy man.

But now let me say this: we feel the Honorable Elijah Muhammad is a modern Moses! Some people say Adam Clayton Powell is a modern Moses and some say Martin Luther King is a modern Moses, but no one can claim to be a modern Moses until he finds out what the first Moses did. And Moses never advocated integration. He advocated complete separation. And he didn't advocate passive resistance, he advocated an eye for an eye and a tooth for a tooth. "Love your enemy." As long as you teach a man that kind of philosophy, he'll remain a slave.

RUSTIN: Well, I am a great advocate of nonviolence, but I think all this talk about whether to integrate or not, and getting involved in the economic life of this country, might be more interesting to me if I knew where you wanted to lead people. But I don't know where you want to go. And I don't think you do, either.

X: Yes we do. We can take some land right here, sir.

RUSTIN: Yes, but if you do not believe in integration, and they don't love you, do you think they are going to give you ten or twelve states?

X: Ah, Mr. Rustin: the predicament that a man is in is what makes him reach certain decisions. America is in the worst predicament of any country in the history of the world.

RUSTIN: I agree....

X: Now what is causing this predicament? The race problem. America's number one problem is the so-called Negro. What must we do? What must I do about this Negro problem? And whenever America is attacked on the race problem, what can she say?

RUSTIN: She can say a lot.

X: What?

RUSTIN: I'll tell you what. I have spent twenty-five years of my life on the race question, and I have been twenty-two times to jail. America can say that until 1954, Negroes could not go to school with whites. Now they can. Negroes could not join trade unions, but now they can. I do not say any of this is perfect, but it is enough for America to be able to answer Russia and China and the rest on the race question and, more important, it is enough to keep the great majority of Negroes feeling that things can improve here. Until you have some place to go to, they are going to want to stay here.

Now, I want to stop right here and get something clear. In [Elijah] Muhammad's mind, this may be a religious matter, but in the minds of his followers the Muslim movement is a psychological and political concept. They do not read the Koran, they read the Bible. They are essentially, culturally, Christian, not Muslims. Why therefore do they call themselves Muslims? Because they do not want to use the same religious terminology that their masters used.

Most Negroes who were brought to America came from the West coast of Africa, long before the spread of Islam to that part of Africa....

X: That is what the white man taught you...after stripping you of your original culture. Now consider the Mali empire—this shows the influence of the Muslim religion in West Africa before the discovery of America.

RUSTIN: I am not putting down the culture of West Africa, I am just saying that the Islamic influence came later. All over West Africa you will find wonderful sculptures which were the sources for much twentieth-century European art, notably Picasso and Cubism. Now these figures could not have been made if the influence of Islam had prevailed, because, as you ought to know, Muslims are not allowed to create figures in their art objects.

X: Let me quote from the *Times* last Sunday. It says that Islam is spreading like wildfire in Nigeria, and Christianity is only skin-deep.

HOST: Does progress involve a greater sense of racial identity?

RUSTIN: I believe it is very important to have a great sense of racial identity because I believe it is quite impossible for people to struggle creatively if they do not truly believe in themselves. I believe that dignity is first. This for me is doubly important because believing in integration and not being told where we are to go, I can see nothing more logical than staying here and struggling for one's rights. Also because of moral principles—but leave them aside for the moment—I can see no way for the Negro to struggle except through nonviolence and a dedication to a strategic nonviolence as a matter of principle. Now therefore if you are going to struggle with nonviolence, to a certain extent you are going to have a certain affection for the people who are mistreating you.

Now affection for the other fellow is not possible without a great sense of dignity of oneself, and therefore the dignity of the Negro for me is not something that is an aside. It is an essential of the struggle. The people in Montgomery were able to struggle and get integration on their buses for a simple reason: ten years before, they could not have done it because they did not believe in themselves. When they believed in themselves they could be socially affectionate to the opposition while at the same time they could be extremely militant and walking and being prepared to sacrifice. I think this is most important and I would therefore agree with Malcolm X that doing away with the ugliness resulting from poverty and their position in society is very necessary and important. We can certainly agree here.

But now let me ask you another question because I want to clarify your position on the Jewish question. Where do you and your group come out on this question? I've been given to understand that your position is—particularly in Harlem—that one of the reasons that Negroes are so oppressed is that the Jews are exploiting them and that the Jews are attempting to exploit the Arab world and stir up difficulties in the Middle East. I'd like to know if this is a misunderstanding I have.

X: If you have read what the Honorable Elijah Muhammad has written and he has written much, I don't think you can find an article where he has ever pointed out the Jew as an exploiter of the black man. He speaks of the exploiter. Period. He doesn't break it down in terms of Frenchmen or Englishmen or a Jew or a German. He speaks of the exploiter and sometimes the man who is the most guilty of exploitation will think you are pointing the finger at him and put out the propaganda that you're anti-this or anti-that. We make no distinction between exploitation and exploiter.

RUSTIN: Now what do you mean that the man who is the most exploited will put out propaganda?

X: I say this, that when a man puts out propaganda against Muslims usually that man feels that the finger is being pointed at him but....

RUSTIN: In other words, you feel that many Jews feel that way.

X: I don't know. But I say that you cannot find anything that the Honorable Elijah Muhammad has written or said that at any time will label the Jew as an exploiter. No sir, but he speaks about the exploitation and oppression and the deception that has been used against the black people in America. Now the man that is guilty [let] whoever is guilty wear that shoe. But he has never made that distinction between a Frenchman—and again—or a Jew or a German. An exploiter is an exploiter, I don't care what kind of label you put on him—you can't duck it.

Making His Mark:
The Autobiography of Malcolm X

◆ ◆ ◆

[1965]

THIS ODYSSEY OF AN AMERICAN NEGRO in search of his identity and place in society really begins before his birth forty years ago in Omaha, Nebraska. He was born Malcolm Little, the son of an educated mulatto West Indian mother and a father who was a Baptist minister on Sundays and a dedicated organizer for Marcus Garvey's Back-to-Africa movement the rest of the week.

The first incident Malcolm recounts, as if it were his welcome to white America, occurred just before he was born. A party of Ku Klux Klanners galloped up to his house, threatened his mother, and left a warning for his father to "stop spreading trouble among the good [Negroes]" and get out of town. They galloped into the night after smashing all the windows. A few years later, the Klan was to make good its threat by burning clown the Littles' Lansing, Michigan, home because Malcolm's father refused to become an Uncle Tom. These were the first in a series of incidents of racial violence...that were to haunt the nights of Malcolm and his family and hang like a pall over the lives of Negroes in the North and South. Five of Reverend Little's six brothers died by violence—four at the hands of white men, one by lynching, and one shot down by Northern police officers. When Malcolm was six, his father was found cut in two by a trolley car with his head bashed in. Malcolm's father had committed "suicide," the authorities said. Early in his life Malcolm concluded that "I too would die by violence.... I do not expect to live long enough to read this book."

Malcolm's early life in the Midwest was not wholly defined by race. Until he went to Boston when he was fourteen, after his mother suffered a mental breakdown from bringing up eight children alone, his friends were often white; there were few Negroes in the small Midwestern towns where he grew up. He recounts with pride how he was elected president of his eighth grade class in an almost totally white school.

But the race problem was always there, although Malcolm, who was light-skinned, tried for a time to think of himself as white or just like anyone else. Even in his family life, color led to conflict that interfered with normal relationships. The Reverend Little was a fierce disciplinarian, but he never laid a hand on his light-skinned son, because unconsciously, according to Malcolm, he had developed respect for white skin. On the other hand, Malcolm's mother, whose father was a white man, was ashamed of this and favored Malcolm's darker brothers and sisters. Malcolm wrote that he spent his life trying to purge this tainted white blood of a rapist from his veins.

Race also set the limits on his youthful ambitions during what he describes as his "mascot years" in a detention home run by whites with mixed feelings of affection and superiority toward him. One of the top students in his school and a member of the debating club, Malcolm went to an English teacher he admired and told him of his ambition to become a lawyer. "Mr. Ostrowsky looked surprised and said, 'Malcolm, one of life's first needs is for us to be realistic...a lawyer, that's no realistic goal for a nigger...you're good with your hands...why don't you plan on carpentry?'" How many times has this scene been repeated in various forms in schoolrooms across the country? It was at this point, Malcolm writes, "that I began to change inside. I drew away from white people."

Too many people want to believe that Malcolm, "the angry black man, sprang full grown from the bowels of the Harlem ghetto." These chapters on his childhood are essential reading for anyone who wants to understand the plight of American Negroes.

Malcolm Little was fourteen when he took the Greyhound to Boston to live with his half-sister, Ella, who had fought her way into the Boston "black bourgeoisie." The "400," as they were called, lived on "the Hill," only one step removed socially, economically, and geographically from the ghetto ("the Town"). Malcolm writes that "a big percentage of the Hill dwellers were in Ella's category—Southern strivers and scramblers and West Indian Negroes, whom both the New Englanders and

Southerners called 'Black Jews.' " Ella owned some real estate and her own home, and like the first Jews who arrived in the New World, she was determined to shepherd new immigrants and teach them the strange ways of city life. There were deep bonds between Ella and her younger brother, and she tried to help him live a respectable life on the Hill.

But for Malcolm the 400 were only "a big-city version of those 'successful' Negro bootblacks and janitors back in Lansing...8 out of 10 of the Hill Negroes of Roxbury...actually worked as menials and servants.... I don't know how many 40- and 50-year-old errand boys went down the Hill dressed as ambassadors in black suits and white collars to downtown jobs 'in government,' 'in finance,' or 'in law.' " Malcolm instead chose "the Town," where for the first time he felt he was part of a people.

Unlike the thousands of Negro migrants who poured into the Northern ghettos, Malcolm had a choice. But from the moment he made it, the options narrowed. He got a job at the Roseland Ballroom, where all the jazz greats played. His title was shoeshine boy but his real job was to hustle whiskey, prophylactics, and women to Negroes and whites. He got his first conk and zoot suit and a new identity, "Red," and his secondary education began before he was fifteen. "I was...schooled well, by experts in such hustles as the numbers, pimping, con games of many kinds, peddling dope, and thievery of all sorts, including armed robbery."

It is significant that it was Malcolm's good qualities—his intelligence, integrity, and distaste for hypocrisy—as well as his sickness that made him choose crime rather than what passed in the Negro community for a respectable bourgeois life. Later he moved on to bigger things in Harlem, became "Detroit Red," went on dope, and at one time carried three guns.

His description of the cutthroat competition between the hustlers and their fraternity is both frightening and moving. "As in the case of any jungle," he writes, "the hustler's every waking hour is lived with both the practical and the subconscious knowledge that if he ever relaxes, if he ever slows down, the other hungry, restless foxes, ferrets, wolves, and vultures out there with him won't hesitate to make him their prey." He summed up his morality at the time: "The only thing I considered wrong was what I got caught doing wrong...and everything I did was done by instinct to survive." As a "steerer" of uptown rich whites to Harlem "sex specialties," he recounts perversions with racial overtones, of white men begging to be beaten by black women or paying large amounts to witness interracial sex that make Genet's *The Balcony* seem inhibited by comparison.

"Detroit Red" was a limited success in his trade for four years. But even in this business, success was limited by race. The big operators, the successful, respectable, and safe executives of policy, dope, and prostitution rackets, were white and lived outside the ghetto.

Malcolm left Harlem to return to Boston, and a few months later was caught as the head of a burglary gang. In February 1946, not quite twenty-one, he was sentenced to ten years in prison, though the average sentence for burglary was about two years—the price for his being caught with his white girl friend and her sister.

Most of the first year in prison, Malcolm writes, he spent in solitary confinement, cursing: "My favorite targets were the Bible and God." Malcolm got a new name from the other prisoners—"Satan"—and plenty of time to think. He went through what he described as a great spiritual crisis, and, as a result, he, the man who cursed God, bowed down and prayed to Allah. It will be difficult for those readers who have never been in prison to understand the psychological torment that prisoners experience, their feelings of isolation, their need to totally commit their minds to something outside of themselves. Men without any of the external economic symbols of status seek security in a religion, philosophy, or ideology. Malcolm particularly, with his great feelings of rebelliousness, hatred, and internal conflict, turned to books and ideas for relief. When his brothers and sisters wrote to him that they had become followers of Elijah Muhammad and sent him Elijah's teachings, Malcolm seized on the tracts. Stimulated, he read other books on religion and philosophy voraciously. In his spiritual and psychological crisis he underwent religious conversion.

He took on a new identity and became Malcolm X, a follower of Elijah Muhammad. Now he had a God to love and obey and a white devil responsible for his plight. Many Negro prisoners accepted the "Messenger," Elijah Muhammad, for similar reasons. Excluded from American society, they were drawn to another one, the Nation of Islam. (This analysis of why Malcolm joined the Muslims is mine, for although Malcolm writes about Muslim ideas, nowhere does he discuss the reasons for his conversion beyond a surface level.)

Out of prison, Malcolm, while remaining religious, arrived at a balanced view of the more fantastic elements of Elijah's teachings and at a deeper understanding of one of the driving forces: "So many of the survivors whom I knew as tough hyenas and wolves of the streets in the old days now were so pitiful. They had known all the angles, but beneath that surface they were poor, ignorant, untrained men; life had eased up on them and hyped them.... I was thankful to Allah that I had become a Muslim and escaped their fate."

Alex Haley, who assisted Malcolm with the book, rightly commends him for deciding not to rewrite the first parts of the book and make it a polemic against his old leader, although in the interim they had broken and now were in competition with each other. As a result, the book interestingly shows changes in Malcolm's thinking.

After seven years in prison, Detroit Red emerged as Malcolm X and was soon to be the brightest star of the Nation of Islam. But as in every conversion, the man himself was not entirely reborn. Malcolm brought with him his traits of the past—the shrewd and competitive instincts learned on the ghetto streets, combined now with the language and thoughts of the great philosophers of Western culture he applied from reading Hegel, Kant, and Nietzsche, and great Negro intellectuals like Du Bois. Remaining, too, with his burning ambition to succeed, was the rebellious anger of his youth for being denied a place in society commensurate with his abilities. But on the other side of the coin was a desire for fraternity, family, and respectability.

Because of his ability, he was sent to New York, where he struck a responsive chord with a great many Harlem Negroes. The Nationalist sects provided an arena of struggle for power and status denied lower-class Negroes in the outside world.

But the same qualities that made him a successful ghetto organizer soon brought him info conflict with other Muslim leaders, especially Elijah's children and prospective heirs. They saw Malcolm as a threat to their domain and apparently were able to convince Elijah that there was a threat to himself as well. For although Malcolm always gave corollary credit to Elijah—and the limits set upon him by Elijah's demands made many underestimate the exceptional nature of his mind—he could not totally constrain his brilliance, pride, or ambition. "Only by being two people could I have worked harder in the service of the Nation of Islam. I had every gratification that I wanted. I had helped bring about the progress and additional impact such that none could call us liars when we called Mr. Muhammad the most powerful black man in America."

As Malcolm's star rose higher in the western sky, Mr. Muhammad saw his eastern star setting and grew jealous. The conflict grew, although Malcolm made efforts toward conciliation. Finally, there was a total break that could be fatal to the erring Muslim who was cast away. Malcolm was aware of the dangers. "I hadn't hustled in the streets for nothing. I knew I was being set up.... As any official in the Nation of Islam would instantly have known, any death-talk for me could have been approved of—if not actually initiated—by only one man." Later, just before his death, Malcolm said the attempt to murder him would come from a much greater source than the Muslims; he never revealed about whom he was talking.

Under a death sentence and without money or any substantial organization, Malcolm opted for action, although it was unclear whether he was running away from or toward something as he began another phase of his odyssey—a pilgrimage to Mecca, where he became El-Hajj Malik El-Shabazz. Throughout his many conversions and trans-formations, he never was more American than during his trip to Mecca. Because his ankles were not flexible enough, he was unable to sit prop-erly cross-legged on the traditional Muslim rug with the others, and at first he shrank from reaching into the common food pot. Like many American tourists, he projected desires for hospitality and fraternity, frustrated at home, on the Muslims he met, most of whom he could not communicate with because of the language barrier. Back in America, he acknowledged that it would be a long time before the Negro was ready to make common struggle with the Africans and Arabs.

In Mecca, Malcolm also dramatically announced that he had changed his view on integration, because he had seen true brotherhood there between black and white Muslims. In reality he had begun chang-ing his attitude on integration and the civil rights movement many months before, as the divisions between him and Elijah Muhammad widened. Partway through the book his attacks on the movement became muted, and in the epilogue Haley concludes that Malcolm "had a reluctant admiration for Dr. Martin Luther King."

The roots of Malcolm's ambivalence were much more profound than personal opportunism. In a touching confession of dilemma he told Haley, "the so-called 'moderate' civil rights organizations avoided him as 'too militant' and the 'so-called militants' avoided him as 'too moderate.' 'They won't let me turn the corner!' he once exclaimed. 'I'm caught in a trap!' " Malcolm was moving toward the mainstream of the civil rights movement when his life was cut short, but he still had quite a way to go. His anti-Semitic comments are a symptom of this malaise.

Had he been able to "turn the corner," he would have made an enormous contribution to the struggle for equal rights. As it was, his contribution was substantial. He brought hope and a measure of dignity to thousands of despairing ghetto Negroes. His extremism made the mainstream civil rights groups more respectable by comparison and helped them wrest substantial concessions from the power structure. Malcolm himself clearly understood the complicated role he played. At a Selma rally, while Dr. King was in jail, Malcolm said, "Whites better be glad Martin Luther King is rallying the people because other forces are waiting to take over if he fails." Of course, he never frightened the racists and the reactionaries as much as he made liberals feel uncomfortable, and moderates used his extremism as an excuse for inaction.

Behind the grim visage on television that upset so many white Americans here was a compassionate and often gentle man with a sense of humor. A testament to his personal honesty was that he died broke and money had to be raised for his funeral and family.

Upset by the comments in the African and Asian press criticizing the United States government for Malcolm's fate, Carl T. Rowan, director of the United States Information Agency, held up some foreign papers and told a Washington audience, according to Alex Haley, "...All this about an ex-convict, ex-dope peddler, who became a racial fanatic." Yes, all this and more, before we can understand. Malcolm's autobiography, revealing little-known aspects of his life and character, makes that tortured journey more understandable.

One of the book's shortcomings is that M. S. Handler and Haley, in their sensitive and insightful supplementary comments, make no comprehensive estimate of Malcolm X as a political leader. His often conflicting roles in the civil rights movement are described rather than analyzed. Perhaps this couldn't be helped, for Haley writes that Malcolm wanted a chronicler, not an interpreter. Obviously, Malcolm was not ready to make a synthesis of his ideas and an evaluation of his political role.

Shortly after Malcolm's death Tom Kahn and I wrote in *New America* and *Dissent:* "Now that he is dead, we must resist the temptation to idealize Malcolm X, to elevate charisma to greatness. History's judgment of him will surely be ambiguous. His voice and words were cathartic, channeling into militant verbiage emotions that otherwise might have run a violently destructive course. But having described the evil, he had no program for attacking it. With rare skill and feeling he articulated angry subterranean moods more widespread than any of us like to admit. But having blown the trumpet, he could summon, even at the very end, only a handful of followers."

Of course we cannot judge political effectiveness by numbers alone, but we cannot ignore his inability to build a movement. As a spokesman for Negro anger and frustration, he left his mark on history, but as a militant political leader he failed—and the Negro community needed both. Till the end, his program was a maze of contradictions. He was a brilliant psychologist when it came to articulating the emotions and thoughts of ghetto Negroes, but he knew virtually nothing about economics and, more important, his program had no relevance to the needs of lower-class Negroes. His conception of the economic roots of the problem is reflected in such remarks as "it is because black men do not own and control their community retail establishments that they cannot stabilize their own communities." And he advocates, as a solution, that Negroes who buy so many cars and so much expensive whiskey should own automobile franchises and distilleries. Malcolm was urging Negroes to pool their resources into small business establishments at a time when small businesses were declining under the pressure of big business and when an unplanned technological revolution was creating massive unemployment for unskilled Negroes. Malcolm's solutions were in fact almost a mirror image of many proposals made by white economic moderates; those advocates of "self-help" without a massive program for jobs remind me of no one so much as those black nationalist sects and their "build it yourself" black economy without capital. In short, Malcolm's economic program was not radical. It was, in fact, petty bourgeois.

Malcolm got a wide hearing in the ghetto because large sections of the Negro working class were being driven into the "underclass" and made part of the rootless mass by the vicissitudes of the economy. He articulated the frustration and anger of these masses, and they admired his outspoken attack on the racists and white hypocrites. But while thousands came to his funeral (I was there, too, to pay my respects), few joined his organization. Nor should it be surprising that the Negro masses did not support his proposed alliance of black Americans, Africans, and

Arabs, including such leaders as Prince Faisal. For what did a Harlem Negro, let alone an Arab Bedouin, have in common with a feudal prince like Faisal? And at home Malcolm maintained an uneasy coexistence with the Harlem political machine. Today Malcolm's organization, the OAAU, hardly exists. In addition, he never clearly understood that, as progress was made toward social integration, the problem for America's Negroes would become just as much one of class as of race.

Malcolm was with the Negro masses, but he was not of them. His experience and ambitions separated him from working-class Negroes. But to say this is not enough. In a sense Malcolm's life was tragic on a heroic scale. He had choices but never took the easy or comfortable ones. If he had, he might today be, as he said, a successful lawyer, sipping cocktails with other members of the black bourgeoisie. He chose instead to join the Negro masses who never had this freedom of choice. And before his death he was working toward a more creative approach to the problems of the ghetto. Perhaps he might have been successful in turning this corner.

After reflecting on the old days at Mosque 7, shortly before he was killed, Malcolm told Haley, "That was a bad scene, brother. The sickness and madness of those days—I'm glad to be free of them. It's a time for martyrs now. And if I'm to be one, it will be in the cause of brotherhood."

Our journey through the madness of racism continues, and there is much we can learn about both the sickness and the cure from Malcolm X.

In Defense of Muhammad Ali

◆ ◆ ◆

[1967]

THOUGH WE MAY NOT AGREE with the politics of the Black Muslims, we cannot contest their right to consider themselves a genuine religious group. In any case, our belief in the principles of individual and religious liberty should be of more importance than any disagreements we might have with the Muslims. That is the basis on which all religious differences ought to be approached, for the more one disagrees with people, the more tempting it becomes to violate their privileges. This has not been sufficiently recognized in the case of Muhammad Ali. His efforts to seek deferment from the armed services are being judged less on their legitimate merits than on the basis of personal and religious animosity.

The most fundamental example of this concerns his application to be deferred on the grounds of his Muslim ministry. There are many precedents for this in our society; hundreds of other ministers have sought deferment on the same grounds and have not been denied it. Because one of our traditions guarantees the separation of church and state, the authorities do not usually seek to determine for themselves the credentials of any Baptist, Presbyterian, or other minister. They recognize not only the definitions supplied by these religions, but also the autonomous privilege of these religions to make their own determinations. In the case of Ali and the Muslims, the authorities seem to be insisting on the right to make their own determination. The Constitution clearly warns against any official establishment of religion, but it would seem that the authorities, by now insisting on the right to determine what is or isn't a legitimate minister, or what is or isn't a legitimate religion, are taking a clear position on the establishment of religion.

Another reason for public hostility toward Muhammad Ali is that he changed his name. The great majority of the press and public have refused to respect his wishes or his right. This is rather strange, considering that no one refers to Cary Grant as "Archibald Alexander Leach who wants to be called Cary Grant" or to Billy Graham as "William Franklin alias Billy Graham." Nor did anyone contest the right of Norma Jean Baker to be known as Marilyn Monroe. The fact that neither the press nor the society shares a belief in Muhammad Ali's way of life is hardly a sufficient excuse for them to violate his personal privilege.

Considering how lucrative it would have been for him to become a "playboy boxer," and the great losses and penalties he now faces by deciding to confront the convictions in himself, his courage is more to be admired than vilified—particularly in a period when there is so little consistency between belief and action.

Finally, the boxing authorities, because of their contempt for due process, have further prejudiced the entire proceedings against Ali by depriving him of his heavyweight championship even while his case is still being determined in the courts. All this aside, we must be horrified, and to some extent amused, that men who control a sport that is not notable for its abundance of ethical scruples should now rush so quickly to cloak it in the mantle of piety and morality.

Dr. King's Painful Dilemma

◆ ◆ ◆

[1967]

ONE OF THE UNDERTONES OF THE ATTACKS in the white press on Dr. Martin Luther King's recent statements on Vietnam may well reveal that America really does not believe that Negroes, as citizens, have yet come of age. Like children, we should be seen but not heard.

I say this because the criticism of Dr. King was not limited to an evaluation of his proposals and his strategy for ending the war. It was, by and large, an attack on his right to debate, or even to discuss, Vietnam. In substance, many editorials seemed to be asking, "What is Dr. King doing discussing Vietnam?" or "Who gave him the right to make proposals about our [meaning white America's] foreign policy?"

In a democracy all citizens have not only a right but also a solemn duty to vote, to advise on domestic affairs, and to address themselves to all aspects of foreign policy. As Americans, Dr. King and all other Negroes have such a duty. First, it is their duty as citizens. Second, it is their duty as black citizens, considering that twice as many Negroes proportionately are fighting and dying in Vietnam.

Equally compelling, for Dr. King, is the fact that he is a Nobel Peace Prize winner. As such he has a moral obligation to speak out for peace according to his insight as a man of God and in keeping with his conscience as a free man.

On the other hand, however, if Dr. King makes proposals that others disagree with, they have the duty to differ with him on the merits or demerits of his proposals. Dr. King knows this, and he will expect no less. Such honest differences may encourage Dr. King to embark upon a reexamination of his position. Such honest discussion will encourage all of us to keep the vexing problem of Vietnam in constant review.

This process might very well turn out to be as illuminating for Dr. King as for the rest of us. But to assume that any individual (particularly any civil rights worker) does not have the right to discuss any problem that affects his nation is to propose that such an individual is still a second-class citizen.

The Negro community should, and I hope will, continue to enter all discussions relative to their experience as Americans. We must, of course, be prepared to accept the political consequences and responsibilities that result from taking such a position.

Perhaps the real question is this: how should Negroes who have a concern for peace organize to express these sentiments? Should they organize through the existing peace organizations, or should they organize within the civil rights movements? I mast say that I would consider the involvement of the civil rights organizations as such in peace activities distinctly unprofitable and perhaps even suicidal.

Yet there must be an opportunity for Negroes to work for peace. For many Negroes do take a deep and genuine interest in the problems of war and peace, if for no other reason than because of the disproportionate number of Negroes in Vietnam.

This is not to say that there is going to be any tremendous onrush of Negroes into the peace movement. The immediate problems facing Negroes are so vast and crushing that they have little time or energy to focus upon international crises.

Nevertheless, when Dr. King speaks out as he recently did, we are forced to recognize and clarify the problems of strategy, tactics, and philosophy that confront the Negro freedom movement in a time of war. Dr. King is, no doubt, more aware today of the subtleties of these conflicts than he was before he made his statement.

Reflections on the Death of Martin Luther King, Jr.

◆ ◆ ◆

[1968]

THE MURDER OF DR. MARTIN LUTHER KING, JR., has thrust a lance into the soul of America. The pain is most shattering to the Negro people. We have lost a valiant son, a symbol of hope, and an eloquent spirit that inspired masses of people. Such a man does not appear often in the history of social struggle. When his presence signifies that greatness can inhabit a black skin, those who must deny this possibility stop at nothing to remove it. Dr. King now joins a long list of victims of desperate hate in the service of insupportable lies, myths, and stereotypes.

For me, the death of Dr. King brings deep personal grief. I had known and worked with him since the early days of the Montgomery bus protest in 1955, through the founding of the Southern Christian Leadership Conference, the Prayer Pilgrimage in 1957, the youth marches for integrated schools in 1958 and 1959, and the massive March on Washington in 1963.

Though his senior by twenty years, I came to admire the depth of his faith in nonviolence, in the ultimate vindication of the democratic process, and in the redeeming efficacy of social commitment and action. And underlying this faith was a quiet courage grounded in the belief that the triumph of justice, however long delayed, was inevitable. Like so many others, I watched his spirit take hold in the country, arousing long-slumbering consciences and giving shape to a new social movement. With that movement came new hopes, aspirations, and expectations. The stakes grew higher.

At such a time, so great a loss can barely be sustained by the Negro people. But the tragedy and shame of April 4 darken the entire nation as it teeters on the brink of crisis. And let no one mistake the signs: our country is in deadly serious trouble. This needs to be said because one of the ironies of life in an advanced industrialized society is that many people can go about their daily business without being directly affected by the ominous rumblings at the bottom of the system.

Yet we are at one of the great crossroads in our history, and the alternatives before us grow more stark with every summer's violence. In moments like these there is a strong temptation to succumb to utter despair and helpless cynicism. It is indeed hard to maintain a clear perspective, a reliable sense of where events are heading. But this is exactly what we are called upon to do. Momentous decisions are about to be made—consciously or by default—and the consequences will leave not one corner of this land, nor any race or class, untouched.

Where, then, do we go from here?

We are a house divided. Of this Dr. King's murder is a stunning reminder. Every analysis, strategy, and proposal for a way out of the American dilemma must begin with the recognition that a perilous polarization is taking place in our society. Part of it is no doubt due to the war in Vietnam, part to the often remarked generation gap. But generations come and go and so do foreign policies. The issue of race, however, has been with us since our earliest beginnings as a nation. I believe it is even deeper and sharper than the other points of contention. It has bred fears, myths, and violence over centuries. It is the source of dark and dangerous irrationality, a current of social pathology running through our history and dimming our brighter achievements.

Most of the time the reservoir of racism remains stagnant. But—and this has been true historically for most societies—when major economic, social, or political crises arise, the backwaters are stirred and latent racial hostility comes to the surface. Scapegoats must be found, simple targets substituted for complex problems. The frustration and insecurity generated by these problems find an outlet in notions of racial superiority and inferiority. Very often we find that the most virulent hostility to Negroes exists among ethnic groups that only recently "made it" themselves or that are still near the bottom of the ladder. They need to feel that somebody is beneath them. (This is a problem which the labor movement has had to face more acutely perhaps than any comparable institution in American life. And it's a problem which some of labor's middle-class critics have not had to cope with at all.)

Negroes are reacting to this hostility with a counter-hostility. Some say the white man has no soul; others say he is barbaric, uncivilized; others proclaim him racially inferior. As is so often the case, such a *reaction* is the exaggerated obverse of the original *action*.

And in fact it incorporates elements of white stereotypes of Negroes. ("Soul," for example, so far as it is definable, seems to consist in part of rhythm, spontaneity, pre-industrial sentimentality, a footloose anti-regimentation, etc.—qualities attributed to Negroes by many whites, though in different words.)

This reaction among Negroes is not so new as many white people think. What is new is the intensity with which it is felt among some Negroes and the violent way it has been expressed in recent years. For this, the conservatives and reactionaries would blame the civil rights movement and the federal government. And in the very specific sense, we must conclude that they are right.

One effect of the civil rights struggle in the past ten years has been to convince a generation of young Negroes that their place in society is no longer predetermined at birth. We demonstrated that segregationist barriers could be toppled, that social relations were not fixed for all time, that change was on the agenda. The federal government reinforced this new consciousness with its many pronouncements that racial integration and equality were the official goals of American society.

The reactionaries would tell us that these hopes and promises were unreasonable to begin with and should never have been advanced. They equate stability with the preservation of the established hierarchy of social relations, and chaos with the reform of that unjust arrangement. The fact is that the promises were reasonable, justified, and long overdue. Our task is not to rescind them—how do you rescind the promise of equality?—but to implement them fully and vigorously.

This task is enormously complicated by the polarization now taking place on the race issue. We are caught in a vicious cycle: inaction on the poverty and civil rights fronts foments rioting in the ghettos; the rioting encourages vindictive inaction. Militancy, extremism, and violence grow in the black community; racism, reaction, and conservatism gain ground in the white community.

Personal observation and the law of numbers persuade me that a turn to the right comprises the larger part of the polarization. This, of course, is a perilous challenge not only to the Negro but also to the labor movement, to liberals and civil libertarians, to all of the forces for social progress. We must meet that challenge in 1968.

Meanwhile, a process of polarization is also taking place within the Negro community and, with the murder of Dr. King, it is likely to be accelerated.

Ironically and sadly, this will occur precisely because of the broad support Dr. King enjoyed among Negroes. That support cut across ideological and class lines. Even those Negro spokesmen who could not accept, and occasionally derided, Dr. King's philosophy of nonviolence and reconciliation, admired and respected his unique national and international position. They were moved by his sincerity and courage. Not, perhaps, since the days of Booker T. Washington—when 90 percent of all Negroes lived in the South and were occupationally and socially more homogeneous than today—had any one man come so close to being *the* Negro leader. He was a large unifying force and his assassination leaves an enormous vacuum. The diverse strands he linked together have fallen from his hands.

The murder of Dr. King tells Negroes that if one of the greatest among them is not safe from the assassin's bullet, then what can the least of them hope for? In this context, those young black militants who have resorted to violence feel vindicated. "Look what happened to Dr. King," they say. "He was nonviolent; he didn't hurt anybody. And look what they did to him. If we have to go down, let's go down shooting. Let's take whitey with us."

Make no mistake about it: a great psychological barrier has now been placed between those of us who have urged nonviolence as the road to social change and the frustrated, despairing youth of the ghettos. Dr. King's assassination is only the latest example of our society's determination to teach young Negroes that violence pays. We pay no attention to them until they take to the streets in riotous rebellion. Then we make minor concessions—not enough to solve their basic problems, but enough to persuade them that we know they exist. "Besides," the young militants will tell you, "this country was built on violence. Look at what we did to the Indians. Look at our television and movies. And look at Vietnam. If the cause of the Vietnamese is worth taking up guns for, why isn't the cause of the black man right here in Harlem?"

These questions are loaded and oversimplified, to be sure, and they obscure the real issues and the programmatic direction we must take to meet them. But what we must answer is the bitterness and disillusionment that give rise to these questions. If our answers consist of mere words, they will fall on deaf ears. They will not ring true until ghetto-trapped Negroes experience significant and tangible progress in the daily conditions of their lives—in their jobs, income, housing, education, health care, political representation, etc. This must be understood by those often well-meaning people who, frightened by the polarization, would retreat from committed action into homilies about racial understanding.

We are indeed a house divided. But the division between race and race, class and class, will not be dissolved by massive infusions of brotherly sentiment. The division is not the result of bad sentiment and therefore will not be healed by rhetoric. Rather the division and the bad sentiments are both reflections of vast and growing inequalities in our socio-economic system—inequalities of wealth, of status, of education, of access to political power. Talk of brotherhood and "tolerance" (are we merely to "tolerate" one another?) might once have had a cooling effect, but increasingly it grates on the nerves. It evokes contempt not because the values of brotherhood are wrong—they are more important now than ever—but because it just does not correspond to the reality we see around us. And such talk does nothing to eliminate the inequalities that breed resentment and deep discontent.

The same is true of most "black power" sloganeering, in which I detect powerful elements of conservatism. Leaving aside those extremists who call for violent revolution, the black power movement embraces a diversity of groups and ideologies. It contains a strong impulse toward withdrawal from social struggle and action, a retreat back into the ghetto, avoidance of contact with the white world. This impulse may, I fear, be strengthened by the assassination of Dr. King.

This brand of black power has much in common with the conservative white American's view of the Negro. It stresses self-help ("Why don't those

Negroes pull themselves up by their own bootstraps like my ancestors did?"). It identifies the Negro's main problems in psychological terms, calls upon him to develop greater self-respect and dignity by studying Negro history and culture and by building independent institutions.

In all of these ideas there is some truth. But taken as a whole, the trouble with this thinking is that it assumes that the Negro can solve his problems by himself, in isolation from the rest of the society. The fact is, however, that the Negro did not create these problems for himself and he cannot solve them by himself.

Dignity and self-respect are not abstract virtues that can be cultivated in a vacuum. They are related to one's job, education, residence, mobility, family responsibilities, and other circumstances that are determined by one's economic and social status in the society. Whatever deficiencies in dignity and self-respect may be laid to the Negro are the consequence of generations of segregation, discrimination, and exploitation. Above all, in my opinion, these deficiencies result from systematic exclusion of the Negro from the economic mainstream.

This exclusion cannot be reversed—but only perpetuated—by gilding the ghettos. A "separate but equal" economy for black Americans is impossible. In any case, the ghettos do not have the resources needed for massive programs of abolishing poverty, inferior education, slum housing, and the other problems plaguing the Negro people. These resources must come primarily from the federal government, which means that the fate of the Negro is unavoidably tied to the political life of this nation.

It is time, therefore, that all of us, black and white alike, put aside rhetoric that obscures the real problems. It is precisely because we have so long swept these incendiary problems under the rug that they are now exploding all around us, insisting upon our attention. We can divert our eyes no longer.

The life and death of Martin Luther King are profoundly symbolic. From the Montgomery bus protest to the Memphis sanitation workers strike, his career embodies the internal development, the unfolding, the evolution of the modern civil rights struggle.

That struggle began as a revolt against segregation in public accommodations—buses, lunch counters, libraries, schools, parks. It was aimed at ancient and obsolete institutional arrangements and mores left over from an earlier social order in the South, an order that was being undermined and transformed by economic and technological forces.

As the civil rights movement progressed, winning victory after victory in public accommodations and voting rights, it became increasingly conscious that these victories would not be secure or far-reaching without a radical improvement in the Negro's socioeconomic position. And so the movement reached out of the South into the urban centers of the North and West. It moved from public accommodations to employment, welfare, housing, education—to find a host of problems the nation had let fester for a generation.

But these were not problems that affected the Negro alone or that could be solved easily with the movement's traditional protest tactics. These injustices were imbedded not in ancient and obsolete institutional arrangements but in the priorities of powerful vested interests, in the direction of public policy, in the allocation of our national resources. Sit-ins could integrate a lunch counter, but massive social investments and imaginative public policies were required to eliminate the deeper inequalities.

Dr. King came to see that this was too big a job for the Negro alone, that it called for an effective coalition with the labor movement. As King told the AFL-CIO convention in 1961:

> Negroes are almost entirely a working people. There are pitifully few Negro millionaires and few Negro employers. Our needs are identical with labor's needs—decent wages, fair working conditions, livable housing, old age security, health and welfare measures, conditions in which families can grow, have education for their children and respect in the community.
>
> That is why Negroes support labor's demands and fight laws which curb labor.
>
> That is why the labor-hater and labor-baiter is virtually always a twin-headed creature spewing anti-Negro epithets from one mouth and anti-labor propaganda from the other mouth.

The duality of interest of labor and Negroes makes
any crisis which lacerates you, a crisis from which we
bleed. As we stand on the threshold of the second
half of the twentieth century, a crisis confronts us
both. Those who in the second half of the nineteenth century could not tolerate organized labor
have had a rebirth of power and seek to regain the
despotism of that era while retaining the wealth
and privileges of the twentieth century.

...The two most dynamic and cohesive liberal
forces in the country are the labor movement and
the Negro freedom movement.

...I look forward confidently to the day when
all who work for a living will be one, with no thought
to their separateness as Negroes, Jews, Italians, or
any other distinctions.

This will be the day when we shall bring into
full realization the American dream—a dream yet
unfulfilled. A dream of equality of opportunity, of
privilege and property widely distributed; a dream
of a land where men will not take necessities from
the many to give luxuries to the few; a dream of a land
where men will not argue that the color of a man's
skin determines the content of his character; a
dream of a nation where all our gifts and resources
are held not for ourselves alone but as instruments
of service for the rest of humanity; the dream of a
country where every man will respect the dignity
and worth of human personality—that is the dream.

And so Dr. King went to Memphis to help 1,300 sanitation workers—
almost all of them black—to win union recognition, dues checkoff,
higher wages, and better working conditions. And in the midst of this
new phase of his work he was assassinated. Since then, the sanitation
workers have won their fight. But the real battle is just beginning.

The Report of the National Advisory Commission on Civil
Disorders is the latest in a series of documents—official, semiofficial,
and unofficial—that have sought to arouse the American people to the

great dangers we face and to the price we are likely to pay if we do not multiply our efforts to eradicate poverty and racism.

The recent recommendations parallel those urged by civil rights and labor groups over the years. The legislative work of the Leadership Conference on Civil Rights, of the National Association for the Advancement of Colored People, and of the AFL-CIO has been vital to the progress we have made so far. This work is now proceeding effectively on a broad coordinated basis. It has pinpointed the objectives for which the entire nation must strive.

We have got to provide meaningful work at decent wages for every employable citizen. We must guarantee an adequate income for those unable to work. We must build millions of low-income housing units, tear down the slums, and rebuild our cities. We need to build schools, hospitals, mass transit systems. We need to construct new, integrated towns. As President Johnson has said, we need to build a "second America" between now and the year 2000.

It is in the context of this national reconstruction that the socio-economic fate of the Negro will be determined. Will we build into the second America new, more sophisticated forms of segregation and exploitation or will we create a genuinely open, integrated, and democratic society? Will we have a more equitable distribution of economic resources and political power, or will we sow the seeds of more misery, unrest, and division?

Because of men like Martin Luther King, it is unlikely that the American Negro can ever again return to the old order. But it is up to us, the living, black and white, to realize Dr. King's dream.

This means, first of all, to serve notice on the 90th Congress that its cruel indifference to the plight of our cities and of the poor—even after the martyrdom of Dr. King—will not be tolerated by the American people. In an economy as fabulously productive as ours, a balanced budget cannot be the highest virtue and, in any case, it cannot be paid for by the poor.

Next, I believe, we must recognize the magnitude of the threat we face in an election year from a resurgence of the right-wing backlash forces. This threat will reach ever greater proportions if this summer sees massive violence in the cities. The Negro–labor–liberal coalition, whatever differences now exist within and among its constituent forces, must resolve to unite this fall in order to defeat racism and reaction at the polls. Unless we so resolve, we may find ourselves in a decade of vindictive and mean conservative domination.

We owe it to Martin Luther King not to let this happen. We owe it to him to preserve and extend his victories. We owe it to him to fulfill his dreams. We owe it to his memory and to our futures.

The Total Vision
of A. Philip Randolph

◆ ◆ ◆

[1969]

SOCIAL STRUGGLE, IF IT IS EFFECTIVELY TO UPLIFT masses of
impoverished and exploited individuals, must articulate and satisfy
their diverse needs as well as reconcile objectives that are often considered contradictory. A people degraded by poverty and a caste system of
segregation, for example, will have the inchoate desire for dignity and
liberation, but that desire will remain unfulfilled until it is given programmatic direction by a political movement. And in the course of
fulfillment, there is always the danger that the felt need deriving from
a perception of fundamental and historic injustices will conflict with
the required political strategy, which by its nature must respond to
circumstances of the moment.

I think it is part of the greatness of A. Philip Randolph that,
throughout his sixty years as a leader of Negro Americans, he has maintained a total vision of the goal of freedom for his people and of the
means for achieving it. From his earliest beginnings as a follower of
Eugene V. Debs and a colleague of Norman Thomas, he has understood
that social and political freedom must be rooted in economic freedom,
and all his subsequent actions have sprung from this basic premise.

He has identified with the spiritual longings of black people, but has
insisted that economic security is the precondition for pride and dignity.
While he has felt that Negro salvation is an internal process of struggle
and self-affirmation, he has recognized the political necessity of forming
alliances with men of other races and the moral necessity of compre-

hending the black movement as part of a general effort to expand human freedom. Finally, as a result of his deep faith in democracy, he has realized that social change does not depend upon the decisions of the few, but on direct political action through the mobilization of masses of individuals to gain economic and social justice.

Randolph thus stands out among Negro leaders of the twentieth century as a man of both principled idealism and practical accomplishment. He has stood firm against racial separatism—whether advocated in the 1920s by Marcus Garvey or in the 1960s by black nationalists—because of his belief in integration and his knowledge that separatism would mean the continued exploitation and degradation of black people. Again, he has rejected elitism—be it in the form of W. E. B. Du Bois's concept of "a talented tenth" or of a proposal for black capitalism—because of his democratic commitment and his opposition to programs that would economically benefit a minority at the expense of the majority. He has adhered to nonviolence as a moral principle and as the most effective means of political struggle.

Pursuing his conviction that the Negro can never be socially and politically free until he is economically secure, Randolph worked to build an alliance between black Americans and the trade union movement. His first efforts met with strong opposition from Southern oligarchs and powerful business leaders who had traditionally tried to use the Negro to subvert the labor movement. Their tactic was to exploit the Negro's grievous need for employment by inviting him to scab on unionized white workers striking for just demands. Realizing that the only beneficiaries of these practices were the exploiters themselves, Randolph embarked upon a crusade opposing any form of strikebreaking by Negroes, advocating instead their full integration into the American trade union movement. Today there are two million black trade unionists in America who have attained economic dignity, job security, and protection against racial discrimination,

Randolph's activities on behalf of black workers, however, did not stop with this broad crusade. In 1925, he began the long and arduous campaign to organize the Brotherhood of Sleeping Car Porters (BSCP). Despite fierce resistance from railway companies and the hardships of the depression, the BSCP eventually won certification in 1937.

This victory not only resulted in the first contract signed by a white employer with a Negro labor leader; it also became a symbol of what could happen if black people organized and bargained collectively. The BSCP enabled thousands of black workers to earn higher wages. What is more important, it became the central focus of the early civil rights protest movement. Brotherhood members, armed with the sophistication they had acquired through their economic battles and making use of the mobility provided by their jobs, carried the message of equality to Negroes in every state in the nation. They formed what was in effect a network for the distribution of political literature. It is hardly surprising, therefore, that E. D. Nixon, one of the main organizers of the 1955 Montgomery, Alabama, bus protest which marked the beginning of the modern civil rights movement, was the head of the local BSCP division and himself a porter.

Since the political strategy of mass protest has become commonplace during the last decade, it is all too often forgotten that this was developed by Randolph at a time when the use of such tactics by Negroes was unheard of. He believed that Negroes could not achieve economic advancement without fighting for it, but he was no less profoundly aware that as an oppressed people, the very act of struggling would confer upon them a dignity they had been denied.

Thus in 1941, with the advent of World War II, Randolph conceived the idea of a massive Negro March on Washington to protest the exclusion of black people from jobs in the defense industries. He wrote of the dramatic plan in the Negro press and agitated for it on the street corners of Harlem and elsewhere. The idea was scoffed at or scorned by most people in the white community, and it was so unprecedented that even many Negroes had difficulty believing it could be made into a reality.

Local March on Washington committees nevertheless began to spring up across the country, and as preparations assumed larger proportions, the pressure on President Roosevelt mounted. On June 20, 1941, less than two weeks before the scheduled date of the march, the President issued Executive Order 8802, banning discrimination in the war industries and setting up the Fair Employment Practices Committee. Once more, thousands of new jobs were opened up to Negroes through Randolph's efforts, and black people began to sense their power as an organized group and the effectiveness of nonviolent direct action tactics.

Even when his actions have seemed to be directed toward noneconomic ends, Randolph has been guided by a persistent concern for the Negro's economic welfare. In 1948, for instance, he traveled to

Washington to speak with President Truman on the problem of segregation and discrimination in the armed forces. Although he was of course concerned that Negroes in the army be treated with dignity, the more fundamental difficulty he saw was that segregation would exclude them from high-paying officer positions as well as from training programs in skills they would need for post-service civilian employment. Such were Randolph's influence and authority that another executive order was issued to comply with his demands.

In 1955, when Randolph urged me to go South to help Dr. Martin Luther King organize the Montgomery bus boycott, he likewise had a dual objective in mind. He naturally felt that Negroes had a right to sit where they wanted to on public accommodations. But he also felt that if the boycott was successful and spread elsewhere, it would create jobs for Negroes as bus drivers and in restaurants, parks, and libraries. His conception was that where Negroes were free to come, they would be free to work; if this proved not to be the case, once having gained access to an institution, they would use the same techniques for obtaining employment that they had originally used to open it up. And this in fact is what has happened throughout the South.

His interest in educational desegregation, too, transcended the problem of dignity or of Negroes and whites attending the same schools together, for he was concerned with the growing threat posed to Negro employment by cybernetics and automation. Since education is the basis for economic advancement, he knew that access to all educational facilities and opportunities was vital to the Negroes. A decade later, we can see even more clearly the devastating effect the combination of automation and inferior segregated education has had on the employment of blacks.

It was Randolph's perception of the economic basis of Negro freedom that enabled him to grasp the unique significance of the 1963 March on Washington. He conceived of it as marking the termination of the mass protest period—during which Negroes had destroyed the Jim Crow institutions in the South—and the inauguration of an era of massive action at the ballot box designed to bring about new economic programs. Aware that the central problem Negroes faced was no longer simply one of *civil* rights but of *economic* rights—for the one would lack social substance without the other—he called for a March on Washington which brought a quarter of a million Americans to the nation's capital to demand "*Jobs* and Freedom."

At the same time President Kennedy introduced what was to become the 1964 Civil Rights Act, and in the minds of some people this became the main focus of the march, Randolph, however, refused to be misled by transient emotion and persisted in his demand for an economic program. At the 1966 White House conference "To Fulfill These Rights," he proposed the Freedom Budget, calling for an annual federal expenditure of $18.5 billion for ten years to wipe out poverty.

Randolph was not speaking here of tax incentives for industry, voluntary assistance by private individuals, or community action programs. He was speaking of full employment and a guaranteed income, the rebuilding of our cities, the provision of superior schools for all of our children, and free medical care for all our citizens. He was speaking, very simply and without rhetoric, of achieving equality in America.

And he was not being unrealistic. He proposed, along with the Freedom Budget, a political strategy for achieving it that calls for building a coalition of Negroes, labor, liberals, religious organizations, and students. If these groups could unite, they would form a majority capable of democratizing the economic, social, and political power of this nation.

Today there are many Negroes and liberals who reject the idea of this coalition. The reason for this, I think, is that they have failed to view the problem of inequality in its totality. Unlike Randolph, their vision is fractured and constricted. Some Negroes, for example, are advocating racial separatism and black nationalism because they are engaged in a very significant psychological quest for identity.

I am in sympathy with this search to a degree, as was Randolph in 1940 when he wrote: "...the Negro and the other darker races must look to themselves for freedom. Salvation for a race, nation, or class must come from within. Freedom is never granted; it is won. Justice is never given; it is exacted. Freedom and justice must be struggled for by the oppressed of all lands and races, and the struggle must be continuous, for freedom is never a final act, but a continuing, evolving process to higher and higher levels of human, social, economic, political and religious relationships."

Randolph did not believe that blacks should isolate themselves, though, so he added: "But Negroes must not fight for their liberation alone: They must join sound, broad, liberal social movements that seek to preserve American democracy and advance the cause of social and religious freedom."

Randolph's position is not only morally correct but strategically necessary, for Negroes today are in danger of letting an emotional imperative destroy the possibility for social and economic liberation. They are emphasizing blackness to the point of isolating themselves from broad political movements for social justice—forgetting that, as one-tenth of the population, they cannot by themselves bring about necessary social changes such as those embodied in the Freedom Budget.

Indeed, many liberals have become obsessed with the psychological aspects of the racial problem to the point of neglecting its economic dimensions. During the early years of the civil rights movement these liberals, unlike Randolph, favored integration primarily as a means of fostering better relations between blacks and whites. Now that the cry of black nationalism has arisen from some Negroes, they have transferred their concern for brotherhood to the need for blacks to achieve pride and identity and for whites to purge themselves of guilt and racism. In both the earlier and the current cases there is a failure to confront the overriding fact of poverty. Most mistakenly, many have now abandoned the objective of building an integrated movement to achieve economic equality.

We are still very much in need of the guidance of A. Philip Randolph. As he reaches his eightieth birthday, this April 14, the freshness and the comprehensiveness of his vision remain evident. And by his presence, he poses a challenge to his followers: to build, through means that are democratic and nonviolent, a just society in which all men need not fear poverty and in which men of all races, graced with the dignity that comes from a full life, need not fear each other. In no other way can we at last become a nation that is at peace with itself.

ELDRIDGE CLEAVER AND THE
DEMOCRATIC IDEA

◆ ◆ ◆

[1976]

SINCE RETURNING LAST NOVEMBER to the United States after
seven years abroad, Eldridge Cleaver has been continuously confined in
various prisons and is currently awaiting trial in the Alameda County jail.
In marked contrast to his days as a leader of the Black Panthers when
the media followed his every pronouncement, only a few random stories
have appeared about Cleaver. More often than not they have merely
reported details on the progress of his trial. There is little real interest
in his thinking, which is penetrating and incisive. If the media once
seemed bent on exploiting Cleaver as good copy, they now seem determined to treat him as a curiosity, when not ignoring him altogether.

The media, with few exceptions, have missed the significance of
Cleaver's return. It was not so startling that Cleaver returned to the United
States, for he had always stated his intention of doing so and he is not the
first black revolutionary to return to the United States. What was surprising was that Cleaver returned with new political views. Once the prophet
of rage and violence, he returned a forceful advocate of democracy.

The political transformation of Eldridge Cleaver is one of the most
profoundly interesting human dramas of our era. Tracing his evolution
is, however, less my concern than the content and clarity of his thinking.
Cleaver is saying many things that badly need saying and which either
are not being said or said so well.

Cleaver's message is to remind us just how revolutionary the
democratic idea really is. His emphasis on the importance of democracy

may seem commonplace, but his views are powerful because they are the result of both theory and experience. His passionately felt beliefs have caused him to perceive the importance of turning the cliches of democracy back into ideals.

Cleaver, who once denounced the United States as "evil," "criminal," and "crazy," now describes himself as a patriot. He is certainly that, but at the same time he is both more and less. Unlike some previous refugees from totalitarian ideologies, Cleaver has not gone over to an opposite and equally as extreme doctrine. Instead he is a radical democrat who sees in the United States the best embodiment of the democratic ideal. "With all its faults," he has declared, "the American political system is the freest and most democratic in the world."

To those who would attempt to stereotype Cleaver as a right-wing super-patriot, he has himself provided the best answer: "The greatest mistake we have made as a nation is to allow our shining principles to lapse so far into disuse that we misname them cliches." Thus, Cleaver's patriotism is not narrow chauvinism but a sophisticated attempt to merge national pride with the fuller implementation of the American principles of democracy, equality, and justice. Cleaver's analysis is remarkably reminiscent of that of George Orwell, perhaps the most astute political observer of the twentieth century. Orwell criticized the British left for denigrating nationalism as necessarily reactionary and provincial. It was the patriotism of the British working class, he argued, that saved Britain from defeat, at the hands of Hitler. In a letter to the *Los Angeles Times* Cleaver advanced the concept of a progressive and democratic patriotism which recognizes that "admitting our weaknesses, does not negate our strengths. And glorifying our strengths, as we rightly should, does not necessitate covering up our weaknesses."

Cleaver has not abandoned his belief in the necessity of fundamental social and economic transformations. He now insists that the method to achieve change is through democratic processes and not by violent revolution. Unlike some American radicals who have recently made a purely tactical endorsement of democracy because revolution is not likely to succeed in the United States, Cleaver has a profound appreciation of the human significance of democracy. Cleaver judges that political democracy is more important than economic democracy. It is easier, he contends, to add economic democracy to political democracy than to add political democracy to the sham economic democracy of the Communist states or the third-world dictatorships.

In the process of altering his views about democracy, Cleaver's feelings about the black struggle in America have also changed. From his experiences abroad he has concluded that the United States is far ahead of the rest of the world in solving its racial problems. In a recent interview, Cleaver outlined his perspective on black progress in the United States thusly: "Black people need to realize very fundamentally that they are full and equal citizens of the U.S. We can no longer afford to 'fence straddle' about where we are going. We can no longer afford to ask: 'Are we going to stay here and be or are we going to go back to Africa, as we have been saying since slavery? Are we going to separate into five states like the black Muslims used to talk about?' ...We are as much a part of the United States as any Rockefeller, and we can no longer afford to ask such questions." Not surprisingly, Cleaver has grown much closer to those mainstream black leaders he used to denounce. He has said, "I want particularly to apologize to Martin Luther King on some points. I now appreciate his awareness that the basic relationship between communities of people has to be one of love."

Cleaver's defense of democracy is all the more persuasive because not only has he lived in totalitarian countries and third-world dictatorships, but he was also once an adherent of those regimes. Indeed, Cleaver's most valuable function may be to dispel the myths about these societies. His idea of proletarian internationalism was but a concentrated version of the still persistent romanticism about the third world and a too common naivete about the nature of Communism. Having lived in the third world, Cleaver is uniquely qualified to communicate the truths that the third world is "an empty phrase," that there are "incredible differences" in the third-world countries, and that many third-world countries are tyrannies.

The analysis which Cleaver makes of Communism is penetrating and insightful. He observes that "communists strap onto people the most oppressive regimes in the history of the world. Regimes that are dictatorships, dictatorships in the name of the proletariat, not by the proletariat." Cleaver criticizes detente for propping up the Soviet regime and concludes that it the United States is truly to be a force for democracy in the world "we have an obligation to help in the disintegration of the Soviet regime." That is a harsh judgment, to be sure, but it flows naturally from Cleaver's commitment to democracy.

Approximately a year ago, as he was preparing to leave Paris, Cleaver speculated about what he planned to do after returning to the United States. He said he wanted to be a philosopher of the left and that he wanted to write rather than become a political activist. Cleaver is, of course, inescapably a political figure. His very presence in this country forces us to confront the meaning of the sixties.

I do not know how many on the left will listen to Cleaver. Certainly they will make every effort to avoid confronting his challenge to their uncritical acceptance of political myths. Sympathizers with the radical currents of the past decade cannot help but be made uncomfortable by Cleaver's proposition that it is time to sum up the questioning process, to abandon mistaken notions, and come to some conclusions. I suspect that nonetheless, the intensity and intelligence of Cleaver's views will force the confrontation whether or not it is desired.

Cleaver, I am convinced, is capable of speaking to a large audience far beyond his former followers and sympathizers. He may well have to endure a long apprenticeship to redeem himself in the eyes of those who still suspect him, or cannot yet forgive his past. Cleaver recognizes that it may be a long time before many people will agree with him.

The return of Eldridge Cleaver to the United States is a summing up of the decade of the sixties and a sign of new possibilities. In the sixties Cleaver became an almost mythical figure for thousands of young blacks and whites, but today, I believe, he is an authentic hero. It is not a simple decision to admit that one was mistaken on fundamental issues as Cleaver has done. Though he could have lived a comfortable life as the puppet of any of a number of totalitarian states, he decided to come home even at the risk of a lengthy prison sentence.

Even in Cleaver's early writings there was a strongly humanistic strain. Unfortunately, his desire for a better world was so strong and consuming he condemned a system that was unable to immediately meet his stringent demands for perfection and justice and embraced an ideology that was destructive of human values. It is to Cleaver's credit that he had the strength and intelligence to reevaluate his beliefs and to avoid the temptations of despair and cynicism. His change is best reflected in his comment, "somehow, man is less grand than I could have thought. He's still OK, but he's less grand." This attitude of realism, responsible optimism, and genuine humanism undergirds Cleaver's political views.

Cleaver presents an opportunity and a test for people committed to realizing the democratic idea. His will not be a political defense; there will be no "Free Eldridge" campaign. But there are many intellectuals, artists, labor leaders, and others who have joined me in working to insure that Eldridge has adequate resources to have a fair trial. Though not all of us may agree with all of his ideas, we believe he can make valuable contributions to the discussion of pressing public issues. He has certainly made a beginning by helping to place the issue of democracy on the agenda.

A Black Presidential Candidacy?

◆ ◆ ◆

[1983]

RECENT WEEKS HAVE SEEN THE EMERGENCE of a spirited discussion about a possible black candidate in the Democratic Presidential race. Clearly, no black or civil rights leader would have reason to quarrel with the entry of a qualified black politician into the Presidential sweepstakes. After all, wouldn't the entry of a popular black candidate raise certain issues of vital concern to the black agenda? Would not a black Presidential candidate serve to galvanize black involvement in the electoral process? Wouldn't a black candidacy increase the number of black delegates to the Democratic Party Convention?

At first glance, the answer to all these questions might appear to be yes. Yet a closer examination of the issue provides a more complicated and less clear-cut picture.

Clearly, a black Presidential candidate would be in a position to raise issues of concern to black Americans. Yet a candidate who entered the Democratic primaries on the basis of a black candidacy and black agenda would deal a substantial setback to black community interests. The issues of greatest concern to black Americans, after all, are not exclusively black issues. The issues of jobs, unemployment, plant closings, education, crime, and poverty are part of the national agenda; they are problems which concern all Americans and must be posed in the broadest possible manner if we are to elect a candidate sensitive to the needs of blacks and all working people. A candidate who runs for President on a black platform, therefore, runs the risk of making such issues appear linked to more narrow special interests.

Clearly, a black Presidential candidacy would galvanize increased black voter interest. Yet the evidence of the 1982 elections is that blacks—who for the first time voted in higher proportions than whites—can also be motivated to vote in greater numbers purely on the basis of political issues and economic interests.

A black Presidential candidacy might increase the number of black Democratic Convention delegates; but not by any significant number. Blacks clearly will be included in substantial numbers within the delegations pledged to the candidates (Mondale, Glenn, Hart, Cranston, Hollings, and Askew). Moreover, because of a shift of delegate strength to the Southern states, where the black vote is more highly concentrated, the number of black delegates to the convention is likely to be augmented.

Thus each of the major advantages of a black Presidential candidacy may not be so substantial as it first appeared. Moreover, there are serious drawbacks to a black Presidential entry:

- Such a candidacy would take away votes from the candidates who, in the absence of a black candidate, are most attractive to the black electorate.
- A black candidacy would mean that the likely nominee won the nomination with less black support and therefore might be less responsive to black interests.
- Blacks who voted for a black candidate would almost certainly be voting for someone who will not be the likely nominee.
- A black candidacy would clearly be perceived by many non-blacks as the candidacy of a special interest and could hurt the Democratic Party by making it appear beholden to special racial, ethnic, or other group interests,
- Because many black political leaders are likely to back other candidates, a black candidacy would add to the division of the black leadership and to the splintering of the black vote.
- A black candidacy might have the effect of heightening racial tensions and weakening the coalition of blacks, labor, and liberals, which is essential to Democratic electoral success.

No one can deny the right of a qualified black or white candidate to enter into the Democratic Presidential campaign. However, any black who might choose to make the run for President should only do so on the basis of a candidacy which appeals to the entire electorate and not only to the black community. An exclusively "black candidacy" not only would end in political failure and split the black electorate, it would do harm to the strategy of coalition politics and to the interests of the black community.

Thus, it is not at all surprising that many prominent black leaders, including the leadership of the NAACP, has expressed serious doubts about the advisability of a black Presidential candidacy in 1984.

THE CURIOUS CASE OF
LOUIS FARRAKHAN

◆ ◆ ◆

[1985]

IN THE RECENT MONTHS NO BLACK FIGURE has excited as much controversy as Louis Farrakhan. Despite the fact that his "Nation of Islam" numbers only a few thousand, Farrakhan's appeal to the irrational, his predictions of "race war," his threats against the life of black reporter Milton Coleman, his anti-Semitic threats against Jews, his praise of Hitler, and his anti-white racism all have made him the object of great attention by the media. Farrakhan, of course, delights in all this publicity. He also recognizes the publicity value of his association with the Rev. Jesse Jackson, an association which has brought him far greater national attention than his sectarian views alone could have. Farrakhan also delights in criticisms from the "white-dominated" press. After all, his strategy stems from a philosophy built on the fundamental principle of black–white separatism, which Farrakhan believes is advanced by promoting chaos within the democratic process.

For many whites, Farrakhan's pronouncements awaken fears about the potential for violence within the black underclass. His rhetoric seeks to exploit the frustration and agony of the black poor, who have been victimized by years of Reaganism and economic decline.

In my view, such fears of violence are not only exaggerated but dangerous. For they bespeak a white stereotyping of blacks as a group somehow outside the society at large. They are a residue of the inner-city upheaval of the 1960s. But they are an inaccurate characterization of the climate within the black community—whether poor, working poor, or middle class—because that community is today energized by increased participation in the political process as evidenced by Jesse Jackson's campaign.

It is precisely for this reason that Louis Farrakhan's message is most strategically damaging to black interests. For Farrakhan's politics of apartness, his racial separatism, come at a time when a decade-long trend of increased black voter participation has tangibly increased black clout within the Democratic Party and within the American political process. Moreover, Farrakhan's racism and anti-Semitism are unconscionable. Thus, for both practical and moral reasons, he should be repudiated by Jesse Jackson.

In recent years, black workers and the black poor have been the victims of an unprecedented series of setbacks, social and economic. A conservative shift in the nation's mood has led to the elimination of vitally needed programs of vocational training, aid to education, and benefits for the poor. Drastic changes in the economy—the stagnation in public-sector job opportunities; a near depression in steel and auto; the loss of labor-intensive jobs; and the effects of a longstanding recession—have hit black workers hardest because it is these sectors which employed the highest proportions of minorities.

Such setbacks, however, are not exclusively limited to blacks. Indeed, far more white steelworkers than black have lost their jobs because of the decline in steel. Far more white Americans are unemployed than are blacks. There are, in absolute numbers, far higher numbers of white poor than black. And although blacks are suffering *proportionally* to a far higher degree, the economic and social setbacks of black Americans are part of a national trend which has affected millions upon millions of white poor, working poor, and middle-income workers.

Thus, this election year is an opportune time for workers and the poor to join together in shaping a strong coalition for political and social change. Today issues can be framed in a way which cuts across racial or religious boundaries and unites the vast majority of Americans. Under such circumstances, Louis Farrakhan's immoral message and behavior are not only demagogic and polarizing, they are anachronistic. He argues for working outside the system at the very moment when blacks are making political gains fighting within that system. Farrakhan's views are anachronistic because they argue for insularity and racial separatism at a time when the only way in which blacks can achieve economic and social gains is through the politics of coalition with their fellow Hispanics, Asians, and whites. Indeed, the modern history of black America is filled with the cautionary examples of separatist figures like Marcus Garvey and Black Power leaders Rap Brown and Stokely Carmichael, who have left hardly anything of permanence to the struggle for black advancement. It has been the integrationist leaders—Martin Luther King, Jr., A. Philip Randolph, and Roy Wilkins—who paved the way for lasting, concrete gains by urging blacks to assert their right to participate fully in American political and economic life.

Assessments of Louis Farrakhan must take into account this legacy of advancement within the democratic system and must accurately reflect Farrakhan's role in the black community as that of a marginal spokesman for a dangerous, out-of-date politics. It's time to recognize that Farrakhan is the quintessential outsider operating outside a con-stitutional system which has often responded effectively to pressures by the civil rights movement to promote needed change. It is that system which once again provides the political means to promote needed social and economic change. Thus, it is time, once again, to pay closer attention to the words and deeds of leaders of such organizations as the Urban League, the NAACP, and the Leadership Conference on Civil Rights. It is also time to listen to elected black leaders who not only have opted to fight for change within the system, but who recognize that change is possible, through a program of coalition politics: through the building of a strong coalition of blacks, Hispanics, women, Christians, Jews, and ethnics.

PART FOUR

◆ ◆ ◆

EQUALITY BEYOND RACE

THE MYTH OF BLACK STUDIES

◆ ◆ ◆

[1969]

IN THE LONG HISTORY OF THE BLACK STRUGGLE, many slogans have emerged which have defined the demands of Negroes at a particular point in time. During Reconstruction, for example, the slogan was "Forty Acres and a Mule." It was both precise and practical. Today's slogans are neither, and Black Studies is a good illustration of this point.

What Black Studies *should* mean is a thorough and objective scholastic inquiry into the history of the black man in America. This history has been scandalously distorted in the past, and, as a field of study, it has been relegated to a second-class status, isolated from the main themes of American history and omitted from the historical education of American youth.

But I am afraid that Black Studies, as it is presently conceived by its proponents on campus, will not correct these errors so much as compound them, for its primary purpose will be to further ends that are fundamentally nonscholastic. It is hoped, first, that Black Studies will serve the *ideological* function of creating a mythologized history and a system of assertive ideas that will facilitate the political mobilization of the black community. Such an ideological undertaking would necessitate the substitution of a glorified version of black history for the present debased version, but *neither* version seems unduly concerned with the discovery of historical truth.

It is also hoped that Black Studies will serve the *political* function of developing and educating a cadre of activists who conceive of their present training as a preparation for organizational work in the black community. One may feel—as I do—that there should be more young Negroes engaging in activities designed to uplift their brethren, but to the extent that Black Studies is used as a vehicle for political indoctrination, it ceases to be a scholastic program.

What I find most distressing about the ideological and political conception of the role of Black Studies is the contempt that is shown toward black history and culture as potential academic disciplines. Faculty members will be chosen on the basis of race, ideological purity, and political commitment—not academic competence. Needless to say this is not the best way to go about developing an intellectually respectable program. Under such conditions, competent black professors will not ever *want* to teach in Black Studies programs—not simply because their academic freedom will be curtailed by their obligation to adhere to the revolutionary "line" of the moment, but because their association with such second-rate programs will threaten their professional status. If such a situation is permitted to develop, Black Studies will become little more than a haven for opportunists and ideologues.

There is, finally, the *psychological* function of Black Studies. It is hoped that by studying Negro history and culture, the self-image of young blacks will improve. Implicit here is the dual assumption that first, young Negroes have a negative self-image because second, they are ignorant of their history. If there is truth to either assumption, then I entirely agree—they should devote many intensive hours to the study of our people's rich heritage of struggle and achievement.

But Black Studies is also serving the psychologically protective function of enabling black students who have been brutalized in the past by segregated education to withdraw from the demanding competition of the university. In this I see little virtue. Providing these students with separate courses of study in soul music and soul poetry—things they can just play with and pass—will enhance neither their competence nor their confidence. Nor will it deal with the fundamental problem of improving the quality of their education in order that they can obtain skills that will be useful in the world they must eventually enter as adults.

To solve this problem would require larger and better trained teaching staffs, remedial efforts, and an expansion of facilities, all of which can be obtained only through a massive increase in present expenditures. And if these changes are not made, the cheap separatist solution will ultimately boomerang, for Black Studies can provide psychic comfort for Negro students only temporarily. When they realize that college administrators are interested more in political accommodation than quality education—when they realize that New Leftist students and faculty members are using black students for their own revolution-by-proxy—and when they realize they are not being given an education but only a paper degree that will hardly improve their intellectual competence or their economic power, then they will rebel with far greater violence and bitterness than anything we have yet seen.

I want to conclude by emphasizing that I am opposed to any program in Black Studies that separates the contribution of black men from the study of American history and society. Racist textbooks and historians have played this game too long for black people to add to the damage that has already been done. The magnificent contribution of black people to America must be recognized and recorded, not only by black people, but also by whites who can benefit at least as much from such knowledge.

THE FAILURE OF BLACK SEPARATISM

◆ ◆ ◆

[1970]

WE ARE LIVING IN AN AGE OF REVOLUTION—or so they tell us. The children of the affluent classes pay homage to their parents' values by rejecting them; this, they say, is a youth revolution. The discussion and display of sexuality increases—actors disrobe on stage, young women very nearly do on the street—and so we are in the midst of a sexual revolution. Tastes in music and clothing change, and each new fashion too is revolutionary. With every new social phenomenon now being dubbed a "revolution," the term has in fact become nothing more than a slogan which serves to take our minds off an unpleasant reality. For if we were not careful, we might easily forget that there is a conservative in the White House, that our country is racially polarized as never before, and that the forces of liberalism are in disarray. Whatever there is of revolution today, in any meaningful sense of the term, is coming from the right.

But we are also told—and with far greater urgency and frequency—that there is a black revolution. If by revolution we mean a radical escalation of black aspirations and demands, this is surely the case. There is a new assertion of pride in the Negro race and its cultural heritage, and although the past summer was marked by the lack of any major disruptions, there is among blacks a tendency more pronounced than at any time in Negro history to engage in violence and the rhetoric of violence. Yet if we look closely at the situation of Negroes today, we find that there has been not the least revolutionary reallocation of political or economic power. There is, to be sure, an increase in the number of black elected officials throughout the United States and particularly in the South, but this has largely been the result of the 1965 Voting Rights Act, which was passed before the "revolution" reached its height and the renewal of which the present administration has not advocated with any noticeable enthusiasm. Some reallocation of political power has indeed taken place since the presidential election of 1964, but generally its beneficiaries have been the Republicans and the anti-Negro forces. Nor does this particular trend show much sign of abating. Nixon's attempt to reverse the liberal direction of the Supreme Court has just begun. Moreover, in the 1970 Senate elections, twenty-five of the thirty-four seats to be contested were originally won by the Democrats in the great liberal surge of 1964, when the political picture was quite different from that of today. And if the Democrats only break even in 1970, the Republicans will control the Senate for the first time since 1954. A major defeat would leave the Democrats weaker than they have been at any time since the conservative days of the 1920s.

There has been, it is true, some moderate improvement in the economic condition of Negroes, but by no stretch of the imagination could it be called revolutionary. According to Andrew Brimmer of the Federal Reserve System, the median family income of Negroes between 1965 and 1967 rose from 54 percent to 59 percent of that for white families. Much of that gain reflected a decrease in the rate of Negro unemployment. But between February and June of 1969, Negro unemployment rose again by 1.3 percent and should continue to rise as Nixon presses his crusade against inflation. The Council of Economic Advisers reports that in the past eight years the federal government has spent $10.3 billion on metropolitan problems while it has spent $39.9 billion on agriculture, not to mention, of course, $507.2 billion for defense. In the area of housing, for instance, New York City needs at the present time as many new subsidized apartments—780,000—as the federal housing program has constructed *nationally* in its entire thirty-four years. The appropriations for model cities, rent supplements, the Job Corps, the Neighborhood Youth Corps, and other programs have been drastically reduced, and the Office of Economic Opportunity is being transformed into a research agency. Nixon's welfare and revenue-sharing proposals, in addition to being economically stringent, so that they will have little or no effect on the condition of the Northern urban poor, are politically and philosophically conservative.

Any appearance that we are in the grip of a black revolution, then, is deceptive. The problem is not whether black aspirations are outpacing America's ability to respond but whether they have outpaced her willingness to do so. Lately it has been taken almost as axiomatic that with every increase in Negro demands, there must be a corresponding intensification of white resistance. This proposition implies that only black complacency can prevent racial polarization, that any political action by Negroes must of necessity produce a reaction. But such a notion ignores entirely the question of what *kind* of political action, guided by what *kind* of political strategy. One can almost assert as a law of American politics that if Negroes engage in violence as a tactic they will be met with repression, that if they follow a strategy of racial separatism they will be isolated, and that if they engage in anti-democratic activity, out of the deluded wish to skirt the democratic process, they will provoke a reaction. To the misguided, violence, separatism, and minority ultimatums may seem revolutionary, but in reality they issue only from the desperate strivings of the impotent. Certainly such tactics are not designed to enhance the achievement of progressive social change. Recent American political history has proved this point time and again with brutal clarity.

The irony of the revolutionary rhetoric uttered in behalf of Negroes is that it has helped in fact to promote conservatism. On the other hand, of course, the reverse is also true: the failure of America to respond to the demands of Negroes has fostered in the minds of the latter a sense of futility and has thus seemed to legitimize a strategy of withdrawal and violence. Other things have been operating as well. The fifteen years since *Brown vs. Topeka* have been for Negroes a period of enormous dislocation. The modernization of farming in the South forced hundreds of thousands of Negroes to migrate to the North where they were confronted by a second technological affliction, automation. Without jobs, living in cities equipped to serve neither their material nor spiritual needs, these modern-day immigrants responded to their brutal new world with despair and hostility. The civil rights movement created an even more fundamental social dislocation, for it destroyed not simply the legal structure of segregation but also the psychological assumptions of racism. Young Negroes who matured during this period witnessed a basic challenge to the system of values and social relations which had presumed the inferiority of the Negro. They have totally rejected this system, but in doing so have often substituted for it an exaggerated and distorted perception both of themselves and of the society. As if to obliterate the trace of racial shame that might be lurking in their souls they have embraced racial chauvinism. And as if in reply to past exclusions (and often in response to present insecurities), they have created their own patterns of exclusiveness.

The various frustrations and upheavals experienced recently by the Negro community account in large part for the present political orientation of some of its most vocal members: seeing their immediate self-interest more in the terms of emotional release than in those of economic and political advancement. One is supposed to think black, dress black, eat black, and buy black without reference to the question of what such a program actually contributes to advancing the cause of social justice. Since real victories are thought to be unattainable, issues become important insofar as they can provide symbolic victories. Dramatic confrontations are staged which serve as outlets for radical energy but which in no way further the achievement of radical social goals. So that, for instance, members of the black community are mobilized to pursue the "victory" of halting construction of a state office building in Harlem, even though it is hard to see what actual economic or social benefit will be conferred on the impoverished residents of that community by their success in doing so.

Such actions constitute a politics of escape rooted in hopelessness and further reinforced by government inaction. Deracinated liberals may romanticize this politics, nihilistic new leftists may imitate it, but ordinary Negroes will be the victims of its powerlessness to work any genuine change in their condition.

The call for black power is now over three years old, yet to this day no one knows what black power is supposed to mean and therefore how its proponents are to unite and rally behind it. If one is a member of CORE, black power posits the need for a separate black economy based upon traditional forms of capitalist relations. For SNCC the term refers to a politically united black community. US would emphasize the unity of black culture, while the Black Panthers wish to impose upon black nationalism the philosophies of Marx, Lenin, Stalin, and Chairman Mao. Nor do these exhaust all the possible shades and gradations of meaning. If there is one common theme uniting the various demands for black power, it is simply that blacks must be guided in their actions by a consciousness of themselves as a separate race.

Now, philosophies of racial solidarity have never been unduly concerned with the realities that operate outside the category of race. The adherents of these philosophies are generally romantics, steeped in the traditions of their own particular clans and preoccupied with the simple biological verities of blood and racial survival. Almost invariably their rallying cry is racial self-determination, and they tend to ignore those aspects of the material world which point up divisions within the racially defined group.

But the world of black Americans is full of divisions. Only the most supine of optimists would dream of building a political movement without reference to them. Indeed, nothing better illustrates the existence of such divisions within the black community than the fact that the separatists themselves represent a distinct minority among Negroes. No reliable poll has ever identified more than 15 percent of Negroes as separatists; usually the percentage is a good deal lower. Nor, as I have already indicated, are the separatists unified among themselves, the differences among them at times being so intense as to lead to violent conflict. The notion of the undifferentiated black community is the intellectual creation both of whites—liberals as well as racists to whom all Negroes are the same—and of certain small groups of blacks who illegitimately claim to speak for the majority.

The fact is that like every other racial or ethnic group in America, Negroes are divided by age, class, and geography. Young Negroes are at least as hostile toward their elders as white new leftists are toward their liberal parents. They are in addition separated by vast gaps in experience, Northern from Southern, urban from rural. And even more profound are the disparities in wealth among them. In contrast to the white community, where the spread of income has in recent years remained unchanged or has narrowed slightly, economic differentials among blacks have increased. In 1965, for example, the wealthiest 5 percent of white and nonwhite families each received 15.5 percent of the total income in their respective communities. In 1967, however, the percentage of white income received by the top 5 percent of white families had dropped to 14.9 percent while among nonwhites the share of income of the top 5 percent of the families had risen to 17.5 percent. This trend probably reflects the new opportunities which are available to black professionals in industry, government, and academia, but have not touched the condition of lower-class and lower-middle-class Negroes.

To Negroes for whom race is the major criterion, however, divisions by wealth and status are irrelevant. Consider, for instance, the proposals for black economic advancement put forth by the various groups of black nationalists. These proposals are all remarkably similar. For regardless of one's particular persuasion—whether a revolutionary or a cultural nationalist or an unabashed black capitalist—once one confines one's analysis to the ghetto, no proposal can extend beyond a strategy for ghetto development and black enterprise. This explains in part the recent popularity of black capitalism and, to a lesser degree, black cooperatives: once both the economic strategy and goal are defined in terms of black self-determination, there is simply not much else available in the way of ideas.

There are other reasons for the popularity of black capitalism, reasons having to do with material and psychological self-interest. E. Franklin Frazier has written that Negro business is "a social myth" first formulated toward the end of the nineteenth century when the legal structure of segregation was established and Negro hopes for equality destroyed. History has often shown us that oppression can sometimes lead to a rationalization of the unjust conditions on the part of the oppressed and, following this, to an opportunistic competition among them for whatever meager advantages are available. This is, according to Frazier, exactly what happened among American Negroes. The myth of Negro business was created and tied to a belief in the possibility of a separate Negro economy. "Of course," wrote Frazier, "behind the idea of the separate Negro economy is the hope of the black bourgeoisie that they will have the monopoly of the Negro market." He added that they also desire "a privileged status within the isolated Negro community."

Nor are certain Negro businessmen the only ones who stand to gain from a black economy protected by the tariff of separatism. There are also those among the white upper class for whom such an arrangement is at least as beneficial. In the first place, self-help projects for the ghetto, of which black capitalism is but one variety, are inexpensive. They involve no large-scale redistribution of resources, no "inflationary" government expenditures, and, above all, no responsibility on the part of whites. These same upper-class whites may have been major exploiters of black workers in the past, they may have been responsible for policies which helped to create ghetto poverty, but now, under the new dispensations of

black separatism, they are being asked to do little more by way of reparation than provide a bit of seed money for a few small ghetto enterprises.

Moreover, a separate black economy appears to offer hope for what
Roy Innis has called "a new social contract." According to Innis' theory,
the black community is essentially a colony ruled by outsiders; there can
be no peace between the colony and the "mother country" until the former is ruled by some of its own. When the colony is finally "liberated" in
this way, all conflicts can be resolved through negotiation between the
black ruling class and the white ruling class. Any difficulties within the
black community, that is, would become the responsibility of the black
elite. But since self-determination in the ghetto, necessitating as it would
the expansion of a propertied black middle class, offers the advantage
of social stability, such difficulties would be minimal. How could many
whites fail to grasp the obvious benefit to themselves in a program that
promises social peace without the social inconvenience of integration
and especially without the burden of a huge expenditure of money?
Even if one were to accept the colonial analogy—and it is in many ways
an uninformed and extremely foolish one—the strategy implied by it is
fatuous and unworkable. Most of the experiments in black capitalism thus
far have been total failures, as, given the odds, they will continue to be.
For one thing, small businesses owned and run by blacks will, exactly like
their white counterparts, suffer a high rate of failure. In fact, they will face
even greater problems than white small businesses because they will be
operating in predominantly low-income areas where the clientele will
be poor, the crime rate and taxes high, and the cost of land, labor, and
insurance expensive. They will have to charge higher prices than the
large chains, a circumstance against which "Buy Black" campaigns will in
the long or even the short run have little force. On the other hand, to
create large-scale black industry in the ghetto is unthinkable. The capital is not available, and even if it were, there is no vacant land. In Los
Angeles, for example, the area in which four-fifths of the Negroes and
Mexican-Americans live contains only 0.5 percent of all the vacant land
in the city, and the problem is similar elsewhere. Overcrowding is severe
enough in the ghetto without building up any industry there.

Another current axiom of black self-determination is the necessity for
community control. Questions of ideology aside, black community control is as futile a program as black capitalism. Assuming that there were
a cohesive, clearly identifiable black community (which, judging by the

factionalism in neighborhoods like Harlem and Ocean Hill–Brownsville, is far from a safe assumption), and assuming that the community were empowered to control the ghetto, it would still find itself without the money needed in order to be socially creative. The ghetto would still be faced with the same poverty, deteriorated housing, unemployment, terrible health services, and inferior schools—and this time perhaps with the exacerbation of their being entailed in local struggles for power. Furthermore, the control would ultimately be illusory and would do no more than provide psychological comfort to those who exercise it. For in a complex technological society there is no such thing as an autonomous community within a large metropolitan area. Neighborhoods, particularly poor neighborhoods, will remain dependent upon outside suppliers for manufactured goods, transportation, utilities, and other services. There is, for instance, unemployment in the ghetto while the vast majority of new jobs are being created in the suburbs. If black people are to have access to those jobs, there must be a metropolitan transportation system that can carry them to the suburbs cheaply and quickly. Control over the ghetto cannot build such a system nor can it provide jobs within the ghetto.

The truth of the matter is that community control as an idea is provincial and as a program is extremely conservative. It appears radical to some people because it has become the demand around which the frustrations of the Negro community have coalesced. In terms of its capacity to deal with the social and economic causes of black unrest, however, its potential is strikingly limited. The call for community control in fact represents an adjustment to inequality rather than a protest against it. Fundamentally, it is a demand for a change in the racial composition of the personnel who administer community institutions: that is, for schools, institutions of public and social service, and political organizations—as all of these are presently constituted—to be put into the keeping of a new class of black officials. Thus in a very real sense, the notion of community control bespeaks a fervent hope that the poverty-stricken ghetto, once thought to be a social problem crying for rectification, might now be deemed a social good worthy of acceptance. Hosea Williams of SCLC, speaking once of community control, unwittingly revealed the way in which passionate self-assertion can be a mask for accommodation: "I'm now at the position Booker T. Washington was about sixty or seventy years ago," Williams said. "I say to my brothers, 'Cast down your buckets where you are'—and that means there in the slums and ghettos."

There is indeed profound truth in the observation that people who seek social change will, in the absence of real substantive victories, often seize upon stylistic substitutes as an outlet for their frustrations.

A case in point is the relation of Negroes to the trade union movement. In their study *The Black Worker*, published in 1930, Sterling D. Spero and Abram L. Harris describe the resistance to separatism among economically satisfied workers during the heyday of Marcus Garvey:

> ...spokesmen of the Garvey movement went among the faction-torn workers preaching the doctrine of race consciousness. Despite the fact that Garveyism won a following everywhere at this time, the Negro longshoremen of Philadelphia were deaf to its pleas, for their labor movement had won them industrial equality such as colored workers nowhere else in the industry enjoyed.

The inverse relation of black separatism and anti-unionism to the quality of employment available to Negroes holds true today also. In the May 1969 UAW elections, for example, black candidates won the presidency and vice-presidency of a number of locals. Some of the most interesting election victories were won at the Chrysler Eldon Gear and Axle Local 961 and at Dodge #3 in Hamtramck where the separatist Eldon Revolutionary Union Movement (ELRUM) and Dodge Revolutionary Union Movement (DRUM) have been active. At both locals the DRUM and ELRUM candidates were handily defeated by black trade unionists who campaigned on a program of militant integrationism and economic justice.

This is not to say that there are not problems within the unions which have given impetus to the separatist movements. There are, but in the past decade unions have taken significant steps toward eliminating discrimination against Negroes. As Peter Henle, the chief economist of the Bureau of Labor Statistics, has observed:

> Action has been taken to eliminate barriers to admission, abolish discrimination in hiring practices, and negotiate changes in seniority arrangements which had been blocking Negro advances to higher-paying

jobs. At the same time, unions have given strong support to governmental efforts in this same direction.

Certainly a good deal is left to be done in this regard, but just as
certainly the only effective pressure on the unions is that which can be
brought by blacks pressing for a greater role *within* the trade union
movement. Not only is separatism not a feasible program, but its major
effect will be to injure black workers economically by undermining the
strength of the union. It is here that ignorance of the economic dimension of racial injustice is most dangerous, for a Negro, whether he be
labeled a moderate or a militant, has but two alternatives open to him.
If he defines the problem as primarily one of race, he will inevitably find
himself the ally of the white capitalist against the white worker. But if,
though always conscious of the play of racial discrimination, he defines
the problem as one of poverty, he will be aligned with the white worker
against management. If he chooses the former alternative, he will
become no more than a pawn in the game of divide-and-conquer played
by, and for the benefit of, management—the result of which will hardly
be self-determination but rather the depression of wages for all workers.
This path was followed by the "moderate" Booker T. Washington who
disliked unions because they were "founded on a sort of enmity to the
man by whom he [the Negro] is employed" and by the "militant" Marcus
Garvey who wrote:

> It seems strange and a paradox, but the only conve-
> nient friend the Negro worker or laborer has in
> America at the present time is the white capitalist.
> The capitalist being selfish—seeking only the largest
> profit out of labor—is willing and glad to use Negro
> labor wherever possible on a scale reasonably below
> the standard union wage...but if the Negro union-
> izes himself to the level of the white worker, the
> choice and preference of employment is given to
> the white worker.

And it is being followed today by CORE, which collaborated with
the National Right to Work Committee in setting up the Black Workers
Alliance.

If the Negro chooses to follow the path of interracial alliances on the basis of class, as almost two million have done today, he can achieve a certain degree of economic dignity, which in turn offers a genuine, if not the only, opportunity for self-determination. It was this course which A. Philip Randolph chose in his long struggle to build a Negro–labor alliance, and it was also chosen by the black sanitation workers of Memphis, Tennessee, and the black hospital workers of Charleston, South Carolina.

Not that I mean here to exonerate the unions of their responsibility for discrimination. Nevertheless, it is essential to deal with the situation of the black worker in terms of American economic reality. And as long as the structure of this reality is determined by the competing institutions of capital and labor (or government and labor, as in the growing public sector of the economy), Negroes must place themselves on one side or the other. The idea of racial self-determination within this context is a delusion.

There are, to be sure, sources beyond that of economic discrimination for black separatism within the unions. DRUM, ELRUM, and similar groups are composed primarily of young Negroes who, like whites their age, are not as loyal to the union as are older members, and who are also affected by the new militancy which is now pervasive among black youth generally. This militancy has today found its most potent form of expression on campus, particularly in the predominantly white universities outside the South. The confusion which the movement for programs in Black Studies has created on campus almost defies description. The extremes in absurdity were reached this past academic year at Cornell, where, on the one hand, enraged black students were demanding a program in Black Studies which included Course 300C, Physical Education: "Theory and practice in the use of small arms and combat. Discussion sessions in the proper use of force," and where, on the other hand, a masochistic and pusillanimous university president placed his airplane at the disposal of two black students so that they could go to New York City and purchase, with $2,000 in university funds, some bongo drums for Malcolm X Day. The foolishness of the students was surpassed only by the public relations manipulativeness of the president.

The real tragedy of the dispute over Black Studies is that whatever truly creative opportunities such a program could offer have been either ignored or destroyed. There is, first, the opportunity for a vastly expanded scholastic inquiry into the contribution of Negroes to the American experience. The history of the black man in America has been scandalously distorted in the past, and as a field of study it has been relegated to a second-class status, isolated from the main themes of American history and omitted in the historical education of American youth. Yet now black students are preparing to repeat the errors of their white predecessors. They are proposing to study black history in isolation from the mainstream of American history; they are demanding separate Black Studies programs that will not be open to whites, who could benefit at least as much as they from a knowledge of Negro history; and they hope to permit only blacks (and perhaps some whites who toe the line) to teach in these programs. Unwittingly they are conceding what racist whites all along have professed to believe, namely, that black history is irrelevant to American history.

In other ways black students have displayed contempt for Black Studies as an academic discipline. Many of them, in fact, view Black Studies not as an academic subject at all, but as an ideological and political one. They propose to use Black Studies programs to create a mythologized history and a system of assertive ideas that will facilitate the political mobilization of the black community. In addition, they hope to educate a cadre of activists whose present training is conceived of as a preparation for organizational work in the ghetto. The Cornell students made this very clear when they defined the purpose of Black Studies programs as enabling "black people to use the knowledge gained in the classroom and the community to formulate new ideologies and philosophies which will contribute to the development of the black nation."

Thus faculty members will be chosen on the basis of race, ideological purity, and political commitment—not academic competence. Under such conditions, few qualified black professors will want to teach in Black Studies programs, not simply because their academic freedom will be curtailed by their obligation to adhere to the revolutionary "line" of the moment, but because their professional status will be threatened by their association with programs of such inferior quality.

Black students are also forsaking the opportunity to get an education. They appear to be giving little thought to the problem of teaching or learning those technical skills that all students must acquire if they are to be effective in their careers. We have here simply another exam-

ple of the pursuit of symbolic victory where a real victory seems too difficult to achieve. It is easier for a student to alter his behavior and
appearance than to improve the quality of his mind. If engineering
requires too much concentration, then why not a course in soul music? If
Plato is both "irrelevant" and difficult, the student can read Malcolm X
instead. Class will be a soothing, comfortable experience, somewhat like
watching television. Moreover, one's image will be militant and, therefore, acceptable by current college standards. Yet one will have learned
nothing, and the fragile sense of security developed in the protective
environment of college will be cracked when exposed to the reality of
competition in the world.

Nelson Taylor, a young Negro graduate of Morehouse College,
recently observed that many black students "feel it is useless to try to compete. In order to avoid this competition, they build themselves a little cave
to hide in." This "little cave," he added, is Black Studies. Furthermore,
black students are encouraged in this escapism by guilt-ridden New Leftists
and faculty members who despise themselves and their advantaged lives
and enjoy seeing young Negroes reject white middle-class values and disrupt the university. They are encouraged by university administrators who
prefer political accommodation to an effort at serious education. But
beyond the momentary titillation some may experience from being the
center of attention, it is difficult to see how Negroes can in the end benefit from being patronized and manipulated in this way. Ultimately, their
only permanent satisfaction can come from the certainty that they have
acquired the technical and intellectual skills that will enable them upon
graduation to perform significant jobs competently and with confidence.
If they fail to acquire these skills, their frustration will persist and find
expression in ever newer forms of antisocial and self-destructive behavior.

The conflict over Black Studies, as over other issues, raises the question of the function in general served by black protest today. Some black
demands, such as that for a larger university enrollment of minority
students, are entirely legitimate; but the major purpose of the protest
through which these demands are pressed would seem to be not so much
to pursue an end as to establish in the minds of the protesters, as well as
in the minds of whites, the reality of their rebellion. Protest, therefore,
becomes an end in itself and not a means toward social change. In this
sense, the black rebellion is an enormously *expressive* phenomenon
which is releasing the pent-up resentments of generations of oppressed

Negroes. But expressiveness that is oblivious to political reality and not structured by instrumental goals is mere bombast.

James Forman's *Black Manifesto,* for instance, provides a nearly perfect sample of this kind of bombast combined with positive delusions of grandeur. "We shall liberate all the people in the U.S.," the introduction of the *Manifesto* declares, "and will be instrumental in the liberation of colored people the world around.... We are the most humane people within the U.S.... Racism in the U.S. is so pervasive in the mentality of whites that only an armed, well-disciplined, black-controlled government can insure the stamping out of racism in this country.... We say think in terms of the total control of the U.S."

One might never imagine from reading the *Manifesto* that Forman's organization, the National Black Economic Development Conference, is politically powerless, or that the institution it has chosen for assault is not the government or the corporation, but the church. Indeed, the exaggeration of language in the *Black Manifesto* is directly proportional to the isolation and impotence of those who drafted it. And their actual achievements provide an accurate measure of their strength. Three billion dollars in reparations was demanded—and $20,000 received. More important, the effect of this demand upon the Protestant churches has been to precipitate among them a conservative reaction against the activities of the liberal national denominations and the National Council of Churches. Forman's failure, of course, was to be expected: the only effect of an attack upon so organizationally diffuse and nonpolitical an institution as the church can be the deflection of pressure away from the society's major political and economic institutions and, consequently, the weakening of the black movement for equality.*

The possibility that his *Manifesto* might have exactly the opposite effect from that intended, however, was clearly not a problem to Forman, because the demands he was making upon white people were

---

* Forman is not the only militant today who fancies that his essentially reformist program is revolutionary. Eldridge Cleaver has written that capitalists regard the Black Panther Breakfast for Children program (which the Panthers claim feeds 10,000 children) "as a threat, as cutting into the goods that are under their control." He also noted that it "liberates" black children from going to school hungry each morning. I wonder if he would also find public school lunch programs liberating.

more moral than political or economic. His concern was to purge white guilt far more than to seek social justice for Negroes. It was in part for this reason that he chose to direct his attack at the church, which, as the institutional embodiment of our society's religious pretensions, is vulnerable to moral condemnation.

Yet there is something corrupting in the wholesale release of aggressive moral energy, particularly when it is in response to the demand for reparations for blacks. The difficulty is not only that as a purely racial demand its effect must be to isolate blacks from the white poor with whom they have common economic interests. The call for three billion dollars in reparations demeans the integrity of blacks and exploits the self-demeaning guilt of whites. It is insulting to Negroes to offer them reparations for past generations of suffering, as if the balance of an irreparable past could be set straight with a handout. In a recent poll, *Newsweek* reported that "today's proud Negroes, by an overwhelming 84 to 10 percent, reject the idea of preferential treatment in hiring or college admissions in reparation for past injustices." There are few controversial issues that can call forth a greater uniformity of opinion than this in the Negro community.

I also question both the efficacy and the social utility of an attack that impels the attacked to applaud and debase themselves. I am not certain whether or not self-flagellation can have a beneficial effect on the sinner (I tend to doubt that it can), but I am absolutely certain that it can never produce anything politically creative. It will not improve the lot of the unemployed and the ill housed. On the other hand, it could well happen that the guilty party, in order to lighten his uncomfortable moral burden, will finally begin to rationalize his sins and affirm them as virtues. And by such a process, today's ally can become tomorrow's enemy. Lasting political alliances are not built on the shifting sands of moral suasion.

On his part, the breast-beating white makes the same error as the Negro who swears that "black is beautiful." Both are seeking refuge in psychological solutions to social questions. And both are reluctant to confront the real cause of racial injustice, which is not bad attitudes but bad social conditions. The Negro creates a new psychology to avoid the reality of social stagnation, and the white—be he ever so liberal—professes his guilt precisely so as to create the illusion of social change, all the while preserving his economic advantages.

The response of guilt and pity to social problems is by no means new. It is, in fact, as old as man's capacity to rationalize or his reluctance to make real sacrifices for his fellow man. Two hundred years ago, Samuel Johnson, in an exchange with Boswell, analyzed the phenomenon of sentimentality:

> Boswell: "I have often blamed myself, Sir, for not feeling for others, as sensibly as many say they do."

> Johnson: "Sir, don't be duped by them any more. You will find these very feeling people are not very ready to do you good. They *pay* you by *feeling*."

Today, payments from the rich to the poor take the form of "giving a damn" or some other kind of moral philanthropy. At the same time, of course, some of those who so passionately "give a damn" are likely to argue that full employment is inflationary.

We are living in a time of great social confusion—not only about the strategies we must adopt but about the very goals these strategies are to bring us to. Only recently whites and Negroes of good will were pretty much in agreement that racial and economic justice required an end to segregation and the expansion of the role of the federal government. Now it is a mark of "advancement," not only among "progressive" whites but among the black militants as well, to believe that integration is passé. Unintentionally (or as the Marxists used to say, objectively), they are lending aid and comfort to traditional segregationists like Senators Eastland and Thurmond. Another "advanced" idea is the notion that government has gotten too big and that what is needed to make the society more humane and livable is an enormous new move toward local participation and decentralization. One cannot question the value or importance of democratic participation in the government, but just as misplaced sympathy for Negroes is being put to use by segregationists, the liberal preoccupation with localism is serving the cause of conservatism. Two years of liberal encomiums to decentralization have intellectually legitimized the concept, if not the name, of states' rights and have set the stage for the widespread acceptance of Nixon's "New Federalism."

The new anti-integrationism and localism may have been motivated by sincere moral conviction, but hardly by intelligent political thinking. It should be obvious that what is needed today more than ever is a political strategy that offers the real possibility of economically uplifting millions of impoverished individuals, black and white. Such a strategy must of necessity give low priority to the various forms of economic and psychological experimentation that I have discussed, which at best deal with issues peripheral to the central problem and at worst embody a frenetic escapism. These experiments are based on the assumption that the black community can be transformed from within when, in fact, any such transformation must depend on structural changes in the entire society. Negro poverty, for example, will not be eliminated in the absence of a total war on poverty. We need, therefore, a new national economic policy. We also need new policies in housing, education, and health care which can deal with these problems as they relate to Negroes within the context of a national solution. A successful strategy, therefore, must rest upon an identification of those central institutions which, if altered sufficiently, would transform the social and economic relations in our society; and it must provide a politically viable means of achieving such an alteration.

Surely the church is not a central institution in this sense. Nor is Roy Innis' notion of dealing with the banking establishment a useful one. For the banks will find no extra profit—quite the contrary—in the kind of fundamental structural change in society that is required.**

Moreover, the recent flurry of excitement over the role of private industry in the slums seems to have subsided. A study done for the Urban Coalition has called the National Alliance of Businessmen's claim to have hired more than 100,000 hard-core unemployed a "phony numbers game." Normal hiring as the result of expansion or turnover was in some cases counted as recruitment. Where hard-core workers have been hired and trained, according to the study, "The primary motivation...is the need for new sources of workers in a tight labor market. If and when the need for workers slackens, so will industry's performance." This has already occurred. The *Wall Street Journal* reported in July of 1969 that the Ford Motor Company, once praised for its social commitment, was forced to trim back production earlier in the year and in the process "quietly closed its two inner-city hiring centers in Detroit and even laid off some

---

** Innis' demand that the white banks deposit $6 billion in black banks as reparations for past injustices should meet with even less success than Forman's ill-fated enterprise. At least Forman had the benefit of the white churchman's guilt, an emotion not known to be popular among bankers.

of the former hard-cores it had only recently hired." There have been similar retrenchments by other large companies as the result of a slackening in economic growth, grumblings from stockholders, and the realization by corporate executives that altruism does not make for high profits. Yet even if private industry were fully committed to attack the problem of unemployment, it is not in an ideal position to do so. Private enterprise, for example, accounted for only one out of every ten new jobs created in the economy between 1950 and 1960. Most of the remainder were created as the result of expansion of public employment.

While the church, private enterprise, and other institutions can, if properly motivated, play an important role, it is the trade union movement and the Democratic party which offer the greatest leverage to the black struggle. The serious objective of Negroes must be to strengthen and liberalize these. The trade union movement is essential to the black struggle because it is the only institution in the society capable of organizing the working poor, so many of whom are Negroes. It is only through an organized movement that these workers, who are now condemned to the margin of the economy, can achieve a measure of dignity and economic security. I must confess I find it difficult to understand the prejudice against the labor movement currently fashionable among so many liberals. These people, somehow for reasons of their own, seem to believe that white workers are affluent members of the Establishment (a rather questionable belief, to put it mildly, especially when held by people earning over $25,000 a year) and are now trying to keep the Negroes down. The only grain of truth here is that there is competition between black and white workers which derives from a scarcity of jobs and resources. But rather than propose an expansion of those resources, our stylish liberals underwrite that competition by endorsing the myth that the unions are the worst enemy of the Negro.

In fact it is the program of the labor movement that represents a genuine means of reducing racial competition and hostility. Not out of a greater tenderness of feeling for black suffering—but that is just the point. Unions organize workers on the basis of common economic interests, not by virtue of racial affinity. Labor's legislative program for full employment, housing, urban reconstruction, tax reform, improved health care, and expanded educational opportunities is designed specifically to aid both whites and blacks in the lower and lower-middle classes where the potential for racial polarization is most severe. And only a program of this kind can deal simultaneously and creatively with the interrelated problems of black rage and white fear. It does not placate black rage at the expense of whites, thereby increasing white fear and political reaction. Nor does it exploit white fear by repressing blacks. Either of these courses strengthens the demagogues among both races who prey upon frustration and racial antagonism. Both of them help to strengthen conservative forces—the forces that stand to benefit from the fact that hostility between black and white workers keeps them from uniting effectively around issues of common economic interest.

President Nixon is in the White House today largely because of this hostility; and the strategy advocated by many liberals to build a "new coalition" of the affluent, the young, and the dispossessed is designed to keep him there. The difficulty with this proposed new coalition is not only that its constituents comprise a distinct minority of the population, but that its affluent and youthful members—regardless of the momentary direction of their rhetoric—are hardly the undisputed friends of the poor. Recent Harris polls, in fact, have shown that Nixon is most popular among the college educated and the young. Perhaps they were attracted by his style or the minimal concessions he has made on Vietnam, but certainly their approval cannot be based upon his accomplishments in the areas of civil rights and economic justice.

If the Republican ascendancy is to be but a passing phenomenon, it must once more come to be clearly understood among those who favor social progress that the Democratic party is still the only mass-based political organization in the country with the potential to become a majority movement for social change. And anything calling itself by the name of political activity must be concerned with building precisely such a majority movement. In addition, Negroes must abandon once and for all the false assumption that as 10 percent of the population they can by themselves effect basic changes in the structure of American life. They must, in other words, accept the necessity of coalition politics. As a result of our fascination with novelty and with the "new" revolutionary forces that have emerged in recent years, it seems to some the height of conservatism to propose a strategy that was effective in the past. Yet the political reality is that without a coalition of Negroes and other minorities with the trade union movement and with liberal groups, the shift of power to the Right will persist and the democratic

Left in America will have to content itself with a well-nigh-permanent minority status.

The bitterness of many young Negroes today has led them to be unsympathetic to a program based on the principles of trade unionism and electoral politics. Their protest represents a refusal to accept the condition of inequality, and in that sense it is part of the long, and I think magnificent, black struggle for freedom. But with no comprehensive strategy to replace the one I have suggested, their protest, though militant in rhetoric and intention, may be reactionary in effect.

The strategy I have outlined must stand or fall by its capacity to achieve political and economic results. It is not intended to provide some new wave of intellectual excitement. It is not intended to suggest a new style of life or a means to personal salvation for disaffected members of the middle class. Nor is either of these the proper role of politics. My strategy is not meant to appeal to the fears of threatened whites, though it would calm those fears and increase the likelihood that some day we shall have a truly integrated society. It is not meant to serve as an outlet for the terrible frustrations of Negroes, though it would reduce those frustrations and point a way to dignity for an oppressed people. It is simply a vehicle by which the wealth of this nation can be redistributed and some of its more grievous social problems solved. This in itself would be quite enough to be getting on with. In fact, if I may risk a slight exaggeration, by normal standards of human society I think it would constitute a revolution.

FEMINISM AND EQUALITY

◆ ◆ ◆

[1970]

THE WOMEN'S LIBERATION MOVEMENT, which has created much controversy in recent months, is not a new phenomenon but part of a long struggle for women's equality. The fact that a major feminist demonstration was held on August 26, 1970, indicates the historical character of this movement, since the date was the fiftieth anniversary of the passage of the Nineteenth Amendment, granting female suffrage.

The modern feminist movement differs from the suffragette movement of a half-century ago in that its demands have to do more with economic equality than with political rights. To a considerable degree, this is a reflection of technological changes that have taken place in the society—changes which have freed the more affluent women from household chores and enabled them to gain a high degree of education. These women are now demanding that jobs and other opportunities be opened to them on a nondiscriminatory basis. The force of their argument is reflected in economic statistics showing that the income differential between men and women is greater than it is between whites and blacks.

If the women's liberation movement should be criticized, it is not because its demands are unjust but because they do not go far enough. The three demands put forth at the August 26 demonstrations were for free abortions, twenty-four-hour day-care centers for children of working mothers, and equal educational and employment opportunities.

I would personally take issue with none of these demands, but they are inadequate in that they are proposed in isolation from the broad social and economic context of American life. The feminists are making the same mistake that many other social protesters have made: they do not relate their demands to the larger issues which ultimately will determine whether the demands are met.

For example, I am entirely for free abortions on demand, since I think women should be able to choose whether they want to have children. But I think that the feminists would be wiser to make this specific demand part of a larger demand for socialized medicine. Our current health system does not permit all women, or all Americans, to obtain adequate medical care, and good health is a prerequisite for "liberation," however one cares to define that word. Similarly, it is not enough to have day-care centers that will free mothers from constant supervision of their children. There should also be a demand for the expansion of preschool education and for high-quality integrated schools that will liberate the minds of the children and enable them to develop their potential to the fullest. Finally, the demand for equal employment opportunities cannot be met in the absence of full employment. As long as a sizable portion of the population is unemployed, workers, regardless of their sex or race, will have to compete for jobs and employers will be able to hire those willing to work for the least pay. Here it should be added that the demand for female equality is too often stated in terms of giving women the same rights as men. What happens then is that women consider their own special rights—such as the legal protection of women workers—to be expendable. Rather than give up these rights, they should be demanding that such provisions be extended to all workers.

Thus far the women's liberation movement has failed to make its demands within this larger social context. That failure is not accidental; it is, in fact, a commentary on the affluent background of many of the feminists. They are, for the most part, women who already have access to adequate health care, whose children (if they have them) probably attend excellent schools, and who don't need jobs, just *better* jobs. This is one reason why so few black women have participated in the feminist movement. If the feminists do not make the larger demands I have suggested, their movement will become just another middle-class foray into limited social reform, the main result of which will be to divert valuable social energies away from the problem of fundamentally transforming our society's institutions. Without such a transformation, leading to full social equality for all Americans—female and male, black and white, poor and rich—our people will not be free.

The Blacks and the Unions

◆ ◆ ◆

[1971]

ONE OF THE MAIN ARTICLES OF FAITH in liberal dogma these days is that the interests and objectives of the American trade union movement are in fundamental conflict with the interests and objectives of black America. One can hardly pick up any of the major journals of liberal opinion without reading some form of the statement that the white worker has become affluent and conservative and feels his security to be threatened by the demand for racial equality. A corollary of this statement is that it is a primary function of the labor movement to protect the white worker from the encroaching black. Furthermore, the argument runs, since there are no signs that the blacks may be letting up in their struggle for economic betterment, a hostile confrontation between blacks and unions is not only inevitable but necessary.

It may well be that historians of the future, recording the events of the past five years, will conclude that the major effect of the civic turbulence in this period has been in fact to distract us from the real and pressing social needs of the nation. And perhaps nothing illustrates the point more vividly than the whole question of the relations between blacks and the unions.

This question itself, however, cannot be properly understood except in the larger context of the history of the civil rights movement. Negro protest in the sixties, if the movement is in its turn to be properly understood, must be divided into two distinct phases. The first phase, which covered something like the first half of the decade, was one in which the movement's clear objective was to destroy the legal foundations of racism in America. Thus the locale of the struggle was the South,

the evil to be eliminated was Jim Crow, and the enemy, who had a special talent for arousing moral outrage among even the most reluctant
sympathizers with the cause, was the rock-willed segregationist.

Now, one thing about the South more than any other has been
obscured in the romantic vision of the region—of ancient evil, of defeat,
of enduring rural charm—that has been so much of our literary and
intellectual tradition: for the Negro, Southern life had precisely a quality of clarity, a clarity which while oppressive was also supportive. The
Southern caste system and folk culture rested upon a clear, albeit unjust,
set of legal and institutional relationships which prescribed roles for
individuals and established a modicum of social order. The struggle that
was finally mounted against that system was actually fed and strengthened by the social environment from which it emerged. No profound
analysis, no overriding social theory was needed in order both to locate and
understand the injustices that were to be combated. All that was demanded
of one was sufficient courage to demonstrate against them. One looks
back upon this period in the civil rights movement with nostalgia.

During the second half of the sixties, the center of the crisis shifted
to the sprawling ghettos of the North. Here black experience was radically different from that in the South. The stability of institutional
relationships was largely absent in Northern ghettos, especially among
the poor. Over twenty years ago, the black sociologist E. Franklin Frazier
was able to see the brutalizing effect of urbanization upon lower-class
blacks: "...The bonds of sympathy and community of interests that held
their parents together in the rural environment have been unable to
withstand the disintegrating forces in the city." Southern blacks migrated
North in search of work, seeking to become transformed from a peas-
antry into a working class. But instead of jobs they found only misery,
and far from becoming a proletariat, they came to constitute a *lumpenproletariat*, an underclass of rejected people. Frazier's prophetic words
resound today with terrifying precision: "...As long as the bankrupt
system of Southern agriculture exists, Negro families will continue to
seek a living in the towns and cities of the country. They will crowd the
slum areas of Southern cities or make their way to Northern cities,
where their family life will become disrupted and their poverty will force
them to depend upon charity."

Out of such conditions, social protest was to emerge in a form
peculiar to the ghetto, a form which could never have taken root in the

South except in such large cities as Atlanta or Houston. The evils in the North are not easy to understand and fight against, or at least not as easy as Jim Crow, and this has given the protest from the ghetto a special edge of frustration. There are few specific injustices, such as a segregated lunch counter, that offer both a clear object of protest and a good chance of victory. Indeed, the problem in the North is not one of social injustice so much as the results of institutional pathology. Each of the various institutions touching the lives of urban blacks—those relating to education, health, employment, housing, and crime—is in need of drastic reform. One might say that the Northern race problem has in good part become simply the problem of the American city—which is gradually becoming a reservation for the unwanted, most of whom are black.

In such a situation, even progress has proven to be a mixed blessing. During the sixties, for example, Northern blacks as a group made great economic gains, the result of which being that hundreds of thousands of them were able to move out of the hard-core poverty areas. Meanwhile, however, their departure, while a great boon to those departing, only contributed further to the deterioration of the slums, now being drained of their stable middle and working class. Combined with the large influx of Southern blacks during the same period, this process was leaving the ghetto more and more the precinct of a depressed underclass. To the segregation by race was now added segregation by class, and all of the problems created by segregation and poverty—inadequate schooling, substandard and overcrowded housing, lack of access to jobs or to job training, narcotics, and crime—were greatly aggravated. And again because of segregation, the violence of the black underclass was turned in upon itself.

If the problems of the ghetto do not lend themselves to simple analyses or solutions, then, this is because they cannot be solved without mounting a total attack on the inadequacies endemic to, and injustices embedded in, all of our institutions. It is perhaps understandable that young Northern blacks, confronting these problems, have so often provided answers which are really nonanswers, which are really dramatic statements satisfying some sense of the need for militancy without even beginning to deal with the basic economic and political problems of the ghetto. Primary among these nonanswers is the idea that black progress depends upon a politics of race and revolution. I am referring here not to the recent assertions of black pride—assertions that will be made

as long as that pride continues to be undermined by white society—
but about the kind of black nationalism which consists in a bitter
rejection of American society and vindicates a withdrawal from social
struggle into a kind of hermetic racial world where blacks can "do their
thing." Nationalists have been dubbed "militants" by the press because
they have made their point with such fervent hostility to white society,
but the implication of their position actually amounts to little more than
the age-old conservative message that blacks should help themselves—a
thing that, by the very definition of the situation, they have not the
resources to do.

The same is true of black proposals for revolution. For to engage
in revolutionary acts in a contemporary America—where, despite a lot of
inflammatory rhetoric, there is not even a whisper of a revolutionary situation—not only diverts precious energies away from the political arena
where the real battles for change must be fought, but might also precip-
itate a vicious counterrevolution, the chief victims of which will be blacks.

The truth about the situation of the Negro today is that there are
powerful forces, composed largely of the corporate elite and Southern
conservatives, which will resist any change in the economic or racial
structure of this country that might cut into their resources or challenge
their status; and such is precisely what any program genuinely geared to
improve his lot must do. Moreover, these forces today are not merely
resisting change. With their representative Richard Nixon in the White
House, they are engaged in an assault on the advances made during the
past decade. It has been Nixon's tragic and irresponsible choice to play
at the politics of race—not, to be sure, with the primitive demagoguery
of a "Pitchfork Ben" Tillman, say, but nevertheless with the same intent
of building a political majority on the basis of white hostility to blacks.
So far he has been unsuccessful, but the potential for the emergence of
such a reactionary majority does exist, especially if the turbulence and
racial polarization which we have recently experienced persist.

What is needed, therefore, is not only a program that would effect
some fundamental change in the distribution of America's resources for
those in the greatest need of them but a political majority that will support such a program as well. In other words, nothing less than a
program truly, not merely verbally, radical in scope would be adequate
to meet the present crisis; and nothing less than a politically constituted
majority, outnumbering the conservative forces, would be adequate to

carry it through. Now, it so happens that there is one social force which, by virtue both of its size and its very nature, is essential to the creation of such a majority—and so in relation to which the success or failure of the black struggle must finally turn. And that is the American trade union movement.

Addressing the AFL-CIO convention in 1961, Martin Luther King observed: "Negroes are almost entirely a working people. There are pitifully few Negro millionaires and few Negro employers. Our needs are identical with labor's needs—decent wages, fair working conditions, livable housing, old age security, health and welfare measures, conditions in which families can grow, have education for their children and respect in the community."

Despite the widely held belief that the blacks and the unions have not the same, but rather irreconcilable, interests—and despite the fact that certain identifiable unions do practice racial discrimination—King's words remain as valid today. Blacks *are* mostly a working people; they continue to need what labor needs; and they must fight side by side with unions to achieve these things.

Of all the misconceptions about the labor movement that have been so lovingly dwelt on in the liberal press, perhaps none is put forth more often and is further from the truth than that the unions are of and for white people. For one thing, there are, according to labor historian Thomas R. Brooks, between 2,500,000 and 2,750,000 black trade unionists in America.* If his figures are correct, and other estimates seem to bear them out, the percentage of blacks in the unions is a good deal higher than the percentage of blacks in the total population—15 percent as compared with 11 percent, to be precise. And since the vast majority of black trade unionists are members of integrated unions, one can conclude that the labor movement is the most integrated major institution in American society, certainly more integrated than the corporations, the churches, or the universities.

Moreover, blacks are joining unions in increasing numbers. According to a 1968 report by *Business Week*, one out of every three new union members is black. The sector of the economy which is currently

---

* "Black Upsurge in the Unions," *Dissent*, March–April 1970.

being most rapidly unionized is that of the service industries, and most particularly among government employees, such as hospital workers, sanitation workers, farm workers, and paraprofessionals in educational and social-welfare institutions. This category of worker is, of course, both largely nonwhite and shamefully underpaid.

Like other workers, blacks have gained from the achievements of their unions in the way of higher wages, improved working conditions, and better fringe benefits. To be sure, in some unions whites still possess a disproportionate number of the higher paying jobs and there is not yet adequate black representation at the staff level and in policy-making positions. But the question of what continues to account for the perpetuation of such inequities cannot properly be answered by the fashionable and easy reference to racial discrimination in the unions. Statistical surveys have shown that the participation of blacks in the work force is no higher in nonunionized occupations than in unionized ones. Indeed, as Derek C. Bok and John T. Dunlop have pointed out in their remarkably informed and comprehensive study, *Labor and the American Community*, even in the automotive and aerospace industries, where the unions have been known for dedication to racial justice, the percentage of blacks, particularly in the skilled jobs, is not appreciably higher than in other industries.

There have, therefore, to be far more fundamental social and economic reasons for present inequalities in employment. Primary among these reasons are certain underlying changes within the entire society which are being reflected in the evolving character and composition of the work force itself. The upsurge of union organization of minority-group workers in the fields of education, sanitation, and health care, for instance, is the result of the rapid expansion of the service sector of the economy.

Another crucial factor here is government economic policy. The tremendous growth in the economy from 1960 to 1968 increased nonwhite employment by 19 percent, 4 percent higher than the increase for whites, and during the same period the unemployment rate for nonwhite adult men dropped from 9.6 to 3.9 percent. A large number of these new black workers entered unions for the simple reason that they had jobs. And now many of them are out of jobs, not because of union discrimination but because the Nixon administration's economic policies have so far caused a sharp increase in unemployment.

All of which is not to exonerate the entire labor movement of any possible charge of wrongdoing. It is rather to put the problem of economic inequality into some useful perspective. The inequalities which persist within the unions must of course be corrected. They are in fact being corrected through the work of the labor movement itself—the role of the civil rights department of the AFL-CIO is particularly noteworthy here—the civil rights activities of the federal government, and the efforts of black trade unionists who are taking over leadership positions in their locals and are playing more of a role in determining union policy. The union drive against discrimination was exemplified by the fight made by the AFL-CIO to have a Fair Employment Practices section written into the 1964 Civil Rights Act. Both President Kennedy and Robert Kennedy were opposed to including an FEPC section because they thought it would kill the bill, but George Meany pressed for it. He did so for a simple reason. The AFL-CIO is a federation of affiliates which retain a relatively high degree of autonomy. The parent body can urge compliance with its policies, but the decision to act is left up to the affiliates. Meany felt that the only way the AFL-CIO could deal effectively with unions practicing discrimination would be to demand compliance with the law of the land. He testified before the House Judiciary Committee that the labor movement was calling for "legislation for the correction of shortcomings in its own ranks." And the passage of the 1964 Civil Rights Act greatly speeded the process of this correction.

Most labor leaders, I believe, are opposed to discrimination against the blacks on moral grounds. But they also have highly practical grounds for their position. They understand that discrimination hurts the entire labor movement as much as it hurts blacks. They know from long experience as unionists that anything which divides the workers makes it more difficult for them to struggle together for the achievement of common goals. Racial antagonisms have undermined solidarity during strikes and have been exploited by management as a means of weakening unions. The following passage from the classic study *The Black Worker*, written in 1931 by Sterling D. Spero and Abram L. Harris, may not be typical of every company's approach to its work force, yet it describes a practice commonly in use till this very day:

> The Negro is now recognized as a permanent factor
> in industry and large employers use him as one of the

racial and national elements which help to break
the homogeneity of their labor force. This, incidentally, fits into the program of big concerns for
maintaining what they call "a cosmopolitan force,"
which frees the employer from dependence upon
any one group for his labor supply and also thwarts
unity of purpose and labor organization.

People no longer lend much credence to the idea that management continues to think and operate in such convoluted terms. But it
does, and so does labor. Indeed, such terms as "labor solidarity" or "labor
disunity" are standard tools of the trade in labor–management relations.
A further error is to imagine that unions might, from such reasoning,
increase unity within their ranks by excluding blacks. On the contrary,
given the character of the American working class, the *only* possibility
for genuine labor solidarity is for the blacks to be fully integrated into
every level of the trade union movement. If they are not, then they will
continue to exist outside the unions as a constant source of cheap labor
exploitable by management to depress wages or to break strikes.

Another notion which has passed into vogue among some blacks as
well as some whites is that the whole problem of integration can be finessed
by organizing the workers into dual unions. This is not a new idea, nor
is its feasibility any greater today than was evidenced by a record of impossibility in the past. For were there to be racially separate unions, it would
naturally follow that the interests of blacks would be diametrically opposed
to those of whites, with whom they would be in competition. And once
again, no matter how innocently or unintentionally, the blacks would
remain in the role of a reserve army that could be called into action whenever companies felt the white workers needed a good kick in the pants.

Of course the blacks would also be victims in this situation, since
they would be at the beck and call of management only if they were
chronically unemployed. Thus, exploitation is as much the effect of poverty
as its cause. It is only the poor, those who are needy and weak, who can
be manipulated at the whim of the wealthy. This introduces another
notion concerning the welfare of black and white workers about which
there has grown up a misplaced skepticism—namely, the function of the
supply of labor. Put very simply, it is in the interests of employers for the
supply of labor to be greater than the demand for it. This situation

obtains when there is high unemployment or what is often called a "loose" labor market. Under these conditions, the bargaining position of the unions is weakened since labor, which is after all the product unions are selling, is not in high demand and also because there are a lot of unemployed workers whom the companies can turn to if the unions should in any way prove recalcitrant. Generally speaking, an excess of supply over demand for labor exerts a downward pressure on wages, and, vice versa, there is an upward pressure on wages when the demand for labor outpaces the supply.

In addition, this dynamic of supply and demand affects the level of racial antagonism within the work force. If supply exceeds demand, i.e., if there is a high level of unemployment, there will be tremendous competition for jobs between white and black workers and racial tensions will increase. Under conditions of relative full employment, there will be little job competition and greater racial harmony. As George Lichtheim recently pointed out, "If economic conflict as a source of political antagonism is ruled out...the residual cultural tensions...need not and doubtless will not fall to zero; but they can be held down to a tolerable level."**

These ideas shape the conceptual universe as well as the behavior of many of the principal actors in our country's economic conflicts. The fact that they tend to be ignored in so much current discussion of blacks and unions is as much a testimony to the naivete of liberal journalists as it is to the public relations skills of corporations. A good example of what I mean is the press treatment accorded the terrible racial conflict in the building trades and the administration's policies in this area.

Racial discrimination exists in the building trades. It is unjustifiable by any moral standard, and as to the objective of rooting it out there can be no disagreement among people of good will. How truly to achieve this objective is another matter. An important distinction here is often overlooked. One cannot set varying moral standards in judging the performance of institutions; the same standard must be applied equally to all—to the unions, the corporations, the churches, etc. But beyond the realm of moral judgement is the crucial question of social utility. Blacks could attack Jim Crow in the South without regard to the welfare of the lunch counters, the hotels, or whatever, because they had little or

---

** "What Socialism Is and Is Not," *New York Review of Books*, April 9, 1970.

no stake in them. This is not the case with the trade union movement, a social force in which blacks *do* have a stake. If blacks attack the unions in such a way as to damage them irreparably, they will ultimately harm themselves. As it happens, certain presently self-styled friends of the Negro are in fact not at all averse to such a possible development.

Writing in the *New York Times*, Tom Wicker reflected the views of many liberals when he described the Nixon administration's strong and forthright position on the building-trades issue as "remarkable." Wicker's analysis, however, never advances beyond this point. He never asks why the Nixon administration, particularly Attorney General Mitchell and most particularly given other administration policies, would suddenly take such an interest in the welfare of blacks. The question is neither gratuitous nor idle. Why, in fact, would a President who has developed a "Southern strategy," who has cut back on school integration efforts, tried to undermine the black franchise by watering down the 1965 Voting Rights Act, nominated to the Supreme Court men like Haynsworth and Carswell, cut back on funds for vital social programs, and proposed a noxious crime bill for Washington, D.C., which is nothing less than a blatant appeal to white fear—why indeed would such a President take up the cause of integration in the building trades?

To begin with, Mr. Nixon's Philadelphia Plan—which requires contractors to make a commitment to hire a certain quota of black workers on a job where over $500,000 of federal funds are involved—actually does nothing for integration. In order to meet this commitment, a contractor could shift the required number of black workers in an area onto a particular job, a procedure known in the trade as checkerboarding. He would thus satisfy federal requirements *for that job*, but no new jobs would be created for blacks and no Negroes would be brought into the building trades. In fact, the contractor can even achieve compliance simply by making an effort of good faith, such as contacting certain people in the area who are concerned about black participation in the building trades. If those people do not produce any workers, the contractor has done his job and can get the federal money. The Philadelphia Plan makes no provision for training, nor does it provide a means for blacks to attain the security of journeyman status within the unions. It is geared only to temporary jobs, and even in this area it is deficient. It is designed primarily to embarrass the unions and to organize public pressure against them.

In simple truth, the plan is part and parcel of a general Republican attack on labor. The same administration which designed it (as well as the Southern strategy) has also sent to Congress a measure that would increase federal control over internal union political affairs. Republican Senators and Representatives have introduced dozens of antilabor bills—one of which, for example, would create a right-to-work law for federal employees; another would restrict labor's involvement in political activities. Moreover, the administration has turned the heat on labor at the same time that it has cooled pressure against discrimination by the corporations.

The advantages to the Republicans from this kind of strategy should be obvious. Nixon supports his friends among the corporate elite and hurts his enemies in the unions. He also gains a convenient cover for his anti-Negro policies in the South, and, above all, he weakens his political opposition by aggravating the differences between its two strongest and most progressive forces—the labor movement and the civil rights movement.

The Philadelphia Plan and related actions are also part of the administration's attempt to pin onto labor the blame for inflation in construction costs. The *Wall Street Journal* has suggested that contractors welcome the thrust for integration in the building trades, since this "might slow inflation in construction by increasing the supply of workers." There is reason to believe that Mr. Nixon thinks in these same terms. It will be remembered that on almost the very day he proposed the Philadelphia Plan, he also ordered a 75 percent reduction in federal construction—thereby reducing the number of jobs available in the industry and producing the twofold effect of exerting a deflationary pressure on wages and increasing competition among workers over scarce jobs. When Nixon finally freed some of the construction funds some months later (a move no doubt designed to improve the economic picture for the 1970 elections), he warned that "a shortage of skilled labor runs up the cost of that labor." He said he would issue directives to the Secretaries of Defense, Labor, and Health, Education, and Welfare to train veterans and others toward the goal of "enlarging the pool of skilled manpower."

It should be pointed out in passing that the President's approach to the problem of inflation in construction costs cannot succeed since he has made the typical businessman's error of identifying wages as the major inflationary factor. According to the Bureau of Labor Statistics, on-site labor costs as a percentage of total construction costs decreased between 1949 and 1969 from 33 percent to 18 percent. During the same period, the combined cost of land and financing rose from 16 percent to 31 percent of the total cost. Thus land and financing, not labor, have been the major causes of inflation in construction. Nevertheless, the President continues his crusade against "wage inflation."

The concern with increasing the supply while reducing the cost of labor is what motivated the Nixon administration's most recent act in the construction field—the suspension of the 1931 Davis–Bacon Act. Here the "deflationary" intention is more evident than in the case of the Philadelphia Plan, but the similarity between the two moves is striking, particularly with regard to the antiunion role envisioned for the unorganized Negro worker.

The Davis–Bacon Act requires contractors on federal or federally assisted projects to pay all workers, union or nonunion, the prevailing union wage rates. The suspension of the Act will not directly affect the wages of unionized workers who are protected by their contract. It will, however, enable contractors to cut the wages of nonunion workers, and this, in turn, should encourage the employment of these workers instead of the higher paid unionists. Thus, there will be fewer jobs for organized workers (there is already an 11 percent unemployment rate in the construction industry), and the bargaining power of the unions will be weakened. Since many of the unorganized workers are nonwhite, it might be argued that this is a boon to their fortunes since they will be more likely to find work. Aside from the fact that they will be working for lower wages, the question is again raised whether it is in the interests of blacks to let themselves be used by employers to hurt unions. I do not think that it is. Their interests lie in becoming part of the trade union movement. Ironically, the current attack on labor may speed the process of their entrance into the labor movement, for in situations where union standards have been threatened by open shops, unions have been spurred on to fully organize their industry.

It should be emphasized that this would only encourage changes that have already been taking place for a number of years as a result of pressure from civil rights groups and union leaders.

Seventy-nine Outreach programs now operate in as many cities and have placed over 8,000 minority-group youngsters in building-trades apprenticeship training programs. Sixty percent have been placed in the highest paying trades—the plumbers, electricians, sheet-metal workers, carpenters, pipe fitters, and iron workers. This is far from sufficient, of course, but within the past two years, these programs have expanded by over 400 percent, and they are continuing to grow. The role of civil rights activists should be to continue to see that they grow.

The blacks have a choice. They can fight to strengthen the trade union movement by wiping out the vestiges of segregation that remain in it, or they can, knowingly or unknowingly, offer themselves as pawns in the conservatives' game of bust-the-unions.

The choice must be made on the basis of a critical assessment of the current economic plight of blacks. More than any single factor, the Nixon administration's policies of high interest rates, "fiscal responsibility," and economic slowdown are undermining the gains which blacks have made during the past decade. Dr. Charles C. Killingsworth, a leading manpower economist, predicted some months ago that within a year the unemployment rate is likely to go up to 8 percent. We could expect the rate for blacks to be twice as high. Nixon's managed recession may calm the fears of businessmen, but it will do so at terrible cost to blacks and to all other working people. There are, no doubt, many well-meaning people who are concerned about the plight of unemployed workers under Nixon, but it is only the labor movement that is fighting every day for policies that will get these workers back on the job.

Thus, it is clear why unions are important to black workers. What may perhaps seem less obvious and must also be sharply emphasized is that the legislative program of the trade union movement can go a long way toward satisfying the economic needs of the larger black community. The racial crisis, as we have seen, is not an isolated problem that lends itself to redress by a protesting minority. Being rooted in the very social and economic structure of the society, it can be solved only by a comprehensive program that gets to the heart of why we can't build adequate housing for everybody, why we must always have a "tolerable" level of unemployment, or why we lack enough funds for education. In this sense the racial crisis challenges the entire society's capacity to redirect its resources on the basis of human need rather than profit. Blacks can pose this challenge, but only the federal government has the power and the money to meet it. And it is here that the trade union movement can play such an important role.

The problems of the most aggrieved sector of the black ghetto cannot and will never be solved without full employment, and full employment, with the government as employer of last resort, is the keystone of labor's program. One searches in vain among the many so-called friends of the black struggle for a seconding voice to this simple yet far-reaching proposition. Some call it inflationary, while to others, who are caught up in the excitement of the black cultural revolution, it is pedestrian and irrelevant. But in terms of the economic condition of the black community, nothing more radical has yet been proposed. There is simply no other way for the black *lumpenproletariat* to become a proletariat. And full employment is only one part of labor's program. The movement's proposals in the areas of health, housing, education, and environment would, if enacted, achieve nothing less than the transformation of the quality of our urban life. How ironic that in this period, when the trade union movement is thought to be conservative, its social and economic policies are far and away more progressive than those of any other major American institution. Nor—again in contrast to most of the other groups officially concerned with these things—is labor's program merely in the nature of a grand proposal; there is also an actual record of performance, particularly in the area of civil rights. Clarence Mitchell, the director of the Washington Bureau of the NAACP and legislative chairman of the Leadership Conference on Civil Rights, a man more deeply involved in Congressional civil rights battles than any other black in America, has said: "None of the legislative fights we have made in the field of civil rights could have been won without the trade union movement. We couldn't have beaten Haynsworth without labor, and the struggle against Carswell would not have been a contest."

Labor's interest in progressive social legislation naturally leads it into the political arena. The committee on political education of the AFL-CIO, the political action committee of the UAW, and the political arm of the Teamsters were active in every state in the last election, registering and educating voters and getting out the vote. This year trade unionists were more politically active than they have ever been during an off-year election. The reason for this is clear. With so many liberal Senators up for reelection, and with political alignments in great flux, 1970 presented itself as a year that would initiate a new period in American politics—a period which would see the regrouping of liberal forces or the consolidation of a conservative majority.

One of the important factors determining the kind of political alignments that will emerge from this period of instability will be the relationship between the trade union movement and the liberal community, and today this relationship is severely strained. Differences over the war in Vietnam are frequently cited as a major cause of this division, but there has been a great deal of misunderstanding on this issue. The house of labor itself is divided over the war, and even those labor leaders who support it have enthusiastically backed dove Congressional candidates who have liberal domestic records, among them such firm opponents of the war as Mike Mansfield, Edward Kennedy, Vance Hartke, Philip Hart, Howard Metzenbaum, and Edmund Muskie.

A better understanding of the trade union movement by liberals may be developing, but for the present the antagonistic attitudes that exist cast an ideological pall over the chances for uniting the Democratic left coalition. It must be said that the vehement contempt with which the liberals have come to attack the unions bespeaks something more than a mere political critique of "conservatism." When A. H. Raskin writes that "the typical worker—from construction craftsman to shoe clerk—has become probably the most reactionary political force in the country"; or when Anthony Lewis lumps under the same category the rich oilmen and "the members of powerful, monopolistic labor unions"; or when Murray Kempton writes that "the AFL-CIO has lived happily in a society which, more lavishly than any in history, has managed the care and feeding of incompetent white people," and adds, "Who better represents that ideal than George Wallace?"; or when many other liberals casually toss around the phrase "labor fascists"—one cannot but inevitably conclude that one is in the presence not of political opposition but of a certain class hatred. This hatred is not necessarily one based on conflicting class interests—though they may play a role here—but rather the hatred of the elite for the "mass." And this hatred is multiplied a thousandfold by the fact that we live in a democratic society in which the coarse multitude can outvote the elite and make decisions which may be contrary to the wishes and values, perhaps even the interests and the prejudices, of those who are better off.

It is difficult not to conclude that many liberals and radicals use subjective, rather than objective, criteria in judging the character of a social force. A progressive force, in their view, is one that is alienated from the dominant values of the culture, not one which contributes to greater social equality and distributive justice. Thus today the trade union movement has been relegated to reactionary status, even though it is actually more progressive than at any time in its history—if by progressive we mean a commitment to broad, long-term social reform in addition to the immediate objectives of improving wages and working conditions. At the same time, the most impoverished social group, that substratum which Herbert Marcuse longingly calls "the outcasts and the outsiders," has been made the new vanguard of social progress. And it is here that liberals and New Leftists come together in their proposal for a new coalition "of the rich, educated and dedicated with the poor," as Eric F. Goldman has admiringly described it, or in Walter Laqueur's more caustic phraseology, "between the *lumpenproletariat* and the *lumpenintelligentsia.*"

This political approach, known among liberals as New Politics and among radicals as New Leftism, denotes a certain convergence of the left and right—if not in philosophy and intent, then at least in practical effect. I am not referring simply to the elitism which the intellectual left shares with the economic right, but also to their symbiotic political relationship. Many of the sophisticated right-wing attacks on labor are frequently couched in left-wing rhetoric. Conservative claims that unions are antiblack, are responsible for inflation, and constitute minorities which threaten and intimidate the majority reverberate in the liberal community and are shaping public opinion to accept a crackdown on the trade union movement.

While many adherents of the New Politics are outraged by Nixon's Southern strategy, their own strategy is simply the obverse of his. The potential for a Republican majority depends upon Nixon's success in attracting into the conservative fold lower-middle-class whites, the same group that the New Politics has written off. The question is not whether this group is conservative or liberal; for it is both, and how it acts will depend upon the way the issues are defined. If they are defined as race and dissent, then Nixon will win. But if, on the other hand, they are defined so as to appeal to the progressive economic interests of the lower middle class, then it becomes possible to build an alliance on the basis of common interest between this group and the black community. The importance of the trade union movement is that it embodies this common interest. This was proved most clearly in 1968 when labor mounted a massive educational campaign which reduced the Wallace supporters among its membership to a tiny minority. And the trade union movement remains today the greatest obstacle to the success of Nixon's strategy.

The prominent racial and ethnic loyalties that divide American society have, together with our democratic creed, obscured a fundamental reality—that we are a class society and, though we do not often talk about such things, that we are engaged in a class struggle. This reality may not provide some people with their wished-for quotient of drama, though I would think that the GE strike or the UAW strike against GM were sufficiently dramatic, and it may now have become an institutionalized struggle between the trade union movement and the owners and managers of corporate wealth. Yet it is a struggle nonetheless, and its outcome will determine whether we will have a greater or lesser degree of economic and social equality in this country. As long as blacks are poor, our own struggle will be part of this broader class reality. To the degree that it is not, black liberation will remain a dream in the souls of an oppressed people.

Black Women and
Women's Liberation

◆ ◆ ◆

[1972]

CONTRARY TO POPULAR IMPRESSION, the woman most discriminated against is not the white suburban housewife but the mother of a ghetto household.

People have argued that the relatively affluent suburbanite would be more vulnerable to the disaffection caused by her sexual role and more likely to embrace the issues raised by the modern feminist movement.

It is hardly difficult to reach such a conclusion, particularly if one's judgment is influenced by the conventional wisdom served by journalists and other opinion molders. For it was the same sort of simplistic analysis, myth making, and stereotyping which convinced many people that working people are the most conservative force in society, when in fact conservative and reactionary attitudes are far more prevalent among the wealthy.

Back women, in reality, hear the drumroll of the movement for female equality much more loudly than do whites. And, contrary to popular myth, poor women respond to a majority of the issues of the feminist movement more fervently and in greater numbers than do the middle-class housewives and professionals who comprise the core of strength of women's activist groups.

But while endorsing the broad aims of feminists, black women differ sharply over which issues they consider most fundamental to equality. While white women find it difficult to define and quantify equality, black women see equality as a less elusive ideal. For black women believe that equality to a large degree can still be measured by more jobs, more and better-quality low and moderate-income housing, improved public education, quality health care, and programs to help the poor and elderly.

I do not mean to imply that feminism's psychological implications do not concern black women. Black women are in fact more dissatisfied with their social roles. More deeply than whites they are distressed that their sexual role may have limited their chances for self-fulfillment, are convinced that doors to success which are open to men are shut for women, and often consider their years of schooling wasted.

These are not subjective evaluations: they are the innermost sentiments of black women as expressed in polls and studies. Yet to accept their validity is to raise significant questions about the course of the women's liberation movement today. For black women, no matter how profound their sympathy for the issues of feminist equality, have largely ignored the women's liberation movement.

When women's liberation rose to prominence several years ago there were those who warned that should it fail to alter the essentially middle-class nature of its appeal it would be unable to win the support of Negroes and white working-class women.

And while some feminist leaders have acknowledged this weakness we still find that black women, poor women, and working women, discriminated against and alienated as they are, remain unenthusiastic and occasionally antagonistic to women's liberation.

Too often they find that women's liberation is concerned with rhetoric and consciousness raising to the neglect of social change. Sometimes Gloria Steinem, Betty Friedan, and other leaders of women's rights arouse focus on issues so irrelevant to the personal lives of working people as to appear dilettantish.

But there is a more basic reason for black disenchantment. Black people, because they have lived with discrimination and struggled to overcome built-in prejudice, cannot relate to a cause which separates and isolates social problems on the basis of sex. They understand from personal experience that discrimination, poverty, and the miseries they bring are not sexually exclusive.

Thus while black women have remained conscious of the special problems they encounter as women, they are also cognizant that discrimination is essentially a matter of class and race.

This is reflected in their choice of social activism. In past years black women played important roles in the civil rights movement. They were the first to respond to Dr. King when he organized the Montgomery bus boycott and assumed leadership positions in this and many other campaigns.

More recently blacks have branched into other areas, organizing domestic workers, hospital workers, and school paraprofessionals, long the most impoverished and exploited of the female work force.

Thus in the most important areas of social activism—civil rights campaigns, labor organization, tenant rights groups, and the like—black women have carved remarkable records of accomplishment. Their leadership has been constructive and responsible, their militancy indisputable. And they bear with them the conviction that what they are doing is important not only in itself but also within the context of the larger movements for human dignity and sexual, racial, and social equality.

AFFIRMATIVE ACTION IN
AN ECONOMY OF SCARCITY

◆ ◆ ◆

[1974]

THE CONTROVERSY OVER AFFIRMATIVE ACTION and quotas has raised a number of important issues for American society. Its critics assert that affirmative action, as currently administered by government, amounts to nothing less than reverse discrimination by forcing employers to give minority groups and female applicants preference over better-qualified white males. Its supporters, on the other hand, see opposition to affirmative action as further proof of the dominant society's resistance to racial advancement. Some deny that affirmative action formulas devised by the government and the courts constitute quotas; others, however, not only acknowledge that quota directives have been issued, but also justify the quota doctrine as a legitimate method for redressing past and present racial inequities.

The A. Philip Randolph Institute believes the affirmative action concept to be a valid and essential contribution to an overall program designed to ameliorate the current effects of racial bias, and, ultimately, to achieve the long-sought goal of racial equality. We do not believe, however, that affirmative action can or should occupy the pivotal role in a strategy for racial progress. Affirmative action, we are convinced, can only succeed when combined with programs which have as their objective a much more fundamental economic transformation than affirmative action could bring about.

We are, furthermore, unalterably opposed to the imposition of quotas or any other form of ratio hiring. Our specific objections will be spelled out later. For now, we would only observe that the implementation of a vigorous affirmative action program which has on occasion included—and we must be honest here—the institution of quota formulas has totally failed to bring about any measurable improvement in the economic condition of the black community. What the imposition of quotas, and the resulting furor they have generated, *have* accomplished is to exacerbate the differences between blacks and other racial and ethnic groups. And to the degree that these tensions and divisions have been provoked, the time when black people are accepted into American social and economic life as full and equal participants has been that much delayed.

The basic issue raised by the quota controversy has less to do with the behavior of the federal bureaucracy, the role of the court system, or even with the persistence of racial discrimination than it has to do with a much more basic consideration. That is the issue of how government is to proceed about the task of fully and peacefully integrating all segments of society and, most particularly, how government is to close the sizable gap between the economic status of blacks and whites.

One of the most striking—although almost always overlooked—aspects of the affirmative action debate is the fact that it has arisen during the tenure of a Republican administration which has demonstrated little enthusiasm for many of the traditional strategies of racial change. We do not see this as a contradiction, however. We believe, in fact, that the troubles which the affirmative action program has encountered are due in large part to a lack of interest and absence of policy of the administration.

We must remember that black people enjoyed steady economic progress in the eight years prior to 1969. There were three basic reasons for this progress. One, obviously, was the passage of laws which laid the legal framework for the abolition of outright discrimination.

A second reason was the decision by the government to intervene on behalf of black people in a broad range of social institutions. Pressure was applied to employers, universities, and other institutions to abolish racially discriminatory hiring and admissions practices and to make special efforts to include those groups that had been previously excluded. This early effort at affirmative action, moreover, was combined with a series of manpower training programs established to help those handicapped by inferior educational opportunity to qualify for better-skilled, higher-paying jobs.

An important point is that this program was not the paramount reason for the economic gains achieved by the black community. The affirmative action effort was essential in breaking society's resistance to racial change. But there was a far more basic reason for the broad economic advancement which black Americans experienced in the middle and late 1960s. We are referring to the policies of economic growth and high employment promoted by the Johnson administration. These policies upgraded the living standards of black and white alike. Jobs were available for the unemployed, and better jobs began to open up for those with special skills and abilities.

For the black community, the consequences of these basic economic policies were profound. To note just a few statistics:

1. The median income of black workers doubled between 1960 and 1970.
2. The median income of black families increased from 51 percent of median white income to 61 percent between 1959 and 1969. By 1970, black husband–wife families whose head was under 35 years old were earning an income 82 percent of corresponding white families.
3. The percentage of black families living in poverty declined from 56 percent in 1962 to 31 percent in 1969.
4. Unemployment in the black community dropped from 12.4 percent in 1961 to 6.4 percent in 1969.

These represent serious changes. They were not produced by persuading a few corporations to hire additional black workers, although the affirmative action effort certainly helped. More important, however, was the availability of jobs, the growing opportunities for higher education, and all the other aspects of an expanding economy.

Today the situation is quite different. The most recent report of the Census Bureau on the social and economic status of the black community reveals that an across-the-board pattern of decline has set in since 1969. Joblessness among black workers has nearly doubled, and the number of blacks living in poverty has increased by nearly 160,000. The earnings gap between black and white workers has once again begun to widen. The real income of black families has failed to keep pace with inflation, while earnings of white families has remained slightly above price increases. Finally, a statistic which relates directly to the problems affecting affirmative action, the number of blacks and other minorities moving into higher-paying jobs has declined significantly during the past five years.

We believe that there is a direct relationship between the economic failures of the past five years and the problems which the affirmative action program has encountered. It seems painfully obvious that an affirmative action program cannot achieve its objectives peacefully and democratically if it must function within the context of scarcity. And we are particularly dismayed by the notion that opportunities can be expanded for some groups at a time when the job market is shrinking for all. You simply cannot elevate significant numbers of backs or women into better-paying, higher-skilled, and more satisfying jobs if those jobs don't exist.

Everyone knows racial discrimination still exists. But the high rate of black unemployment and the reversal of hard-won economic gains is not the result of discrimination. All indications, in fact, show that racial prejudice, particularly in the area of employment, is decreasing year by year. Black economic decline is a function of much broader economic failures; failures which, moreover, have left their mark on all Americans regardless of race. But as long as inequality is treated as the product of racism, instead of economics, it will seriously divert the attention of society from difficult issues which ultimately must be faced.

An important reason why the affirmative action program has evoked the criticism of those who, on almost every other occasion, would have supported programs which seek the upgrading of minorities, is that its basic function has been changed to meet new economic realities. Originally conceived as a means of discouraging racial and sexual bias, affirmative action has been transformed, by design or otherwise, into a strategy which attempts to deal with the effects of a faltering economy.

Two areas which have drawn the most scrupulous attention of contract compliance officials have been the universities and the construction industry, both of which also happen to be suffering quite seriously from the recessionary economy. To fully integrate the construction and education field has long been a prime goal of the civil rights movement. But it simply cannot be accomplished when there are fewer jobs for everyone, or where the industry's growth is insufficiently strong to meet employment demands.

There are those who argue that, on a short-term basis, quota hiring schemes represent an effective and expedient means of resolving a difficult social problem. But we are convinced that the inherent dangers of the quota principle far outweigh any temporary gains they might bring.

One of the most serious dangers of the quota doctrine is that it will perpetuate the stereotypical—and profoundly mistaken—view that blacks lack the ability and the will to make it on their own. Should quotas become institutionalized as government policy, society, as black educator Thomas Sowell has warned, would no doubt conclude that Negroes "must be given something in order to have something."

Quotas would further entrench the tendency of society to respond to the call for equal opportunity with tokenism. Quotas, in fact, are tokenism taken to its logical conclusion. Blacks object to the token because it downgrades the dignity and abilities of the individual, cheapening both his or her accomplishments and the accomplishments of other blacks to follow. The same is true of the quota, only to a greater degree. The black who benefits from the quota suffers the uncertainty of never knowing whether he made it on his merits, or was simply hired to meet a government decree. As for the dominant white society, it would automatically question the abilities of all blacks, including the overwhelming majority who have succeeded because of their intelligence, skills, and self-discipline.

We also believe that the widespread application of quotas would unquestionably lead to the weakening of the merit principle. We recognize that what has been referred to as "merit" often works to the unfair exclusion of certain racial or sexual groups. Thus one of the affirmative action program's most signal accomplishments is to force society to reevaluate the standards which determine who is hired, admitted to college, and so on.

But we are determinedly opposed to a broad assault on the concept of qualifications and standards. For where legitimate standards are weakened, or abolished altogether, it is those who are most vulnerable to discrimination or whimsy who will suffer the most severe consequences. It should be kept in mind that blacks have entered many skilled trades and professions in significantly large numbers. Very often they won their position precisely because their qualifications were superior to other applicants. That blacks are underrepresented in a particular profession does not by itself constitute racial discrimination. Very often the inability of large numbers of blacks to qualify for a particular job is a function of poor educational background. It is for this reason that we believe it is essential for government to expand its efforts to compensate for the inferior education in the inner cities.

We would like to conclude by offering some conclusions about basic strategies of racial advancement.

1. Affirmative action efforts should be largely directed to instances of racial discrimination. In place of ratio or quota formulas, those institutions that have been found guilty of practicing discrimination should be given stiff fines; in other instances of recalcitrance, such as have been exhibited by Southern police departments, government should consider asking the courts to institute racially blind lotteries to determine hiring procedures. We also favor the cancellation of government contracts in cases where racial or sexual bias has been proven.

2. Federal manpower and education programs should be expanded. In the manpower area, we would like to point to the success of the Recruitment and Training Program, which has helped place over 12,000 minority youths with apprenticeship programs in the building trades, as a possible model for other programs.

3. Government should continue to question the standards and qualifications for hiring. But it should keep in mind that standards are most important to those who are the likely victims of discrimination. The reforming of standards should not mean their weakening or abandonment.

4. Finally, there should be a realization that affirmative action, by itself, can do little to help blacks unless it operates in a positive economic framework. An affirmative action program cannot find jobs for the unemployed or help the underemployed into better jobs if those jobs do not exist. The most important issue is an economy of growth and expansion. Above all, it must be an economy providing a job for all.

CIVIL RIGHTS AND UNCIVIL WRONGS

◆ ◆ ◆

[1982]

ACCORDING TO A RECENT REPORT in the *New York Times*, the Harvard Black Law Student Coalition and the Harvard Third World Coalition are calling for a boycott of a Harvard Law School course on race and legal issues because that course will, in part, be taught by a white civil rights lawyer. The lawyer in question is Mr. Jack Greenberg, executive director of the NAACP Legal Defense and Educational Fund.

The leaders of the boycott are protesting Jack Greenberg's appointment for two reasons. Because he is white, the students believe that Mr. Greenberg is, in the words of the Third World Coalition, unable to identify and empathize with the social, cultural, economic, and political experiences of the third world communities. Secondly, the students are opposed to Mr. Greenberg's serving as director of the NAACP Legal Defense and Educational Fund, again presumably because he is not black.

The objection to Mr. Greenberg's role in teaching the Harvard course and to heading the Legal Defense Fund simply because he is white amounts to nothing more than blatant racism: the denial of a person's right to pursue certain activities solely on account of his race. Blacks, as victims of racial discrimination, should be the first to reject the view that race can disqualify one from any particular pursuit.

Anyone who objectively examines the record will conclude that Jack Greenberg is eminently qualified to teach civil rights law and to direct an important civil rights organization. Indeed, during his twenty years as head of the Legal Defense Fund, Mr. Greenberg has shown himself to be one of our country's most effective fighters for racial justice and civil rights. Over the years he has directly participated in many of the landmark civil rights victories which have been won in our nation's courts.

What, then, one might think, has provoked the militant protest of Harvard Law School's young blacks? Today, black law students at Harvard feel frustration at the fact that their less privileged counterparts in the ghetto are suffering unemployment rates approaching 50 percent. They feel great unease over the current administration's callous disregard for such matters as equal employment opportunity. They are angry at what they rightly perceive as an abandonment by the federal government of its legitimate role as a leading advocate of civil rights. In this context it is entirely understandable that these students would seek to make their voices heard. It is regrettable, however, that their militancy and sense of social responsibility manifests itself in this fundamentally destructive and irresponsible way.

Harvard's young blacks are pursuing their education not only as a result of their abilities, but also as a consequence of the opportunities opened to them by the civil rights battles waged both inside and outside the courts. It is ironic—indeed perhaps tragic—that they would vent their rage on Jack Greenberg, a talented and sensitive man who has contributed in no small measure to the freedom and dignity of young black Americans.

There is something else underlying the black protest at Harvard. It is the mistaken view that somehow the issue of civil rights is an issue which is exclusively black. Nothing could be further from the truth. Civil rights is an issue of universal significance and, as such, should be important to all Americans. Civil rights, moreover, is an area in which progress cannot be attained without the building of a strong and wide-ranging coalition of blacks and whites, Christians and Jews. Blacks, despite their large numbers, constitute a minority in American life. They cannot achieve progress by going it alone. Attacks such as the one against Jack Greenberg may have the harmful effect of discouraging idealistic whites from participating fully in the battles for civil rights and social justice.

We don't need to worry about Jack Greenberg. He will not be discouraged and his organization will continue to make a contribution to the advancement of racial justice and human rights. We have more cause to worry about the leaders of the Harvard Black Student Coalition. Unless they change their perspectives they will be ill equipped to serve the cause of civil rights, a cause which their recent actions have served to undermine.

Civil Rights: Twenty Years Later

◆ ◆ ◆

[1983]

TWENTY YEARS AGO this week, 250,000 black and white Americans gathered in Washington's sweltering heat to assert their commitment to an America based on the principles of racial and social justice. The 1963 March on Washington for Jobs and Freedom was a landmark in the decades-long struggle for civil rights, economic justice, and due process for all Americans.

Yet twenty years after that pivotal day on which our consciences were stirred by the eloquence of Martin Luther King, Jr., and A. Philip Randolph, the economic status of black Americans is deteriorating, black unemployment stands at nearly 20 percent, and our civil rights leaders appear to be incapable of developing broad-based support for their agenda.

It would be convenient to ascribe all the problems confronting black Americans to the persistence of racism. But while racism continues to exert a baneful influence upon our society, the plight of black Americans today is more and more the consequence of a number of important nonracist, structural features of our economy:

- The decline in labor-intensive industries and the displacement of unskilled and semiskilled black workers as a consequence of automation and robotization.
- The elimination, because of unfair foreign competition and a severe recession, of hundreds of thousands of jobs in industries such as steel and autos that have historically provided well-paying jobs for large numbers of black workers.

- The collapse of black family structures—a result as well as a cause of the black plight—and the alarming increase in the number of unwed black mothers, most of whom live in poverty.
- The decline in the size of the public sector, which in recent years has employed some 60 percent of all black college graduates and has been a major factor in the emergence of a black middle class.
- The shift from heavy industry and manufacturing toward high-technology industries for which many blacks are ill prepared.
- The continued growth of a black underclass of poor and indigent which in 1978 stood at 30 percent but today stands at approximately 36 percent.

It would, of course, be easy to pin the blame for all this on the current administration. Although President Reagan's policy of blind reliance on the marketplace has worsened the plight of blacks, the deteriorating conditions of the black poor and particularly of the working poor began before Reagan took office and would have continued, perhaps at a slower pace, even had President Carter been re-elected.

Some may argue that the problems I have outlined are too large ever to be solved. Yet, paradoxically, the dilemmas confronting black Americans *are* solvable, for the very reason that they are now intimately linked with the overall performance of our national economy. Although blacks are disproportionately represented among the poor, there are ever-increasing numbers of white poor. Although many blacks are joining the ranks of the jobless because of the decline in our basic industries, far larger numbers of whites have lost their jobs.

An important opportunity exists to develop a broad coalition based on a nonracial strategy for dealing with the decline of basic industries, with the significant growth in poverty and with the high rates of unemployment that will persist even after our projected economic "recovery." Unlike twenty years ago, when discrimination was the most significant obstacle to black economic well-being, the latest available figures show that except in the South, the median wage of blacks who are lucky enough to hold jobs is 99 percent that of the median white wage. This rarely acknowledged fact is a consequence of the civil rights legislation of the 1960s. It is also a consequence of the high rate of black participation in organized labor. For as the late black labor leader A. Philip Randolph noted, a union contract provides equitable, nonracial wage standards for ell employees. Unlike twenty years ago, when we marched to protest the racist denial of black access to the voting booth, today, as a result of the 1965 Voting Rights Act, black voters are a cohesive and increasingly significant national political force with a rate of voter participation approaching that of the white electorate.

Each of these developments confirms the correctness of Randolph's view in 1963 that civil rights would be supplanted by economic rights as the fundamental issue for black Americans. Today the recession and the long-term crisis our nation confronts suggests that economic issues are not solely an item for the black agenda. They are a matter of concern for white blue-collar workers, for recent college graduates anxious about a stagnant job market, and for the growing ranks of black and white poor.

It can therefore be asserted that the goal of the participation of large numbers of blacks in the economic mainstream has been achieved. Yet when in 1963 we marched under the banner of integration we did not envision that participation to be within industries and occupations that are in substantial decline.

Thus today's black agenda must be part and parcel of an agenda for all Americans. It must be an agenda that includes such items as national commitment to excellence in education, federal programs in vocational training, increased federal aid for higher education, and a national industrial policy in which government plays an active role in fueling the growth of expanding industries, easing the transition of workers displaced by the changing economy, and developing a more highly skilled work force able to compete in the international marketplace.

Clearly such an agenda is not specifically black. Rather it is an agenda that can unite a potent coalition of blacks and whites, Christians and Jews, workers and the poor. Only such a coalition can help attain the goals that twenty years ago brought 250,000 of us to the edges of Washington's reflecting pool on a scorching August Saturday. Only such a coalition can help us achieve our centuries-long dream of "Jobs and Freedom."

PART FIVE

◆ ◆ ◆

GAY RIGHTS

From Montgomery to Stonewall

◆ ◆ ◆

[1986]

IN 1955 WHEN ROSA PARKS sat down and began the Montgomery Bus Protest, if anyone had said that it would be the beginning of a most extraordinary revolution, most people, including myself, would have doubted it.

But revolutionary beginnings are often unpredictable. Consider, for example, Russia. In 1917 Lenin was in Switzerland writing a book indicating that the Russian Revolution could not possibly begin before 1925. Then, a most unusual thing happened. Some women in a factory were cold, and to warm themselves they decided to go out into the street and parade around the plaza. Some Russian soldiers, upon seeing these women, assumed that they were making a protest and joined them. Thus the Russian Revolution began!

Consider now gay rights. In 1969, in New York of all places, in Greenwich Village, a group of gay people were in a bar. Recall that the 1960s was a period of extreme militancy—there were antiwar demonstrations, civil rights demonstrations, and women's rights demonstrations. The patrons of the bar added gay rights demonstration to the list. The events began when several cops moved into the bar to close it down, a very common practice in that period, forcing many gay bars to go underground. The cops were rough and violent, and, for the first time in the history of the United States, gays, as a collective group, fought back— and not just that night but the following night, and the next, and the night after that.

That was the beginning of an extraordinary revolution, similar to the Montgomery Bus Boycott in that it was not expected that anything extraordinary would occur. As in the case of the women who left the Russian factory, and as in the case of Rosa Parks who sat down in the white part of the bus, something began to happen. People began to protest. They began to fight for the right to live in dignity, the right to resist arbitrary behavior on the part of authorities, the right essentially to be one's self in every respect, and the right to be protected under law. In other words, people began to fight for their human rights.

Gay people must continue this protest. This will not be easy, in part because homosexuality remains an identity that is subject to a "we/they" distinction. People who would not say, "I am like this, but black people are like that," or "we are like this, but women are like that," or "we are like this, but Jews are like that," find it extremely simple to say, "homosexuals are like that, but we are like this." That's what makes our struggle the central struggle of our time, the central struggle for democracy and the central struggle for human rights. If gay people do not understand that, they do not understand the opportunity before them, nor do they understand the terrifying burdens they carry on their shoulders.

There are four burdens, which gays, along with every other despised group, whether it is blacks following slavery and reconstruction, or Jews fearful of Germany, must address. The first is to recognize that one must overcome fear. The second is overcoming self-hate. The third is overcoming self-denial. The fourth burden is more political. It is to recognize that the job of the gay community is not to deal with extremists who would castrate us or put us on an island and drop an H-bomb on us. The fact of the matter is that there is a small percentage of people in America who understand the true nature of the homosexual community. There is another small percentage who will never understand us. Our job is not to get those people who dislike us to love us. Nor was our aim in the civil rights movement to get prejudiced white people to love us. Our aim was to try to create the kind of America, legislatively, morally, and psychologically, such that even though some whites continued to hate us, they could not openly manifest that hate. That's our job today: to control the extent to which people can publicly manifest antigay sentiment.

Well, what do we have to do that is concrete? We have to fight for legislation wherever we are, to state our case clearly, as blacks had to do in the South when it was profoundly uncomfortable. Some people say to me, "Well, Mr. Rustin, how long is it going to take?" Let me point out to you that it doesn't take a law to get rid of a practice. The NAACP worked for sixty years to get an antilynch law in this country. We never got an antilynch law, and now we don't need one. It was the propaganda for the law we never got that liberated us.

> *Editied from a talk presented to a gay*
> *student group at the University of*
> *Pennsylvania, April 9, 1986.*

THE NEW "NIGGERS" ARE GAYS

◆ ◆ ◆

[1986]

TODAY, BLACKS ARE NO LONGER THE LITMUS PAPER or the barometer of social change. Blacks are in every segment of society and there are laws that help to protect them from racial discrimination. The new "niggers" are gays. No person who hopes to get politically elected, even in the deep South, not even Governor Wallace, would dare to stand in the schoolhouse door to keep blacks out. Nobody would dare openly and publicly to argue that blacks should not have the right to use public accommodations. Nobody would dare to say any number of things about blacks that they are perfectly prepared to say about gay people. It is in this sense that gay people are the new barometer for social change.

Indeed, if you want to know whether today people believe in democracy, if you want to know whether they are true democrats, if you want to know whether they are human rights activists, the question to ask is, "What about gay people?" Because that is now the litmus paper by which this democracy is to be judged. The barometer for social change is measured by selecting the group which is most mistreated. To determine where society is with respect to change, one does not ask, "What do you think about the education of children?" Nor does one ask, "Do you believe the aged should have Social Security?" The question of social change should be framed with the most vulnerable group in mind: gay people.

Therefore, I would like to be very hard with the gay community, not for the sake of being hard, but to make clear that, because we stand in the center of progress toward democracy, we have a terrifying responsibility to the whole society.

There are four aspects to this responsibility. First, the gay community cannot work for justice for itself alone. Unless the community fights for *all,* it is fighting for nobody, least of all for itself. Second, gay people should not practice prejudice. It is inconsistent for gay people to be anti-semitic or racist. These gay people do not understand human rights.

Third, gay people should look not only at what people are doing to us but also what we are doing to each other. Fourth, gay people should recognize that we cannot fight for the rights of gays unless we are ready to fight for a new mood in the United States, unless we are ready to fight for a radicalization of this society. You will not feed people *à la* the philosophy of the Reagan administration. Imagine a society that takes lunches from school children. Do you really think it's possible for gays to get civil rights in that kind of society? Do you really think that a society that deprives students of food will confer rights to gay people? And what about people my age who don't have my vigor at seventy-five, who are not provided with adequate Social Security? These economic concerns must go hand-in-hand and, to a degree, precede the possibility of dealing with the most grievous problem—which is sexual prejudice.

Edited from a speech delivered to the
Philadelphia chapter of Black and White
Men Together, March 1, 1986.

BROTHER TO BROTHER:
AN INTERVIEW WITH JOSEPH BEAM

◆ ◆ ◆

[1986]

JOSEPH BEAM: How instrumental were you in getting Jesse Jackson to embrace lesbians and gays in the Rainbow Coalition of his 1984 Presidential campaign?

BAYARD RUSTIN: Well I played a very, very limited role in the Jesse Jackson campaign. I do not look upon myself as one who supports this or that politician to get in office, but as a person who says if and when you get into office you must do these things. So that my only real contribution to the Jesse Jackson campaign was that when he went to talk with the trade union leader of the AFL-CIO, Mr. Lane Kirkland, I accompanied him largely because I felt it important that if Jesse were going to run that he hear from trade unionists as to what their basic program was and why.

BEAM: Over the years, as an openly gay black activist, what kind of treatment has been afforded you by the black press?

RUSTIN: Well, that's an interesting question. The first real interest that the black press showed in me as a gay was soon after I made my first trip to India in 1946, and worked with the Gandhi movement. Several pictures were shown in the American press with me sitting with Mr. Nehru. Soon afterwards, *Jet* magazine had a big throw under the title, "Is Homosexuality Becoming Respectable?" One of the things they concentrated on was the fact that I had been meeting with Nehru. That was a first. Following that I would say except when I have been attacked the black community has seldom seen fit to even mention the gay aspect. And since when I have been attacked I have usually been defended by the black community, I would say that the black newspapers have played it very straight. If I was attacked they simply published that I was attacked, if I was defended they simply said I had been defended. But I don't think they have taken any effort at maligning me or maligning gays or making any effort to give to people anything that wasn't news.

BEAM: Did you ever attempt to add sexual orientation to the agenda of the civil rights movement?

RUSTIN: No I didn't, and because I believe there are certain types of movements which cannot be married, but rather to go about it the other way. To say to the gay rights movement, if you want to win you must join us as individuals into the civil rights movement and to say to the civil rights people if you really want to get freedom for blacks don't think you can do it by getting freedom for blacks alone. You have to join every other movement for the freedom of people. Therefore join the movement as individuals against anti-Semitism, join the movements for the rights of Hispanics, the rights of women, the rights of gays. In other words, I think that each movement has to stand on its own feet because it has a particular agenda, but it can ask other people.

Now there's another reason for that. And that is if people do not organize in the name of their interest, the world will not take them as being serious. And that is the chief reason that every person who is gay should join some gay organization. Because he must prove to the world that he cares about his own freedom. People will never fight for your freedom if you have not given evidence that you are prepared to fight for it yourself. Incidentally, that's the reason that every gay who is in the closet is ultimately a threat to the freedom of gays. I don't want to seem intolerant to them and I think we have to say that to them with a great deal of affection, but remaining in the closet is the other side of the prejudice against gays. Because until you challenge it, you are not playing an active role in fighting it.

BEAM: In 1958, after having worked closely with Dr. King for some time, how did it feel when he failed to offer you the directorship of the Southern Christian Leadership Conference (SCLC), an organization whose structure was principally drafted by you?

RUSTIN: To say I was not disappointed would be a lie. To say I was in any way disturbed other than somewhat disappointed would also be untrue. Back then is not now. There was not a gay liberation movement; there was tremendous prejudice to gays and I think that Dr. King had every right to raise questions as to whether prejudice to gays would affect what he looked upon as a very important movement at the moment. I think the likelihood is, had he made me the executive director, it would have created some problems for him, so he declined. But let me say in Dr. King's defense that a few years later, when the question emerged in 1963, he stood behind me 100 percent and my right to continue organizing the March on Washington for Jobs and Freedom. I think that was, in part, because times were changing, but also because Dr. King felt unhappy with what he had to do earlier.

BEAM: Do you think that black people generally know that a black gay man was the deputy director of that March?

RUSTIN: Everybody finally knew it because when Strom Thurmond stood in the United States Senate and talked for more than three-quarters of an hour, it appeared on the front pages of all the major papers in the country including the *Wall Street Journal,* the *New York Times,* and the *Washington Post.* So those people who read the papers knew.

BEAM: What remarks do you have for other black gay activists who hope to follow in your footsteps?

RUSTIN: Well, I think the most important thing I have to say is that they should try to build coalitions of people for the elimination of *all* injustice. Because if we want to do away with the injustice to *gays* it will not be done because we get rid of the injustice to gays. It will be done because we are forwarding the effort for the elimination of injustice to all. And we will win the rights for gays, or blacks, or Hispanics, or women within the context of whether we are fighting for all. A good example of this is the present Reagan administration. If anyone thinks they're going to get anything out of the Reagan administration for any particular group, they're wrong! You have to all combine and fight a head-on battle—in the name of justice and equality—and even that's going to be difficult. But if we let ourselves get separated so that we're working for gays or school children or the aged, we're in trouble.

Black and Gay in
the Civil Rights Movement:
An Interview with Open Hands

◆ ◆ ◆

[1987]

OPEN HANDS: Starting back at the beginning, in West Chester, Pennsylvania, what did you absorb, spoken or unspoken, about homosexuality in your upbringing?

BAYARD RUSTIN: My early life was that of being a member of a very, very close-knit family. I was born illegitimate. My mother was about seventeen when I was born, and, consequently, my grandparents reared me. The family members were largely Democrats, long before most other black families. My grandmother was one of the leaders of the NAACP; she had helped found the Black Nurses' Society and the black community center.

There were two homosexual boys in high school that were rather flamboyant, and the community, I think, looked down on their flamboyance much more than on their homosexuality. But, in general, the question of homosexuality never emerged as a social problem until I got to college. What I heard in high school was: Why don't those guys behave themselves? Why are they always doing something outlandish?

As far as my early life is concerned, there was one other incident. There was one young man who was very highly respected in the community that I can remember as a child hearing whispering about. But I never could put my finger on what it was that made him, in the eyes of people, different. One of the reasons that this was confusing to me was that he was highly respected—he was a member of the church, sang in the choir, played the organ, and seemed to be such a responsible, talented, and charming person that I could never get quite what it was that was being whispered about him. I asked my grandmother once, and she said, "Oh, well, he's just a little different from other people and I wouldn't pay any attention to it." On one occasion this fellow was visiting our home, and when he was leaving he put his arms around me and kissed me (which had never happened to me with a man before). Later when I was discussing him with my grandmother, I said, "You know it's very interesting, but this is the second time that he has hugged me and tried to kiss me." My grandmother simply said, "Well, did you enjoy it?" And I said, "No, I felt it very peculiar." And she said, "Well, if you don't enjoy it, don't let him do it." That's all she said. And that was the extent of it.

Now it was in college I came to understand that I had a real physical attraction to a young man.

OPEN HANDS: This attraction was to a particular young man?

RUSTIN: Oh yes, very definitely. He lived in California. We were both at Wilberforce College in Ohio. He used to come home with me for the holidays. I had a bedroom of my own, but it had twin beds in it—he slept in his bed and I slept in mine. We never had any physical relationship but a very intense, friendly relationship. At that point, I knew exactly what was going on, but I did not feel then that I could handle such a physical relationship. But I never went through any trauma about coming out because I realized what was going on. I was also strong and secure enough to be able to handle it. But I have always sympathized with people who, for one reason or another, go through the great trauma that I never experienced.

OPEN HANDS: Can you say a little more about how you handled your coming out?

RUSTIN: There was one young man at home who was interested in me when I came back from college. (This is what makes me know that my grandmother knew what was happening.) My grandmother called me into the kitchen one Saturday morning (we always had sort of weekly talks on Saturday morning in the kitchen while we were preparing lunch), and she said, "You know, I want to recommend something to you. In selecting your male friends, you should be careful that you associate with people who have as much to lose as you have." And I said, "What do you mean, as much to lose as I have?" She said, "Well, you have a very good reputation, so you should go around with people who have good reputations. You are being educated; you must make friends with people who are being educated. You have certain values, and you must make certain that people you go out with hold those values. Otherwise you could find yourself in very serious trouble. Because very often people who do not have as much to lose as you have can be very careless in befriending you because they are careless in befriending themselves." I think that a family in which the members know and accept one's lifestyle is the most helpful factor for emotional stability. They were aware that I was having an affair with my friend from college, and they obviously approved it. Not that anybody said, "Oh, I think it's a good thing." But they would say, "Friends have invited us over for dinner tonight, and we told them that your friend is here, and they said it's quite all right for you to bring him along." There was never any conflict. And yet there was never any real discussion.

OPEN HANDS: A few years later you moved to New York City. The clubs in Harlem in the 1930s and 1940s were known as meccas for gay men and lesbians. Did you interact in that world?

RUSTIN: Well, Harlem was a totally different world than I had known. When I came to New York, I lived with a sister (really my aunt) who lived on St. Nicholas Avenue, which was at that time the main thoroughfare of black New York aristocracy—it was called Sugar Hill. That's where the black doctors, the lawyers, the professionals, and ministers lived. In the black upper class there were a great number of gay people. So long as they did not publicize their gayness, there was little or no discussion of it. A number of the poets, artists, musicians were gay or lesbian. And the clubs paid little attention. In that early period there were few gay clubs because there didn't need to be. The gay clubs came later, with World War II and after. I think that the black community has been largely willing to accept its gay elements so long as they were not openly gay. It was later when the gay clubs came, and gay men and lesbians wanted the right to come out of the closet, that I think the black community became quite as intolerant as the white community.

OPEN HANDS: Why is that, in your estimation? What caused the resistance to acceptance?

RUSTIN: Well, I think the community felt that we have, as blacks, so many problems to put up with, and we have to defend ourselves so vigorously against being labeled as ignorant, irresponsible, shufflers, etc., there's so much prejudice against us, why do we need the gay thing, too? I remember on one occasion somebody said to me, "Goodness gracious! You're a socialist, you're a conscientious objector, you're gay, you're black, how many jeopardies can you afford?" I found that people in the civil rights movement were perfectly willing to accept me so long as I didn't declare that I was gay.

OPEN HANDS: During those years in New York were there any gay or lesbian role models for you?

RUSTIN: Hall Johnson, leader of the Hall Johnson Choir, was gay and one of the most important black musicians of his time. He was probably the key role model for me. He was responsible for helping train people like Leontyne Price and all kinds of other opera singers, and was the inspiration for many other musicians. I used to go to his apartment. It was never a hangout for gay men and lesbians; it was a hangout for musicians and artists. And if you were gay or lesbian (and there were many of us) you were there too.

OPEN HANDS: As you began working for the Fellowship of Reconciliation, did it seem like you were leading a double life—moving in the artist and musician circles in New York and becoming involved in the different sphere of human rights activists?

RUSTIN: It was amongst the Fellowship people that there was hypocrisy—more so—called love and affection and nonviolence toward the human family, but it was there that I found some of the worst attitudes to gays. I experienced this personally after I'd been released from working with the Fellowship when I was arrested in California on what they called a "morals charge." Many of the people in the Fellowship of Reconciliation were absolutely intolerant in their attitudes. When I lost my job there, some of these nonviolent Christians despite their love and affection for humanity were not really able to express very much affection to me.

Whereas members of my family (a couple of them had actually fought in the war) were loving, considerate, and accepting. So there are times when people of goodwill may find it difficult to maintain consistency between belief and action. This can be very difficult for some people when faced with a homosexual relationship.

OPEN HANDS: Later, in the early '60s, Adam Clayton Powell threatened to expose you, and Strom Thurmond did make accusations against you. Did you experience many other incidents like these?

RUSTIN: Yes, for example, Martin Luther King, with whom I worked very closely, became very distressed when a number of the ministers working for him wanted him to dismiss me from his staff because of my homosexuality. Martin set up a committee to discover what he should do. They said that, despite the fact that I had contributed tremendously to the organization (I drew up the plans for the creation of the Southern Christian Leadership Conference and did most of the planning and fundraising in the early days), they thought that I should separate myself from Dr. King.

OPEN HANDS: When was this, the late 1950s?

RUSTIN: This was about 1960 actually. This was the time when Powell threatened to expose my so-called homosexual relationship with Dr. King. There, of course, was no homosexual relationship with Dr. King. But Martin was so uneasy about it that I decided I did not want Dr. King to have to dismiss me. I had come to the SCLC to help. If I was going to be a burden I would leave—and I did. However, Dr. King was never happy about my leaving. He was deeply torn—although I had left the SCLC, he frequently called me in and asked me to help. While in 1960 he felt real pressure to fire me, in 1963 he agreed that I should organize the March on Washington, of which he was one of the leaders.

OPEN HANDS: During those tumultuous times when your private life was threatened to be exposed, how did you deal with that? Whom did you find support from?

RUSTIN: In June of 1963, Senator Strom Thurmond stood in the Congress and denounced the March on Washington because I was organizing it.

He called me a communist, a sexual pervert, a draft dodger, etc. The next day Mr. A. Philip Randolph called all the black leaders and said, "I want to answer Strom Thurmond's attack. But I think we ought not to get involved in a big discussion of homosexuality or communism or draft dodging. What I want to do, with the approval of all the black leaders, is to issue a statement which says: 'We, the black leaders of the civil rights movements and the leaders of the trade union movement and the leaders of the Jewish, Protestant, and Catholic church which are organizing this march, have absolute confidence in Bayard Rustin's ability, his integrity, and his commitment to nonviolence as the best way to bring about social change. He will continue to organize the March with our full and undivided support.'" He said, "If any of you are called, I do not want any discussion beyond that—Is he a homosexual? Has he been arrested? We simply say we have complete confidence in him and his integrity." And that's exactly what happened.

Someone came to Mr. Randolph once and said, "Do you know that Bayard Rustin is a homosexual? Do you know he has been arrested in California? I don't know how you could have anyone who is a homosexual working for you." Mr. Randolph said, "Well, well, if Bayard, a homosexual, is that talented—and I know the work he does for me—maybe I should be looking for somebody else homosexual who could be so useful." Mr. Randolph was such a completely honest person who wanted everyone else also to be honest. Had anyone said to him, "Mr. Randolph, do you think I should openly admit that I am homosexual?," his attitude, I am sure, would have been, "Although such an admission may cause you problems, you will be happier in the long run." Because his idea was that you have to be what you are.

OPEN HANDS: You were involved in many civil rights groups in the '40s, '50s, '60s, '70s. Did any of them at least begin to internally think about lesbian/gay rights?

RUSTIN: After my arrest (in California in '53), I tried to get the black community to face up to the fact that one of the reasons that some homosexuals went to places where they might well be arrested was that they were not welcome elsewhere. I wanted to get people to change their attitudes, but they always made it personal. They would say, "Well, now, Bayard, we understand—we know who you are and we know what you are, but you're really different." And I'd say, "I don't want to hear that. I want you to change your attitudes." But there was little action, and even now it's very difficult to get the black community doing anything constructive about AIDS because it is thought of as a "gay" problem.

OPEN HANDS: Looking back over your whole life, in what ways did your being a gay man affect the person that you are, the person you have been?

RUSTIN: Oh, I think it has made a great difference. When one is attacked for being gay, it sensitizes you to a greater understanding and sympathy for others who face bigotry, and one realizes the damage that being misunderstood can do to people. It's quite all right when people blast my politics. That's their obligation. But to attack anyone because he's Jewish, black, a homosexual, a woman, or any other reason over which that person has no control is quite terrible. But making my peace and adjusting to being attacked has helped me to grow. It's given me a certain sense of obligation to other people, and it's given me a maturity as well as a sense of humor.

You were asking about role models earlier—I think one of the best, most helpful, black men in the '20s and '30s and '40s was a professor at Howard University whose name was Alain Locke. I got to know Alain Locke very well. He was gay and held open house for the literati and for young people like young Langston Hughes and Richard Wright. I suspect that he was probably more of a male role model for me than anyone else. He never felt it necessary to discuss his gayness. He was always a friend to those who were aspiring to be writers. Therefore, he universalized his affection to people. And he carried himself in such a way that the most people could say about him was that they suspected he was gay, not that he was mean or that he was in any way unkind. So I find that it's very important for members of a minority group to develop an inner security. For in that way we become fearless and very decent human beings.

I shall never forget once at a meeting, a chap from the Fellowship of Reconciliation accused me of impairing the morals of minors and stated that the organization should not permit me to associate with all the youngsters in the organization. A young man stood up at this meeting and said something which was so amazing I have never forgotten about it. He said, "I want this group to know that I am now twenty-two, and I went to bed with Bayard Rustin last year. And it was a culmination of five years of the most profound and deep friendship and love that I have ever known. And I am *not* homosexual, and I will marry, and I promise you now, if my first child is a boy, I'm going to name him Bayard. I learned so many important and good things from him. That's why I want my firstborn named Bayard." Now that took a tremendous amount of nerve on his part. Four years later he named his firstborn Bayard.

OPEN HANDS: If you had to do it all over, if you had to live life knowing what you know now, would you want to be gay?

RUSTIN: I think, if I had a choice, I would probably elect not to be gay. Because I think that I might be able to do more to fight against the prejudice to gays if I weren't gay, because some people say I'm simply trying to defend myself. But that's the only reason. I want to get rid of all kinds of prejudices. And, quite frankly, one of the prejudices which I find most difficult is the prejudice that some black homosexuals have to white homosexuals, the prejudice that Oriental homosexuals have to everybody but Oriental homosexuals, and certainly the tremendous amount of prejudice that some white gay men and lesbians have to blacks. And the reason this is sad to me is not that I expect homosexuals to be any different basically than any other human being, but it is sad because I do not believe that they know that it is not prejudice to any one group that is the problem, it is prejudice itself that is the problem.

That brings me to a very important point—people who do not fight against all kinds of prejudice are doing three terrible things. They are, first of all, perpetuating harm to others. Secondly, they are denying their own selves because every heterosexual is a part of homosexuality and every homosexual is part of this so-called straight world. If I harm any human being by my bigotry, I am, at the same time, harming myself because I'm a part of that person. And, finally, every indifference to prejudice is suicide because, if I don't fight all bigotry, bigotry itself will be strengthened and, sooner or later, it will turn on me. I think that one of the things we have to be very careful of in the gay and lesbian community is that we do not under any circumstances permit ourselves to hold on to any indifference to the suffering of any other human being.

The homosexuals who did not fight Hitler's prejudice to the Jews finally got it. Now they may have gotten it anyhow. But when the Gestapo came up the stairs after them, they would have died knowing that they were better human beings if only they had fought fascism and resisted when the Jews were being murdered.

OPEN HANDS: Are you hopeful for the human race? Do you think prejudice will be overcome? Do you think it's improved during your lifetime?

RUSTIN: Oh, I think, it's improved some places; it's gotten worse in others. But I have learned a very significant lesson from the Jewish prophets. If one really follows the commandments of these prophets, the question of hopeful or nonhopeful may become secondary or unimportant. Because these prophets taught that God does not require us to achieve any of the good tasks that humanity must pursue. What God requires of us is that we not stop trying. And, therefore, I do not expect that we can do anything more than reduce prejudice to an irreducible minimum. We have the responsibility to try to improve economic and social conditions which I believe may well reduce human problems. As long as there's this much unemployment amongst blacks and poor Hispanics and poor whites, they will prey on each other. Secondly, we can try to deal with problems of injustice by setting up a legal structure which outlaws them and causes people to be punished if they violate them. There's a third way, and this is what I call the way of reconciliation. If you can get enough law and you can get an economic structure, then you can get people to live together in harmony, to go to school together, and they will cooperate in the work force. Then there is a deep learning process in which new stimuli will create new responses. Now these are three of the ways in which I believe we can try to reduce prejudice.

I want to say a word while I'm on this, about the uniqueness of the gay and lesbian community today. The gay community now becomes the most important element when it comes to answering the question that you have raised about hope. Because the gay community today has taken over where the black community left off in '68 or '69. In those days black people were the barometer of social change; black people were the litmus paper of social change. At that time if a person was prepared to accept blacks then it followed that that person was prepared to look at Jews, Catholics, and other persons. Today gay men and lesbians have taken over that social role. Because theirs is now the central problem and, if you are to go to the bottom line, if people cannot accept gay men and lesbians, they may not be able to accept anybody who is different

That is what makes the homosexual central to how much progress we can make in human rights. That means there must be among gay men and lesbians themselves tremendous political activity. And that means now that we have an additional good reason for coming out of the closet. We cannot really respect ourselves unless we're willing to state quite honestly who we are. Beyond this there's now another reason why we must come out of the closet, and that is to help carry on the real political struggle for acceptance. Because if you do not fight for yourself in a very vigorous way, you cannot expect anybody to join in a fight with you.

OPEN HANDS: Do you have any observations, looking historically, at the black civil rights movement and the lesbian/gay civil rights movement— where have there been similarities; where have there been differences?

RUSTIN: Well, I think the moral question is similar. But after you get beyond that question, I think there are not many similarities. The gay and lesbian community is not a community which looks any one way; it is not a community which behaves in any one way. Wherein blacks all look black (which is not true, but people think so) and they have certain things you can point to—they were once slaves, they were once uneducated—gay men and lesbians tend to belong to a more educated, college-trained group. Gay men and lesbians are not all in that group, by any means, but the visible ones are.

The prejudice to gay men and lesbians is much deeper. Those who fight against gay men and lesbians carry a propaganda which is designed to strike deeply at the most fundamental concerns of our society. Antigay/-lesbian proponents will argue that humanity must have the family and gay men and lesbians are antifamily. The society advances only as there are children. Gay men and lesbians will not produce children. The society will only exist as long as there is a high standard of moral behavior. Gay men particularly are pictured as running around having sex with everybody in sight and not concerned with anything other than their own immediate pleasure and satisfaction. Now you and I know that much of that is decidedly untrue. But gay men and lesbians are looked on as being an unstable element when what you need in the society is stability. As I said this propaganda has been carefully designed.

Beyond all this, the bigots argue that segments of both the Old and the New Testament have denounced homosexuality as an abomination. If one goes through the scriptures and picks out little pieces of this and that, it's possible to distort. You know, those who believe you shouldn't have anything to drink find the little place in the Bible that justifies that attitude. Those who want to drink will quote St. Paul and say, "A little wine is good for thy stomach's sake." People will pick out what they want rather than seeing the scriptures as a growth in spiritual insight. The people who want to carry on racial prejudice will no longer talk about this as the way that God wants it. But people will still tell you that homosexuality is ungodly and destructive. That's what I mean when I say that gay men and lesbians have now become the barometer and the litmus paper of human rights attitudes and social change.

Martin Luther King's
Views on Gay People

◆ ◆ ◆

[1987]

IT IS DIFFICULT FOR ME TO KNOW what Dr. King felt about gayness except to say that I'm sure he would have been sympathetic and would not have had the prejudicial view. Otherwise he would not have hired me. He never felt it necessary to discuss that with me. He was under such extraordinary pressure about his own sex life. J. Edgar Hoover was spreading stories, and there were very real efforts to entrap him. I think at a given point he had to reach a decision. My being gay was not a problem for Dr. King but a problem for the movement.

He finally came to the decision that he needed to talk with some people in his organization. Reverend Thomas Kilgore, a good friend of mine and pastor of Friendship Baptist Church, was a man Dr. King turned to. Reverend Kilgore asked Martin to set up a committee to advise him. The committee finally came to the decision that my sex life was a burden to Dr. King. I think it was around July when they advised him that he should ask me to leave. I told Dr. King that if advisors closest to him felt I was a burden, then rather than put him in a position that he had to say leave, I would go. He was just so harassed that I felt it was my obligation to relieve him of as much of that as I could. Someone sent his wife a tape in which he was supposedly having an affair with another woman.

There was also another problem: some of the people in the Democratic Party were distressed at Dr. King's marching, as he did in 1960 and in 1964, against the conventions of both of the major parties calling for more immediate relief to black people through Congress. Adam Clayton Powell, for some reason I will never understand, actually called Dr. King when he was in Brazil and indicated that he was aware of some relationship between me and Dr. King, which, of course, there was not. This added to his anxiety about additional discussions of sex.

I don't want you to think that Dr. King was the only civil rights leader who raised these questions. Although Dr. King had been relieved by my officially leaving, he continued to call on me as Mr. Garrow makes clear in his book, *Bearing the Cross,* over and over. Now this all took place around 1960; but in 1963 when the question came up whether I should be the director of the March on Washington, I got 100 percent cooperation. On this occasion, it was Roy Wilkins who raised the question. Roy was my friend. He told me he was going into the meeting to object. He made it quite clear that he had absolutely no prejudice toward me or toward homosexuality; but he said: "I put the movement first above all things, and I believe it is my moral obligation to go into this meeting and say that with all of your talent, I don't think you should lead this important march. They are not only going to raise the question of homosexuality. Although I know you are a Quaker and I know you paid a heavy price for your conscientious objection, they are going to call you a draft dodger." He was referring to my three years in prison as a conscientious objector in 1943, '44, and '45. "But," Mr. Wilkins also said, "you were once, and you've never said you weren't, a member of the Young Communist League. Therefore, they are going to raise three questions: the question of homosexuality, the question of draft-dodges, the question of your being a Communist. The fact that you are a Socialist is a problem, because people in the United States don't differentiate between Socialism and Communism." We also had a long discussion about how the Communists had co-opted the term Socialist, although the two systems are totally different: one is democratic and one is totalitarian.

Mr. Randolph [who was president of the Brotherhood of Sleeping Car Porters and president of the A. Philip Randolph Institute] took the view that it was important for him to have me. Mr. Randolph was finally made director of the march. "But I want to warn you before you vote that if I'm made leader, I'm going to be given the privilege of determining my staff," he said. "I also want you to know I'll make Bayard Rustin my deputy." He turned to Martin and said: "Dr. King, how do you vote?" And Dr. King said: "I vote yes." He turned to Jim Farmer. Jim

Farmer said: "I vote yes." Then he turned to Roy Wilkins. Roy said: "Phil, you've got me over a barrel, I'll go along with you." So, it was never a prejudicial situation; it was that given the attitude at that time, people felt this was a problem. I think there were others who felt: How many problems can a guy have and expect us to elevate him to the directorship of this march?

From an interview conducted by
Redvers Jeanmarie, March 1987.

THE IMPORTANCE OF GAY RIGHTS
LEGISLATION

◆ ◆ ◆

[1987]

Statement on Proposed Amendments to Law Banning Discrimination on the Basis of Sexual Orientation

I am Bayard Rustin, Chairman of the Randolph Institute and Chairman of the Executive Committee of the Leadership Conference on Civil Rights, which is composed of over 150 national groups dedicated to human rights for all. As one who has been active in the struggle to extend democracy to *all* Americans for over fifty years I am opposed to any attempt to amend the recently enacted law banning discrimination on the basis of sexual orientation.

I have been arrested twenty-four times in the struggle for civil and human rights. My first arrest was in 1928 merely for distributing leaflets on behalf of Al Smith's candidacy for President in a climate of anti-Catholic hysteria. Since that time I have fought against religious intolerance, political harassment, and racism both here and abroad. I have fought against untouchability in India, against tribalism in Africa, and have sought to ensure that refugees coming to our shores are not subject to the same types of bigotry and intolerance from which they fled. As a member of the U.S. Holocaust Memorial Council I have fought anti-Semitism not only in the United States but around the world.

On the basis of such experiences, I categorically can state and history reveals that when laws are amended to provide "legal loopholes" that deny equal protection for any group of citizens, an immediate threat is created for everyone, including those who may think they are forever immune to the consequences of such discrimination. History demonstrates that no group is ultimately safe from prejudice, bigotry, and harassment so long as any group is subject to special negative treatment. The only final security for all is to provide now equal protection for every group under the law.

I therefore call upon all New Yorkers to give this new law a chance before considering any revisions.

I call upon the City Council to reject amendments to the law that would deny to lesbians and gay men protections that are enjoyed by all other citizens.

I call upon Mayor Koch to veto any amendments designed to weaken this law should such amendments be passed.

❖   ❖   ❖

Twenty Reasons to Support a Gay Rights Bill for New York City

1. Lesbians and gay men need protection of their basic civil rights.
2. Government should stand on the side of the victims of prejudice, not for those who would discriminate or persecute.
3. Government has a legitimate interest in people being known as who they are rather than encouraging dishonesty and hiding.
4. Fifty cities and the state of Wisconsin have passed gay rights legislation with nothing but positive effects.
5. Everyone has a sexual orientation and this bill would protect straight people as well as lesbians and gay men.
6. People should not be persecuted for who they are. Since a gay rights bill would cover sexual orientation and not actions, people would still be responsible for living their sex lives legally and responsibly.
7. The people want it. Poll after poll—even in presumably conservative areas—show that the public supports an end to antigay discrimination.
8. It is the politically wise thing to do. The vocal minority that is against gay rights does not treat it as a single issue when voting the

way people do on, say, the abortion issue. Lesbians and gay men—
who live in every district in this city—will never vote for a candidate
who votes against their rights.

9. It signals tolerance and openness.

10. Lesbians and gay men are not going to go away. They will achieve
    protection of their civil rights sooner or later. Those who stand in
    the way now will become targets for defeat in the next election.
    With gay political organizations in every borough now, those who
    vote against us now will only be helping those clubs to begin the
    work against them earlier.

11. No Councilmember has ever lost his or her seat because of voting
    for this bill. On the other hand, many opponents of gay rights have
    lost elections and, coincidentally, four Council opponents were
    removed for malfeasance in office.

12. No one runs for higher office in this City without supporting les-
    bian and gay rights. The bill is supported by all Citywide officials,
    most of all the Assembly delegation, most of the State Senate and
    Congressional delegations, Senator Moynihan, Governor Cuomo,
    Attorney General Abrams, and so on. If you think you're going any-
    where in politics with an antigay record, think again.

13. The violence against lesbians and gay men is a scandal and outrage.
    The thugs who prey on gay people think they are justified because
    lesbians and gay men have no civil rights protection. The bill doesn't
    address the violence problem specifically, but passage would cer-
    tainly signal people that the government stands on the side of those
    who are victimized.

14. The discharge motion should be passed so that the full Council can
    express its true opinion on this issue. The 6–3 Committee defeat
    certainly doesn't reflect the full Council's feelings on this issue.
    This bill has not had a floor vote since 1974 when it was the first bill
    in the history of the Council to pass Committee and lose on the
    floor. Justice demands that the issue be given a fair debate in the
    full Council. No one will be allowed to hide behind voting against
    the discharge motion purely on procedural grounds. Rule 7.10 of
    the Council provides that discharge is simply an alternate route to
    bring a bill to the floor—not a violation of the Committee system.
    No Committee should be permitted to bottle up a bill for nine
    years when everyone in the Council has strong opinions on it.

15. If you have children and they turn out to be gay or lesbian, would
    you want them to grow up in a place where their basic civil rights
    were not respected?

16. It is the position of the national Democratic Party, adopted in con-
    vention in 1980 and 1982, that discrimination on the basis of sexual
    orientation be brought to an end. All the major Democratic candi-
    dates for President support gay rights.

17. Lesbians and gay men are contributing members of this society. It
    is imperative that we protect their basic civil rights.

18. Most religious denominations support a gay rights bill. No matter
    where these religions stand on the practice of homosexuality—and
    many of them prohibit it—they understand sexual orientation as
    morally neutral and feel that discrimination on the basis of sexual
    orientation is unjust.

19. It brings gay people into the mainstream of society and discourages
    ghettoization and a lack of trust in government.

20. It is the right thing to do.

TIME ON TWO CROSSES: AN INTERVIEW WITH GEORGE CHAUNCEY, JR.

◆◆◆

[1987]

GEORGE CHAUNCEY, JR.: How did your homosexuality affect your work in the civil rights movement, particularly after your arrest in Pasadena in 1953 on a "sex perversion" charge?

BAYARD RUSTIN: There is no question in my mind that there was considerable prejudice amongst a number of people I worked with. But of course they would never admit they were prejudiced. They would say they were afraid that it might hurt the movement. The fact of the matter is, it was already known, it was nothing to hide. You can't hurt the movement unless you have something to reveal. They also said any more talk would hurt me. They would look at me soulfully and say, surely you don't want to go through any more humiliation? Well, I wasn't humiliated. Even at the time of the arrest, I was not humiliated. The fact of the matter is, in my case it was an absolute setup.

CHAUNCEY: Do you mean you were entrapped?

RUSTIN: Yes, that's very definite. But that's unimportant. Let's assume I was completely guilty. It wouldn't matter.

CHAUNCEY: A lot of gay men were entrapped in those days. Do you think you were targeted for political reasons?

RUSTIN: I think so. Because way back as far as 1946, '47, I had organized all over the country, even in the deep South, and I was in California at the time of the arrest, leading demonstrations against discrimination in theaters, hotels, and restaurants.

CHAUNCEY: Could you tell us about specific incidents when your being gay became an issue for the other leaders in the movement? For example, when you and Dr. King were organizing demonstrations at the Democratic and Republican conventions in 1960.

RUSTIN: Actually, [A. Philip] Randolph asked me to organize the marches. I decided that Mr. Randolph ought to get Dr. King to join us, on the simple principle that the other civil rights leaders would feel they had to join in. Dr. King was at the press conference announcing the marches, and then left for Brazil. Later he called me from Brazil very, very agitated indeed, and said that on second thought maybe we ought not to proceed with the marches. At that point, he did not tell me why, straightforwardly. I went to see Mr. Randolph, and asked him to give me permission to say to Dr. King that he was very sorry, but that he and the others were going to go ahead anyhow. I thought that Dr. King would have no choice but to stay in.

I called Martin back and told him this, whereupon he told me the whole story. A woman who was well known in the movement had called him and said that [Congressman Adam Clayton] Powell was going to call a press conference and implicate me and Dr. King in some sort of liaison if Dr. King did not call off the marches. Now, obviously this is a case where Powell had been promised something by the Democratic Party if he'd get rid of me. Dr. King asked for a delay and I said we couldn't afford to delay. In the end, he decided not to go ahead and Powell did not go to the press. This is the kind of thing Adam did.

CHAUNCEY: What about the 1963 March on Washington, when your homosexuality was used publicly in an effort to discredit the movement? The leadership seems to have stood by you then.

RUSTIN: Here again, Mr. Randolph had asked me to organize the march. I proceeded to line up people; it was always a matter of boxing in the civil rights leadership, because each had his own turf. In any event, it was

Mr. [Roy] Wilkins [Executive Director of the NAACP], whom I happen to admire greatly, who raised the question this time. He called me to his office and said, "I don't think you should lead this march because they will try to stop it, and the most important thing they have to stop it with is that the director of it is gay." I said, "Roy, I just disagree with that, and I think that the time has come when we have to stand up and stop running from things. And I don't believe that if this is raised by the Southern Democrats, that it will do anything but spur people on. We can issue a statement which says they will use anything to try and stop us in our march to freedom, but no matter what they use we will win." He disagreed and called a meeting of all the civil rights leaders. Finally, a compromise was reached. Mr. Randolph would be the director of the march, but he made me his deputy.

Then, Strom Thurmond stood in the Senate speaking for three-quarters of an hour on the fact that Bayard Rustin was a homosexual, a draft dodger, and a communist. Newspapers all over the country came out with this front-page story. Mr. Randolph waited for the phone to ring. And it did indeed ring. I went immediately to Mr. Randolph, and we agreed he would make a statement for all the civil rights leaders which basically said, "We have absolute confidence in Bayard Rustin's integrity and ability." He read the statement to the labor leaders and the Jewish and Catholic and Protestant leaders involved in the march and they all agreed to it.

CHAUNCEY: Why do you think the press didn't come down harder on you? Thurmond charged there was a whitewash.

RUSTIN: They had a great deal of respect for our creating the march out of nothing. They just felt that why is this son-of-a-bitch from the South mouthing all of this shit that everybody knows. They thought he was just trying to get us to call off the march. And they didn't like it.

CHAUNCEY: What private conversations did these incidents lead to with Dr. King? Did you ever talk at length with him about your homosexuality?

RUSTIN: Oh yes, yes, of course.

CHAUNCEY: What was his attitude?

RUSTIN: Dr. King came from a very protected background. I don't think he'd ever known a gay person in his life. I think he had no real sympathy or understanding. I think he wanted very much to. But I think he was largely guided by two facts. One was that already people were whispering about him. And I think his attitude was, look, I've got enough of my own problems. I really don't want to be burdened with additional ones. Secondly, he was surrounded by people who, for their own reasons, wanted to get rid of me—Andy Young in particular, and Jesse Jackson.

CHAUNCEY: What reasons? Because of your homosexuality?

RUSTIN: No. Definitely not. It was because we didn't agree on some issues—whether or not King should go north to Chicago, and also the Poor People's Campaign.

CHAUNCEY: Did your being gay interfere with your relationship with Dr. King?

RUSTIN: Dr. King was always terrified of the press. His first question would be what is the press reaction going to be? He would normally have preferred never to discuss any of it. And he never did except when he was pressured in some way into doing so. And on two occasions, I went to him and said I can tell you're deeply agonized by this. So I think that I'm going to get out of the way now. If you need me later, call me back. And on two occasions, he called me back because he needed me.

CHAUNCEY: Did he ever compare your problems to the rumors about his extramarital affairs?

RUSTIN: I wouldn't think there was any possibility of him comparing them, because I don't think he saw them as having any relationship whatever. Oh, the crap that was going on in those motels as the movement moved from place to place was totally acceptable. The homosexual act was not.

CHAUNCEY: What about Mr. Randolph? How much did you talk with him about your being gay?

RUSTIN: Never! Mr. Randolph was a man who drew very strict lines. He would not discuss anybody's personal life. He was a gentleman, of the old order.

PART SIX

◆ ◆ ◆

EQUALITY BEYOND AMERICA

AFRICAN REVOLUTION

◆ ◆ ◆

[1958]

THE STRUGGLE FOR FREEDOM AND JUSTICE against imperialism must be based on power. There are two types of power: one is violent, the other nonviolent. In each, suffering, imprisonment, and death are inevitable. The leaders of the violent revolution seek to inflict the inescapable suffering upon the exploiters. In the nonviolent struggle, the exploited, in spirit and tactic, voluntarily accept the irreducible suffering upon themselves. Their aim is to win over the so-called enemy to the side of truth and justice.

This was the aim and the success of Gandhi and Nehru in India. It is now the hope of thousands of men and women in South Africa who daily refuse to use violence in their struggle against tyranny. The heroic story unfolding in South Africa is becoming known throughout the world. Everywhere men of justice pray for its success. But already in the Gold Coast nonviolence has had remarkable success. This effort, in fact, gave courage to the leaders of South Africa.

Based on Courage

Dr. Kuame Nkrumah, American-educated leader of the Convention Peoples Party (CPP), became Prime Minister of the Gold Coast as a result of the indomitable will of thousands of unarmed black men and women. They faced prison, guns, and death rather than remain colonial subjects.

I want to recall that brilliant page of history as told me not only by Dr. Nkrumah and the leader of the political opposition, Dr. Dangah, but also by many of the simple men who were shot at and imprisoned during the struggle.

In June 1949, after considerable political jockeying for position, Dr. Nkrumah emerged as the dominant and most colorful personality in the Gold Coast. He captured the now almost defunct United Gold Coast Convention (UGCC) by his organizational genius, his personal magnetism, his honesty, and his judgement of the temper of his people. The UGCC slogan was "Self-government in the shortest possible time." To many young men impatient for action this slogan indicated confusion and equivocation. Nkrumah, quick to feel the common pulse and revolutionary by nature, resigned from the UGCC. On June 12, 1949, he established the Convention Peoples Party urging "Self-government Now."

For some months earlier, the UGCC had asked for a new constitution, and the government had set up the Coussey Committee on Constitutional Reform. On October 26, 1949, the Committee's report was released. It pleased no one, but the UGCC was reluctantly prepared to go along with it. The CPP denounced it as "bogus." Dissatisfaction with the report increased. Meantime, Nkrumah toured the country urging nonviolent resistance to the new constitution outlined in the Coussey Report.

On November 20, 1949, the CPP held its first mass meeting. Ninety thousand people attended. Three things happened at that meeting that were to change the history of the Gold Coast and the life of Kuame Nkrumah. First, the meeting went on record as rejecting the Report of the Coussey Committee, and proposed radical reforms. Secondly, Nkrumah called for civil disobedience if these reforms were not made. Finally, Mr. Pobee Biney, vice-president of the Gold Coast Trades Union Congress, sought the support of the CPP in asking the government to reinstate several scores of meteorological workers who had been dismissed a few days earlier when they had struck for better conditions. At this point in the mass meeting pandemonium broke loose. The people met the suggestion with such enthusiasm that it was several minutes before order could be restored. Responding with equal intensity, Mr. Biney took the platform and threatened a general strike if the workers were not reinstated. The people had given leadership to the leaders.

The attitude of the government was to laugh at the CPP. British officials were overheard to refer to the "animal emotion of the mass meeting," which they considered had "spent itself with talk and drumbeating," and flatly refused to reinstate the workers.

The CPP and the Trades Union Congress promptly announced a general strike to begin at midnight, Sunday, January 8, 1950. Nkrumah went to the towns and villages calling for "political action without violence for full self-government now" and for the reinstatement of the strikers who had been dismissed.

He called for boycotts, strikes, civil disobedience, and noncooperation. Hundreds of his young lieutenants went to the bush (countryside) to educate the masses in the meaning and tactics of nonviolence. People were advised to save food, not to waste money at Christmas time. Market women were asked not to sell to European cooks. Stevedores were organized. Domestic workers were educated on the part they had to play. The aim was to stop business throughout the Gold Coast.

British Change Tactics

The British, sensing a real struggle, swiftly changed their tactics from ridicule to negotiation. They called Nkrumah alone to the Government House. Nkrumah would not attend without "the representatives of the people." Finally Nkrumah and a number of young men went to confer. They presented the two demands Nkrumah had taken to the people. The British would not budge and used the conference first to soft-soap and finally to threaten.

Although the conference ended in a stalemate, the CPP won the day psychologically. Everywhere the people said: "The government is weak. Nkrumah is strong. They can't settle without him and they know it. Nkrumah has caused the government to compromise."

Nonviolent March

Meanwhile, the Gold Coast's ex-servicemen had decided to stage a nonviolent march on Government House the day of the strike's start, carrying a petition of grievances to the Governor. Their chief concern was with the high cost of living and low salary scales. The Government's permission for the march was granted and the route of the parade agreed to.

Sunday afternoon came. The veterans, marching four abreast, were followed by thousands of bush- and townspeople, many of whom had traveled miles to the capital to witness the beginning of the general strike. As the veterans, marching slowly and with discipline, reached a spot near the sea about a half mile from the Governor's palace, they were met by a British officer, with a contingent of African police and soldiers with fixed bayonets.

The war veterans closed ranks and began to sing, moving more slowly but still moving. The officer ordered them to stop, but they pressed on. The officer then ordered his men to shoot. The war veterans moved ahead, still singing.

"Shoot," cried the officer.

Not one African soldier or policeman fired. "Shoot! Shoot!" he cried again. As the ex-servicemen continued on, the African soldiers and police broke ranks. They would not fire upon their brothers and cousins, who merely marched and sang, but who carried no weapons.

Demonstrators Fired Upon

The bewildered officer himself opened fire. Four men lay mortally wounded or dead upon the ground. Most of the veterans continued forward. No one harmed the officer, but the thousands behind the veterans became a mob. In panic, fear, and revenge they ran back to the business district of the city. They broke the windows and doors of the European shops. They burned automobiles, they tore down signs. By evening they had begun to loot. A million dollars in property and foodstuff went up in smoke. The property of African merchants was not disturbed. The government was incapable of handling the situation. Soon soldiers and police were themselves looting. It took four days to restore a semblance of order. By refusing to accept a nonviolent Grievance Committee, by shooting down well-disciplined men, the British administration had shown itself incapable of governing.

A committee of men, members of both CPP and UGCC, wired London that the government had broken down. They asked that an interim government of Africans be set up while a new constitution was written, granting full self-government. London took the situation lightly and delayed.

By Monday, the workers had fulfilled their promise. North, south, east, and west, the country's trade came to a standstill. The workers of the Gold Coast had gone on strike.

The government declared martial law, and established a six P.M. curfew for Africans. Hundreds ignored the curfew and were jailed. Anywhere lights were seen burning after six o'clock the army battered down doors and dragged men off to prison. Finally orders went out to "shoot to kill" anyone at large after curfew.

The Strike Suspended

Some small-minded and jealous Africans began to attack Nkrumah. Sincere men, fearing further reprisals, began to preach submission. Food problems arose. The strain became greater and greater as the days wore on. Discipline began to break down. Violence seemed imminent. As Gandhi before them had done, the leaders decided to suspend action. Their aim was revolution, not by violence, but by peaceful means. On January 19, after eleven days, the strike was called off.

The following day's newspapers attacked Nkrumah and the labor leaders for "leading the people to destruction and hunger." The British, misinterpreting the newspapers' hostility as "grassroots" sentiment, resolved to break the back of the CPP and the Trades Union Movement once and for all. One by one the trade union leaders were arrested, charged with inciting an illegal strike. On February 22, Nkrumah and all the executive members of the CPP were arrested and put in jail for "inciting an illegal strike to coerce the government." Only Mr. K. A. Gbedemah, the vice-chairman, who was already serving a term in prison for seditious publication, escaped the new arrest. All who took part in the strike were dismissed from their jobs. Unemployment mounted. A state of emergency was proclaimed and all organized political and labor action became illegal. All CPP files and those of the labor unions were confiscated.

In March, Mr. Gbedemah was released. Under his direction the CPP began quietly to organize underground. The curfew, martial law, and other emergency acts had been lifted. Gbedemah toured the country speaking in the name of the CPP leaders "who by their imprisonment had demonstrated their love of the Gold Coast, the people and God."

Gbedemah had four objectives: (1) to rebuild the scattered party; (2) to win the local elections beginning in April; (3) to win CPP control of the National Assembly; and (4) to effect the release of the imprisoned leaders.

Gbedemah's Campaign

If these aims could be realized, he argued, nonviolence would be vindicated and freedom ultimately assured. He campaigned throughout the country. He pointed out the failure of the British to negotiate. He called attention to the bogus constitution. He eulogized those shot down on January 8. He emphasized the fact that the most militant men in the nation had been arrested. He was careful always to speak in the name of Nkrumah.

On the day the curfew was lifted 30,000 people attended a mass meeting called by the CPP. Mass demonstrations were held outside prisons. The people were told that only their actions could release the leaders. They were encouraged not to hate the British but to "go to the polls for independence." This they must do "for Ghana [the Gold Coast] and for God." By April the job was well done.

Progressive Victories

On April 1, CPP voters swarmed to the polls and won the local elections. At Accra, the seat of the government, "the capital was taken without a gun," one leader said. On June 1, CPP won the by-election in Cape Coast. On June 14, Mr. Kwesi Plange captured a vacant seat in the Legislative Council for CPP. Gbedemah then brought out the CPP flag of red, white, and green, symbolizing the victory (white) and the determination (red) to free the virgin country (green) from alien exploitation. The flag was hoisted over every village and town.

Meantime Mr. Plange succeeded in getting the Legislative Council to lower the voting age from twenty-five to twenty-one, an important victory since CPP strength was among youth.

These successes were followed by the November 1 sweep of the Kumasi Town Council, and the December 11 election that filled a vacancy in the Cape Coast Council. To emphasize the dignity of going to prison, Gbedemah introduced the PG (Prison Graduate) cap.

Meantime the Coussey Committee on Constitutional Reform Report was to be implemented, and on the basis of it general elections were announced for February 8, 1951. The CPP decided to run candidates. They had concluded that although the constitution was bogus, it could be used to release the leaders and to reveal to the British government that the people desired independence. Their slogan was "Vote CPP for self-government now."

In the middle of January the names of the candidates for national elections were released. The entire country was electrified. Gbedemah announced that Nkrumah, a prisoner in James Fort, had been nominated as first candidate for the Accra municipality.

The Prisoner Elected

On February 8, the CPP won thirty-one of the thirty-three seats in the rural area and all five seats in the Municipal towns. Dr. Kuame Nkrumah led the lot with 22,000 votes. The British officials, who had underestimated the movement's strength, were shocked and confused. When the people heard the returns they assembled outside the prison and began to call for their leaders. Hurried meetings were arranged at Government House.

London decided to release the leaders. To save face, the announcement indicated that the men were being released "as an act of grace on the eve of the inauguration of the new constitution." No one was taken in. On the morning of February 12, news of their release flashed across the country.

Thousands of cheering enthusiasts met the prisoners, Nkrumah, Baako, Nortey, Nketsia, Provencal, Quarshie, and Reuner, at the gates. They were carried shoulder-high among the people. They were fanned by singing women with costly white cloths as a sign of victory over the imperialist.

Nkrumah, now freed, had a very real problem: could CPP take over the government under a constitution that was not in keeping with the desires of the people? After careful consideration by the CPP Working Committee it was decided that, in keeping with nonviolent strategy, they could form a government. There were two reasons for this decision. First, to accept would give CPP time to "clear up several internal problems" before twisting the lion's tail further. Secondly, CPP could "demonstrate that they would leave no stone unturned in their effort to meet the British half way." The Working Committee then went to the people and explained why they were changing tactics from one of "civil disobedience" to "strategic cooperation." The people understood.

Black Prime Minister

On Tuesday, March 20, 1951, the Legislative Assembly opened. Dr. Nkrumah had become the first black prime minister of the Gold Coast and the first in Africa. The men who had been jailed with him became ministers of state.

Nkrumah knows that the struggle in one sense has just begun, that perhaps there will be prison again. But he and his ministers are prepared to push on to freedom, come what may.

As Gandhi and Nehru before them, Nkrumah, Gbedemah, and a handful of black men have demonstrated once again that no array of guns and prison walls can prevent men from pursuing freedom and justice when they have rejected guns and depend on the spiritual power that springs from forgiveness and an indomitable will.

How Black Americans See
Black Africans—and Vice Versa

◆ ◆ ◆

[1969]

THE RELATIONSHIP BETWEEN AFRICANS and Afro-Americans is one of ambivalence. It is an ambivalence that derives from a great tension between, on the one hand, a shared ancient heritage and racial identification and, on the other, profound differences in the historical, cultural, and political circumstances of the two peoples which make them almost incomprehensible to each other. This tension has produced in the Negro a poignant desire to reach backward to Africa in search of his roots, and the forward-looking need to achieve full economic and social equality on his native soil—which is America.

The central experience that binds Africans and Negroes together is their common understanding of the brutality of racism. The difference here, however, is that while the African's knowledge of racism has grown out of his experience with imperialism and colonialism, Afro-Americans have been concerned with it in the context of slavery, segregation, and social inequality. As a result, both have found it necessary to develop political strategies of opposition appropriate to the different circumstances surrounding the development of racism in their respective lands. The fact that they have had to employ different strategies in order to destroy the same evil has led to much confusion.

Africans, we must never forget, are the majority in societies which until very recently were dominated by a white minority. (In South Africa, Rhodesia, Mozambique, and Angola, the anachronistic injustice of white domination still persists.) Their fundamental concern, therefore, was to seize national power through violent or nonviolent revolutionary action. The African political context of imperialism, in other words, provided the conditions for a genuine revolution.

Many American Negroes have tried to use the independence movements in colonial territories as the model for their own political actions. Consequently, we have had black nationalist movements for "self-determination" and "black power," which some people have called anti-imperialist and revolutionary. This revolutionary rhetoric is misplaced, however, and the movements have inevitably failed to achieve their goals for two simple reasons: Negroes can have no geographical focus for national sentiment and they do not constitute a majority of the population. They constitute but 11 percent of the American people, and they are dispersed throughout every state in the nation. Negroes, therefore, must be concerned with obtaining that degree of power which one-ninth of the population should expect. They must do this through constitutional and democratic means, for to attempt a revolution would bring on a counterrevolution of the sort that I do not wish to contemplate.

Beyond these political distinctions, there are differences in cultural and social patterns of behavior that are so profound as to make it almost impossible for Africans and Negroes to understand one another. This situation is illustrated by a conversation I had with a seventeen-year-old boy during a recent visit to Nairobi, Kenya. He said to me, "Mr. Rustin, I am a Kenyan and I belong to the Kikuyu tribe. You are an American, and I would like to know what tribe you belong to."

Being taken aback, I replied, "I belong to the Negro tribe," upon which he asked me to speak some Negro to him. I tried to explain to him that Negroes had originally been Africans at which time they spoke their tribal languages, but that after 300 years in America we had forgotten our tribal tongue and now spoke the common American language of English. Incredulously, he asked, "How can you be of the Negro tribe if you do not speak the Negro language? I am a Kikuyu and I speak Kikuyu as my first language and Swahili as my second."

Our conversation lasted for over an hour, and though I made every effort to be explicit and explanatory, it was impossible for me to identify myself to him in any way that he could understand. He found me as strange a being as he might find a white American, a European, or an Asian.

Just as Africans have difficulty understanding Negroes, so many of our own people do not know that there is not *one* Africa but many, including many tribes that are now within the borders of African states. The extent of the American Negro's failure to understand Africa was articulately described in *Ebony* by Tom Mboya, Kenya's minister for economic planning and development:

> ...I find sometimes there is a complete misunderstanding of what African culture really means. For example, some people think that to identify as an African, one has to wear a shaggy beard or a piece of cloth or skin on the head, or has to wear one's hair natural. These are conditions imposed on the African today by the circumstances of poverty, limitations in technical and educational and other resources. These must not be confused with culture.
>
> An African walks barefoot or wears sandals made of old tires not because it is his culture, but because he lives in poverty. He lives in a mud or wattle hut, but these are signs of poverty which must not be mistaken for cultural heritage. Culture is something much deeper. It is the total sum of your personality, outlook, and attitude to life.

Mboya made these remarks as part of a larger statement discouraging American Negroes from expatriating to Africa "because they are black." His words are relevant today because there is again talk among some Negroes of going back to Africa. While relatively few Negroes realistically consider expatriation a possibility, the fact that it is being discussed is significant, for it is part of a much broader movement by black Americans to separate themselves from the mainstream of society.

There is a reason for this movement which has to do far less with the Negro's relation to Africa than to America. The "Back to Africa" and separatist tendencies are always strongest at the very time when the Negro is most intensely dissatisfied with his lot in America. It is when the Negro has lost hope in America—and lost his identity as an American—that he seeks to reestablish his identity and his roots as an African.

This period of despair has historically followed hard upon a period of hope and of efforts to become integrated—on the basis of full equality—into the economic, social, and political life of the United States. The present separatist mood, as we know, has come after a decade in which the Negro has achieved enormous and unprecedented gains through the civil rights struggle, and it has coincided with a right-wing reaction that has obstructed further measures toward equality. The combination of progress, aroused hopes, frustration, and despair has caused many Negroes to withdraw into separatism and to yearn for Africa.

Three times in the past the Negro has been similarly disenchanted. During the period of social stress following the founding of this nation, the humanitarian ardor which had been aroused by the independence movement disappeared. Negroes who had hoped for progress turned inward, and it was during this period that the African Church was formed. The separatism of Booker T. Washington rose upon the ruined expectations that had been aroused by the Civil War and its aftermath but dashed by the Compromise of 1876. And when Negroes expected but were denied justice after fighting for their country in World War I, Marcus Garvey organized a movement of over 2,000,000 blacks to buy ships that would carry them back to Africa.

Many who joined the Garvey movement, I believe, did not really wish to return to Africa. Rather, they wanted to express to other Americans their intense dissatisfaction with the injustices that they had been subjected to in this country. For to the Negro Africa is a vague memory and a misunderstood reality. He is an American. His ancestors have suffered here and have died here. He has roots in this country as deep as—or deeper than—any other American. However much the Negro searches for his African heritage, he can never escape his American identity. He has no choice, therefore, but to struggle for the establishment of the economic and social conditions that will enable him to realize fully his potential on this soil. Not until this struggle is successful will he entirely reject the illusion of Africa and accept the reality of his American selfhood.

American Negroes and Israel

◆ ◆ ◆

[1974]

THE PERSISTENCE OF THE DEBATE over the relationship between black people and the State of Israel is a perplexing and troublesome phenomenon. For one would think that the historic bonds which link blacks to Jews—the common heritage of discrimination and oppression, the cooperation during the protest campaigns of the civil rights movement, and the fact that blacks and Jews occupy pivotal roles within the liberal coalition—would be sufficiently powerful and enduring to preclude serious differences over Israel's fate. Added to this is Israel's democratic and egalitarian character, which stands in marked contrast to the conservatism and authoritarianism of the Arab regimes.

Yet one cannot dismiss the existence of a controversy even if, as I believe to be the case here, its relevance and magnitude are of questionable dimension. Since her establishment twenty-five years ago, Israel has enjoyed a remarkable level of support from the leadership of the black community, including elected officials, civil rights leaders, and church and labor figures. Nor is there any significant evidence to suggest that this support diminished during the most recent outbreak of fighting. Quite the contrary. Shortly after the Yom Kippur War began, thirteen of the fifteen black members of Congress agreed to co-sponsor a resolution urging the U.S. Government to resupply Israel's hard-pressed military forces. In addition, seventy-five black trade union leaders issued a statement which was published in the Sunday *New York Times* (October 21, 1973) calling on black Americans "to stand with Israel in its struggle to live and be free." A similar statement was issued by a group of leading black elected officials.

But while traditional black leadership has been generous in embracing Israel's cause, the same cannot be said for black nationalists or separatists. Following the Six Day War in 1967, the Black Panthers, the Student Nonviolent Coordinating Committee, and other such organizations denounced the "imperialist" and "genocidal" nature of Israel and proclaimed the necessity of black–Arab solidarity. Others, employing language that avoided the coarseness and irrationalism which marked the Panther rhetoric, equated black support for Israel with subservience to Jewish interests in the United States. Thus in criticizing black Congressmen for their endorsement of military aid to Israel, Robert S. Browne, who is the director of the Black Economic Research Council, asked whether "black leadership is so intimidated by its ties to the Jewish community that it cannot articulate positions which might collide with Jewish aspirations." What Browne is suggesting is obvious: that not only is there no validity to the Israeli cause, at least insofar as blacks are concerned, but that black politicians, by supporting Israel, are placing the wishes of American Jews above their own sense of what is right and wrong.

To express such strong doubts about the principles of black elected officials is to tread on dangerous territory. One might as easily ask whether the voting records of Senators Javits and Ribicoff, both of which are impeccably pro–civil rights, reflect nothing more than a bowing to black "aspirations." Only the most cynical or the most foolish would deny that Javits and Ribicoff have demonstrated an abiding, personal commitment to racial equality during their public careers. It takes equal cynicism to impugn the motives of black elected officials, as Browne and others have done.

Israel's black critics have misrepresented Israel's policy towards black African nations. The suggestion, for example, that Israel has systematically supported and aided Portugal against the liberation forces in its African colonies is simply not true. Israel has in fact been a consistent supporter of the freedom movements in Angola and Mozambique and has demonstrated this support through her anticolonialist votes in the United Nations and through technical aid extended to the liberation forces themselves. The Afro-Asian Institute,* for example, has from the

---

* The Afro-Asian Institute is operated by Histadrut, the general labor federation of Israel. It offers training and work-study programs to those active in the labor and cooperative movements in Africa, Asia, and Latin America.

outset carried out a policy of recruiting trainees from the freedom movements in nations still under minority white dominance.

Furthermore, the critics generally fail to analyze in any depth the nature of Arab and Israeli societies. To propose, as some have, that the Arab nations in general and the Palestinians in particular represent a revolutionary vanguard for the underdeveloped world is simply to ignore the realities of the Arab social structure. And to assert that there are historic ties of brotherhood linking black Africans to Arab Moslems requires both a substantial rewriting of history and a disregarding of the tensions between blacks and Arabs which exist to this day.

The conflict between Africans and Arabs dates back many centuries; Moslems were in fact one of the first outside forces to enslave and uproot tribal Africans on a wide scale. As John Hope Franklin, the distinguished black historian, has noted:

> When the Mohammedans invaded Africa, they contributed greatly to the development of the institution of Negro slavery by seizing Negro women for their harems and Negro men for military and menial service.
>
> By purchase as well as by conquest, the Moslems recruited Negro slaves and shipped them off to Arabia, Persia, or some other land of Islam....
>
> Long before the extensive development of the slave trade in the hands of the Europeans, many of the basic practices of the international slave trade had already been established.

It is true, of course, that the slave trade as practiced by the Moslems was not as severe or extensive an institution as it later became under the Europeans. A much more serious indictment of the attitudes of Arab society is its continued tolerance for the slave trade at a time when the rest of humanity has condemned and abandoned the practice. The Anti-Slavery Society, headquartered in London, an organization committed to the eradication of slavery around the world, reports that Arab nations are the most flagrant violators of the 1956 United Nations Convention on the Abolition of Slavery, the Slave Trade, and Practices Similar to Slavery. In Saudi Arabia alone there are

500,000 persons living in slavery or enforced bondage, according to Society estimates, and slavery is known to exist in a number of other Arab lands, including Kuwait, Oman and Muscat, Yemen, Algeria, and Lebanon.

The pattern of modern slavery, according to journalist Noel Mostert, "is the age-old one. The source is still mainly Africa, the essential difference being that the routes of the slave traders run eastward instead of westward."

One of the most disturbing aspects of modern slavery is that despite its almost universal condemnation and the sanctions of the United Nations, it has undergone a steady increase during the past twenty-five years, a period which coincides with the era of growing wealth for the oil sheikdoms of the Persian Gulf. The Anti-Slavery Society believes that chattel slavery has increased threefold since 1947, and it ascribes the increase to the growing affluence of the oil nations.

The world reaction to the phenomenon of modern slavery is a textbook case of how the dictates of *realpolitik* drown out the cries of the oppressed. The United Nations, the only agency with jurisdiction sufficiently broad to provide an effective policing mechanism, has treated the slavery question with the utmost care. The Big Powers—the United States and the Soviet Union, in particular— are unwilling to risk a confrontation with the Middle Eastern states with which they hope to form economic and political alliances. In addition, Russia fears that opening the question of slavery might ultimately lead to an examination of its own political trials and slave labor camps.

The myth of Arab–African brotherhood is further belied by Moslem oppression of non-Moslem blacks in Nigeria and the Sudan. During the war of Biafran secession, Egyptian pilots flew bombing missions in which the principal targets were inhabited villages rather than military installations of Biafran troops. In the Sudan, the Moslem north carried out a near-genocidal campaign of terror against the black pagans and Christians of the south. The Sudanese civil war was provoked by the efforts of the Moslems to force their language, religion, and culture on the non-Moslem blacks. Between 500,000 and 1,000,000 Sudanese were slain in the conflict; countless others, after watching their villages burn, fled to the bush or sought sanctuary in neighboring countries. The Sudanese government was able to conduct its military campaigns because of a $5,500,000 gift from Kuwait, and because of arms shipments from

Algeria, Egypt, and the Soviet Union. Thus we had an example of Arab unity in which black people, not Jews, were the victims.

For their part, African nations are aware of the long history of conflict between Arab and black; they recognize that forming alliances with the Arabs is a matter of pragmatic politics, not the result of "brotherhood." African leaders, moreover, do not share the sentiments of black nationalists here who look on Israel as imperialist or racist. Until the Yom Kippur War, African nations enjoyed close and often beneficial relations with Israel, which for years had provided aid and technical advice that was of considerable value to states just emerging from colonialism's yoke. Thus the fact that all but a handful of African nations have broken off diplomatic ties with Israel in the past few months must be evaluated in the light of the shifting political forces in the Middle East, rather than in terms of political ideology.

Just as oil is in large measure responsible for the upsurge of slavery in the Middle East, so is oil a principal cause of the shifting political alliances of African nations. One must keep in mind that oil was a powerful enough weapon to evoke anti-Israel responses from Great Britain, France, and other European countries. Small wonder that the same weapon is sufficiently imposing to bring about a reversal in the foreign policies of the struggling, impoverished, and often politically unstable nations of Africa.

The power of oil—particularly as wielded by Libya since the ascension of Colonel Muammar el-Gaddafi as chief of state—becomes evident upon examining a chronology of recent Arab–African relations. In 1967 nearly all African nations retained diplomatic ties with Israel. And when the United Nations debated the question of which side was the aggressor in the Six Day War, most black African nations supported Israel.

But in 1970, after Gaddafi had assumed power, support for Israel began to wane. Libya promised aid to economically unstable countries, such as Uganda, and threatened to finance Moslem revolutionary movements in militarily weak nations, like Chad, but only if the governments would quickly sever relations with Israel.

Israel also had the growing influence of Mohammedanism to contend with. Many African countries have sizable and ever-increasing Moslem populations that represent a potential source of unrest. It is far simpler, in the view of African chiefs of state, to appease the Moslem communities by denouncing Israel than to risk internal disorder or an insurgent movement financed by Libya or Kuwait.

The African nations were also motivated by the promise of the Arabs to extend the oil boycott to Portugal, Rhodesia, and South Africa. As we shall see, however, the boycott, and the ensuing spiral in oil prices, threatens the economies of African and other underdeveloped nations far more seriously than countries which practice colonialism or apartheid. In the case of South Africa, furthermore, it is the blacks who will suffer most severely; one of South Africa's most respected tribal leaders, Chief Gatsha Buthelezi, has already asked that the boycott be called off, asserting that "it would end up being the blacks in South Africa who would end up bearing the brunt if the taps were turned off."

Of the African leaders who have publicly criticized Israel, the most widely publicized has been Uganda's General Amin, who once asserted that Hitler had not gone far enough in his annihilation of the Jews. Amin's voice, however, finds few echoes. (It should be noted that Amin broke off relations with Israel only after Israel had refused to provide Uganda with military aid which, it is believed, was to have been used for a war against neighboring Tanzania.) As the *New York Times* reported: "Amin...was the only one to accompany the break with a diatribe against Israel, to expel all Israelis, and to terminate all economic relations. Those African countries that followed said more or less clearly that they hoped to continue trade and economic relations.... Some African leaders told Israelis that the ruptures should not be interpreted as breaches of friendship."

Under a different set of circumstances, the intense pressure that Arab governments have applied to African lands would be called "imperialist blackmail." But there seems to be an almost conscious desire by many blacks and liberals to believe in the unity of underdeveloped nations, and any evidence to the contrary is ignored or dismissed.

And yet in raw economic terms, it is the world's developing nations that will suffer most severely from the oil embargoes and price increases which have been imposed by the Arabs. The *Development Forum*, which is published by the Centre for Economic and Social Information of the United Nations, notes that prior to the energy crisis the poorest countries were already paying 20 percent more for imported fuel than the industrialized world. The *Forum* further observed:

> The recent price rises have greatly aggravated
> their [the underdeveloped nations'] plight. Unless
> the upward spiral in the price of oil is halted, or

some measure of relief provided, it could bring
development of the Third World to a dead halt....
Industrial countries are also affected, but they have
fallback positions: e.g., rich coal deposits that can
be reactivated, and the technology to speed up the
development of new resources from nuclear to geo-
thermal and, eventually, solar energy. Above all,
they have the financial means to meet the rising
price of oil. No such escapes are open to the poorer
nations.... Oil, which flows so easily from well to
pipeline into tanker, refinery and pump, and eventually, into furnace or generator, is a convenience
for the industrial countries. For the developing world,
it is a lifeline which is essential to their survival.

It should be added that this was written before the oil-producing
nations announced a doubling of the price of crude oil at the wellhead.
The *New York Times* reported that these increases would cost the developing world $5 billion, an amount which represents approximately half
of what it receives annually in development aid from the industrialized
countries. A further dimension to the plight of the poorer nations is the
fact that countries like the United States and Great Britain will undoubtedly reduce foreign-aid allocations, particularly to those nations which
have the least to offer in return, because of the domestic problems
created by the oil crisis. World Bank officials have already predicted that
India will have a negative growth rate for years to come because of oil
prices; the impact on the less affluent nations of Africa could be even
more shattering.

A point I have been trying to make is that there are differences not
just between Arab and white cultures, but differences, which in some
ways run just as deep, between Arab traditions and the traditions of
black people in Africa and in the Americas.

The reason for exposing these differences is to address, as directly
as possible, the myth of a cohesive, universally progressive "Third World"
of underdeveloped countries. In that the term connotes a group of
governments with which black people should identify, the Third World
does not exist. Some developing nations are profoundly militaristic
and reactionary; others are feudalistic; still others, although they call

themselves socialistic, are headed by brutal and dictatorial regimes which differ little from the most repressive authoritarian states.

Some of Israel's critics, of course, would argue that they distinguish between the oil sheikdoms (such as Kuwait and Saudi Arabia), military governments (Iraq and Syria, for instance), and the Palestinians. The latter, according to the current mythology, are a genuinely revolutionary force whose ideals might ultimately reshape Arab society along progressive lines.

I will not here dwell on the question of whether a truly revolutionary movement would employ the strategies of international terror which have become the trademark of the Palestinians. A more substantive and far-reaching issue is the relationship of the Palestinians to the rest of the Arab world, and particularly to its most conservative elements. Shlomo Avineri, an authority on Middle East political systems, has written of this relationship:

> Trained mostly by regular Arab army officers, financed by Saudi Arabian or Kuwaitian money, [the Palestinians] are—for all their left-wing rhetoric— poor substitutes for a real revolutionary force. In order to be able to exist and operate they have to make their peace with the powers that be. Imagine Castro having a *tête-à-tête* with the Brazilian dictators in the same way in which Yasir Arafat appears together with King Faisal at an Arab summit. The most reactionary Arab rulers pay danegeld to the proponents of social revolution—and it is a shrewd investment on the part of the Saudis—for otherwise dangerous revolutionary fervor is thus channeled into an exclusively anti-Israel direction. What better way is there than this to divert the revolutionaries from truly revolutionizing Arab society!

It is, ironically, Israel, with her socialistic society and expanding democratic institutions, which most nearly has achieved the egalitarian ideal. Israel has already established a pattern of society and government which could serve as a model for other Middle East nations in their struggle to reduce widespread poverty and to bring democracy to their people.

I am not uncritical of some of Israel's policies and particularly deplore the continued plight of the Palestinian refugees. But it is important to keep in mind that the misery of the refugee camps is as much a result of the unwillingness of the Arabs to agree to a permanent solution to the Middle East situation as it is of Israeli policies. One cannot be certain if the Arab vow to "push Israel into the sea" is mere rhetoric designed to arouse the patriotism of the masses, or an acknowledgment of their ultimate objective. But there can be no doubt that the Arabs have exploited the refugee problem as a means of legitimizing their aggression. The refugee camps, with their squalor and overcrowded conditions, are for the Arabs a means of mobilizing moral opinion against Israel. And while liquidation of the camps and resettlement of the refugees might serve the cause of humanity, it would also deprive the Arabs of an effective propaganda weapon.

One hopes, above all, that a just and permanent peace emerges from the current negotiations. The achievement of that peace, however, requires a recognition of the legitimacy of both forms of nationalism—Arab and Israeli—that are now competing in the Middle East. Both have their historical roots in the Middle East, and are capable of co-existing, as indeed they did co-exist in the years between World War I and the establishment of the State of Israel in 1948.

Until these rights are acknowledged and accepted, however, there will be no peace, nor justice for the Palestinian refugees, nor social progress for the impoverished of the Middle East. Society cannot be remade while governments are in a perpetual state of military alert. If there is to be true progress for the peoples of the Middle East, it must come about because peace is achieved, and because both Arab and Israeli accept and cooperate with each other. Social progress cannot be won in the battlefield.

A U.S. Coalition on Human Rights

◆ ◆ ◆

[1977]

We meet as individuals active in major American organizations involved in social, economic, or political improvement, to join with leaders of organizations with a long and honorable tradition in promoting international human rights.

We have come together to consider whether we should form an American coalition for human rights; and, if so, to begin the discussion of what its purpose, structure, and functions should be.

The idea for this meeting originated when a few of us met to plan an educational conference on the meaning of the human rights provisions of the Helsinki Accords which are being discussed at the Belgrade Conference that opened earlier this week. As we explored with others the idea of such a conference on the Helsinki Accords, it became clear that concern in America for human rights is now so strong that there was a need for a far broader organization than we had originally anticipated.

At the outset, I would like to suggest a moral philosophy for your consideration as a basis for the coalition that is being proposed.

I believe we must oppose suppression of human rights anywhere, *whatever the ideology of the oppressor.* We must, in my view, oppose dictatorships *of both the right and the left*—unequivocally and without qualification.

In addition, I would like to propose that such a coalition stress the importance of social and economic well-being for all peoples. We must, in my view, look to the development of human well-being that embodies the *full* range of human rights and aspirations. I point out that this means stretching the definition of human rights beyond civil and political considerations to include all matters which affect human welfare.

We have called together today people whom we believe to be committed to the principles I have suggested.

It is my hope that this coalition will be concerned *whenever* governments, including our own, restrict the rights of people for advocating or exercising:

Freedom of speech and of the press; *or*

Freedom of assembly and association, including the right to form free trade unions; *or*

An independent judiciary; *or*

Freedom of artistic and intellectual expression; *or*

Religious liberty and freedom of movement.

We must also begin to lay a groundwork for education about minimum social and economic standards. These are the tasks for the coalition.

It is also my hope that our coalition would oppose violations of human rights whether they take place in Chile *or* Cuba—that is, in dictatorships of the right *or* left; in South Africa *or* Uganda—that is, in dictatorships that are white *or* black; in South Korea *or* Vietnam—that is, in dictatorships that are authoritarian *or* totalitarian. In order for this coalition to be successful and morally consistent, it must oppose dictatorships of every kind.

Let those of us here today not forget that, if we lived in a dictatorship, we could be among the first to be jailed, or interned in some island prison, or sent to the Gulag Archipelago. We are the counterparts of the human rights advocates who are chemically lobotomized in Soviet mental institutions or trapped in the brutalized serfdom of the apartheid system that tyrannizes the vast majority of South Africans.

We are not in South Africa, or Chile, or the Soviet Union, or Uganda. We are in America, and here we can provide moral sustenance to those who suffer afflictions because of their beliefs in elected governments and in an open society.

Just two days ago, a voice cried out to us, the voice of Andrei Sakharov, one of the true heroes of our time, who said: "We are going through a period of history in which decisive support of the principles of freedom of conscience, an open society, and the rights of man, have become an absolute necessity." I want to express my total solidarity with this statement, and with the admirable man who made it. And I hope that we here can provide such support, and help develop it elsewhere. We can also provide economic sustenance, both to relieve human suffering and to sustain democracy wherever it exists.

The people of India have shown recently that even the most poverty-stricken demand both bread and freedom. And as we celebrate the bloodless democratic restoration in that ancient land, we must not forget that the people of India need our bread, and our support of their economic and social development. Yet I have not detected a commitment in our nation to greater assistance, on anywhere *near* the scale that I believe is required to reinforce political democracy in India with the solid foundation of economic development.

Although our government must do more in this area, our president, Jimmy Carter, deserves great credit for expressing eloquently the concern which many Americans have for human rights. Indeed, our president has raised the spirit of this country and given renewed hope to millions throughout the world who suffer from political oppression.

Most of the people in this room today were active in the civil rights movement a decade and a half ago.

We marched together in Washington in 1963 and in Selma in 1965.

We protested together. We lobbied together. We mourned together.

We have friends who are not here today—Protestant, Christian, Jewish, black, white, yellow, brown—who lost their lives in that great struggle.

But, despite suffering, we accomplished a revolution in American society. We learned what can be done when peoples join together to work for democratic change.

It is my hope that the proposed coalition will be formed, and that we *all* will enlist in this struggle for human rights. Yet we should remember, as we enter this arena, that we are really the second or third wave in a battle long led by others, whose significant contribution has, I am happy to report, recently begun to be appreciated.

I speak, of course, of the major human rights organizations, many of whose leaders are here today. I particularly want to welcome our friends from Amnesty International, the International League for Human Rights, the International Commission of Jurists, Freedom House, the International Rescue Committee, and the leaders of human rights efforts sponsored by some of our nation's principal religious and trade-union organizations. We came to these human rights organizations for advice and assistance in planning this conference, and we will assuredly need their cooperation in the future, if such a coalition as is proposed here is to prosper.

May I also add that many of us are deeply concerned about the campaign launched by some of the worst oppressors in the world to remove United Nations consultative status from such principal human rights organizations as the International League for Human Rights. I hope I speak for all of us when I urge representatives of the organizations in this room *not to fail* to bring to the attention of other leaders and members of their organizations this despicable effort launched by such champions of police-state terrorism as Argentina, Chile, and the Soviet Union.

We should watch this situation carefully. If the professional human rights organizations request our assistance, I hope all of us will communicate to the Carter administration our concern at this expulsion effort, and our strong support of what we hope will be a determined effort by President Carter to organize multilateral backing for protecting the present United Nations status of the independent human rights consultative organizations.

With respect to the function and structure of the coalition, we have in mind the model developed by the Leadership Conference on Civil Rights, founded by Roy Wilkins over twenty-five years ago and still going strong. The Leadership Conference is a broad coalition of more than 150 organizations, many of which are represented here today. At its core are the major black organizations, and surrounding them are the labor, religious, liberal, professional, service, and youth organizations that make up that body.

It has been our experience in the Leadership Conference that all involved have benefited from such an arrangement. The civil rights groups have been strengthened by having immediate access to a permanent coalition of organizations which might otherwise not be involved in an ongoing basis in the civil rights cause. Equally, the non-civil rights organizations benefit by having a means of informing themselves about civil rights issues and of participating effectively in this field.

Yet, in the Leadership Conference, we do not pretend to have unity on every issue, and we issue statements or take actions only where there is a consensus. However, when the Leadership Conference does act in consensus, its effectiveness is far, far greater than any single organization could ever hope to achieve acting alone.

We hope that the human rights coalition proposed today could serve similar purposes. For those organizations that are relatively new to the human rights field, the proposed coalition could provide valuable, reliable information and a means of becoming active. For those organizations with extensive human rights traditions and programs, the coalition can provide a national framework for cooperation. For professional human rights organizations, it can help increase their influence by expanding the number of leaders and organizations who receive their materials, endorse their statements, and promote their appeals.

In another connection, there are profound differences in the way in which many people here approach the problem and meaning of social and economic human rights. The coalition can be an agency to stimulate research to help define and clarify these important areas.

As to the proposed coalition's specific objectives and structure, they are, for discussion purposes, spelled out in two sheets of paper you should all have, one called the statement of *Purpose and Goals,* the other the statement of *Structure and Function.*

You are no doubt aware that the problems we address today are vast and complex. Thus, I have suggested to all panelists that they consider commenting on these two papers in the course of their remarks, where they feel it appropriate. I also stress that the suggested goals, structure, and function are tentative and are presented to open the discussion.

Some people may say that we should not presume to concern ourselves with conditions in other countries which have different histories from our own, different cultures, different levels of social and economic development, different forms of governments, and different political ideologies. The expression of such concern, some maintain, constitutes interference in the internal affairs of other countries. I am in this context reminded of the criticism which eight Alabama clergymen leveled against the Rev. Dr. Martin Luther King, Jr., for "interfering" in the internal affairs of Birmingham. I was deeply moved by Martin's reply when he illuminated John Donne's "no man is an island." In Martin's famous "Letter from a Birmingham Jail," he said:

"I am in Birmingham because injustice is here.... Moreover, I am cognizant of the interrelatedness of all communities and states. I cannot sit idly by in Atlanta and not be concerned about what happens in

Birmingham. Injustice anywhere is a threat to justice everywhere. We are caught in an inescapable network of mutuality tied in a single garment of destiny. Whatever affects one directly, affects all indirectly."

That, I trust, is our common belief. May we move to the task ahead.

Opening address to a human rights conference organized by Rustin and cosponsored by Freedom House, October 6, 1977.

The War Against Zimbabwe

◆ ◆ ◆

[1979]

NO ELECTION HELD IN ANY COUNTRY at any time within memory has been more widely or vociferously scorned by international opinion than the election conducted last April in Rhodesia, now Zimbabwe Rhodesia. In scores of other countries, non-democratic governments periodically stage elections whose predetermined results are never challenged or questioned, even by the world's democracies. Indeed, just two weeks before the Rhodesian election, the Iranian government held a referendum in which the people were asked to approve the establishment of an "Islamic republic." Though a constitution had not yet been drafted, and though the vote took place during a period of growing repression of civil liberties, widespread separatist rebellions, and a reign of terror by semi-secret courts dispensing "revolutionary justice," no government raised objections to the whole procedure or questioned the validity of its predictable outcome.

In contrast to the silent acquiescence in what passes for elections in the world's tyrannies, the outcry against the Rhodesian election has been deafening. The United Nations Security Council immediately passed a resolution condemning it and calling upon all countries not to lift economic sanctions against Zimbabwe Rhodesia. And the *New York Times*, urging no change in the Carter administration's Rhodesia policy, announced that it would be "a moral and diplomatic disaster" for the United States to recognize the legitimacy of the election or of the government resulting from it. The *Times*'s wish has since been granted.

Few critics of the election have even pretended to have an open mind on the subject. United Nations Ambassador Andrew Young, who had earlier described as "neofascist" both the interracial transitional government in Rhodesia and anyone who supported it, announced that the election was "rigged" and called for "new elections without pressures." Congressman Stephen Solarz, the chairman of the House African Affairs Subcommittee, said the election no more expressed the will of the people than did the elections of the Soviet Union. (He had earlier helped defeat a move to send a Congressional observer team to Rhodesia to determine if, in fact, such a harsh judgement of the election were warranted.) Columnist Tom Wicker, who had predicted that the civil war would prevent the Rhodesian government from conducting any election, let alone a fair one, dismissed the absence of major disruption during the voting as immaterial, and observed that the newly elected government of Bishop Abel T. Muzorewa simply could not be accepted as "a legitimate member of the family of nations." And a group of ninety-nine Americans, ranging from intellectuals and others on the far Left to liberal civil rights and labor leaders, issued a statement the month *before* the election calling it a "fraud" since "the people of Zimbabwe cannot vote freely with a gun at their heads."

Contrary to these predictions and opinions, however, the people of Zimbabwe did vote in an election that was freer than most held in the developing world—freer, certainly, than elections held anywhere in Africa with the exception of Gambia, Botswana, and possibly several other small countries. Moreover, not only did they not vote with "a gun at their heads," many voted with genuine, unmistakable enthusiasm. The contrast between how the election was viewed by most Zimbabweans (the name preferred by the blacks) and how it was described by critics outside the country is nothing less than extraordinary.

As one of the nine members of the Freedom House delegation which observed the election (others included the journalist Roscoe Drummond, former Congressman Allard K. Lowenstein, and Professor Maurice C. Woodward of Howard University), I had the opportunity to speak on the spot with hundreds of voters in different election districts, as well as with leaders of the participating parties, knowledgeable correspondents, and other international observers. I also met with opponents of the election who were part of the so-called external forces or the Patriotic Front and with professors and students at the University of Salisbury, most of whom boycotted the election. Our delegation stayed throughout the five-day election, visiting more than 100 polling stations throughout the country. Three members remained in Zimbabwe Rhodesia until all the votes were counted and any complaints of irregularities could be received.

The delegation, whose members had professionally monitored previous elections in twenty-six countries, was excellently qualified to make an informed and objective judgment about the fairness of the election and the attitude of the people toward it. Our conclusion, reached unanimously, was that "the election represented a significant advance toward multiracial majority rule" and was "a useful and creditable step toward the establishment of a free society in Zimbabwe Rhodesia."

To be sure, the election was held under extraordinary circumstances. The Patriotic Front had vowed to use violence to disrupt the voting— Joshua Nkomo, the leader of one wing of the Front, had predicted a "bloodbath" at the polls, a warning repeated by many of the guerrillas— and so martial law was in force throughout most of the country. The security forces at the polls protected voters and gave them a feeling of reassurance. Their presence may also have had a coercive effect, but we saw no evidence that they compelled people either to vote or to vote for a particular candidate. (The voting was by secret ballot.) In many localities where people did not vote in large numbers, the government did not try to increase the turnout. Moreover, it was in the large urban centers, where the voters were the most sophisticated and the least subject to exhortation and coercion, that the highest levels of participation occurred.

This is not to say that the government took a passive role in the election. Everyone eighteen years of age and older was allowed to vote, and the government encouraged participation through publicity about the election and voting procedures. But these actions were not inappropriate in a situation where most people were voting for the first time in their lives; and their overall effect was to increase majority control over the results. At the same time, the government sharply curtailed the nonviolent expression of opposition to the election. Such expression was allowed in some places, such as at the University of Salisbury where we witnessed a demonstration urging a boycott of the voting. But on the whole, the opponents of the election were not allowed freely to communicate their point of view.

What effect this restriction had on the election is hard to say, since voters were subject to many conflicting pressures. White farmers and employers encouraged people to vote, as did the local militias (the security forces organized by the black political parties). But voting was also discouraged by the fear of disruption at the polls and by the Patriotic Front's warnings that it would punish anyone who participated. While the disruptions did not occur on a large scale, some voters were killed in transit to the polls by land mines which the guerrillas had laid.

No one can say with certainty what influence these different pressures had on the voters. But clearly a very large proportion of the population felt free to participate or not to participate in the election. Taking into consideration disputes over the size of the voting populations in some districts and voting by some teenagers under the qualifying age of eighteen, the turnout was still well over 50 percent and was most likely nearer the official figure of 64.5 percent. The turnout was unexpectedly high, well above the minimum figure the government felt was necessary to demonstrate majority support for the election. Since opponents of the election would undoubtedly have used a low turnout as evidence of majority opposition to the election, they are hardly in a position to deny the significance of the turnout that did take place.

Moreover, the voters had, in the view of the Freedom House delegation, "a sense of meaningful choice." The nearly 1,900,000 black votes were divided among four competing parties, with Bishop Muzorewa's United African National Council (UANC) receiving an overwhelming 65 percent majority. The post-election charge by the Reverend Ndabaningi Sithole that there were "gross irregularities" during the election only underscores the fact that the competition was keen, since he was deeply disappointed by his party's distant (14 percent) second-place finish. (Significantly, his allegations did not focus on the mechanics of the election, which no one has challenged, but on the methods used by Muzorewa's party to increase its vote; and the allegations have not been supported by the evidence or testimony of the overwhelming majority of international observers.)

It is true, of course, that the two external parties—Nkomo's Zambia-based Zimbabwe African People's Union (ZAPU) and Robert Mugabe's Mozambique-based Zimbabwe African National Union (ZANU)—did not appear on the ballot. But the common belief that they were excluded from the election is simply inaccurate. Not only were Nkomo and Mugabe invited to participate, they were both offered seats on the transitional government's Executive Council, along with Prime Minister Ian Smith, Bishop Muzorewa, Reverend Sithole, and Chief Jeremiah

Chiraw. But Nkomo and Mugabe refused to have anything to do with the election. Still, voters were allowed to cast protest votes by spoiling their ballots or leaving them blank. Some did, since the number of spoiled blank ballots was highest in districts where the external parties have the most support. Yet the percentage of such ballots never reached 10 percent in any single district, and nationally only 3.35 percent of the voters chose to protest in this way.

While the election thus did not meet the rigorous standards that one would apply to elections in Western democracies, it was remarkably free and fair, especially considering that a civil war was in progress and that most of the population had never before participated in an election. But the opponents of the election—not just the Patriotic Front, the front-line states (Zambia, Mozambique, Botswana, Tanzania, and Angola), the Communist world, and the United Nations, but also political leaders and publicists in Western democracies, including the United States—have not shown the least interest in the question of how democratic the voting process was. As the *New York Times* put it, "The real issue is not how the election was conducted, but what it was about."

In this connection, two major objections have been raised, the first having to do with the new constitution. It is charged that this constitution was never submitted to the black voters for approval; that it reserves, for a period of ten years, 28 of the 100 parliamentary seats for the 4 percent white minority; and that it preserves white domination over the army, police, judiciary, and civil service. The second objection is that the internal settlement, under which the constitution was adopted and the election was held, did not include the Patriotic Front, and so would not end the civil war but lead to its escalation, with the likely involvement of Cuban troops. Summing up these objections, the *Times* has charged that the internal settlement "is little more than a device for keeping real power in the hands of Rhodesia's small white minority" and is, therefore, "rightly suspect in black African eyes" and "a recipe for civil war."

Here again, the views of the opponents of the election outside Zimbabwe Rhodesia and the views of the people inside the country diverge in a most extraordinary way. The Zimbabweans participated in the election with enthusiasm precisely because they felt it marked the beginning of real majority rule and would also bring an end to the war. Virtually all the people I spoke with gave these reasons to explain why they were voting.

The "internal leaders" who negotiated the settlement with Ian Smith felt that the agreement reached on March 3, 1978, established, in the words of Bishop Muzorewa, "the machinery for dismantling the structures and practices of colonialism and racism and of minority rule." They went into the negotiations with the objectives of destroying the legal foundation for institutionalized racial discrimination and winning the transfer of power from the minority to the majority in an election based on the principle of one person/one vote. The first objective was achieved on October 10, 1978, with the abolition of all statutory discrimination, including the Land Tenure Act which reserved land for white ownership. The second objection was achieved with the election in April.

The argument that the constitution was never submitted to the black voters for their approval is weak. Throughout the talks, black negotiators reported back to the executive bodies of their respective parties to get their approval for any agreements that were made. At one point in the negotiations, when Bishop Muzorewa walked out in a dispute over the number of white seats in the new parliament, a special meeting of the UANC's Provincial Council was called which was attended by 800 delegates from all over the country. These delegates represented local constituents who were kept informed about the progress of the talks. In the view of the *black* parties, a referendum on the constitution would simply have delayed independence and exposed their party workers to increased guerrilla violence. Ant it would have been redundant, they felt, since participation in the election was itself a vote in favor of the constitution and the internal settlement—a point implicitly recognized by those who opposed the election because of "what it was about." * The black negotiators

---

* It is true that a referendum on the internal settlement was held for whites. This was done to fulfill Smith's 1977 electoral pledge that whites would be consulted on any agreement negotiated with internal black leaders—a pledge made to shore up the confidence of the whites, whom Smith had promised only a few years before that there would not be black majority rule "for a thousand years." In this connection, Andrew Young's repeated claim that 40 percent of the whites preferred the Anglo-American plan to the internal settlement is without foundation. In the 1977 election in which Smith had sought a mandate to negotiate an internal settlement, his Rhodesian Front party won 85.4 percent of the votes. The Rhodesian Action party, which opposed any move toward majority rule, won 9 percent of the votes, while the National Unifying Force, which backed the Anglo-American plan, received only 4 percent. In the subsequent referendum, held in January 1979, over 84 percent of the whites voted in favor of the internal settlement, and once again the opposition consisted overwhelmingly of those who opposed majority rule altogether.

compromised on the issue of the twenty-eight white seats; they were, after all, *negotiating*, and they did not feel that they had sacrificed their fundamental position. In the first place, such an arrangement was in the tradition of Britain's African decolonization policy of "multiracialism." (In Zambia, for example, the special allotment of parliamentary seats to the non-African minority was not discontinued until 1968, four years after independence.) Then, too, all the plans that have been introduced for a negotiated transition to majority rule have made a special provision for white representation in parliament. Even the now obsolete Anglo-American plan, which is vigorously defended by Ambassador Young, reserves twenty of the 100 seats for the white minority. During Nkomo's bilateral talks with Smith in 1976, he proposed an election with three different voting rolls which would have assured the whites a substantial minority of legislative seats. He did so, as he said, "to meet fears expressed by the Rhodesian Front" (Smith's party) and "in spirit of compromise." In the talks leading to the internal settlement, Smith demanded thirty-four seats for the whites. Muzorewa wanted the number limited to twenty but reluctantly compromised at twenty-eight after his black negotiating partners, Sithole and Chirau, accepted that figure.

The blacks agreed to this arrangement for a ten-year period; they also agreed to clauses in the constitution which protected the institutional interests of the whites for an equal period, in order to reassure the white minority that its political and economic position would be stabilized under an African-dominated government. The alternative to this kind of settlement would have meant the inevitable flight of whites from the country and the collapse of the economy, as happened recently in Angola and Mozambique. Muzorewa has made the point that if independence is not to be a "hollow shell," Zimbabwe must not repeat the mistakes of other African countries which drove out indigenous skilled whites, and then in desperation rehired at three times the cost "economic mercenaries who were inevitably failures in their own countries and who came to Africa for what they could milk out of their hosts."

The internal settlement, then, was designed to provide a period of stable transition during which blacks could acquire the experience and skills they were denied under white rule. Muzorewa has promised training programs for Africans to achieve "*both*...the necessary efficiency and the necessary organization to black majority rule" (emphasis added). He is not impatient, since black control over the institutions now dominated by whites is inevitable in a country 96 percent black. Already the army is 85 percent black and the police force is 75 percent black, and the cabinet minister responsible for each force is also black. Moreover, all white officials are now answerable to a black head of state and to a parliament and cabinet which have over a two-thirds black majority.

While Muzorewa and the other internal black leaders have expressed a practical interest in retaining the skills and energies of the whites for Zimbabwe, expediency has not been their only consideration. Whites who have been four generations in Zimbabwe, Muzorewa has said, and who have no other home, must not be "driven out to nowhere." In an open letter to American blacks, Muzorewa has emphasized that Zimbabweans had never "fought the white man's skin. We fought his evil system. We fought his racism." Some people, he said, feel that we should "be ruthless with the white race. But I wish to warn against the reversal of discrimination…It makes us hypocrites to turn into black racists ourselves. It makes us oppressors and not liberators."

Ordinarily one might expect such sentiments to be applauded by Western liberals. But in fact, as Bishop Muzorewa said recently, while Zimbabweans "are prepared to forget the past and work together with our white brethren…some people in Britain, America, Africa, and other parts of the world appear unwilling to allow us to do so." Little attempt has been made to understand the practical and moral aspects of the Bishop's position, which is viewed as a rationalization for continued white control of Zimbabwe Rhodesia. As a result, we have the paradoxical situation that a settlement which has been accepted by most people inside Zimbabwe Rhodesia as the best and only realistic course for their country to take is opposed by foreign advocates of "majority rule"!

The negotiations leading to the internal settlement succeeded, where all previous attempts to negotiate a solution to the Rhodesian crisis failed, because three conditions prevailed. First, by the fall of 1976, the Smith regime had been forced by events to concede the principle of black majority rule. No single event broke the back of white resistance. Rather, it was a series of developments: the energy crisis and the Western economic recession which magnified the impact of sanctions on the Rhodesian economy; the collapse of Portuguese colonialism and the emergence of pro-Communist regimes in Angola and Mozambique; a sharp change in policy toward Rhodesia by both the United States and South Africa; and not least, the steady escalation of the guerilla insurgency and the increased rate of white flight from the country. All these together compelled Smith to abandon his position of intransigence.

The second factor was the involvement in the talks of black leaders with a broad following in the country, in particular Bishop Muzorewa. The earliest talks (aboard the HMS *Tiger* in 1966 and the HMS *Fearless* in 1968, and the negotiations in 1971 between Smith and Alec Douglas-Home, the British Foreign Minister) had been between Britain and Rhodesia and had bypassed the black majority entirely. Subsequent talks between Smith and Nkomo in 1975 and 1976 similarly lacked the involvement of broadly representative nationalist leaders. Nkomo certainly had long experience in the nationalist movement. But he had only limited support in the country, partly because of his narrow tribal base among the Ndebeles who make up only about 15 percent of the black population. In addition, the talks were viewed by other nationalists as an attempt by Zambia's President Kaunda to impose his own candidate, Nkomo, as the leader of the internally divided nationalist movement. If fact, resentment against Zambian interference in Zimbabwean affairs has been one of the elements in the Rhodesian talks least understood by outsiders.

Muzorewa, unlike Nkomo, had for some time been thought to have the broadest popular support among Zimbabweans. Elected Rhodesia's first black bishop in 1968, he quickly earned the reputation of being a resolute defender of black interests and was barred by the government from visiting tribal trust lands. When the British appointed the Pearce Commission in 1971 to test the acceptability to blacks of the Smith–Home constitutional proposals, he was the only figure the different nationalist factions could agree upon to head the new African National Council (ANC), which was organized to mobilize the campaign for rejection. The campaign was successful, and during the course of it Muzorewa emerged as the preeminent black leader in the country.

Combining strong criticism of the Smith regime with appeals for racial reconciliation, Muzorewa has frequently drawn huge crowds at rallies, at times as many as 200,000 people, and his popularity was confirmed by his overwhelming victory in the election. He also has support among the guerrillas, most of whom left Rhodesia in the period following 1972 when his popularity was at its height. This helps explain why he is seen as the only nationalist leader capable of unifying the country.

After the collapse of the all-party Geneva talks in January 1977, Smith announced that he would seek talks with "moderate blacks," chiefly Muzorewa's ANC. Muzorewa refused to take part in any talks unless Smith was prepared to surrender power "immediately and unconditionally" to the black majority. But the decision of the five frontline presidents to give exclusive backing to the Patriotic Front produced great resentment in Muzorewa's party, which accused them of "launching a civil war" that would cause the slaughter of Zimbabweans. When the Organization of African Unity, at its Libreville meeting in July 1977, also decided to back the Patriotic Front, an internal settlement became the only course open to those who still wanted a negotiated solution. Sithole, a dedicated nationalist who had spent ten years in prison for his political activities and was, in fact, the founder of ZANU, had already agreed to negotiate with Smith. So when Smith, on November 24, 1977, conceded the principle of one person/one vote elections as the starting point for negotiations, Muzorewa announced that he was ready "to test him out."

Muzorewa's desire for free, universal-suffrage elections was naturally strengthened by his confidence that he would win them convincingly. Similarly, not least among the reasons Nkomo and Mugabe have opposed such elections as the basis for a transfer of power from the white minority is their fear that they could not win on those terms. Both, in fact, have said that they would only consider holding elections *after* power had been transferred to the Patriotic Front. This, if anything, is a sure "recipe for civil war," since an election policed by the two guerilla forces of the Patriotic Front would quickly degenerate into a war between them, a prospect that even Zambia's Kaunda is thought to fear.

Moreover, it is hardly likely that either Nkomo or Mugabe would govern democratically. Nkomo, given his narrow base, could only rule through force. And his close ties to Russia and Cuba, which have equipped and trained his army, make it inevitable that both countries would have a decisive influence in any government he headed. Mugabe, even more than Nkomo, favors totalitarianism out of ideological conviction. He has made no secret of his belief that "the multiparty system is a luxury," and he has announced that if the blacks of Zimbabwe do not like his ideology, "then we will have to reeducate them."

The absence, then, of Nkomo and Mugabe from the talks with Smith was the third factor which made it possible for the negotiations to succeed. There simply was no basis for a political compromise which included the Patriotic Front, a reality which the frontline states and the OAU recognized (and helped bring about) when they endorsed the Front and announced that an independent Zimbabwe could only be created through armed struggle.

For this reason, the insistence by both the British and American governments that any political solution which did not include the Patriotic Front was unacceptable can most generously be described as naive. If Nkomo and Mugabe had any interest at all in a political settlement, they would not have rejected out of hand the Anglo-American plan which called, among other things, for Smith's resignation in favor of a British resident commissioner who would head a transitional government; for a UN peace-keeping force which would supervise elections; and for the replacement of the Rhodesian army by a new Zimbabwe army which would, according to the then British Foreign Secretary David Owen, "be based on the liberation forces." Smith called the plan "a very cunning scheme" to hand power over to the Patriotic Front. But Nkomo and Mugabe did not think so, partly because they did not believe as Andrew Young said they did, that they would win free elections. (Only Muzorewa and Sithole welcomed the plan, though they expressed concern that African elements in the UN peace-keeping force might aid the Patriotic Front, even to the extent of assisting in a coup.)

Similarly, Nkomo and Mugabe both reacted with manifest contempt to the subsequent British–American call for an all-party conference. Nkomo said he would have nothing to do with "all-party nonsense" and declared on September 11, 1978, that "We mean to get that country by force and we shall get it." Mugabe said he would attend such a conference, but only on the condition that "the entirety of the Salisbury regime must go and the enemy forces must be completely dismantled." Then, shortly after the announcement in Washington by the four members of the Rhodesian Executive Council that they would attend an all-party conference without preconditions, Mugabe's organization (ZANU) made public a death list which included fifty Zimbabweans associated with the internal settlement, including the three black members of the Executive Council. The document described these people as "Zimbabwean black bourgeoisie, traitors, fellow-travelers, and puppets of the Ian Smith regime, opportunistic running-dogs and other capitalist vultures."

Nkomo and Mugabe have adopted an equally uncompromising attitude toward each other, thus making a political compromise *within* the Patriotic Front no more likely than one between it and the parties to the internal settlement. The presidents of the frontline states have made repeated attempts to impose "unity" on ZANU (Mugabe) and ZAPU (Nkomo), but with little success. The formation in 1975 of a united army, the Zimbabwe People's Army (ZIPA), resulted in violent clashes between the ZANU and ZAPU forces and eventually in their complete separation. The Patriotic Front, established the following year, is a paper political alliance that has done nothing to increase military cooperation between the two guerrilla forces. On the contrary, Mugabe and his aides have long resented Nkomo's failure to commit his heavily armed forces to the war effort, alleging that he is conserving his army's strength for what he expects will be the final showdown with ZANU. In a statement directed at Nkomo, Mugabe recently warned that "Those who have not fought cannot reap the rewards of a victory to which they have contributed nothing."

The current division within the guerrilla ranks—which persists despite a new effort to coordinate their military effort—must be seen against a background of fifteen years of splits, splits within splits, tribal/ regional conflicts, fierce internal violence, and meddling by neighboring African states.** Indeed, in a curious, sordid, and illuminating way, the creation of the Patriotic Front can be traced to the most notorious act of internal violence, the murder of ZANU chairman Herbert Chitepo in Zambia on March 18, 1975. The killing, which was preceded by a mini–civil war within ZANU's ranks and by mass executions of a rebel group, prompted President Kaunda of Zambia to establish an international commission of inquiry consisting of representatives of

---

** Dr. Masipula Sithole, the brother of Ndabaningi Sithole and a ZANU activist for eight years, has just published an honest and courageous book, *Zimbabwe Struggles within the Struggle* (Rujeko Publishers: Salisbury, 1979), which tells the history of the conflicts within the Zimbabwe nationalist movement.

thirteen African states. After nine months of investigation, the commission found members of ZANU's high command guilty of the murder.*** Mugabe, furious at the verdict and at the jailing of his ZANU comrades, denounced Kaunda and withdrew from Zambia to Mozambique where he consolidated ZANU's guerrilla forces. Shortly thereafter, Kaunda, hoping to resurrect Nkomo (whose reputation had been badly damaged by the failure of his talks with Smith), offered to release Chitepo's murderers if Mugabe would agree to a joint ZANU–ZAPU delegation at the Geneva talks. The deal was consummated and the Zambian high court acquitted the assassins who promptly joined Mugabe in Geneva, and the Patriotic Front came into being.

This incident may help explain why many Zimbabweans resent Zambian interference in their affairs, and do not regard the Patriotic Front as their chosen instrument for bringing peace and majority rule to their country. It may also explain why there is distrust of international institutions which have endorsed the Patriotic Front as the sole legitimate representative of the people of Zimbabwe; and of Western "progressives" who, as Muzorewa has said, "extol the armed struggle, especially from some safe distance from the death and the bloodshed and the tears and the misery."

In the wake of the election, the continued support of the Patriotic Front must be viewed as morally unconscionable. At the time the internal settlement was announced, Conor Cruise O'Brien commented (*New York Review of Books*, March 8, 1978) that if the Patriotic Front continued to kill people after free elections were held and a black majority government sat in Salisbury, then its behavior would be "morally equivalent" to that of such antidemocratic European terrorist groups as Baader-Meinhof

---

*** The commission described one of the assassins, Josiah Tongogara, as a "man possessed of inordinate ambitions" who had engaged in "the systematic process of eliminating possible rivals by death...." According to the commission's report, Tongogara had openly remarked that "he saw no reason why he should not be the first President in an independent Zimbabwe through the barrel of the gun." Remarkably, when Andrew Young was asked by interviewer Jonathon Powers (London Times, May 22, 1978) if he saw any parallels between the American civil rights movement and the Patriotic Front, he replied: "Nonviolence is in many ways being practiced by the Patriotic Front.... I asked one of their commanders, Tongogara, what they actually do in Rhodesia, and he said they're not doing much fighting, except when they are fired upon, or when the Rhodesian defense forces find them and try to run them out. Basically, what they're doing is moving around the villages and conducting political seminars and singing songs—which is exactly what we did."

and the IRA. All this has now come to pass, yet the Patriotic Front retains the support of the UN and other international bodies, while the elected government of Zimbabwe Rhodesia is viewed as an "illegal" pariah state.****

It is especially interesting that the excommunication of Zimbabwe has been decreed in the name of racial self-determination, but in total disregard of the views of that country's black majority; and that the Patriotic Front is favored in the name of majority rule, but in total disregard of that group's antidemocratic outlook. Thus, we have the spectacle of the United Nations denying a platform to an "illegitimate" black African leader (as it did to Muzorewa), who is then greeted upon his return home by a cheering throng of over 150,000 blacks; and of the *New York Times,* ordinarily a proponent of political democracy, asserting that for the U.S. to "pressure" the Patriotic Front to come to terms with the newly elected black government in Zimbabwe Rhodesia "would be a betrayal of American support for majority rule."

One can account for such anomalies only if it is understood that the issue is not whether or not there shall be rule by the black majority, but what form such rule shall take. And here the alternatives are as clear as they were at an earlier time between white minority and black majority rule. For if the presidents of Zambia, Mozambique, Tanzania, and Angola have their way, majority rule will take a form more or less similar to what exists in their own countries; which is to say that it will be a dictatorship by a small black elite over a destitute black population. It is, of course, precisely this kind of "majority rule" that Muzorewa has said would be a betrayal, for it would have "the mere trappings of independence—a brand new flag, sleek and shiny limousines, black faces in parliament, the OAU, and the United Nations—while those in power are not accountable to the governed for their actions." In fact, it has been Muzorewa's rejection of "worn-out ideologies," of "political philosophies which could make people secondary to the state—which

**** The charge of illegality, which is contained in the two UN Security Council resolutions on the internal settlement and the election, is more than a little ironic, since it implicitly accepts the legality of British colonial rule in Rhodesia. "To the black majority," Muzorewa has said, "illegality was imposed on the country at the onset of British colonialism in 1890 and not in 1965 [when the Smith government issued its Universal Declaration of Independence from Britain]. We do not accept that there is any other authority than the black majority which can bestow legality to Zimbabwe."

would regard people as expendable," which constitutes his indictment of the postcolonial experience in much of Africa, and which accounts for the antagonism to him and to Zimbabwe Rhodesia among those who cling to such ideologies and who rule uneasily over the increasingly disillusioned and discontented black masses. And it is, not least, the need to conceal the betrayal of independence and the self-infliction of poverty and political oppression which explains why the struggle for "majority rule" is proclaimed with such strenuous devotion.

Into this essentially internal African debate have stepped the Soviet Union and its Cuban and East German proxies, seeking to exploit African conflicts and frustrations to advance Moscow's geopolitical ambitions. And into it also has wandered the United States, newly sensitive, as it would like to think, to the aspirations of black Africa and determined, as Secretary of State Vance has put it, not to "mirror Soviet and Cuban activities." The foremost U.S. objective has been to preserve American "credibility" in black Africa, the assumption being that this is the measure of our influence on the continent and is also the best and the only way (all military options having been ruled out) to deter the Russians. Anything we might do to undermine that credibility, it is thought, would only invite further Soviet intervention which we would not (and should not, given our Vietnam experience) be prepared to counter.

With respect to Zimbabwe Rhodesia, the price for maintaining American credibility among the frontline presidents and with Nigeria has been that we support—or at the very least, do nothing to oppose—the Patriotic Front. As a result, we have found ourselves, until now, tacitly aligned with groups armed by Moscow, hostile to America, antagonistic to democracy, and unpopular within Zimbabwe Rhodesia itself. And we have opposed the internal parties which look to us for support, share our professed belief in an open multiracial society, and have genuine popularity within the country. We have defended this policy in terms of our historic commitment as a nation to human rights and, more practically, in terms of protecting our country's vital interest in Africa and of preventing the escalation of civil war. Yet it has been hard for most Americans, or for the United States Congress, to understand how any of these objectives is served by promoting the Patriotic Front.

The fact is that this has not been the only practical course open to us. The psychology of appeasement is now so deeply rooted among most American officials and political commentators that they have, almost as a matter of course, underestimated our own strengths and the strengths of our friends, as well as the weakness of the Soviet position. U.S. officials tremble at the thought of a Nigerian oil embargo, forgetting the fact that Nigeria needs American capital and technology at least as much as America needs Nigerian oil. Most importantly, within Zimbabwe Rhodesia itself, there is now less sympathy for the guerrillas than ever before. The people are simply tired of violence, especially violence which has no purpose, since there is now a black majority government. If this government takes steps, as it has promised, to improve the social and economic position of the black population, the rate at which guerrillas will defect to become part of the new order could increase dramatically. It is also possible that the Patriotic Front leaders will now negotiate with the Bishop if, as the London *Economist* has observed, they "are not to risk becoming the 30-year Arafats of southern Africa." Moreover, Zambia and Mozambique, which have suffered badly from the fighting and are heavily dependent on the much stronger economies of Zimbabwe Rhodesia and South Africa, are already under pressure internally to end their support of the Patriotic Front and to accommodate to the new reality. Zambia is particularly vulnerable, since more than half its trade and most of its food imports are now carried by rail through Zimbabwe Rhodesia.

Whether Moscow would be prepared, under these circumstances, to escalate the war is doubtful. At present, the army of Zimbabwe Rhodesia is, in African terms, a strong fighting force and more than a match for the divided Patriotic Front. To defeat it would require a major commitment by Soviet proxy forces at a time when the Cubans are overextended in Angola (where they now maintain a force of 45,000 military and civilian personnel). An intervention of this kind would be deeply resented in most of Africa, and it would strengthen opposition to détente in this country and weaken whatever chance there is for Senate ratification of SALT.

The Russians will, more likely than not, remain cautious and wait for an opportune moment to strike. The point is that it should not be our policy to create opportunities for them and to encourage the guerrillas to continue fighting, which is what the President's repudiation of the Muzorewa government in his June 7 statement has already done. Beyond the narrow issue of economic sanctions against Zimbabwe Rhodesia, there is the larger question of whether we will do anything to help the new black government to survive and continue to evolve in a democratic direction; or whether, by our inaction and failure of nerve, we will embolden its enemies and thus destroy any hope for democracy in the country. If we take the latter course, we will have done nothing to increase the credibility of the United States either in Africa or elsewhere. On the contrary, we will have raised a signal to all the world that this country no longer has the capacity to defend or even understand its interests, or to help those who, unlike ourselves, continue to believe in freedom.

A WAY OUT:
SOLUTIONS FOR SOUTH AFRICA

◆ ◆ ◆

[1983]

THE ONGOING CRISIS IN SOUTH AFRICA continues to befuddle American policymakers. While the American people seem to be united against apartheid and appear to be willing to exert American influence in dismantling this odious system, there is by no means a consensus on the appropriate strategy of how to do so.

The groundswell of popular opposition to the Pretoria regime has forced the Reagan administration into a *de facto* desertion of its much maligned "constructive engagement" policy; yet, the government has thus far failed to devise an acceptable alternative. And even though the Senate decision to override President Reagan's veto on sanctions did serve to clarify a previously divided policy, it is equally clear that punitive economic measures alone—while psychologically satisfying—cannot create democracy and a more just society in that troubled land.

It is by now apparent that sanctions and the recent spate of divestment by major American corporations may, in fact, be exacerbating the plight of blacks and other victims of apartheid, as well the economic viability of the front-line states. Moreover, it is a dubious proposition to assume that outside economic pressure can do much to eliminate apartheid or enhance the chances of a democratic transition. However, such selective pressure may be useful if accompanied by a fundamental shift in our approach. U.S. policy can be effective only if our primary objective is to help foster the growth of democracy in South Africa, not merely to dismantle apartheid.

The American public and policymakers must understand that if our interest is simply to eliminate apartheid, then virtually any tactic and strategy will do, including violence and terror. But if our goal is democracy, then a strategy consistent with democratic ideals and practices is required. And it must be anchored on the supposition that, while U.S. policy may help, the final outcome of the struggle is in the hands of South Africans of all races.

The major objective of U.S. policy, and of its citizens, must be to assist, both financially and morally, groups within South Africa committed to peaceful and progressive change. All too often our foreign policy efforts have been frustrated because we failed to recognize the importance of nurturing and encouraging a democratic center. There are literally hundreds of grass-roots organizations in South Africa—community associations, women's organizations, trade unions, and religious groups—that form the fragile foundation of democratic institutions. These groups serve to broaden the democratic center and ultimately to support constitutional arrangements that will deal with both the fears of those who have dominated and the aspirations of those who have been oppressed. But the middle ground is rapidly eroding. Moderate elements are caught between a brutal white regime and an extremist black segment which advocates violence as the only means to abolish apartheid. Unfortunately, such polarization has caused many whites who had hoped for a progressive solution to either close ranks with the Botha government or to emigrate.

To arrest this process, to enhance meaningful change, and to reduce violence depends on the development and implementation of constitutional arrangements that will allay the anxieties of the white minority while expanding the rights of the nonwhite majority. Each side will tend to resist change until there is guaranteed protection for all.

In light of recent oppression, internecine violence, and polarization, it is clearly time for Americans in and out of government to examine approaches to the problems of South Africa in the context of pragmatic solutions. It is now time to raise a number of difficult questions concerning the possible structure of a postapartheid South Africa. Among the questions: Can a new Constitution ensure freedom for all, and what kind of document would it be? Is a Bill of Rights essential for individuals? Is a Bill of Rights essential for groups? Is there a consensual basis for the elimination of apartheid? Is there anything to be learned and applied from the Zimbabwe experience or the Swiss-style canton system? If, in light of recent developments, "constructive engagement" has failed, what kind of policy does the U.S. need to develop? Can U.S. policy be directed merely to South Africa, or must it include economic and other considerations that deal with the whole of southern Africa? What can the American people do to strengthen the democratic center?

Today, South Africa is a tinderbox. It may become one of history's most tragic episodes, no matter what America does. But there are yet avenues of hope if new approaches can be applied. These essays are an invaluable contribution to that process.

AFTERWORD

IT IS A TESTAMENT to Bayard Rustin's true excellence that he played such as major role in America's civil rights movement. I knew him and respected him a great deal. Despite living as an openly gay black man in a time of enormous prejudice, he embraced the nonviolent principles of Gandhi and acted as a guide to John Lewis and many others in the movement. He was vital to the movement, bringing about great change alongside Dr. Martin Luther King. Bayard Rustin was a great leader, and a great American. He is an example for young people today of how social justice can happen with commitment and conviction.

Barney Frank

SELECTED BIBLIOGRAPHY

Anderson, Jervis. *A. Philip Randolph: A Biographical Portrait*. Berkeley: University of California, 1986.

——. *Bayard Rustin: Troubles I've Seen*. New York: HarperCollins, 1997.

Branch, Taylor. *Parting the Waters: America in the King Years 1954–63*. New York: Touchstone, 1988.

——. *Pillar of Fire: America in the King Years 1963–65*. New York: Simon & Schuster, 1998.

D'Emilio, John. *Lost Prophet: The Life and Times of Bayard Rustin*. New York: Free Press, 2003.

Garrow, David J. *Bearing the Cross: Martin Luther King, Jr., and the Southern Christian Leadership Conference*. New York: Morrow, 1986.

Hampton, Henry, and Steven Fayer, eds. *Voices of Freedom: An Oral History of the Civil Rights Movement from the 1950s through the 1980s*. New York: Bantam, 1990.

Haskins, James. *Bayard Rustin: Behind the Scenes of the Civil Rights Movement*. New York: Hyperion, 1997.

Henthoff, Nat. *Peace Agitator: The Story of A. J. Muste*. New York: Macmillan, 1963.

Jeanmarie, Redvers. "An Interview with Bayard Rustin" in *Other Countries: Black Gay Voices*, vol. I. New York: Other Countries Collective, 1988.

Kapur, Sudarshan. *Raising Up a Prophet: The African-American Encounter with Gandhi*. Boston: Beacon Press, 1992.

Levine, Daniel. *Bayard Rustin and the Civil Rights Movement*. New Jersey: Rutgers, 2000.

Lewis, John, and Michael D'Orso. *Walking with the Wind: A Memoir of the*

Movement. New York: Simon & Schuster, 1998.

Morris, Aldon. *The Origins of the Civil Rights Movement: Black Communities Organizing for Change.* New York: The Free Press, 1984.

O'Reily, Kenneth, and David Gallen, eds. *Black Americans: The FBI Files.* New York: Carroll & Graf, 1994.

Rustin, Bayard. *Down the Line: The Collected Writings of Bayard Rustin.* Chicago: Quadrangle, 1971.

————. *Strategies for Freedom: The Changing Patterns of Black Protest.* New York: Columbia, 1976.

Tracy, James. *Direct Action: Radical Pacifism from the Union Eight to the Chicago Seven.* Chicago: University of Chicago, 1996.

Weisbrot, Robert. *Freedom Bound: A History of America's Civil Rights Movements.* New York: Norton, 1990.

About the Editors

DEVON CARBADO is Professor of Law and African American Studies at the University of California–Los Angeles. He teaches and writes in the areas of constitutional law, critical race/feminist theory, and gay and lesbian studies. His scholarship appears in law reviews at, among other institutions, Harvard, UCLA, Cornell, and Michigan. He is coeditor of *Black Like Us: A Century of Lesbian, Gay, and Bisexual African American Fiction* (Cleis Press, 2002), winner of the 2003 Lambda Literary Awards and the Independent Publisher Award, and editor of *Black Men on Race, Gender, and Sexuality: A Critical Reader* (New York UP, 1999). He lives in Los Angeles.

DONALD WEISE is coeditor of *Black Like Us: A Century of Lesbian, Gay, and Bisexual African American Fiction* (Cleis Press, 2002), as well as *The Huey P. Newton Reader* (Seven Stories, 2002) with Black Panther Party founding member David Hilliard. He is also editor of Gore Vidal's *Los Angeles Times* best-seller *Gore Vidal: Sexually Speaking—Collected Sex Writings* (Cleis Press, 1999). He lives in San Francisco.